Priests of the French Revolution

JOSEPH F. BYRNES

Priests of the French Revolution

SAINTS AND RENEGADES IN A NEW POLITICAL ERA

THE PENNSYLVANIA STATE UNIVERSITY PRESS
UNIVERSITY PARK, PENNSYLVANIA

FRONTISPIECE: "Put 'er there, Father, I knew you would be on our side" might well translate the French caption "Touchez-là, M[onsieur] l'Curé. J'savais ben qu'vous seriais des nôtres," the words of a poor French peasant. This simplified the story somewhat, because the Revolution was mainly a revolution of the middle class, but the commoner class included everyone who was not an aristocrat, making it possible to suppose that the Revolution belonged to the poor—and that good priests would work on their behalf in particular. (Bibliothèque nationale de France)

Library of Congress Cataloging-in-Publication Data
Byrnes, Joseph F., 1939– , author.
Priests of the French Revolution : saints and renegades in a new political era / Joseph F. Byrnes.
p. cm
Summary: "Explores how priests and bishops who embraced the French Revolution creatively followed or destructively rejected traditional versions of priestly ministry"—Provided by publisher.
Includes bibliographical references and index.
ISBN 978-0-271-06377-5 (cloth : alk. paper)
1. France—History—Revolution, 1789–1799—Religious aspects.
2. Christianity and politics—France—History—18th century.
3. Church and state—France—History—18th century.
4. Priests—France—History—18th century.
5. France—Church history—18th century.
I. Title.

DC158.2.B97 2014
940.2'71—dc23
2014004247

Printed in the United States of America
Published by The Pennsylvania State University Press,
University Park, PA 16802-1003

The Pennsylvania State University Press is a member of the Association of American University Presses.

It is the policy of The Pennsylvania State University Press to use acid-free paper. Publications on uncoated stock satisfy the minimum requirements of American National Standard for Information Sciences—Permanence of Paper for Printed Library Material, ANSI Z39.48–1992.

This book is printed on paper that contains 30% post-consumer waste.

For VERONICA AND MICHAEL

Contents

List of Illustrations / *ix*
Acknowledgments / *xi*
Prologue / *xiii*

PART I: ENGAGEMENT, 1789–1791 / *1*

1 The Formation of a Revolutionary Priest: Sieyès and Grégoire / *7*
2 The Priests in Action: From Estates General to National Assembly / *28*
3 Claude Fauchet at the Bastille / *47*
4 The Church of Adrien Lamourette and His Allies / *60*

PART II: SURVIVAL, 1791–1795 / *75*

5 The Failed Relationship of Revolutionary Church and State / *82*
6 The Tragic Convention Years / *100*
7 Terrorists and Abdicators: Ultimate Renegades / *127*

PART III: REVIVAL, 1795–1802 / *151*

8 The New Constitutional French Church / *158*
9 Stabilizing the Constitutional Church: Claude Le Coz and the Council of 1797 / *175*
10 Constitutional Irresolution in the See of Paris: Jean-Baptiste Royer and the Council of 1801 / *192*
11 Constitutional Clergy in the Church of Napoleon's Concordat / *211*
12 The Afterlife of the Constitutional Church: Hopes and Reality / *227*

Appendix: Administration of the Constitutional Church and Oath Adherence by Department / *243*
Notes / *259*
Bibliography / *293*
Index / *305*

Illustrations

FIGURES

1 Priest patriot swearing oath of loyalty to the nation, the law, and the king / *xv*
2 Tennis Court Oath, the abbé Henri Grégoire in the foreground / *8*
3 The abbé Emmanuel-Joseph Sieyès in clerical dress / *12*
4 The abbé Grégoire intervening before the Constituent Assembly / *26*
5 The abbé Jacques Jallet, priest and diarist / *33*
6 Canon lawyer Pierre Durand de Maillane / *38*
7 Caricature of clergy refusing the oath of loyalty in the Assembly / *45*
8 Fauchet preaching at Mass for Bastille victims / *49*
9 Title page of Fauchet's book *De la religion nationale* / *51*
10 A front page of Fauchet's publication *Bouche de fer* / *55*
11 The abbé Adrien Lamourette / *62*
12 Mirabeau with Franklin and Enlightenment philosophes on the Champs Élysées / *66*
13 Canon lawyer Armand-Gaston Camus / *70*
14 The Kiss of Lamourette in the Legislative Assembly / *72*
15 Bishop Louis-Alexandre Expilly / *83*
16 Caricature of a priest refusing the oath of loyalty at Sunday service / *87*
17 King before the Constituent Assembly after his attempt to flee the country / *89*
18 Cover of *La Feuille villageoise*, a forum for radical priests / *95*
19 The episcopal vicar Yves-Marie Audrein in a mock procession of Jacobins / *105*
20 The episcopal vicar François Chabot as Franciscan and corrupt politician / *110*
21 Bishop Jean-Baptiste Saurine / *113*
22 Bishop Jean-Baptiste Massieu / *117*
23 Jacques Roux with Louis XVI and official entourage about to bring the king to execution / *135*
24 Joseph Le Bon caricatured as blood-drinking executioner / *141*
25 Formal ordination papers turned in by an abdicating priest / *146*

26 First page of first issue of *Annales de la religion* / *160*
27 The revolutionary calendar / *171*
28 Bishop Claude Le Coz / *177*
29 First manuscript page of the minutes of the 1797 Council / *186*
30 Bishop Jean-Baptiste Royer / *195*
31 Caricature of the 1801 Council gathered in Notre-Dame Cathedral / *205*
32 Jean Gerson, late medieval hero of the constitutionals at the 1801 Council / *207*
33 Signing of the Concordat / *213*
34 Pope Pius VII and Cardinal Caprara, head of papal delegation to reconcile former constitutionals / *222*
35 Commemorative image of Pope Pius VI (burial at Valence) / *234*

MAPS

1 The oath of loyalty to the nation, the law, and the king / *43*
2 Estimated number of abdicating priests, 1793–1794 / *143*
3 The revived Constitutional Church—six areas of activity / *209*

All maps after Langlois, Tackett, and Vovelle, eds., *Religion*, vol. 9 of *Atlas de la Révolution française*, © 1996 Éditions de l'École des Hautes Études en Science Sociales.

Acknowledgments

In my prologue I praise—and none too much, I might say—the colleagues and friends whose books have provided the bases and parameters essential for the structuring of my own research. To add thanks to praise, I want to express my gratitude to Rodney J. Dean, who carefully read through earlier versions of my book; Timothy Tackett, who instantly responded to all my questions about his own extensive research *sans pareil*; and Paul Chopelin, whose support, encouragement, and generous welcome to his own remarkable private library facilitated my manuscript revisions these past few years. Paul and his wife, Caroline Chopelin-Blanc, also a leading scholar of the Revolution, graciously received me into their home, where I made new contacts, Michel Biard in particular; renewed old contacts, Daniel Moulinet in particular; and met members of the Université de Lyon III group RESEA (Religions, sociétés et acculturation). Bernard Hours, director of RESEA when I arrived, assuming thereafter the headship of the more extended LARHRA (Laboratoire de recherche historique Rhône-Alpes), arranged my situation as a guest associate of RESEA and LARHRA with generosity and great good humor. Thanks to the Chopelins, Bernard Hours, Yves Krumenacker, and Christine Chadier, we were able to arrange for a colloquium on the constitutional bishops, the springboard for our continuing work on both bishops and priests of the Revolution. It is not possible to name all the participants here, but I do wish to note the patronage of the virtual dean of church–state studies of the revolutionary era, Bernard Plongeron, whose unparalleled erudition I was finally able to encounter face to face; the assistance of Jacques-Olivier Boudon, the Sorbonne scholar who years ago encouraged the pursuit of any useful prosopography of the clergy of the era; and the expertise of Philippe Bourdin, cordial *érudit* of the Université Blaise Pascal. It was also the occasion to integrate into a wider framework the accomplishments of our original research group for the study of the constitutional bishops, Rodney Dean, Jean Dubray, Emmanuel Lecam, Michel Deblock, Valérie Murger, and Guillaume Colot. Both Valérie Murger and Fabien Vandermarcq of the Bibliothèque de Port-Royal were the principal insurers of my successful work at that veritable shrine of Constitutional Church sources.

I have had several extended conversations with Jacques Guilhaumou, to whom I am especially indebted for interpretation of the complexities of the early career of the abbé Sieyès and for delivering me from the redoubtable task of transcribing all of Sieyès's *Sur Dieu ultramètre*, the centerpiece of my study of Sieyès in chapter 1. Alyssa Sepinwall graciously supplied guidance at every turn on the career of the abbé Grégoire—along with encouragement and the example of a scholar at the service of the field of history and the fellow scholars who work there.

This is not my first experience publishing with Penn State University Press: in fact, brief portions of chapters 5, 7, and 11 derive from chapter 1 of my *Catholic and French Forever* (Penn State, 2005). I continue to be amazed, however, at the intelligence, dedication, and cordiality of the whole *équipe*, beginning with Kendra Boileau, omnicompetent and a lover of French history and literature, who has been at once my history editor, editor-in-chief, and ever-encouraging adviser. Whatever faults this book may have are certainly, then, mine alone.

At Oklahoma State University, my essential aid in working up the *présentation* of my work has been the master of illustration and digitizing, David Thompson of the OSU Library. From my early attempts to get the relevant illustrations from the Bibliothèque nationale into my first manuscript through the digitizing of the final version for the Penn State Press, David has furnished expertise, lots and lots of time, and unfailing good humor. And Michael Larson of the Geography Department refined for my needs the maps that I have used in this book. The History Department has provided funds for research on several my chapters, and the supervising secretaries, Susan Oliver and Diana Fry, have handled all the logistics of manuscript production carefully, rapidly, and with salt-of-the-earth kindness; furthermore, colleagues have been uniformly supportive of the book. Overall, I want to highlight in particular the support of my dear friend Tonia Sharlach.

Across the many years, my daughter Veronica Byrnes and my son Michael Byrnes have been at the center of my real life, as much in Boston and Chicago as at home. I have here neither adequate words nor sufficient space to express my love and appreciation. To them I dedicate this book.

Prologue

"People get the priests they deserve" is the old Russian proverb, which is true if a good-living and successful community of people is served by a good priest, or a troubled and failed community by a bad priest. But you do not have to study history to know that the proverb is not always true. French aristocrats of the revolutionary era would have denied it, some of them complaining, "It is the screwed-up priests who have caused the Revolution," and wondering how could they have deserved *that*?

There were about 115,000 priests on French territory in 1789, certainly a large professional class.[1] They made what they could of the long and evolving tradition of priesthood, at its double levels of priest and bishop: mediators with another world, moral guides, or simple teachers. There is no reason to assume that in their day-to-day lives they were innocent of the regular run of personal deficiencies stemming from upbringing, sexual development, and competitiveness. The challenge of making sense of the Christian tradition can be formidable in any era, but this challenge was especially formidable for those priests required at the very beginning of 1791 to take an oath of loyalty to the new government, and thereby to accept the religious reforms promoted in a new Civil Constitution of the Clergy. More than half did so at the beginning (recent calculations put the number as high as 61 percent), and those who were subsequently consecrated bishops became the new official hierarchy of France.[2] Their writings, public testimony, and recorded private confidences furnish the story of a national Catholic church, the so-called Constitutional Church, which was rejected as schismatic by Rome and eventually rejected as an alien force by the revolutionary government.

These men lived out creative and sometimes destructive versions of priestly ministry as it had been handed on to them. Haunted by the besetting ghosts of the monarchical past, priests and bishops had to deal with the radical revolutionary conversation that quickly dominated their national and local government assemblies, coursed along their city streets, and quietly or noisily entered their villages. Certainly resentment of Old Regime episcopal power animated some of the most outspoken and politically effective curés—parish priests—in 1789. Those who were deputies to the Estates General railroaded their own First Estate into revolutionary partnership with the Third (commoner) Estate, to the chagrin of the aristocracy of the Second Estate. As the Estates General was transformed into the official French legislature, priest diarists recorded the heated discussions of the clergy among themselves. Then, once the Constituent Assembly was established, a special ecclesiastical committee began work on church reform.

The resulting Civil Constitution of the Clergy coordinated church dioceses with the new system of counties (*départements*) in France. Curés and bishops (previously ordained or consecrated within the church system, of course) were to be elected to their parishes and their dioceses, the bishops no more needing a mandate from the pope to occupy their sees than they did in the early church. The state was guaranteed freedom from church interference and the right to help with reform. The pope had begrudgingly supported Old Regime Catholicism, which gave the papal court general ecclesiastical jurisdiction while reserving certain prerogatives in the appointment of bishops for the monarchical state. But the Constituent Assembly reserved for itself and its ecclesiastical committee every operative decision, and the pope and his entourage considered this an unacceptable arrangement.[3] It is clear that whatever chance there had been to sell genuine republic-oriented Catholicism to the legislators of the Republic quickly failed in the face of high-level enthusiasm for republic-oriented deism: a civil religion presented earlier by Jean-Jacques Rousseau and promoted in the first half of the revolutionary decade by Maximilien Robespierre. The move to Rousseau had been natural enough, given the diffusion of Rousseauian ideas, among both the intelligentsia and broad areas of the population.[4] Deistic religion continued on, of course, as a major competitor to the Constitutional Church, all the more potent because the campaign against Catholicism, the famous "dechristianization" efforts of the central years of the revolutionary decade, gave a pass to deism even as it persecuted Catholicism. But the constitutional bishops and priests believed that they were the last great hope for revolutionary, or republican, Catholicism in France. The French church they administered, in coordination with the revolutionary government, tried to avoid the Scylla of Old Regime Catholicism with its assumption of papal control moderated only by monarchical order, if not divine right monarchy, and the Charybdis of the civil religion that ex-Catholic or post-Catholic political leaders promoted all across the revolutionary decade.

Figure 1 A priest before an altar and cross, swearing the oath of loyalty to the nation, the law, and the king, in accordance with the Civil Constitution of the Clergy, a legislative document that projected a major reform of French Catholicism. This was the dividing moment separating the revolutionary clergy from the clergy who refused the oath—and with it, active pastoral engagement with the new religious and political regime. In 1791, a new roster of bishops was chosen from among the priests who took the oath. (Bibliothèque nationale de France)

In fact, our revolutionary priests were not always participants in the Constitutional Church nor were all constitutional priests so very revolutionary. This is not primarily a prosopography of the constitutional clergy or an organizational history of the Constitutional Church before the separation of church and state, and the Second Constitutional Church after 1795. Some of the great personalities who pass in review, beginning with the abbé Sieyès, were little involved in the church reforms of 1790 and 1791. Others who took the oath, such as the violent populist Jacques Roux and the virtual terrorist Joseph Le Bon, spun out of the organizational church into their own secularized apostolates. Histories of the Constitutional Church as such do not include these men. Subtler even is the problem of the continuity of the original Constitutional Church and the Second Constitutional Church. The great dominating bishops of the Constitutional Church such as Henri Grégoire and Claude Le Coz referred to the foundational value of the first oath to the government in accordance with the Civil Constitution of the Clergy, but they had to give that oath symbolic value when it was no longer operative. At times the old label for a French Catholic church structured with its own specific prerogatives was used, and the Second Constitutional Church was simply called the Gallican Church. In part III of this book, after clearly noting that I am talking about a "Second" version of the Constitutional Church, I will continue to use the single adjective "Constitutional."

Instead of the label "revolutionary priest," I have used in my title the most open expression possible, "priests of the French Revolution." The priests who moved into, out of, or parallel to the constitutional clergy had their own degrees of dedication to the revolution as represented by the governments between 1789 and 1802. Those priests who detested the national government after the disappearance of the reformed monarchy, those priests who lost all political interest after the trauma of the Terror, those priests who supported the different extremes of Directory politics . . . were they all the same kind of revolutionary? Hardly. In fact, the word "revolution," with its implications of violence, was never in full favor, and, after the Terror, was more a label for violence than reform. We could just as well have used the label "republican," for it was in a republic, or at the beginning in a constitutional monarchy, that the bishops and priests wanted to activate their mission.

But then, why "*priests* of the French Revolution," when so many of my featured "saints and renegades" are presented as bishops? In fact, most all of them were priests as the Revolution began, and were chosen and consecrated bishops precisely because they were *revolutionary priests*. A Catholic theological tradition, dating back to the early Christian church, would have it that bishops possess the fullness of the priesthood. The bishops necessarily saw their ministry as priestly.

For this book, I take my cue from John McManners, who more than forty years ago published the first sympathetic study of the constitutional priests, as well as the refractory priests (i.e., those who refused to take oath), urging further attempts to understand the motivation of the apparent "renegades" from the constitutional clergy.[5] Here I study of the religious attitudes and psychological experiences that underpinned the behavior of representative bishops and priests on the constitutional/revolutionary side, some of them major players on the political and church scene and some of them near-anonymous figures whose intense commitment to or rejection of the constitutional experiment merits attention even so. I play individuals against groups and religious teaching against political action, in order to tell a balanced story of saints and renegades. They were not *all* saints and renegades, of course. Those labels may seem somewhat fanciful, but certainly the priests of France, as revolutionaries or at least as republicans in a new and radically changing political era, were driven to creatively serve or creatively, and often destructively, reject the versions of the priestly ministry that had been handed down to them. *I have researched and studied the archival and primary source material to explain the priests of the French Revolution precisely as priests, on the premise that their priestly commitment, with its mutations, is the primary explanation of their behavior.*[6] It is a study of what these priests and bishops made of priesthood, Catholic and French, and what they tried to accomplish in their priestly ministries, across the revolutionary decade.

Readers will naturally question at times my choice of personalities and events, and here I issue a promissory note: this book is of a piece with two other projects that involve encyclopedic completeness, a dictionary of the 118 bishops of the Constitutional Church, both the original and the reconstituted versions, and an online repertoire of all the priests of France who engaged themselves by oath in the constitutional apostolate—beginning with those thousands who figure in the already published repertoires. As this book goes to print, the initial dictionary entries are being edited, and a search committee has set up the collaborative structures for the online dictionary.[7] For now, I offer a simple appendix with a complete listing of constitutional bishops by dioceses, and full statistics on the priests' initial oath taking in these dioceses, and all constitutional bishops who are presented in the body of the book will be asterisked in the appendix.

This study stands on its own and in relationship to the monumental contributions made by my fellow historians over the years: the institutional histories of the Constitutional Church by Rodney J. Dean, the political and theological interpretations of the constitutional enterprise and leading constitutionals by Bernard Plongeron, and the fundamental sociography and social analysis of the tens of thousands of priests who took the oath of loyalty that originally gave the church its identity by Timothy Tackett. Dean's *L'Église constitutionnelle, Napoléon et le Concordat de 1801* is a reconstruction of developments within the Constitutional Church before and during the negotiations between the pope and Napoleon, and *L'Abbé Grégoire et l'Église constitutionnelle après la Terreur, 1794–97* is a record of the first years of revival after the fall of Robespierre: two masterful theses that now stand as the fundamental reference works for all future studies of the Parisian and nationwide functioning of the Constitutional Church after the Terror. Bernard Plongeron and generations of his students have made available an enormous range of archival data on religion and the Revolution, and established several basic politico-theological orientations for Constitutional Church study. Plongeron's prodigious output begins with his dissertation, published as *Les Réguliers de Paris devant le serment constitutionnel*, through his general but highly original study in volume 10 of *Histoire du Christianisme*, up to his recent work, gathered together in *Des Résistences religieuses à Napoléon (1799–1813)*. The fundamental contemporary research on the constitutional clergy remains Timothy Tackett's *Religion, Revolution, and Regional Culture in Eighteenth-Century France: The Ecclesiastical Oath of 1791*, for all practical purposes a definitive study of the priests' revolutionary motives, some of it handily resumed in the *Atlas de la Révolution française*, vol. 9: *Religion*, which Tackett edited with Claude Langlois and Michel Vovelle.

Other important studies include the early work of Catholic clergy who in varying degrees felt obliged to point out the dogmatic and moral errors of the constitutionals. The abbé Augustin Sicard and Dom Henri Leclercq found little of value in the "schism," whereas the Institut Catholique priest–historian Paul Pisani, although writing in an ultramontane Catholic mode, tried to be evenhanded in his dictionary of all the constitutional bishops, *Répertoire biographique de l'épiscopat constitutionnel* of 1907 and in his multivolume *L'Église de Paris et la Révolution*, published in the years immediately following. Building on Pisani's *Histoire de l'Église de Paris*, the abbé Jean Boussoulade published after World War II a history of the church in revolutionary Paris with special attention to the years after the Terror, *L'Église de Paris du 9 thermidor au Concordat*. Three major Anglophone historians have offered vital interpretations of the religion in the revolutionary era as part of their own agendas: Dale Van Kley in *The Religious Origins of the French Revolution*, with a chapter on the role of residual Jansenism in the shaping of the Constitutional Church; Suzanne Desan in *Reclaiming the Sacred: Lay Religion and Popular Politics in Revolutionary France*, which deals with Constitutional Church influence in the context of independent lay Catholic religious activity; and Nigel Aston's particularly valuable study of bishops at the waning of the Old Regime, *The End of an Elite: The French Bishops and the Coming of the Revolution, 1786–1790*, originally a dissertation done under the direction of John McManners, which can be complemented by his more recent *Religion and Revolution in France, 1780–1804*, an omnium-gatherum of specialized studies of specific national and local Constitutional Church events and personalities. However, a new generation of scholars has focused the agenda for study of church and state during the Revolution on regions, cities, and individual personalities in context. Paul Chopelin examines with profound insight the values and problems of both the constitutional and the refractory clergy on the regional level in his *Ville patriote et ville martyre: Lyon, l'église et la Révolution, 1788–1805*. And the most notable study of an individual clergyman is his local setting is Caroline Chopelin-Blanc's *De l'apologétique à l'Église constitutionnelle: Adrien Lamourette (1742–1794)*.[8]

Priesthood: The Catholic and French Heritage

The book is not only for historians. Members of the Catholic, Orthodox, and Anglican Churches have an active, personal interest in the identity and behavior of the priests of their traditions, because so much of the health and wealth of these churches has depended on that very identity and behavior. Full parishes and successful universities can be indications of a vital faith and successful priests, both together. Countries where Catholic Christianity played a major role in shoring up dynasties, reinforcing ethnic communities, and directing charities would periodically go into political crises that played back into religious crises. The French story I tell here, of the enterprise and heroism of the priests who tried to ensure the safety and good health of their people, and the cruel mutation of some of the priests into men of violence, may well have bearing on today's religious dramas, both American and European. In Europe, for example, note the end of Catholic clerical control of both Irish and Polish popular culture, and the even more dramatic cases of the destruction of the all-embracing Orthodox Christian culture in Russia in the years following 1917 (with its striking recovery following the fall of the Soviet Union, to be sure) or the diminishment to minuscule numbers of churchgoers in the Anglican Church in England and the Lutheran Churches of Scandinavia. Note, too, the intensity of priests' engagement in politics as a form of religion, and religion as a form of politics in the Yugoslav states, where clergy of the different traditions have used Catholicism to define Croatian politics and culture and Orthodoxy to define Serbian politics and culture.

Historians of religion and sociologists have collected examples of "priestly" identities from across the literature and traditions of ancient, medieval, and modern cultures. Historical scholarship is vague on the religious functionaries of the Egyptian kingdoms, the Jewish Second Temple, or the Roman Republic. In the performance of their duties, priests overlapped with government figures, teachers, healers, magicians, and soldiers.[9] We know their sacred books, their myths, and their rituals, but not the direct effect of this religious practice on political, social, and individual life. The challenge in examining the tradition of Christian or Catholic priesthood is that each succeeding generation of believers has altered the priestly job profile to meet the needs of its own era. In fact, the Christian priest was not to be the sacred figure of the old Jerusalem priesthood. Rather he was called *presbyteros* or elder (presbyter), helping the *episcopos* or superintendent of local Christian communities in directing, teaching, and presiding at worship. This person was never called *iereus*, the term used of the temple priest, though the Christian community as a whole was labeled "priestly." Both superintendents and elders took on the qualities of priestly sacredness and the role of mediator. The function, panoply, and theology of the Old Testament priesthood was appropriated, along with the function, panoply, and theology of the Sabbath. We can assume that images of sacrificial blood and ascending smoke were never far away, but the presbyter was not strictly speaking a priest, nor was Sunday (the first, not the last, day of the week and the day of the Resurrection) the Sabbath.

The roles of priest as prayer leader at Eucharist and bishop as guarantor of apostolic succession (transferring spiritual authority from the apostles) became central only gradually. If we stay in the Roman world, in order to get a look at modern France, we have some solid information on papal Rome, monastic Ireland, and parts of Gaul. From the fourth century onward, we have sermon collections of noted bishops, liturgical sources, and archeological remains. But clear evidence of the development of the parish priest as we now know him comes only from the eighth century, when systems of parishes were put in place: in urban centers at the beginning and later to outlying areas.[10] Writings from Charlemagne's era make the parish priest a model of pastoral concern and personal holiness.[11] Here, monks, canons, and other priestly functionaries were as likely to staff parishes as much as some kind of "pure" parish priest. In fact, the curé in the strict sense of the word, with a system of parish priests under the bishop (to go with an already long existing system of randomly staffed parishes), was a development of the twelfth and thirteenth centuries. It could be said that the status of the French priest in society was established by the Concordat of 1516 between Pope Leo X and King Francis I, making the whole system depend on papal and monarchical authority. The Edict of Nantes, although according basic but limited rights of worship to Protestants, did not diminish the priority of Rome. Public worship was reserved for Catholicism alone and legal cases involving churchmen were in a class by themselves. In the realm of finance, churchmen experienced both privilege and subjugation. Estimates of the extent of church properties range from one-tenth to one-sixth of the national territory; churchmen paid minimal taxes. But these goods basically originated with crown and government. And in return for control of education, the Church, naturally, had the duty of providing it.

The major Catholic Church Council of Trent (1545–63) stated that "the priest is a mediator between the faithful and God; set aside for the ministry of the Eucharist and forgiveness of sins, he must identify himself completely with Christ the mediator, at once sacrificial victim and intercessor for his flock."[12] Until the twentieth century, eucharistic ministry was more important than preaching ministry, of course, and the Eucharist was seen more as an act of sacrifice than a sacramental encounter. Bishops were expected to ensure the quality of this new priest, but the records they kept reveal curé resistance to the reforms. The ultimate goal of clerical enlightenment was popular enlightenment. The old residency foibles were looked into, and attempts were made to monitor preaching, all these efforts issuing in effective change of clergy behavior, even though the Council of Trent was not officially promulgated in France due to political complications. The best of the curés of the seventeenth and eighteenth centuries, formed in a specifically French school of spirituality associated with the name of Cardinal Pierre de Bérulle, combined ideals of sanctity and intellectuality with a concern for the masses of believers.

Bérulle, from the highest levels of the aristocracy, was a marvel of spiritual engagement and political clout. He sustained all dramatic Counter-Reformation efforts, whether in championing the work of the Jesuits or in establishing the French version of St. Philip Neri's Oratorians. He was politically prominent enough to be the temporary political nemesis of Cardinal Richelieu, chief minister of Louis XIII. The central Christian teaching of the Incarnation was concretized in a theology of total submission to God, striving to interpret and relive the interior spiritual states of the divine–human Christ. This theology cum spirituality was further institutionalized in the preaching, writing, and organizational work of the most prominent French clerical leaders of the generations to follow, including Jean-Jacques Olier, founder of the Sulpicians, and Louis Grignion de Montfort, a missionary preacher in some measure responsible for the high-profile traditional Catholicism in the Vendée.[13]

Beyond the Bérullian spirituality of the dedicated clergy, three diffuse and vague sets of attitudes—Gallican, Jansenist, and Richerist—complicated clerical life and authority. Gallicanism promoted a distinct French structure and style of Roman Catholicism. The Latin *Ecclesia Gallicana* was simply a problem-free label for the French church, which was obviously part of the Latin Western, and therefore Roman, tradition. Political Gallicanism prioritized government rights over church structure and style, and an ecclesiastical Gallicanism prioritized the French bishops' rights to control their own ecclesiastical destinies within the Roman ecclesiastical system. Jansenism was a profoundly moral reform movement that had marked French religion since the 1600s in much the same way as Puritanism had marked English religion. Distrustful of a hierarchical church structure that counted on worldly success and human righteousness, Jansenism had been condemned by Rome as antiauthority and Protestant, even though it was, in fact, a Catholic response to the values of Calvinism. Jansenists believed that they were promoting the true Catholic Christian theology transmitted by Augustine from the early church. Years of controversy, of dissembling, and, from time to time, of underground existence had given the movement a fluid shape and scattered demography that made it impossible to clearly condemn and round up: even so, the pope had condemned Jansenism in his Bull, *Unigenitus*, and the government of Louis XV had outlawed both public organization and expression. Richerism (after the sixteenth- and seventeenth-century Sorbonne theologian Edmond Richer) demoted the authority of bishops to promote the authority of priests. Episcopal authority as such was not rejected, but Richer developed a theology of priestly character and rights that, he believed, came from apostolic times: Christ gave a commission to the apostles to be the first bishops, but other disciples (the seventy, according to the Gospel of Luke, chap. 10) were commissioned separately, with their own rights and duties.[14] At times, Gallican, Jansenist, and Richerist influences dominated priestly identity and behavior and must be noted, but certainly not as much as the earthy, human attempt to live up to church-wide models for priesthood and the expectations of local parishioners.

Clergy were too much a part of society to protect themselves from its worldliness. The aristocratic bishops and the commoner priests belonged to different social teams, each of which required its own theological backing. There were the scandalous extremes, where bishops' palaces were frequently the setting for worldly pleasures and poor curés were totally unwelcome, but even in good times, the split was all too obvious. Priests, too, could sometimes ensure their fortune by procuring good positions in cathedral chapters or by currying favor with the aristocracy. Parish priests and members of religious orders were at odds within their own circles and across the divide, their jealousies deriving from their funds, their education, their workload, their social status, and such. Curés had special sources of money, orders had wealthy chapters at times. A dedicated curé could resent an idle monk; a learned and prayerful monk could be scandalized by a benefice-hunting curé.

Priests and Bishops in 1789

By the end of the Old Regime, the object of seminary education, in conformity with the decrees of the Council of Trent, was to make of the priest, a *being separate* from the world, the "religious [as if in a religious order] of God according to the priestly spirituality of the French school of the seventeenth century."[15] Sulpicians, Spiritains (Congregation of the Holy Spirit), Lazarists

(Vincentians), and Doctrinaires (Fathers of Christian Doctrine, disbanded during the Revolution) ran the 130 to 140 French seminaries in place in 1789. This does not take into account the minor seminaries, earnestly promoted after 1750.[16] But education for priesthood did not mean years in a seminary; there were other means of acquiring the requisite knowledge and getting experience necessary for the métier. The obligation to spend time in the seminary dated from 1696, at least for Paris; by 1789, the average amount of time spent in a Parisian seminary was sixteen months.[17] Boys could not be tonsured before their fourteenth year. Later they received the four minor orders, then subdiaconate with the obligation to continue on to diaconate and priesthood. Even the great central Paris seminary of Saint-Sulpice was often little more than a career opportunity for young men, concerned more about intellectual and cultural development. In this setting, wigs and musical studies often weighed more heavily than did prayer and theology. Priesthood was conferred, in principle, at twenty-four years of age. And the majority of the ordinands came from the middle classes, which gave importance to recruitment in an urban setting.[18]

Priests attracted both criticism and praise. The *bon curé* of eighteenth-century France was praised by both Catholic reformers and Enlightenment rationalists. John McManners cites Edmé-Nicholas Restif de la Bretonne, brother of the notorious revolutionary-era writer and erotic roustabout Restif de la Bretonne.[19] As curé of Courgis, he prayed for hours, was totally and constantly available to his parishioners, lived abstemiously, and did everything to improve the physical and spiritual lives of his flock. The country curé was an idyllic hero and the city curé was a man of substance. On the other hand, there are records of all kinds of tipsiness, dishonesty, and vulgarity. Where there were local aristocrats to serve, receive, or otherwise appease, the curé who was on his toes had a number of proprieties to learn and observe. Generosity with parishioners and kindness to the poor stood high on the list of qualities attributed to the *bon curé*. Even the peasant *cahiers* of 1789, for all their complaints, could praise the simple, good pastor of souls.[20] Looking more closely at priests of the era, we note that they tended to be local, though some regions could not generate enough vocations for their needs and needed to look elsewhere, even to foreign lands. But the majority came from the town bourgeoisie and the well-off farming class. Depending on the size of the parish and its location, there could be great variations in income, with some of the clergy terribly underpaid. The *Traité des devoirs d'un pasteur* (1758) included a suggested list of books that every curé should have.[21] In fact, a curé could have everything from a minimal four or five books through the library necessary to do his own research and writing in history and theology.[22]

The bishops did indeed, virtually all of them, come from the aristocracy at the end of the Old Regime. By 1789, only one commoner priest had been elevated to the episcopacy, and in 1790 the brilliant Jean-René Asseline was consecrated a bishop, just in time to refuse the constitutional clergy oath, and so lose the bishopric.[23] The same pecking order of greater and lesser aristocratic dignity obtained for the noble bishops as for nobles in general: the older the pedigree and the closer connection to military service to the kings of old, the more highly honored the family name. An aristocratic family could try to obtain a good church position for a family member by appeal to the aristocratic bishop, and naturally bishops helped their own. Riches and affluence often translated into worldliness, but the ideal was a bishop who was generous to his people, protective of his clergy, and charitable across the board in his last will and testament. Stories of episcopal scoundrels are better known: Cardinal Louis de Rohan hoping for a secret tryst with Marie Antoinette, or the ethical chameleon and shameless (if brilliant) diplomat Charles-Maurice de Talleyrand. John McManners retells the story of this young, clubfooted aristocrat taking over the see of Autun with a great show of piety, earnest preaching, and commitment to service, only to pack up and leave forever, right after his hold on the position was assured.[24] Yet, it did make sense to have a bishop who could stand up for the diocese at the highest levels of political, economic, and social life—and all the trappings of the episcopacy cost plenty of money. The problem was that many of the bishops were seldom if ever back in their dioceses, being off in Paris or elsewhere—post–Council of Trent rules for residency, parish visitations, and confirmation be damned. Of course, even dedicated bishops maintained a clear distinction between themselves and their commoner clergy.

And so, now, to the saints and renegades of the French Revolution, the priests and bishops who played an ecclesiastical and sometimes political game of constitutional or republican reform *at some point* in their careers regardless of their status in the Constitutional Church. I feature the star performers (often constitutional bishops) and the dramatically important priestly activities in the government or in high-profile church work. Readers will find in these chapters the personalities, writings, and activities of national leaders, local mavericks, and whole sections of the clergy that rebelled, resigned, retracted, or totally dedicated themselves to an apostolate that was at once revolutionary and priestly. It is a drama divided into three acts, or sections—each section furnished with a general orientation, chapter introductions, and a selective chronology of state–church events[25]—which I characterize simply as *engagement*, *survival*, and *revival*.

Part One

ENGAGEMENT, 1789–1791

Bad harvests and the high cost of food staples pushed King Louis XVI and his advisers to convoke the Estates General, France's first parliamentary assembly in 175 years, obviously a dramatic bid for help in resolving chronic financial crises. Few in the clerical First Estate, the aristocratic Second Estate, or the commoner Third Estate were aware of the revolutionary risks they were courting. Well before the first session, scheduled for the beginning of May 1789, meetings were held all over France, not only to elect delegates but to draw up lists of complaints and goals for the Estates to consider: the famous *cahiers de doléances*. The clergy of the First Estate expressed very few deep political or social anxieties that could result in political upheaval, and no real hints that a transformed church should go hand-in-hand with a transformed government. The actual opening of the Estates General was first of all a church event, with a procession to the church of Saint-Louis in Versailles. The Third Estate marched first, followed by the other two Estates; King Louis walked at the end of the procession, preceded by the Blessed Sacrament, which was carried under a canopy by the archbishop of Paris.

Successful power bids by the Third Estate at Versailles in June, violent manifestations in Paris with the attack on the Bastille in July, and the Declaration of the Rights of Man and of the Citizen in August overshadowed the first legislative moves toward church reform. Before this Declaration of Rights, the clergy had abandoned the tithe, and several months later, church properties and lands were nationalized—to be used as collateral for the new bonds (eventually used as currency), the assignats. The church reform was one of the surprises of the early Revolution, its causes residing in the personal and religious orientations of the priests and the experts in church law who dominated the Estates General and the Constituent Assembly.

With the new year, 1790, random but radical church-reform proposals of different stripes continued apace: to withdraw recognition of monastic vows, to recognize Catholicism as the official religion of France, and to attach Avignon, the papal enclave, to France. The new Civil Constitution of the Clergy was approved, to be rejected soon enough by a substantial minority of priests. Even so, most priests, whether of revolutionary or counterrevolutionary orientation, supported a festival celebration of the first anniversary of the fall of the Bastille, and Archbishop Boisgelin of Aix tried to reconcile all sides—really Rome and the French government—with a compromise document. Dialogue, if it ever existed, certainly ended when an oath of allegiance to the nation, the law, and the king was imposed on all priests engaged in active apostolates; swearing the oath meant acceptance of the Civil Constitution at the Clergy. Anticipating resistance, the government, at the beginning of January 1791, ordered the clergy to take the oath of allegiance on the next day. The French Catholic Church as envisaged by the authors of the Civil Constitution was now a reality, albeit with a major problem: only a small handful of French bishops agreed to be part of this reformed Catholicism. Finally, the minimally religious maverick bishop of Autun, Charles Talleyrand, along with two auxiliary bishops, agreed to consecrate new bishops, and followed conscientiously the time-honored church ritual for these consecrations. Roman authorities rejected these consecrations as illegitimate (but valid), with the pope finally and officially condemning the Civil Constitution.

Whether in response or on their own, legislators passed laws proclaiming religious liberty—hitherto limited in Catholic France—and restricting professional organizations in a way that could neutralize the efforts of the French clergy who refused to take the oath.

Priests and Bishops

Chapter 1. Emmanuel-Joseph Sieyès and Henri Grégoire, two priests with strong and visible personalities, worked for government reform in the months of preparation for the Estates General, France's first parliamentary assembly since 1614. Their personal orientations reveal the polarities of revolutionary priesthood in 1789: the cranky and secular Sieyès, in fact minimally a priest, trying to bracket religion to bring about a new political era; and the imposing and pastoral Grégoire trying to reform religion to bring about a new political era as well. As a seminarian, Sieyès had developed a distinct philosophy, or rhetoric, of religion, as well as a refined musical taste. His tract *Sur Dieu ultramètre et sur la fibre religieuse de l'homme* (*On God beyond Measure and on Man's Religious Fiber*) is a suggestive dialogue on religion that bears comparison with later German philosophy. Grégoire, three years before ordination, produced an essay on poetry as a way to beauty, truth, and, through scripture, to God. Their early lives and seminary educations gave both of them the opportunity to develop the roles they played as members of the Estates General and thereafter.

Chapter 2. The political efforts of Sieyès and Grégoire were abetted by the great numbers of priests in France who demanded reforms in the clerical *cahiers de doléances*, collected and submitted as part of the national program to inform the deputies to the Estates General of the complaints and demands of their constituencies. When the priests who were actual deputies to the Estates General began their own official discussions of religious and political change, they took sides, for and against this change, in weeks of clerical haggling recorded best by the abbé Jacques Jallet but also by other priests who were present at the Assembly meetings. The decision of these members of the First Estate, the clergy, to join the Third Estate, the commoners, in a new National (Constituent) Assembly was a confused affair: a wide range of assumptions and misunderstandings was behind the actual move. Subsequently, priests and bishops on the Ecclesiastical Committee, appointed by the National Assembly, were dominated by lay canon lawyers. Together, they were responsible for the Civil Constitution of the Clergy, the founding document for the July 1790 revolutionary reorganization of French Catholicism in the Constituent Assembly.

Chapter 3. Henri Grégoire's highly influential colleagues were Claude Fauchet, the most visible of the revolutionary priests in Paris, and Adrien Lamourette, mentor to Grégoire across the years and a theological adviser to key members of the Constituent Assembly. The derring-do of Fauchet as he scampered about in a rain of gunfire during the taking of the Bastille can be partly explained by his theology, but more from his personal and political engagement in the new political era. His major book, *De la religion nationale*, had been published a month and a half before the attack on the Bastille. In the very first years of the Revolution, he was at the center of radical political dialogue and journalism. But he was above all a constitutional bishop, high profile of course, given his earlier deeds and publications, and creative in his response to opponents of the Constitutional Church with its new bishops.

Chapter 4. Lamourette's work alongside a leading figure of the early Revolution, the comte de Mirabeau, is displayed both by his theology and by his day-to-day practical ministry. He articulated both the role of the church for a new political era and a more-or-less systematic theology—"ecclesiology" is the technical label—for a renewed and enlightened church. Lamourette should be situated between Mirabeau, whom he advised, and Camus, the lay canon lawyer, whose work was one of the bases of his own theology. Elected as constitutional bishop of the primatial see (first in dignity of the French dioceses) of Lyon, he is best known for his intervention as a delegate to the successor to the Constituent Assembly, the so-called Legislative Assembly; it was a passing moment of reconciliation in 1792, and so, a flash forward in this part of the narrative (see Chronology, Part II: Survival, 1791–1795) on behalf of a constitutional monarchy, only a month before both assembly and monarchy disappeared.

Chronology

1789

24 January	Modalities of election to the Estates General officially set up.
February	Publication of Sieyès's *What Is the Third Estate?*
4 May	Procession and Mass for opening of Estates General.
30 May	Publication of Fauchet's *De la religion nationale.*
13 June	Three curés led by Jallet join the Third Estate.
17 June	The Third Estate led by Sieyès proclaims itself the National Assembly.
19 June	Vote of the clergy to join the National Assembly.

20 June	Tennis Court Oath, with Grégoire and Sieyès in attendance.
9 July	The National Assembly proclaims itself the Constituent Assembly.
14 July	Fall of the Bastille.
4 August	Renunciation of aristocratic privileges by members of the former Second Estate.
11 August	Clergy abandon the tithe, which was paradoxically defended by Sieyès.
26 August	Declaration of the Rights of Man and of the Citizen.
2 November	Nationalization of church lands.

1790

5 February	The Assembly adds new members to its Ecclesiastical Committee.
13 February	Law proposed by Jean-Baptiste Treilhard, a delegate especially engaged in church reform, withdrawing official recognition of monastic vows.
12 April	Motion of the Carthusian Dom Gerle to recognize Catholicism as the religion of the French.
12 June	Avignon, the papal enclave, asks to be attached to France.
13 June	Counterrevolutionary insurrection at Nîmes with massacre of Protestants.
12 July	Text of the Civil Constitution of the Clergy approved.
14 July	First revolutionary festival, supported by both revolutionary and conservative clergy.
30 October	Archbishop Boisgelin's *Exposition des principes* attempts to bridge gap between Rome and the Constituent Assembly.
27 November	Decree imposing clerical oath of allegiance to the nation, the law, and the king, implying acceptance of the Civil Constitution of the Clergy.
26 December	King sanctions the decree of 27 November.

1791

3 January	Clergy ordered to take the oath of allegiance to the nation, the law, and the king within twenty-four hours.

February	Beginning of election and consecration of the constitutional bishops (through May), the first consecration performed by Talleyrand of Autun with two auxiliary bishops.
10 March	Pius VI condemns the Civil Constitution.
2 April	Death of Mirabeau.
13 April	Pope reiterates his condemnation of the Civil Constitution.
7 May	Proclamation of religious liberty.
14 June	Le Chapelier Law forbidding worker/professional organizations and strikes is invoked by constitutional bishops to control refractory clergy.

Chapter One

THE FORMATION OF A REVOLUTIONARY PRIEST

Sieyès and Grégoire

The educational and spiritual formations of Emmanuel-Joseph Sieyès and Henri Grégoire were similar, and both men possessed a worldly intellectual independence in their seminary days, Sieyès searching for meaning in philosophy and Grégoire in poetry. They were formed in an era when Catholic seminary education was a combination of the high ideals reset for priests at the Council of Trent and the practical worldliness of French social life at all levels. According to Trent, priests were to be mediators between God and the people in a ministry of preaching the gospel and presiding at worship, Mass, confession, and the other sacraments. The preaching and sacramental activity in the early careers of Sieyès and Grégoire has left few traces, especially for Sieyès, but even his silence about his priesthood could not hide the years of saying Mass. A major Sieyès biographer, Jean-Denis Bredin, writes, "One can doubt that he stayed away from [celebration of] the sacraments, for it was not that easy for an important *vicaire* to never 'do' priest. It is sure in any case that at Chartres he said Mass."[1] Though Grégoire was the totally dedicated priest and revolutionary, either one of two other major figures might have been considered as alternates to Sieyès: (1) Charles-Maurice de Talleyrand, one of those priests by default from the aristocracy, who in his last act as bishop of Autun assured the valid consecration of the first constitutional bishops, and thus apostolic continuity; (2) Joseph Fouché, member of the Catholic teaching congregation of the Oratorians, who emerged as a thoroughly secularized, even violent promoter of revolution, and who, under Napoleon, helped assure the incorporation of the constitutional bishops into the concordatory church. But of Talleyrand's seminary days no documentation of intellectual and quasi-spiritual developments has

Figure 2 Sieyès and Grégoire at the center of the Tennis Court Oath, whereby the commoner Third Estate members vowed to ensure their successful transformation into the National Assembly—in effect, then, the legislative branch of the French government. It was in no small measure the influence of the abbé Sieyès that brought about all this. In this small center foreground of Jacques-Louis David's illustration of the event, Sieyès is seated, calmly holding his hat, just to the right of the presiding officer on the table, and Grégoire is standing with two other men in front and to the left of the table. The monk is Dom Gerle, who was actually absent, and the other figure is Rabaut Saint-Etienne, who was a Protestant pastor. (Bibliothèque nationale de France)

survived, and Fouché was not an ordained priest. The theme here is *formation*, in any case.[2]

In major writings, published before the opening of the Estates General, Sieyès laid down a program for the rehabilitation of the state, and Grégoire, a program for the rehabilitation of religion in general by the regeneration of the Jews (of Europe) in particular. Sieyès and Grégoire were arguably the most influential priestly voices in French public life in the first three years of the revolution. They are impossible to miss in Jacques-Louis David's unfinished yet famed canvas of the Tennis Court Oath of 12 June 1789: Sieyès seated at the central table *faite* podium for the reader of the oath (Jean-Sylvain Bailly, dean of the Third Estate) and Grégoire standing in the foreground slightly left, in a common embrace with the Carthusian monk, Dom Christophe Gerle, and the Protestant pastor Jean-Paul Rabaut Saint-Etienne. Dom Gerle, painted in as an appropriate actor by David, was absent that day, which leaves Sieyès and Grégoire as the featured priests. When they both arrived on the national scene, Sieyès had jettisoned the minimal God talk of his earlier years and Grégoire had jettisoned the worldly cultural discourse of his earliest essays. Whereas Sieyès was a political revolutionary for whom priesthood was little more than a job category, Grégoire was an engaged priest who was at the same time a political revolutionary. Sieyès and Grégoire represented the two polarities of revolutionary priesthood—total secularism and total commitment to ministry in the new political era—with Sieyès far above the religious "isms" in his own realm of philosophy and political theory, and with Grégoire firmly planted in mainline Gallicanism, leaning Jansenist in some ways, and much more Richerist when he was opposing Old Regime bishops than when he was presiding as a bishop of the Constitutional Church.[3]

Emmanuel-Joseph Sieyès

Neither before nor after ordination did the abbé Sieyès appear to have any of the formal religious commitment promoted in the Catholic theological and spiritual writings of the day. But he was the last in a long line of Old Regime priests who balanced their secularism and even, at times, total lack of religious faith with dedication to their intellectual and administrative tasks.[4] As a young man, his drive for social advancement was uncomplicated by moral or professional vision. Short in stature, plain in looks, afflicted with poor skin, his physique and personality were perhaps no worse than average. His parents were dedicated churchgoers in Fréjus, the southern French city of Sieyès's birth and upbringing, and his two older sisters, whom he said he loved more than all the other siblings, eventually joined the convent. The father, Honoré Sieyès, was the one who talked of God and morality in his correspondence with the future priest. Sieyès himself had only those practical, "get ahead" concerns, accepting the clerical state as a natural setting for the realization of social status and financial security, and any efforts he made on behalf of his brothers were geared toward the same goals.[5] Neither as a youth nor as an adult of any age did Sieyès display any interest in female companionship or sexual pleasure. A misanthrope on the personal level, he eventually became, nevertheless, a passionate student of the human condition.[6]

Formation and Clerical Life

The Jesuits at Fréjus were Sieyès's first teachers, but whether he left their school because his father wished it (as is said in the autobiographical *Notice* that has come down to us from the mature Sieyès) or because he simply was not invited to go on there, we do not know.[7] He continued his studies at Draguignan with the Doctrinaires, a congregation that in southern France was on a par with the Jesuits, and he flirted briefly and fancifully with the idea of a military career. Inasmuch as priesthood was his family's goal for him from the beginning, he prepared, in the totally unsystematic way of his day, for entrance into the clerical state. When he arrived at the seminary of Saint-Sulpice in Paris at the age of seventeen and a half, he had already been tonsured—officially, then, a cleric. The top seminary in France at that time, Saint-Sulpice had never fully realized the goals of the Council of Trent or the hopes of its founder, Jean-Jacques Olier. Instead, there was at best a conflict of disciplinary styles and at worst an apparent certification of spiritually directionless hangers-on.

Sieyès worked out his own range of studies and readings, primarily philosophical and social scientific. Music had real importance for him then; theology, none. In a manuscript labeled *Projet de bibliothèque*, he set about structuring his intellectual life. Otherwise he went about his serious study at the nearby Sorbonne (transferring from Saint-Sulpice to the nearby Vincentian seminary of Saint-Firmin) before taking on the full clerical obligations that came with ordination to the subdiaconate. The range of courses that were prerequisites to his licentiate forced him back into theology and church history, to the detriment of his social scientific studies. But, even so, by the time he was ordained in 1772, two years before finishing the licentiate, he had already laid the foundation of his future intellectual life.

Charles-Augustin Sainte-Beuve highlights, in his *Causéries de lundi*, Sieyès's culture and originality: "Sieyès was a *born master*" in the sense that "he did not make use of any of the masters of his day: neither Encyclopedists nor Condillac nor Rousseau. Even politically, one cannot say that Sieyès had been a disciple of Rousseau; he had early passed judgment on, and refuted, him."[8] Probably he was preoccupied more with the observation of himself in the act of analyzing society, the economy, and the possibilities of revolution. Sainte-Beuve wrote that Sieyès's *sciences sociales* consisted above all in the divisions of work, applied to the different functions and powers in society, and that an *art social* consisted in controlling popular energy: "Sieyès, the enemy of every privilege and of all aristocracy, had nonetheless distanced himself from pure democracy. And he believed that the *art* [*social*] consisted primarily in making popular energy reasonably applicable for modern nations, by means of a system of representation that he put together with infinite ingenuity."[9] His tabula rasa approach to politics and the economy extended to history also: "It seems to me that judging what is taking place by that which has already happened, is to judge the known by means of the unknown. It is better to judge the past on [the basis of] the present, and to acknowledge that so-called historical truths have no more reality than so-called religious truths."[10]

Therefore, people as social, political, and economic actors were the objects of his interest. Later, in the autobiographical *Notice*, he wrote, "I really believe that I am traveling among an unknown people; I have to study the customs."[11] Even supposing the everyday lives of people to be "unknown" to him, he was not heartless. His genuine concern for the poor was probably related to his hatred of nobility and his vestigial identity as a cleric.

Humiliation by, and jealousy of, the highborn and well-off haunted him all his life, even into old age. His aversion to noble titles was intense, and the reason for the aversion clear. Without the money needed to compete for a canonry (*canonicat*) early in his career, he and his father groveled to obtain a miserable benefice. Shortly thereafter, he went north, to Tréguier in Brittany in 1775, beginning there a long association with Bishop Jean-Baptiste de Lubersac that was to end in the diocese of Chartres. Sieyès appears to have been happy there. Though he attended every diocesan chapter meeting, he was never made vicar general of the diocese of Tréguier as he had hoped. More important for his later career was his attendance at the États de Brétagne, a proximate preparation for his maneuvering at the Estates General. Bastid says, "From this moment on, Sieyès embraced the cause of the

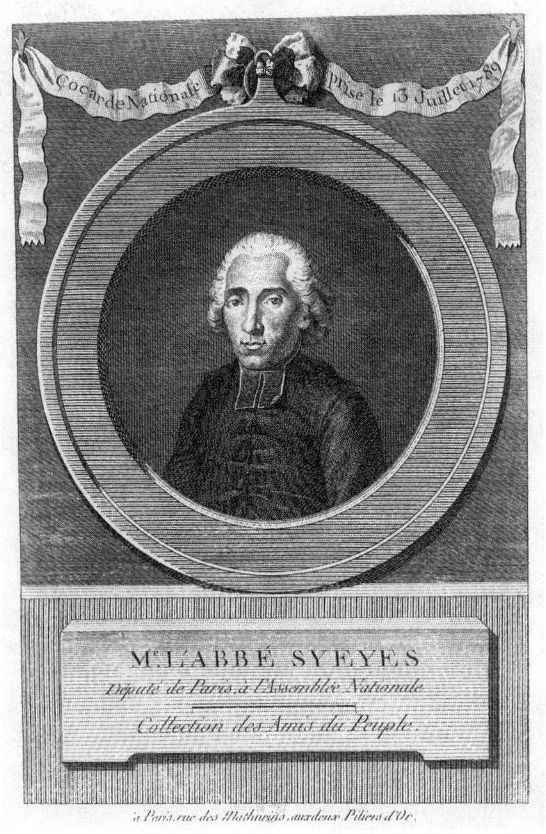

Figure 3 An unusual image of the abbé Sieyès in priestly attire. The irony of the image is that Sieyès avoided a public priestly apostolate most of the time, even as he was a full-time functionary within priestly administrative settings. He was elected one of the Paris deputies of the Third Estate, although he was from Chartres and a member of the clergy. Undoubtedly this was because of his crucially important publication *What Is the Third Estate?* (Bibliothèque nationale de France)

people. He who disdained history, consecrated two notebooks to a study of the origins of the Estates General."[12] But the great preoccupation and disappointment of his early clerical career was his failure to become chaplain for the king's aunt, Madame Sophie, in 1778. In a letter to his father, he said, "He [the bishop] is not thoughtful [*délicat*] enough to help me in any way that does not turn to his own profit. . . . It is the only reason that can have caused him to fail to support me plain and simple, to miss the Madame Sophie appointment, to astonish all who know me."[13]

The bishop and the canons of Chartres had different reservations about the man. Lubersac was overheard excluding Sieyès as a potential candidate for an office because he was not a "gentilhomme." And by 1790, the canons of Chartres wanted him removed as vicar general: "In view of the scandalous principles spread throughout the writings of M. Sieyès, chancellor of this diocese, is it not appropriate to write to the bishop to ask him to withdraw his support from M. Sieyès and to rescind his appointment as vicar general of this diocese?"[14] But this was 1790, and Sieyès had a high secular and political profile. In his formative years, religious life was philosophical life and he never envisaged religious activity as anything other than social and political action. One might say that the life and ministry promoted by the Council of Trent mutated into a purposeful living and political engagement, *and* this did not disqualify someone as a priest in Sieyès's era. While at Chartres, he participated, naturally, in the ecclesiastical "chamber" in his area, but his political experience of the period came more from membership in the Orléanais provincial assembly.

Interpreting Religion

For Sieyès, religion was one small part, but an important one, of the great world of philosophy, economics, and political thought.[15] According to Jacques Guilhaumou, "It is a matter of scattered remarks about religion, unexpected in the *Grand cahier métaphysique* but which send us to the 'religious' manuscripts of Sièyes, that are few in number but quite significant."[16] Sieyès did not ignore the abstractions of metaphysics and the problem of God, keeping over the years the aforementioned *Grand cahier.* First in line is Condillac and the sensing statue that engendered major discussion of the reality of the self and self-knowledge. Here, Sieyès enthusiastically worked out a philosophical position that owed less to French philosophy than it did to German and Anglo-Scottish empiricism, fashioned in conformity with Sieyès's long-term understanding of language and rhetoric. At the end of the first half of the *Grand cahier,* Sieyès limns a set of religious reflections—dating, it would appear, from 1773. On the uselessness and usefulness of religion as such, Sieyès wrote, "Revelation of supernatural dogmas, useless," and this, for two reasons: (1) the "revelation of truths that are useful in the arts and sciences" belongs to reason; and (2) the "revelation of moral precepts, or ways leading to happiness, founded on the nature of man and of physical laws," are clear from observation and experience. Religion can be useful as part of an open natural learning experience, but in an informed and ordered society it is not necessary. In such a society, the individual is guided by a combination of self-interest and common interest, and needs no religious sanctions to get him to behave.[17] Societies can actually eliminate religion and maintain morality by wholesome teaching about the meaning of human actions. If, however, society does want to make use of the religion in its midst, then that religion should be enlisted in "teaching the means of arriving at natural happiness." For, on its own, natural religion "has no foundation; everything is false in the exposition and refutation of all that is said to belong to the worship of the divinity." As far as revealed religion is concerned, Sieyès says that "nothing in all of that can be useful,"[18] and that Christianity, in comparison with other religions, "has done the most harm": "(1) by the dogmas to which people must submit in faith, (2) by its precepts and counsels, (3) because in replacing the natural motives for human actions it has annulled the force [of the actions], (4) by the ignorance of morality that it foments in forbidding the use of reason, (5) by its maintenance of ministers [of religion]."[19]

The most substantial text for viewing Sieyès's unique combination of Enlightenment rationalism and vestigial religious sentiment, a formal set of reflections on God, is *Sur Dieu ultramètre et sur la fibre religieuse de l'homme* (*On God beyond Measure and on Man's Religious Fiber*), written, in would appear, around 1780.[20] In this work, Sieyès continues to decry "the revelation of useless supernatural dogmas" promoting "natural morality" as the "revelation of moral precepts or the ways leading to happiness." Only this latter kind of religion is useful because here "man is guided by his own self-interest; in an ordered society, public interest results from individual interests, for which there is no need of religious sanction." That Sieyès considered ethics to be religion at all is intriguing. He does hold out for calling some good behavior and attitudes "religion."[21] Condemning the standard philosophical and theological presentations of God, he searches for the only type of useful religion, the only God-reality. Although he refuses to promote full-fledged atheism, he sees clericalism as a major obstacle to the functioning of an otherwise healthy society: "Do not tolerate the existence of a clergy, by which I mean a corporation, for every corporation other than the open establishment of a large national alliance [*association*] is an evil in the social machine."[22]

Disarmingly, Sieyès says that he is attacking the opinions of no one. He is only searching, and can make mistakes himself. This being a personal search, he is not trying to become the teacher of all. To the basic question, "Can I come to the knowledge of God without the aid of reason?" he offers sentiment as the alternative to reason and use of cognitive faculties: "Because I cannot *understand* God, nor come up with any ideas of him, I search to see if one can get there by *sentiment*." God is unknowable and no amount of verbal dexterity can make it otherwise: "It is certain and acknowledged that no human idea, supposing even the most exalted, can attain God. You would add if you could *infinity* to all human faculties and imagining, and you would not have any better idea of God. We have here two different natures. It involves the existence not only of the unknown but of the unknowable."[23]

The reality of God is found in the reality of the human being, for the simple reason that there is no reality outside of the world of human beings. Under these conditions, it makes no sense to Sieyès to negate the reality of God: God may be incomprehensible, but he is real.[24] Of course, Sieyès would need to push further than this, because a reality in the mind does not necessarily mean a reality outside the mind, although philosophers from Anselm through Descartes to Kant have managed to get to the reality of God from this same starting point. But here Sieyès cleverly sketches a dialogue on the strengths and weaknesses of words to express reality. We note that the Q[uestioner] and the R[esponder] do not always play their roles; it is a mixed-up conversation, cited here at length:

> Q. Are you an atheist?
>
> R. What do you mean by that?
>
> Q. In other words, do you believe in an intelligent, infinite, eternal, and immense being who is not nature, but from whom nature derives its temporal existence?
>
> R. What a pile-up of words that do not bring any distinct idea to mind. All my reflections bring me back to the clear idea that I am only a human being and that any idea of the *superhuman* means nothing to me; that it is not even an idea. I can thus answer you that I do not understand you. But now let me ask you what *patîma* or other nonsense syllables might mean.
>
> Q. Let us see where you want to lead me. All right, *patîma* is only a word.
>
> R. This is the reproach I made to you when I asked what is God. It is only a word unless you explain it to yourself.
>
> Q. But your word signifies nothing, whereas the name God doubtlessly signifies something because I deny his existence.
>
> R. It will mean as much or as little as you wish. Can a word contain anything other than the ideas that you can put there? And can you put there anything other than human ideas? I can also mark with

the label *patîma* a completely different range of ideas, or what I will name, following your example, ideas that are unknown; that is, I cover over as you did, an empty space . . . physical syllables that strike my ear without imprinting anything on, or recalling anything to, my brain.

Q then says that intellection counts more than desire here, without adding to the observation, but R continues on the drawbacks of any God discussion:

R. If what you understand is a *reality*, then why do you deny it? If it is nothing, then you have made a great discovery. You declare to me that by the word *God*, you do not mean anything real; I believe that. It is as if you said to me, "Nothing is nothing."

Q. Well, we will soon not even be able to discuss this together. From your side of things, tell me what your thought is on God.

R. I would like to, even without hope of giving you satisfaction. I have, like many others and for a long time, talked nonsense about these matters and beaten about in empty space. The research was in vain. So I have come back to *man* as the central goal of philosophy, as the source from which every human activity proceeds.[25]

So, there is no *concept* of God that works. "God" is a nonsense syllable, and the search for ultimate meaning in human reality must start elsewhere.

The essence of the human being is found, however, in his or her needs, which are at the center of all human faculties. Sieyès concludes the section on "the *needs* of man" with this admonition: "Everything is there. Every search, every movement that does not go toward this goal is a false step, a loss of human strength. The need for subsistence, the need for protection against changes in the atmosphere, the need for social exchange, the needs arising from curiosity, the imagination, and hope. Man is, therefore, a *being with needs.* Around him nature has placed an infinity of concentric circles that are so many depositories open to his needs, open to the *progressive* development of his faculties and whatever is useful for life."[26] Here, then, hope expressed as God is the ultimate need of humans. If you stay with science and the material reality, thinking that you can go from the known to the unknown, you will never come to God as reality/idea.[27] You cannot simply *study* the evidence: you have to pose questions and then arrive at some kind of state where curiosity rests; that is, you have to traverse those concentric circles of reality. The need to live, the need to ask, the need to know, is a drive that takes a person beyond any concept of truth: "It is not in the order of truths, but in the order of *needs* that I have placed myself. . . . The order of truths must remain outside of every idea of God, it is true, but its necessity is visible to the human being in the order of his needs."[28]

Our needs are useful, in that they lead us to the "beyond": "Can we get something out of it for our own needs? Certainly if I am only speaking of the closest *beyonds* and not of the farthest, the response is indubitable."[29] Sieyès uses strange terminology whereby he assures us that the discussion does not shoot for the ineffable infinite. The "beyond" is outside human measure, but it can serve as some kind of goal: "Let us not dream of discovering the *beyond*, or discovering if there is a question of a true *beyond*, that which I can call God or what is better designated by the name of *ultramètre*, beyond human measure. . . . Can the *ultramètre* be useful to our needs? I would like to respond with clarifications that will give you all my thoughts on the topic"[30] Does an attempt to look beyond this world serve any useful religious purpose? "No," answers Sieyès, "if religion kills the energy that has its own animation; yes, if it has added to and continues to add to this [energy]." Priests regularly kill the energy when they say such things as "your sufferings are the will of God."[31]

God is attained through intuition and feeling, not through reasoning: "Everything that is not in the order of our needs we can reject, I see; but God *felt* and not *conceptualized* seems to be part of this order [of needs]." God is not a "*rational truth*," which does not mean that he is in opposition to truth.[32] There are parallels to other disciplines here. You can say that "God is heterogeneous to the order of truths," but you can say the same thing about geometry relative to sentiment, about color or hardness relative to abstract geometric shapes: "Everyone carves out this notion in his own way; it [the notion] is relative to what each person can best believe." God is "beyond all senses [*hypo-sens*]," beyond all goodness, beauty, virtue, knowledge, justice, and power.[33] And yet in the end, God is a reality: "God is incomprehensible and unknowable, agreed. Thus he is a *reality* grasped by the sentiments."[34]

In sum, God is at the heart of human action, human exchange, human goodness, at the heart of the action of the religious "fiber." The God that is experienced, or felt, here does not interfere, however, with the progress of reason. He is the reality of goodness in moral activity. With Sieyès, the Frenchman, we see a teaching that presages German liberal religion and philosophy from Schleiermacher to Fichte.[35] But for Sieyès it was a dead end, probably because with his lexical acumen there were too many elements *within* measuring distance and not *ultramètre*, especially politics and economics, that won his attention.

Political Commitment

Less than ten years later, in *Qu'est-ce que c'est le tiers état?* Sieyès promoted the political rehabilitation of the social majority, in effect, the entire population, apart from the clergy and nobles.[36] Looking forward to the revival of the old parliamentary legislature, which had not assembled since 1614, Sieyès hammers away at the obvious: the legislature is divided into three Estates or houses, two of them (clergy and nobles) representing only a tiny portion of the total French population. The Third Estate, which ideally should be representing the commoners, would have at best a third of the political clout on the national scene. And Sieyès found that this derisory one-third of the legislative force was yet further limited by unfair voting practices.

Why did Sieyès want so much to rehabilitate the majority? Probably because he identified with the majority in its suppressed state, and avenging them certainly had to do, in part, with avenging himself. In his personal life, he had used the church as a stand-in for the broader society, and now, trying to make his mark in that broader society, he was working for all his compatriots. Sieyès placed the word *nation* in high relief in this (and other) writings, defining it in this text as "a body of associates living under *common* laws and represented by the same *legislative assembly*."[37] "What does a nation require to survive and prosper," he asks, and he proceeds to enumerate the principal private activities that "support society."[38] Public services are the army, the law, the church, and the bureaucracy, and even there, with aristocrats and clergy so often in charge, it is the common people who do all the work. "What, then, is the Third Estate? All; but an 'all' that is fettered and oppressed," because "the privileged have succeeded in usurping all well-paid and honorific posts."[39] There follows a tirade against the aristocracy which, "from infirmity, incapacity, incurable idleness, or a collapse of morality, performs no functions at all in society."[40] Aristocrats are a burden for the nation without being part of it. They hold themselves exempt from any common obligations and they have political rights distinct from all the other members of the population.

In his third chapter, "What Does the Third Estate Want to Be? *Something*," Sieyès complains bitterly about the humiliating control of this estate by the aristocracy, even as he works on the primary theme of the Estates General voting methods.[41] Instead of voting by head, so that a critical mass of commoner and commoner-sympathetic votes could be secured, the voting was to be done by orders. The First Estate with its aristocratic bishops dominating, and the Second Estate made up completely of aristocrats, would always outvote, two to one, the Third Estate. Consequently, "First claim of the Third Estate: that the representatives of the Third Estate be chosen solely from among citizens who really belong to the Third Estate."[42] It has been too easy for aristocrats, new and old, to be chosen by their districts, where they dominate the local people, as representatives in the Third Estate. And even if they do not go themselves, they can make sure that their Third Estate representatives do their dirty work. The "second claim" that Sieyès lays down is that the deputies to the Third Estate "be equal in number to those of the two privileged orders."[43] Apparently tolerant of the disproportions in representation that occurred in much earlier centuries, he is indignant that two hundred thousand clergy and nobles of his own day should be allowed to dominate twenty-five or twenty-six million citizens. Voting by head, then, is, of course, the third claim of the Third Estate: "It is quite certain that unless votes are counted by head the true majority may be set aside, which would be the supreme difficulty, since it would render legislation null and void."[44]

Naturally, a government dominated by aristocrats could not fairly and successfully go about reform, even though they have at times seemed more eager for reform than have been the torpid members of the Third Estate itself. In his fourth chapter, Sieyès finds once again that the members of the other Estates can do no right. If they want to help, it is in their own interest. If they make a move to pay taxes, it will be so that the Estates General will not have to meet at all: "More likely, one suspects, the nobility is trying to hoodwink the Third Estate at the price of a kind of anticipation of justice, in order to divert it from its current demands and so distract it from its need to be *something* in the Estates General."[45] Other major examples of the unequal treatment meted out by the government are the use of taxes (to help poor nobility) and the tracking down and sentencing of criminals: "Who are the citizens the most vulnerable to personal harassment by the regular agents [*agents de file*] and by their subordinates in all parts of the administration? The members of the Third Estate."[46]

Basic principles of operation and a statement of future agenda constitute the last two chapters. The nation is not part of some other entity; it *is* the whole. Consequently, the orders who stand apart from the citizenry are not part of the nation, and means for getting to and tabulating the population are essential. Another shot at the nobles, then: "There was once a time when the Third Estate was in bondage and the nobility was everything. Now the Third Estate is everything and the nobility is only a word."[47] He is chagrined that, even so, the aristocracy can pretend to a new authority, more repressive than the previous authority. The Third Estate has to be true to itself. It should not see itself as an order, one of three Estates. It is the nation, and "its representatives constitute the whole National Assembly."[48] More immediately, Sieyès's expressed intransigence in discussion of the role of the Third Estate, equating it with the legislature, energized the Tennis Court scenario. Others, such as the comte de Mirabeau, feared going all the way, but on 17 June 1789 the Third Estate affirmed its identity as the National Assembly.

Henri Grégoire

Grégoire was born in the commune of Vého, which was once a province of the Holy Roman Empire known as Les Trois Évêchés, a region distinct from Lorraine proper. He complained that historical errors had led to misunderstandings about the entire western region of France, about Alsace-Lorraine in general and Les Trois Évêchés in particular. Yet he called Lorraine "our Lorraine" when he reviewed some of the hurts visited upon it from the Middle Ages onward.[49] His earliest religious experience would have been colored by the Jansenism of his mother, who herself was simply following the local curé.[50] Receiving his early education from the Jesuits, he clearly distinguished, in his *Mémoires*, the role of good Jesuits in his own formation from the role played by the whole order in church life. "I will carry with me to my grave a respectful attachment to my teachers, even though I do not at all like the spirit of the defunct society," he wrote, in the belief that a revival of the society might well bring new problems to Europe.[51] Youthful intellectual impressions stayed with him across the years. Antimonarchical texts such as *De justa Henrici tertii abdicatione* and *Vincidiae contra tyrannos* were the foundation of his antipathy to the monarchy of Louis XVI. And he never forgot how one elderly librarian responded to his search for books to "to amuse" himself with: "We only give out books here *to learn from*."[52]

From Humanist to Pastor

Both Pierre-Joseph de Solignac, secretary of the Polish king, Stanislaus, and author of a five-volume history of Poland, and Canon Gautier, who had published studies in science and history, helped Grégoire in his early attempts at poetry. He said that he loved "the joyful allure [*aspect riant*] of the Vosges, made to stir up the imagination."[53] At Nancy, he studied one year of philosophy, and was then introduced by De Solignac to the "Jewish question" of the day. On to Metz for a second year of philosophy, a year of fundamental theology, and the lively influence of Adrien Lamourette, who believed that a return to the ways of the primitive Jerusalem church would bring about a golden age of Christianity. Antoine Sutter says of Lamourette's early influence on Grégoire, "He not only hoped for regeneration and the primitive purity [of the church], he sang its praises, and his student was not deaf to the song."[54] Grégoire ended his studies with two years of dogmatic theology at Pont-à-Mousson under the abbé Sanguiné, who won him over to Richerism, with its exaltation of the priest's role in the church.

In 1773, Grégoire entered a major essay contest sponsored by the Academy of Nancy with his *Éloge de la poésie*, recently cited by Alyssa Sepinwall as a capital text in distinguishing the early from the later Grégoire.[55] Here, too, there was little religious reference, certainly no specific Christian religious reference, but in its engaged, perhaps overheated, aestheticism it parallels Sieyès's philosophically engaged, perhaps overblown, discussion of religion. Poetry is his "faithful lover," the embodiment of perfection because it conjoins usefulness and pleasure.[56] Philosophical treatises, in contrast, have produced much less: "Philosophy persuades the mind and makes little progress; the poet leads the heart and wins over the person."[57] There is praise of Virgil, Homer, Corneille, and the muses, and condemnation of those he considered promoters of vice: Catullus, Tibullus, and Ovid. Biblical poetry is praised subsequently: "The most sublime poetry, the most majestic, and all the riches of the secular Muses will never equal it."[58] This was followed by virtually the only extended reference to God in the text: "Sometimes I see a merciful God who opens his hand, and the earth swims in abundance. Sometimes it is a terrible God who arms himself with wrath and makes the universe tremble from the sound of his lightning."[59] Grégoire invokes the great and ringing sounds of praise in the Temple and the laments of the Jews in exile: "I open David's Psalms. What energy, what nobility, what images."[60] Nevertheless, as Sepinwall puts it, in this essay

"Grégoire sounded like any classically trained young man using romantic metaphors."[61]

In the *Éloge*, there is a non-moralizing appreciation of the tenderness of women: "To hold back the destructiveness of your charms, must we add oriental cruelty to our own ways."[62] There is also great discretion in talking of the depths of his soul. One assumes he is speaking of Christ in the following lines, but is he necessarily? "For a long time my wavering heart searched for repose in the bosom of a friend." There were other bonds of love that he broke when, as he said, "I learned to discern a true friend from those muddied souls that have only the tawdry jewelry of friendship; after such effort, I found my dear J. . . .[*sic*]."[63] Grégoire exalts the role of poetry as a moral guide, but also shows its didactic importance in such diverse areas of life as astronomy, painting, and agriculture. Beauty is understood to be found in every area of life. He interpolates words of praise for Stanislas, father-in-law of the French king and ruler of the Les Trois Évêchés: "O Stanislas . . . an immortal crown is on your head, and the wishes of Lorraine are at your feet. The rare geniuses who have enlightened the universe are there."[64] Cultures and empires have celebrated and consolidated their greatness through poetry: Greece, Rome, the France of Louis XIV, and the Russia of Peter the Great. Fallen cultures, such as the Trojan, or even corrupt cultures can be later celebrated and valorized by the muses. Poetry can delight and transform the old as well as the young, and has something for people of all walks of life.

After ordination in 1776, Grégoire became preoccupied by the far-from-poetic abuses inherent in an aristocratic society. Witnessing the death of an old man who had masqueraded as a salt worker, the priest Grégoire was hardened against a regime that would hound the poor with a heavy tax on salt pits and streams. Prison life had killed the old fellow, "a poor octogenarian who had pulled up a little water to make his wretched soup."[65] As pastoral assistant at Marimont-lès-Bénestroff, Grégoire completely dropped his work in poetry for the sake of the great causes. When he joined the Société philanthropique at Nancy, he was constitutionally attracted to the 1779 Strasbourg *concours* of the society, using the occasion to prepare a report on the "Jewish question," based on a study tour of parts of Alsace. Then he combined a pilgrimage to Notre-Dame des Ermites near Zurich with a study of Swiss democracy. He became the friend of the social work–oriented Protestant pastor Jean-Frédéric Oberlin of Ban-de-la-Roche, and then began a study of the treatment of Gypsies in Europe. His apostolate as curé of Emberménil, begun in 1782, remained for him the happiest and most fulfilling period of his career, serving his Catholic parish and working to know and understand the Ashkenazi Jewish communities of Lorraine, concentrated in Metz, Nancy, and Lunéville.

Out of his own formation Grégoire fashioned a life and ministry that was priestly and pastoral in the tradition of the Council of Trent: there's no question that he saw himself as mediator and teacher. If he wrote little about his celebration of Mass as a young priest, he exalted the values of confession, which "establishes in the Catholic religion relations that are more direct between pastors and the faithful than in societies that have suppressed this element of the sacrament of penance. In general, the confidence of my parishioners was such that if I had not placed some limits on their spontaneous revelations, they would have gone too far."[66]

Regenerated Political Society: Jews and Christians

In 1788, Grégoire put together a treatise that promoted the acceptance of Jews into European society, with the accompanying training and restraints necessary to make this reform work.[67] On the one hand, he insists that if these people are treated fairly they can fill all roles, accomplish all tasks. But on the other hand, he seems to accept all the old prejudices. Christian Europeans, he says, have contributed in no small measure to the physical, moral, and political plight of the Jews of his day, but the majority of the condemnations and criticisms of Jewish physical, moral, and political degeneration are valid. God has made them pay for their past sins. It is not for Christians to replay God's vengeance, but to offer the Jews justice, charity, and the possibility of a happy life. The low estate of the Jews is not permanent: they can be regenerated.

To begin with, Grégoire evokes the destruction of Jerusalem and the persecutions in Europe. He makes the case that many Christian bishops, and the popes themselves, were defenders of the Jews against the murderous attacks of princes and populations. Wherever they have gone, they have been massacred, burned alive, victims of pillage and pursuit. The Jews have suffered the equivalent of the St. Bartholomew's Day Massacre hundreds of times. Grégoire does note, however, that here and there Jewish society did bring on persecution by its reprehensible behavior. And he does accept the notion that "the blood of Jesus Christ has fallen upon the Jews as they once desired: since the day of blood at Calvary, they have become a spectacle to all the earth as they wander across it looking for a Messiah."[68]

More often than not, the Jews were made to suffer unjustly, "for imaginary crimes."[69] How could they, then, love their rulers, or the peoples who made common cause against them? They could only be jealous of Christians, whose religion has completely eclipsed their own. When you persecute a religion, you render it more precious to its members; they become more committed to the values for which they have suffered. Grégoire admits that Jews, like everyone else, are given to vice, but he lists also their many virtues, and he rehearses many persecutions they have endured, concluding that "in their place we would have perhaps been worse."[70]

Then Grégoire paints a collective portrait of decadence and degradation, in which he lists a wide variety of dangerous, even murderous, rabbinical influences, with no real questioning or downplaying of reports he transmits. "What to conclude from all of this?" he asks. "That we must hunt down the Jews and destroy them: No! which clearly proves that we need to regenerate this people."[71] And thus, beginning with the perversion of usury and working down the list of their evil tendencies, recognizing that in the end their usury in particular resulted from the oppression they suffered. It is the "height of inconsequence" to reproach them for their crimes "after having forced them to commit them."[72] The many governments of Europe have taken away from them all other means of subsistence.

Enlightenment has already begun among the Jews, he says, citing the case of Moses Mendelssohn and the attempt to return to the purity of the law: "Already a number of Jews disgusted with rabbinical mess, prune away all the human additions to the law, without harming the truth of the basic principles."[73] The Jews must be formed in the arts and crafts, as well as in agriculture. In other times and in other places they have excelled in these things. Give them a chance, he says. Grégoire combines a language of safeguards against their supposed natural tendencies and a hope for community with Christians. Ensure a sensible education and solid moral training for them, surround them with good will, and "they will learn to love enemies too generous to be hated, and they will thereby acquire a [new] sociability, sentiment, and virtue, without losing the simplicity of their ancient ways."[74] Limits can be set on Jewish commerce, but, properly integrated into life, they will be in a good position to revive languishing areas of the economy. Grégoire proposes legislation that will be fair and yet keep them away from the types of business dishonesty to which they are prone. Let commercial transactions be done in cash, but allow for old debts to be paid. When Grégoire proposes to keep the Jews away from functions that will draw them back to the old ways, he adds, "For we should never lose sight of the character of the people we are hoping to set straight."[75] His project, after all, is regeneration, and not simple liberation. Opposing ghettos, he continues his argument that the company and goodness of Christians will have a salutary effect. They should be given freedom of expression, although those elements of Mosaic practice that would not be acceptable in modern government (e.g., stoning of adulterers) are not negotiable Should they be admitted to civil office, the nobility, the academies, education, and the ownership of buildings? Yes, to all the above, and he would permit Jewish/Catholic marriages if the children could be raised Catholic.

In sum, Grégoire preaches love and fraternity: "Children of the same father, eliminate every pretext for aversion to your brothers, who one day will be reunited into the same sheepfold; open to them places of refuge when they can peaceably lay down their heads and dry their tears. And may the Jew at last, granting to the Christian a return of affection, embrace in me his fellow citizen and his friend."[76]

Across the months intervening between his full engagement with the Jewish question and his first weeks in the 1789 assemblies, Grégoire did not lose his central concern for Jewish regeneration. During the 13–15 July session of the Constituent Assembly, he reprised his ideas in a motion on behalf of the Jews, published and entered into the minutes: "Now allow a Catholic pastor to raise his voice on behalf of the fifty million Jews in the kingdom, who, being men, demand the rights of citizens."[77] As Alyssa Sepinwall puts it, Grégoire was "radically inclusive" as he developed his project of regeneration with successive attention to the rights of blacks and the status of women.[78]

Polarities of Revolutionary Priesthood

Polarities do not define "typical," of course, but they do define a range of priestly types, from jobber through apostle. Clear in politics and primed for revolution, the abbé Sieyès had a minimal and mutated pastoral orientation. But he was a philosophical soul who made what sense he could of the religious sentiment, everywhere present around him. His *Sur Dieu ultramètre* was really a window on his formation in religious thinking, abstract and random in its meandering, and ultimately separate from his public life—separate with good reason, because it was not usable within the church

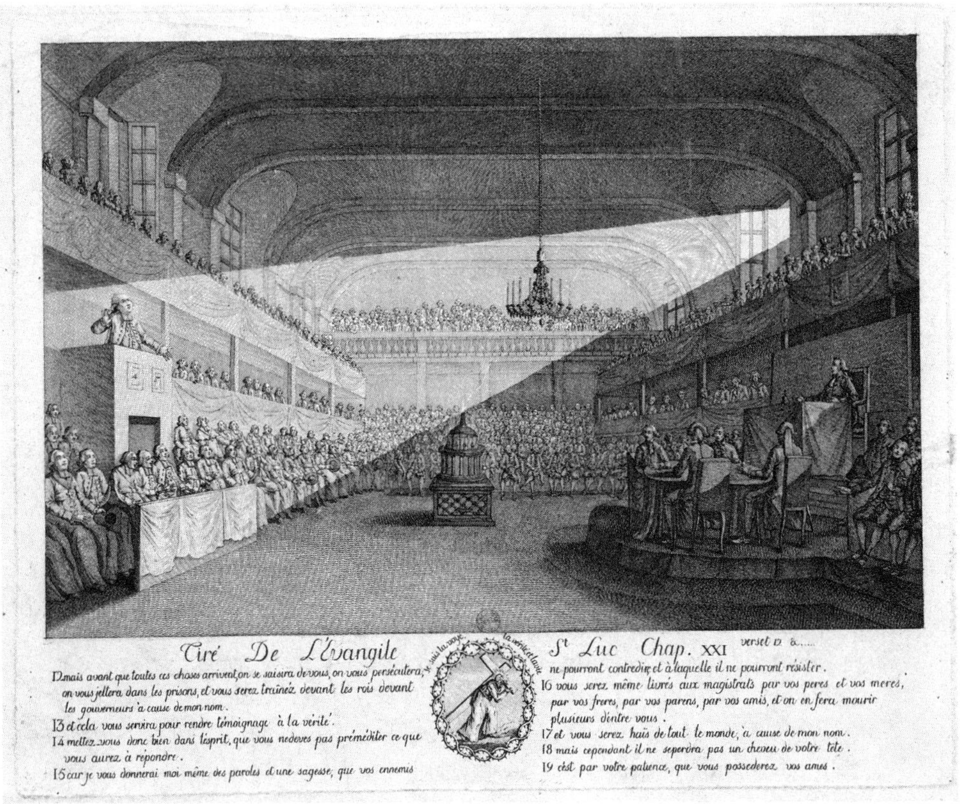

Figure 4 The abbé Grégoire intervening before the Constituent Assembly. Underneath the image are verses taken from the twenty-first chapter of the Gospel of Luke, wherein Christ tells his apostles that they will be handed over into prison and brought before kings (21:13–15). The image, published in 1791, presages a later Grégoire speech. His dramatic confession of faith and priestly loyalty in the Convention might be appropriately captioned with these verses, but for that occasion Grégoire wore his bishop's regalia. (Bibliothèque nationale de France)

apostolate of his day, revolutionary or otherwise. He undoubtedly knew this, and so had no other recourse but to minimalize as much as possible a formal pastoral identity of preaching and sacraments. It was not specifically as episcopal vicar of the diocese of Chartres nor as a delegate from the clerical First Estate that he primed for action the delegates of the Third Estate, of which he was surprisingly a member (thanks to his triumphalist pamphlet *Qu'est-ce que c'est le tiers état?*). After weeks of tension, members of the Third Estate, believing they were locked out of their regular meeting hall, adjourned to a nearby tennis court and proclaimed themselves the final arbiter in the formation of a new government—without *really* posing for David's take on them, of course. Members of the clergy and aristocracy who were already reform-minded (looking for a constitutional monarchy or even a republican government) prevailed on the recalcitrant majorities of both their estates to come over to the new assembly, soon to be called the Constituent Assembly. Immediately the Committee for Public Instruction and the Ecclesiastical Committee began work on reform documents, recasting the old French unity of throne and altar into a new state and church relationship. The reworking of church and state came to be dominated by the abbé Grégoire, standing fast for a reformed Catholicism and a solid constitutional government.

Henri Grégoire arrived at Versailles in 1789 as the First Estate delegate from the *bailliage* of Nancy, already known as pastorally, intellectually, and politically engaged. His youthful preoccupation with poetry was an exploration of the religious sentiment that he straightaway, but with delicacy, labeled specifically Christian. Two years before the opening of the Estates General, he had already begun to meditate on a specifically Catholic Christian program for cultural transformation, because a transformed French Catholic Church could and should bring about the regeneration of the Jews of France and the rest of Europe. His election to the Estates General was an indication of his reputation for this engagement in church and society, although his first pastoral letters of the new decade and his later memoirs of the era are clearer indications of his specifically priestly qualities than anything he wrote before the opening of the Estates General. As fate would have it, however, the abbé Grégoire, priest and revolutionary, was taking his brief turn as secretary of the Constituent Assembly at Versailles when the Bastille was stormed and taken in Paris.

Catholic priests across the revolutionary years could strip down to the pure political secularism of Sieyès, or enliven their politics with Catholic Christian faith and experience, like Henri Grégoire. Preoccupied with their parish work, the curés' engagement with political change began during the months of preparing the *cahiers de doléances* locally, and, for a limited few, participation in the Estates General and subsequent Constituent Assembly.

Chapter Two

THE PRIESTS IN ACTION
From Estates General to National Assembly

No one was ready for the convocation of the Estates General, so far beyond living memory was the activity of a parliament. When elections were held in all the electoral districts in the first months of 1789, the *bailliages* and *sénéchaussées*[1] of France, the clergy had to work out their own problems of power and politics, which were further complicated by theology and religious sentiment. Strong reformist priests were able to dominate from the beginning, although individual bishops were occasionally astute enough to maintain their control over clergy meetings within their own dioceses.[2] At the opening of the Estates General there was an unexpectedly high percentage of curés, even given the ground rules set in place by Finance Minister Jacques Necker in order to ensure a high priest-to-bishop ratio. Curé words and deeds are recorded in the *cahiers de doléances*, those official lists of complaints and hopes, in the diaries kept during the meetings of the First (clergy) Estate, and in the records kept by the Comité ecclésiastique after the Estates General became the Constituent Assembly. After many months of work in 1790, the members of the Comité ecclésiastique produced the founding document of church reform, the Civil Constitution of the Clergy.

Reform Within the Church: The *Cahiers de Doléances*

Very few revolutionary demands or complaints are in the clergy *cahiers*, according to Timothy Tackett, who scanned them to establish the frequency of such demands and complaints. There was some minor concern for the rights of the poor and antagonism toward the systems of rich and noble bishops, but no straightforward expression of bona fide revolutionary ideas.[3] Tackett says that "grievances anticipating the most radical measures of the Civil Constitution were scarcely to be found anywhere."[4] Still and all, Philippe Grateau, in his "cultural rereading" of the *cahiers*, highlights a tradition of contempt for luxury and a clerical caste, and Nigel Aston notes a pervasive desire that the state might possibly "order matters thought formerly to be the preserve of the Church."[5] Ever stricter rules were required for the celebration of religious festivals, fasting, and control of immoral behavior in its usual forms of sex, drinking, and blasphemy. There was much demand for press censorship and little thought about toleration of non-Catholicism.[6] There was little clarity about the distribution of powers needed to accomplish the reforms, with only a small minority of the *cahiers* suggesting that the decisions of the Estates General should be handled and ratified by the bishops or a national council or diocesan synods. At times the Estates General were considered the final authority. To highlight regional differences, Tackett recalculated his figures to apply geographically to departments instead of the old electoral districts. The highest level of demand for curé rights was found in western Normandy, Maine, the Touraine, then between the Massif Central and the Pyrénées. In these regions, the north looked more to "honorific" rights; the south, to political rights—but rights in any case. It is striking that these regions did not, on the one hand, end up with a high percentage of constitutional clergy or successful dechristianization, or, on the other hand, with high levels of revolutionary demands.[7]

There were, to be sure, expressions of resentment and rebellion, recorded by Charles Chassin in his book on the clergy *cahiers*.[8] Class differences always counted for something. The *cahier* from Arles indicates that "the diverse classes of ecclesiastics put forward their individual *doléances* in contradiction to one another."[9] In Aix and several other towns, little opposition to the bishop was recorded; but, even so, a simple village curé *was* chosen to accompany him to the Estates General.[10] The curé, Father Cousin, helped prepare the parish *cahier* that was sent to the Third Estate—with provisions for the election of curés. In Marseilles, a supplementary *cahier* was sent in because the bishops would not sign some of the formulations that had been crafted by the lower clergy. From Puy-en-Velay came the strange *cahier* that was episcopal in tone, but noted the complaints of curés demanding that bishops and others who were rewarded for their services should actually provide those services.[11] From time to time, a group of clergy would produce a very moderate document but choose a strongly political curé to represent them. Antagonism to the bishop is evident in the *cahier* that expects, not from the higher clergy, but "from the nation the concern to improve the lot of curés and assistants."[12] In Périgord the curés of Libourne also look to the nation "to remedy the abuses that have made their way into the church administration."[13]

From the Auvergne came the plea that the bishops be well chosen: "Since bishops must be the lights and model of the clergy, the king should be begged right away to take effective measures, so that in choosing [these] first pastors, the minister charged with this task experience no coercion or fear, due to the intrigue, money, or power of the powerful."[14] Opposition to the bishop also featured in the letters from the curés of Poitiers and Luçon. When Father Guilleminet wrote to Necker, the king's finance minister, he said, "Monseigneur, the Lord Bishops of Poitiers and Luçon are always opposed to admitting into the minutes all the demands, requests, and protests that the curés want relative to the aforesaid *cahier.*"[15] The Norman priest Crosnier roundly criticized episcopal immorality: "The people are indignant, scandalized to see that riches taken for the altar serve the secular luxury, sensuality, and intemperance."[16] Rather, the money "could have been used to put their children in a position to serve the fatherland, rather than to support the idleness of clergy useless to church and state."[17]

Curés projected their own key roles in church and society. The *cahier* from Caen was a pure Gallican document highlighting the importance of the curés and urging a separate but equal status for the French church relative to pope and king.[18] The *cahier* from Beauvais provided for limited elections, Chassin says, in order to avoid the formula of the curé from Saventin demanding that gold and silver be taken from the churches in order to pay the national debt![19] In the *cahier* of the *sénéchaussée* of Anjou the curés call for the restoration of all Gallican liberties, including "freedom of election."[20] But seldom does one find a *cahier* such as the two brief articles from the Angoulême region, wherein the curés said nothing of church or clergy, dealing only with taxes and—in a surprising expression in these documents—"the legitimate liberty of the press."[21] In Lorraine, the curés of Toul offered to pay taxes, "considering themselves citizens and children of the fatherland."[22] In Lille, the curés demanded that all pastors of the city church "participate in the administration of the properties and revenues of the *fabrique* of the diocese."[23] In Metz, however, though favorable to a constitution, they wanted the rescinding of Protestant civil status, just granted in 1787.[24] And opposition to the corruption of the religious orders was juxtaposed to the demand for curé rights. In the Southwest, curés wanted formal assemblies of their own resembling the religious-order assemblies, noting the "decline that threatens the religious orders with imminent dissolution," and suggesting the convocation of a national council to work on the problem.[25] In Bigorre, the curés claimed the right to be the "only genuine preachers, instead of monks and religious."[26]

Curés highlighted the lot of their parishioners. The poor in their charge should benefit from the tithe, some of them said.[27] The clergy of the *bailliage* of Mirecourt even demanded that the king himself listen to his people: "They will tell you for how long these children of the best of fathers [the king] groan under oppression. They will recount the rapport possessed by the church in the Vosges. It is a cruel stepmother that torments the inhabitants of the countryside and takes from them all the money it can."[28]

In any case, the priests of France had yet to try their hand at revolution when they arrived at Versailles in May 1789 for the opening of the Estates General. The expression of opposition to domination by bishops allowed little room for other church and government reforms. Confrontations developed across the meetings of the Estates General, where the curés of the First Estate acquired most of their spirit of revolution in asserting their religious and social rights against the aristocratic bishops.

Clergy Journals: Jacques Jallet in Particular

Lively records of the clergy sessions of the Estates General and the common sessions of the Constituent Assembly, minutes and diaries in effect, were kept by the curés Sigisbert-Etienne Coster and Anne-Alexandre Thibault, and then Jacques Rangeard and Jacques Jallet.[29] There were contrasts here. Coster feared the radicality of the group's decisions and refused the oath; Thibault, despite his appreciation of revolution and reform, wrote a matter-of-fact journal. Rangeard, although keeping his editorializing to a minimum, complained of the unjust distribution of tithes—so much taken by the aristocratic bishops and so little received by the hardworking priests.[30] Jacques Jallet's journal was, from beginning to end, the work of a priest revolutionary. On 13 June 1789, he had led the first curés (there were two others) to the hall of the Menus-Plaisirs to join the Third Estate.

Jallet put much more of himself in his journal, noting with satisfaction that the head of the small Third Estate deputation addressed the gathered members of the First Estate as *Messieurs*; even though there were a number of aristocratic bishops present, he never once said *Messeigneurs*. It was May 1789 and some of the bishops were hoping for good relations with the two other Estates. The trouble began with those efforts to unite the clergy and noble Estates as an intermediary between the king and the Third Estate. This would have considerably strengthened the control of the aristocratic bishops over the commoner priests: "We easily saw the real goal of this writing. If the plan were adopted, the clergy of the second order [priests], overcome by the higher clergy and the nobles, would have not the least force, even for resistance, in the chamber."[31] The bishops were also unwilling to renounce their tax privileges; to Jallet they seemed to oppose the Third Estate and protect the old union of throne and altar. It was then that Jallet undertook to show the Assembly that "all the cahiers insisted on the preservation of the throne and of religion, but they insisted on the reform of abuses, of the intolerable and scandalous luxury of the bishops; on the amassing of benefices, nonresidency, the exclusion of commoners from the episcopate; it made clear that the clergy themselves should take on the honors of planning the reforms, but those who live off the abuses endeavor to defend them."[32]

And it got rough at times, such as when a canon from Marseilles told the bishop of Langres, "I've forgotten more about this than you know now" (in fact, the canon was an aristocrat and conservative, whereas the bishop was open to change). This all took place in the confusing time between the first invitations to join the Third Estate and the dramatic unification of the First and Second Estates to the Third Estate; the memorable day was 19 May 1789. The indefatigably conservative abbé Maury, urging caution, "calumniated" (Jallet's word) the intentions of the Third Estate. But Grégoire said that delays had already jeopardized the reform, and Lubersac of Chartres promoted a careful but rapid restructuring. The continued fussing of Maury and powerful logic of Lubersac took center stage until a weepy curé from Bordeaux drew some snickers as he warned of the dangers religion was facing.[33] Jallet believed that the bishops were stonewalling the curés' efforts to "reconcile" the First and Third Estates. He reported that "an episcopal curé was bold enough to treat the Assembly of the Third Estate as seditious; a bishop had said the previous day that it was a cave of robbers."[34] The radical curés won out, with the final vote 148 for union with the Third Estate and 136 against; "the bishops exited quickly before the news of the defeat could be reported."[35] The crowd did not know what had transpired, but they

Figure 5 A strong personality in the clergy circles, Jacques Jallet was a leader in promoting the passing over of the clergy of the First Estate into the Third Estate, a stance that made him the second great priestly influence on the clergy, after Grégoire. In his journal, he recorded with great zest the haggling and confrontations attendant upon the move to the Third Estate. (Bibliothèque nationale de France)

were still looking for a fight with the abbé Maury: he "could not get away from the boos of the crowd; he made a threat and they were ready to attack him; some spoke out saying that it would be better not to dirty one's hands by touching such a despicable person."[36] But at least the forces for change had won the day: "Then the joy and the applause were universal; the archbishop of Vienne [Le Franc de Pompignon], that of Bordeaux [Champion de Cicé], and the bishop of Chartres [de Lubersac] we put at the head of the winners."[37] The aristocratic bishops who lost went to the king to protest that the vote had not been legal, but the archbishops of Vienne and Bordeaux and the bishop of Chartres held fast in their defense of the change.

The curés were anxious to finish the union project, and the bishop of Chartres suggested that all repair to the church of Saint-Louis for the official ceremony. And so it was, to Jallet's clear joy: "The union of the clergy with the Third Estate will bring life and action to the National Assembly; and it is noteworthy that this union has been accomplished in a church that is under the patronage of good Saint Louis; a situation that no one has noticed, as far as we know."[38] The king then tried to stop the proceedings, ordering the three Estates to return to separate assemblies the next day. The Third Estate and a large number of clergy in favor of union remained. There was a profound silence for several minutes. The marquis de Brézé entered at the king's behest and declared with the accord of the president that the will of his Majesty was that the different orders separate. The president answered that the session could not be closed except with the consent of the National Assembly. One of the deputies rose and said, "Only bayonets could get us out of here."[39]

The business of getting the final union worked out was a drawn-out affair, a tug of war between curé eagerness and episcopal reserve. But on 25 May forty-seven nobles ("among whom figure the names of the first families of the kingdom," wrote Jallet) reinforced the clergy for Estate unification.[40] In the final discussion, Cardinal de La Rochefoucauld protested against the elimination of his right to meet separately with his Estate (his fellow bishops), and Mirabeau rose to say that no one had the right to protest his own will, or even cite the king's will to the Assembly. The archbishop of Aix wanted to refute Mirabeau, but in his melodrama drew some laughter. Other bishops decided against continuing the contest, but Jallet referred to it all as an episcopal final attempt, a "swing of a club" to prevent the union of the Estates.[41]

And when the secretaries for the united National Assembly were chosen for the first period on 8 June, the short list comprised two nobles, two members of the Third Estate (Le Chapelier, a founder of the Jacobin Club, was one), and . . . the abbés Sieyès and Grégoire! These were troubled times, nevertheless. In the first days of July plans were made to call in more than thirty thousand troops to maintain the peace. Mirabeau, believing that the order would arouse the people, demanded its cancellation, Grégoire wanted to know who could have given the king such pernicious advice, and Sieyès wondered how the Assembly could have free and open discussion when surrounded by bayonets.[42] Then came the storming of the Bastille, consternation at Versailles, and the deliberations as to what to do, with the coming and going of the king. Jallet combines reports of the people's and delegates' esteem and expressed enthusiasm for the king, with the subtle insertion of reserve and antagonism—primitive reverence and primitive rebellion in a unique alloy only two days after the storming of the Bastille. A delegation was sent from the Assembly to Paris with an archbishop at its head: "It had been received with lively joy; taken down to the Place Louis XV, they were conducted by an honor guard of the Paris militia, to the acclamations of an immense crowd demanding the return of Necker, to the Hôtel-de-Ville, where the archbishop of Paris announced the dispatching of troops."[43]

The next delegation had the king at the center, but the clergy who were committed to reform were squeezed out of membership, Jallet himself finding that his name had been proposed but then arbitrarily removed.[44] After a full presentation of the precautions taken against insurrection and violence in Paris, and a comment on the popularity of the duc d'Orléans, Philippe Egalité, Jallet posts his negative assessment of the king's behavior: "The king revealed himself to the Assembly, not with the dignity of a monarch who considers it an honor to surround himself with the counsels of a noble nation, not with the goodness of a father who has just taken his place, but with the weakness of a despot, humbled by the evil success of his unjust and violent enterprises, and who has just humbled himself before those he cannot destroy, or rather with the faintheartedness of a weak king, without character, whom the counsels of those around him can make proud or craven, alternately, according to circumstances."[45]

Records show, then, that the priests' discussions were sometimes reform-oriented and sometimes intimidated by the aristocratic bishops. Only a minority felt comfortable making common cause with the Third Estate, and few, apart from reflexively fearful conservatives, fully realized the magnitude of the changes they were bringing about. One of the outspoken curés, Jean-Louis Gouttes, author of *Considérations sur l'injustice des prétentions du Clergé et de la Noblesse*, changed his mind within ten days, from no to yes, on the question of joining the Third Estate.[46]

What had happened was this. The regular run of lower clergy were clearly anxious about their relationship with the aristocratic bishops, first in their own Estate and then in the Constituent Assembly; those curés with the greatest resentment of the aristocracy were the most ready to reject their status as a separate Estate. Their suspicion of episcopal self-interest waxed and waned, depending on the liveliness of the communal discussions and the reconciliation achieved in them. All this meant that the clergy were less unified in their stand for or against union with the Third Estate than were the nobles. Back at the end of May, one of the great motivators of debate had been the *Essai sur la réforme du clergé*, an attack on the bishops by the curé Laurent; published probably on 20 May, it ensured intense debate by 25 and 26 May.[47] Archbishop (of Aix) Raymond de Boisgelin's warning that the clerical order would be swallowed up in a general assembly persuaded the majority of the clergy that loss of collective clout was the greater danger.[48] By the middle of June, those promoting union with the Third Estate garnered enough votes to win, after several divided and inconclusive—perhaps gerrymandered—votes.[49]

Maurice Hutt decades ago insisted that union with the Third Estate was not what the curés had voted for: "They had voted to cross to the Third Estate's chamber to check election returns. It was not a decision to merge the Order with that of the Third Estate. . . . The leaders of the 'curé party' were prepared for voting by head and urged acceptance of verification in common to bring this about. But they realized quite clearly that this was not a view common among the lower clergy and in their speeches and pamphlets they took care to 'manage' this opinion."[50] This interpretation has been substantially qualified in subsequent years by Ruth Necheles, William Doyle, and Nigel Aston, who wrote that the clergy "were certainly aware of the implications of their behavior."[51] The Third Estate had actually decided two days before that they were the French "National Assembly" plain and simple, but at least some of the clergy (Hutt was not totally wrong) thought, right up through the fall of the Bastille, that they would be maintained as a distinct order. On 19 July, Cardinal de La Rochefoucauld announced the full participation of the clergy in the Assembly sessions and debates, and the First Estate was no more. A number of these *patriote* clergy who had voted *nolens volens* for the crossover in June had changed their minds by the beginning of 1791, when only one-third of them (compared to more than one-half of the clergy in general) were willing to take the oath of loyalty to the Constitution and accept the Civil Constitution of the Clergy.

With the union of orders, the Estates General became the Constituent Assembly. One-quarter of the curés seated there came from peasant or artisan families, representing, then, humbler levels of society. Grégoire's father was a tailor; Jallet's father, a gardener; Thibault's father, a cobbler. More than half of the curés came from families that were considered *notable* in the Old Regime, and the rest came from merchant or professional families.[52] Some of the curés were widely read, and some had managed to publish their own works, with or without university degrees. Work with the Estates General and Constituent Assembly developed the political inclinations of some. Priests belonged, too, to the Jacobin Club, although some of them went along with the Feuillants, constitutional monarchists, when the Jacobins turned antireligious after the end of the Constituent Assembly.[53] This was late June 1789, and in the following months there was no lack of strife.

Reform in the National Assembly: The Ecclesiastical Committee

Paris militias and mobs had stormed the Bastille on 14 July. Nobles surrendered their legal and tax privileges in August, after months of rumored and real peasant attacks on the great landed estates. After issuing a balanced "Declaration of the Rights of Man and of the Citizen," inspired by the American founding documents, an enthusiastic reforming assembly directed that all church property was to be placed at the disposal of the nation. Radical active churchmen, reinforced and even dominated by enthusiastic laymen, worked into the following year to reform and revolutionize church structures. They established the Comité ecclésiastique on 12 August to work out the shape of the church for the new regime.

Committee members wanted a democratic church that would have as close a relationship to a constitutional monarchy as had the Old Regime church to the Old Regime state. Coming from all three Estates, they were a mixture of nobles, bishops and priests, and laymen trained in canon law—in particular, Jean-Denis Lanjuinais, Jean-Baptiste Treilhard, and Pierre Durand de Maillane. Before long, a new rostrum of members included the future constitutional bishops Thibault, Louis-Alexandre Expilly, and Jean-Baptiste Massieu. According to Durand de Maillane, the Committee continued to hammer out the contents of the future Civil Constitution of the Clergy, trying to ensure a democratically elected roster of clergy. Dioceses were reorganized to conform to the new distribution of departments, with administrative units replacing the old regions: eighty-three uniformly divided and politically operative units in place of the old ramshackle set of dioceses that included great and small, rich and poor, well and poorly administered, dedicated and charlatan bishops. Curés and bishops were to

Figure 6 Pierre Durand de Maillane was a layman but a specialist in church law. He was a major influence in the Ecclesiastical Committee of the Constituent Assembly as it gradually produced the Civil Constitution of the Clergy. Durand de Maillane's full report on the discussions and decisions of the Committee is a look behind the scenes, sometimes criticized for its neglect of anything with which he did not agree. (Bibliothèque nationale de France)

be elected, and the bishops duly constituted without a mandate from the pope. Financially supporting the whole system, the state was to ensure an equitable distribution of income.[54] This setup was an amalgam of political and ecclesiastical Gallicanism, an independent church–state polity that gave churchmen relative independence from Rome while keeping them submissive to the state.

Durand de Maillane, reporting on the whole affair, insisted that the state could not let clerical domination and religious abuses continue as it went about the job of cleaning up the other problems. The state could not tolerate any ecclesiastical self-defense from the bishops and priests who were the source of the abuses, no more than it could tolerate any offensive actions against the government. The Catholic Church response could not be taken seriously, because it was offered by "the court of Rome" and not really by the "Holy See." When False Decretals and new laws unjustly extended Roman authority over the years, "the more learned bishops in these latter days have complained"; and this was one of the glories of the Gallican Church, always holding out against Roman abuses. Durand scorns the lavishness of church ornaments as one major example of clerical self-indulgence.[55] Rather, he envisions a new episcopate, elected after the manner of the early church, "half ecclesiastical, half popular." It appears, too, that Durand would expect that choices could fall outside the regular rostra of bishops and priests: "I thought that if the choice for the episcopate should fall upon others, it could only be by divine inspiration because of outstanding virtues such as those of Ambrose and Augustine, which appeared to me more in conformity with the minds of the church, and electoral liberty, and ancient customs."[56]

Gallican bishops had always insisted that their church dignity was founded by Christ and, hence, not arbitrary. Durand insists that, consequently, authority cannot be exercised arbitrarily, and so sets the bishop in the proper context to benefit from his priests: "It is precisely because of the new cathedral arrangement that we have come to place the bishop and his presbytery in a happy and paternal relationship."[57] But the aristocratic French bishops were refusing to countenance any loss of dignity and so rejected everything the Assembly tried to do to return to the discipline of the early church, and to assure the care of souls and the preaching of the gospel. Apropos, Durand is especially concerned to ensure the care of souls and the preaching of the gospel, and consequently, to elevate the wretched state of the country priests.[58]

As he drafted the document, Durand knew that a principal complaint against election of bishops was based on the possibility of a non-Catholic vote: "But after the explanations that I have given on the real meaning of the acts of *election*, *institution*, and *consecration*, a single response will be enough to refute one or another of the objections."[59] The regular voters can be trusted to supply a good moral and political foundation for the election; then it is up to the hierarchy to decide what best serves the spiritual interests of their people. Inasmuch as the decrees presupposed the celebration of a Mass before the election, one would expect non-Catholics to vote in very limited numbers. Durand builds on the commonplace that a special dynamism resided in the bishops of the early church. And in its carefully maintained freedom, the Gallican Church is a counterweight to the abuses of the Roman court. So, the "pope is neither infallible nor superior to a general council, which alone represents [the church]."[60] He has no civil or temporal rights over kings, nor can he insist that people set up any particular form of society or government. The pope is not to make any particular judgments about the French. That is for the local hierarchy to do, and this in conformity with "natural law and ancient custom."[61]

The Civil Constitution of the Clergy

The central church reform document, and the subsequent cause of all the strife, was the Civil Constitution of the Clergy, adopted by the Constituent Assembly on 12 July 1790 and ratified, in effect, by all clergy who professed the oath of loyalty to the nation, the law, and the king, at the very beginning of the following year.[62] Pierre Durand de Maillane and Jean-Baptiste Treilhard, the lay canon lawyers, were the outspoken members of the Ecclesiastical Committee across the weeks of debate in 1790, 29 May to 12 July. But the top orator was Armand-Gaston Camus, lay canon lawyer and polymath, whose theology of the church was the principal inspiration for Adrien Lamourette, the future constitutional bishop, a major influence on Henri Grégoire and Claude Fauchet all along, and on the comte de Mirabeau in the National Assembly.

The Civil Constitution fundamentally restructured French dioceses to coordinate with the new subdivision of the country into departments. Special attention was given to the independence of the French church from outside domination: "No church or parish of France, and no French citizen, may, under any circumstances or on any pretext whatsoever, acknowledge the authority of an ordinary bishop or archbishop whose see is established under the name of a foreign power."[63] Cities of less than six thousand people were to have one parish only; cities of more than six thousand were to have as many parishes as necessary to take care of the needs of the people. All titles and offices were to be abolished.

In providing for the election of church officials, the Civil Constitution revived much earlier custom. Priests who served fifteen years within a diocese were eligible for election as bishop and, if elected, would receive confirmation from the metropolitan bishop; if election was to the metropolitan see itself, confirmation would come from the oldest bishop of the arrondissement. Each bishop with his council constituted the regional church authority. The election of the local curé was to take place in each parish, following the form established for election of members of the district administrative assembly.

Set between the rules for the election of the bishop and the election of the curé were two major elements of the Civil Constitution. First, the bishops were to report in (and *only* report in) to the pope: "The new bishop may not apply to the Pope for confirmation, but shall write to him as the Visible Head of the Universal Church, in testimony of the unity of faith and communion which he is to maintain therewith."[64] Second, the bishop was to take an oath of loyalty to the nation, the law, and the king: "The bishop-elect shall take a solemn oath, in the presence of the municipal officials, the people, and the clergy, to watch with care over the faithful of the diocese entrusted to him, to be faithful to the nation, to the law, and to the king, and to maintain with all his power the Constitution decreed by the National Assembly and accepted by the king."[65] All clergy were to be salaried by the state but held to laws of residency: "No bishop may absent himself from his diocese for more than fifteen consecutive days during any year."[66] The same time limits were to apply to curés and vicars in their parishes.

When the time came, the elections themselves were conducted as part of the new governmental electoral structure. Selection of bishops and curés was actually accomplished by electors who were themselves chosen by voters who met in primary assemblies. There would be one elector for every one hundred citizens, and the electors tended to be relatively well-off, with enough leisure time to take part in the somewhat lengthy process. Later constitutional writers seldom acknowledged this two-tier system, but preferred, rather, to evoke a golden age of early church history, when the faithful would in all freedom and innocence choose their clergy, sometimes by acclamation. In fact, the system tended to produce bishops and priests that appealed to the more radical bourgeoisie.[67]

If one label is to be used to explain the motivations or at least the orientation of the champions of the Civil Constitution, it would be "Gallican," the grand old tradition of a national church wherein the French bishops would establish and carry out their own agenda, in conformity with the bishop of Rome (and so, Roman Catholic) but not under his direct jurisdiction. The old Jansenists in the Committee and legislative discussions cobbled together as many usable parts as possible from the old multiform and sometimes self-contradictory ideology, and the old Richerist tendencies were considerably diffused—all of which has led Catherine Maire to write, "Jansenism dissolved into its own proper contradictions."[68]

Even so, the bishops in the Constituent Assembly, with Boisgelin at their head, constrained to oppose any final church–state structures that the state would set up unilaterally, circulated an *Exposition des principes* on 30 October 1790. They insisted that the legislature should work with either a church council or the pope, for without that no redistribution of religious authority would be possible.[69] Roman cardinals, in special session that September, were weighing the potential for schism of the redrawing of the diocesan boundaries, episcopal elections, and the relationship of bishops to Roman authority; they were to advise the pope, whose considered response the French bishops anxiously awaited.[70] The king, however, was forced to approve the 27 November decree obliging the clergy to swear the oath of loyalty to the nation, the law, and the king (implying acceptance of the Civil Constitution of the Clergy). Henri Grégoire actually took the oath ahead of schedule, believing that it was the only way to reconcile the church and the revolutionary government. A minority of the priests and only two of the bishops in the Assembly took the oath. In the end, only seven of the Old Regime bishops took the oath: Talleyrand and Jean-Baptiste Gobel, the Assembly members, and then Étienne-Charles de Loménie de Brienne of Sens, Louis-François-Alexandre Jarente of Orléans, Charles de la Font de Savine of Viviers, and the non-jurisdictional bishops Jean-Baptiste Dubourg-Miroudot (titular bishop of Babylon) and Pierre-François Martial de Loménie (titular bishop of Trianopolis). The massive refusal of the bishops came out of motivations theological and psychological, but aristocratic family background certainly weighed in here. More than 50 percent of the priests in public ministry (a much higher percentage than the priests in the actual Constituent Assembly) complied. Their motives, mapped by Timothy Tackett, were more varied than the motives of the bishops, of course, and can be conjectured with reasonable confidence by reference to authority and financial stability of church appointment, theological orientation, ecclesiastical milieu, age, social position, and location of diocese. The map of the wildly varying percentages of oath takers in the different regions of France, derived from Tackett's broad sociography of oath takers, does not show these motivational factors, and must be supplemented with his other statistics.[71]

Priests in their thirties and those over sixty took the oath in greater numbers, probably because they were more vulnerable financially. Curés from the aristocracy unsurprisingly rejected the oath, and curés from the formerly Jansenist—and so, still relatively anti-episcopal—areas accepted it, but those from the lowest economic strata took the oath in greatest numbers. A seminary education was an investment that poorer families did not want to lose.

Map 1 The oath of loyalty to the nation, the law, and the king: A referendum on the Civil Constitution of the Clergy

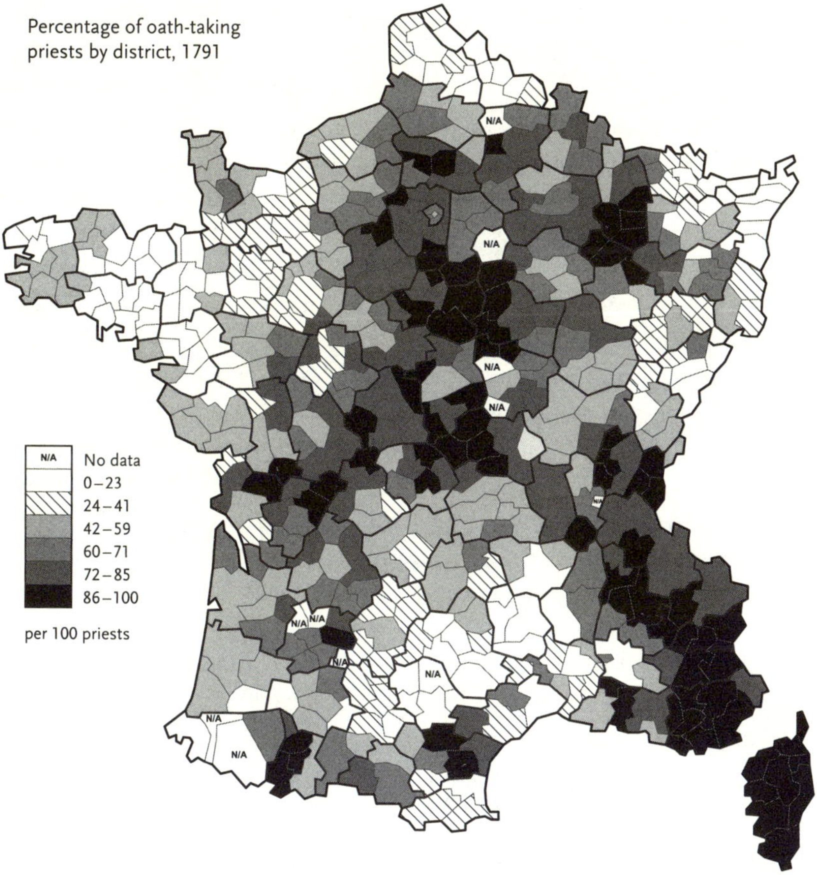

Statistics of priestly loyalty to the new regime in the eighty-three departments of France (subdivided into districts). Taking the loyalty oath indicated acceptance of the Civil Constitution of the Clergy. Pastors, and those exercising public functions, were held to the oath, whereas other priests had some choice in the beginning. An oath for all clergy, regular and secular, was instituted in August 1792.

As for milieu, priests who lived in close proximity to colleagues were less likely to take the oath than were isolated curés, who identified more with the lay community. Personality traits are harder to pin down, although, after a sampling of ten provinces, Tackett noted "that of those young men specifically cited for their 'piety,' only about a fourth would take the oath. . . . On the other hand, some two thirds of the young priests described with the relatively neutral adjective 'honnête' or criticized for their 'haughtiness' or 'quick temper' would ultimately emerge oath takers. . . . There was apparently a tendency to those least amenable to ecclesiastical discipline to later accept the Civil Constitution."[72]

With eighty-three dioceses and only a handful of Old Regime bishops available, new bishops had to be chosen from the ranks of the constitutional priests. Talleyrand, assisted by Gobel and Miroudot, consecrated Fathers Louis-Alexandre Expilly and Claude-Eustache-François Marolles, who then got right to the task of producing more new bishops, consecrating around fifty by the end of the first month.[73] When regional governments organized the election of the curés, immediate problems ensued. Only a limited number of parishioners took part in the elections, incumbent curés were unwilling to go, and elected curés were often unwilling to take up the posts to which they were called. Most often a nonjuror was replaced with a juror, although many nonjurors proved impossible to replace. Antagonisms quickly multiplied, with violence perpetrated by rough-and-ready types offended by the constitutional clergy, their anger heated up by some of the more embittered or extreme refractories. Constitutional bishops, in their new dioceses, were met sooner or later with mockery, accompanied at times by violence.

Accepting or rejecting their new priests, the common people were inevitably engaged: in some regions the peasants were quite fond of their old curé or the traditional modes of church life. Constitutional bishops and priests themselves were resentful of troublesome refractories, but occasionally reached out with, or responded to, kindness. As far as the government was concerned, the constitutionals were the real priests of France. They were to control all the parish registers, and thus records of baptisms, marriages, deaths—matters of vital public record. Refractories were occasionally emboldened to resist, and the political clubs struggled with them all the more. The parish of Saint-Sulpice in Paris was able to get around the restrictions by turning over jurisdiction to a religious order, the Theatines. Constitutional bishops, their authority so often in question, could maintain that authority only by formal rejection of refractory ministries; they were aided by the passage on 14 May 1791 of the Le Chapelier Law requiring that recalcitrant clergy be brought to court.[74]

In Paris, the only other bishop in the Constituent Assembly who had taken the oath with Talleyrand, Jean-Baptiste Gobel, was elected bishop, receiving five hundred votes, as opposed to the fifty-six votes for Louis

Figure 7 An artful caricature of the swearing of the oath to the nation, the law, and the king, and acceptance of the Civil Constitution of the Clergy. On the "left"—that is to say, the left of the chairman, though on the right side of the image here—are the good bishops who swore the oath; on the left and in the center of the image, the bad bishops and priests who refused and railed against the oath. The Holy Spirit hovers over the good bishops; snakes, bats, and other unsavory creatures issue from or settle around the others. (Bibliothèque nationale de France)

Charrier de la Roche, then a canon from Lyon, and the twenty-six votes for Sieyès, who declined to be a candidate anyway. Gobel had an indifferent reputation in Alsace, where he was serving as bishop after a position as auxiliary bishop of Bâle: the main problem seemed to be his debts, resulting from high though probably not immoral living. Income was a factor in his choice of the see of Paris over those of Colmar, Langres, and Agen. There were even some reports that he was willing to negotiate his submission to the Holy See for a certain sum. He turned out to be an inconsistent leader, alternately showing pastoral concern and submission to revolutionary dechristianization. His correspondence with government officials contained little explicit talk about spirituality, theology, or ministry. His priestly personality can be glimpsed only in a few rare texts, such as one letter to a local government committee about his Paris seminarians, who straddled residency in the nearby parish of Saint-Magloire and liturgy in the cathedral. A principal issue for Gobel was their health! "There is no one who does not feel that we would endanger the health of the young men by forcing them, in winter especially, to come back to Saint-Magloire after the morning office, only to return to Notre-Dame for the [evening] office after dinner, and by requiring [subsequently] that they remain for two or three hours after they arrive soaked by rain or covered with snow."[75] The seminarians are good for the cathedral and the cathedral is good for them, because they assist in teaching catechism (Gobel developed four catechisms since taking charge of the diocese), and they get the opportunity to hear good preachers. It all might have worked out in less trying times.

One revolutionary priest who had established his reputation in Paris before Gobel was elected bishop there was Claude Fauchet. Right in the middle of the violent storming of the Bastille, Fauchet, the churchman closest to the men who fought and died there, was at the center of Parisian political and religious life. Later bishop of Calvados, he was the revolutionary priest and constitutional bishop who animated the radical activity that spread from the capital to the provinces. Both by his life and by his writings, he proved to be an essential "priest of the French Revolution."

Chapter Three

CLAUDE FAUCHET AT THE BASTILLE

Brilliant as a young student and pious as a seminarian, Claude Fauchet taught members of the nobility early in his clerical career, and even preached before the king and queen. Yet he championed the Revolution as a Christian enterprise by animating a powerful political circle and several political journals. He eventually became the high-profile *vicaire prédicateur* of the Paris church of Saint-Roche, appropriately responsible, then, in 1789 for the clergy *cahier de doléances*, and one of the electors who chose delegates to the Estates General.[1] A large minority of the Paris clergy, and a genuine majority of the clergy around Paris, eventually followed in his revolutionary footsteps.[2]

On 14 July 1789, Fauchet was a member of the deputation, sent by a Paris assembly headquartered at the Hôtel de Ville, to negotiate with the marquis de Launay, governor of the Bastille, in order to forestall violence and bloodshed. Although the story got about that he was in the front lines of the attackers, saber in hand, reports agree that he was a member and then leader of the two deputations that tried and failed to get through to the governor. Fauchet himself told the story during a funeral commemoration on 5 August for those who died at the Bastille. First, he had proposed the decree ordering the commander of the Bastille to turn over the place to the care of the city. He was then given the dangerous task of delivering it: "We flew across those perils; we placed ourselves beneath the blazing guns; with our entreaties we held back the desperate people who were vainly trying to get to the top of the battlements and the cowardly assassins who were raining down death upon them. We then handed over the pacification decree." There he was, Claude Fauchet, "a legal expert, and a priest, accoutered only for peacemaking," whereas "they responded with weapons of war." Back he went with the others three times, and three times they were fired upon:

"We stayed alive, by some miracle of providence." Then a second deputation with a more obvious identification, a lowered flag, was sent with the same results. On the third try, he could only encourage his companions, "intrepid warriors, invincible soldiers of France, worthy of this great name which you justify by ranging yourself on the side of the fatherland to oppose its oppressors."[3] One year later, he added details about his narrow escape from death: "I saw the Bastille artillery fire at me, its murderous shells piercing my clothing and felling those citizens who were by my side; I did not fall back; I pressed on."[4] He was more precise about dates in the *Journal des Amis* at the beginning of 1793: "On 12 July, the people who had gathered at the Hôtel-de-Ville named me one of the principal officials of the insurrection. On 14 July, I wrote out and I myself carried the civil injunction to the governor of the Bastille, asking him to hand over immediately and without bloodshed that fortress of despotism; three times I braved outbursts that the artillery fired at me."[5] He saved his bullet-torn, long black cassock, subsequently seeing himself as "permanently at the Bastille."

Later, as constitutional bishop of Calvados, Fauchet set his memories of the Bastille drama in a talk on the union of gospel and revolution: "The gospel, too, is incendiary. The liberator of the human race wanted to extend to all the earth the sacred fire of universal fraternity. He held despots in horror: he was their victim; he loved all peoples; he is their savior."[6] This, of course, makes Christ a victim of despotism and an authentic revolutionary. Fauchet is not promoting violence here, but "equality, fraternal love, and divine liberty." In that first revolutionary community, the disciples were "brothers, friends, equals, and free." Christ and his disciples, and the early Christian community, were a real republic, which "should serve, in the fullness of time, for a universal republic."[7] The great symbol of the triumph of the republican way was the fall of the Bastille, in which Fauchet, no humility here, played a key role: "My eyes have seen the battlements of despotism thrown over. My voice is strong with all the power of a great people, who have chosen me to be their voice and have ordered the destruction of the Bastille in the name of the law, the true law, or the general will."[8] Not that he led the siege, but that he voiced the popular will for its destruction. It was a sublime moment, not only in the history of France but in the history of the world: "National sovereignty was born on that day, and now is immortal, invincible from its first moment: all of France embraced it at that moment. All the tyrants in the world were unable to harm it, and it will actually swallow them up."[9]

Figure 8 Claude Fauchet was the priest who was at the center of the violence in the taking of the Bastille. Since he played the role of mediator, his cassock (or clerical robe) was pierced by musket balls. Not long afterward, he was appropriately chosen as the preacher for a memorial service in the Paris church of Saint-Jacques et les Saints Innocents for those who died at the Bastille. At that point, Fauchet was probably the most publicly known priestly advocate of the new revolutionary order. (Bibliothèque nationale de France)

Priest and Politician

When he was ten years old, Claude Fauchet was sent to the Jesuits at Moulins for secondary school, where, the story was told, he preached his first sermon at age sixteen. At Bourges he went through all levels of seminary education, up to and including his doctorate. Jules Charrier describes him, then, as "a young man, kind to everyone, of pleasing manner, noted for the gentleness of his features and his athletic build, who was, besides, genuinely pious."[10] Like many other talented young priests from the provinces, he moved to Paris in search of greater openness and opportunities. In his sermons and writings he managed sound explanations of nature and grace, sorted out the moral complications of the Crusades, and in general gained a reputation for intelligence and eloquence. Before the king and queen he preached a theologically and politically unremarkable sermon that concluded with a prayer that in no way presaged the future enemy of kings. He received a substantial clerical income, but there is no record of lavish living: "Having a sensitive and generous heart, he could not see an unfortunate person and not help out."[11]

With talents recognized early in his career, Fauchet had both political and ecclesiastical clout that brought him into conflict with another high-profile ecclesiastic in the Constituent Assembly, his opposite number, the conservative abbé Maury. Fauchet was the rising star who was later elected to both the Legislative Assembly and the Convention. He was even asked to preach at the funeral of Philippe d'Orléans, father of Philippe Egalité. His principal theme was forgiveness of sinners and generosity to all. In several of his talks he rejected Jansenist notions of salvation, yet he also espoused a sort of Richerism in his enthusiasm for the story of St. Ambrose's popular election to the episcopacy. He said, "I am completely dedicated to the Revolution; you will find me at it until death."[12] He objected to the nobility's monopoly of the episcopate, although he was able to make sense out of the life of an Old Regime bishop. In the presence of the king he had preached a concern for the poor using, ten years before the Revolution, the words *people*, *freedom*, and *fatherhood*.[13] Contemporary enthusiasm for his preaching may have derived somewhat from its social character: "Voltaire himself, if he could have heard him, would have embraced him and cried out, 'I am a Christian.'"[14] It is clear from his writings that the social and economic welfare of people was at the heart of his morality.

On National Religion

Jules Charrier called *De la religion nationale* a type of manifesto of Fauchet's orientations on religion, philosophy, and the economy.[15] Like most of the tracts of the times, it lacks philosophical originality and narrative grace, but has—Fauchet was a deservedly esteemed preacher of the period—a certain rhetorical flourish. To begin with, he says, "in order to have full rights of the citizen, one must profess the national religion,"[16] which, ratcheting it up a notch, means "one is a citizen, that is to say French, to the extent that one is a Catholic."[17] The first part of the book deals with the vital importance

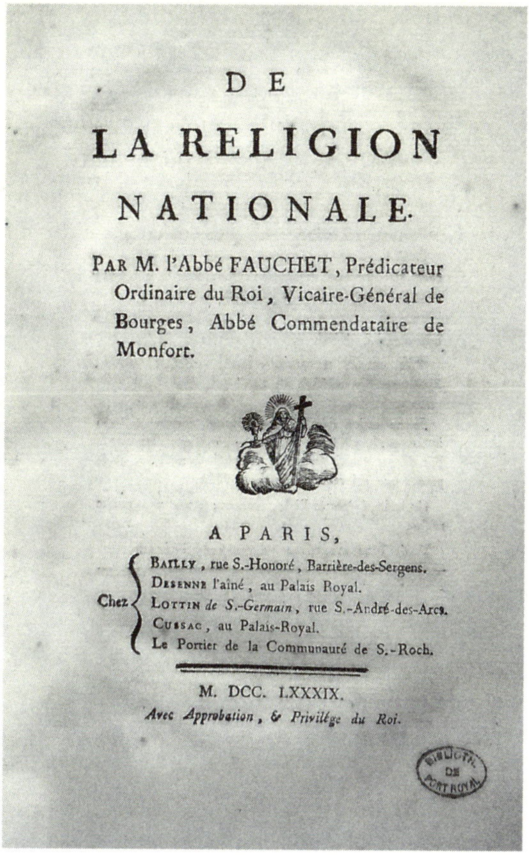
DE
LA RELIGION
NATIONALE.

PAR M. l'Abbé FAUCHET, Prédicateur Ordinaire du Roi, Vicaire-Général de Bourges, Abbé Commendataire de Monfort.

A PARIS,

Chez { BAILLY, rue S.-Honoré, Barrière-des-Sergens.
DESENNE l'aîné, au Palais Royal.
LOTTIN *de S.-Germain*, rue S.-André-des-Arcs.
CUSSAC, au Palais-Royal.
Le Portier de la Communauté de S.-Roch.

M. DCC. LXXXIX.
Avec Approbation, & Privilège du Roi.

Figure 9 The title page of Fauchet's book on the role of Catholicism in French national life. It was published in May 1789, before the taking of the Bastille in July. He gives a substantial role to the state and to the king in the promotion of a national Catholicism, but in some ways prefigures the revolutionary and republican ways of the future Civil Constitution of the Clergy.

of religion in supporting the "laws" against human passions, here meaning in particular the rule of law as protection against the passions of tyrants and crowds. In the second part, he analyzes the "combination of the laws of the Catholic church with the laws of the temporal power."[18] Here Fauchet considers public need and religious orders, universities, appropriate titles for bishops, the value of celibacy, and most of all, the role of the government in the choice of church leaders. The third part of the book takes on the relation of religion to the temporal order embodied in civil law, a jumble of issues having to do with tolerance, agrarian law, marriage law, paternal authority, legal successions, the theater, and Sunday rest. Here, too, he defended freedom of the press.

People have the right to choose their ministers. Fauchet privileges the assemblies of the faithful, based on the historical commonplace that orderly, fair elections were the norm in the early centuries of Christianity. But of course, simple elections could reinvigorate the French church at all levels, limited as it was by the top-heavy aristocratic domination of all areas of public and private life. Fauchet's promotion of elections—in particular elections of bishops—came to be the norm in the new Constitution of the Church. A principal target of his work here was the Concordat between Pope Leo X and King Francis I that gave the monarchy such great control. As a countermeasure, Fauchet proposes a structure for episcopal elections, with all parts of the diocese getting together to propose three candidates, the king choosing one of them, and the pope providing "canonical investiture."[19] Fauchet gives the king a substantial role even in the elective system because he believes monarchs have a good chance of rising above local intrigues. The pope simply gives rubber-stamp ecclesiastical approbation. The state, then, has a considerable role to play in controlling the abuses of religion, but it does not have arbitrary authority. Religious properties cannot be taken away, for example, when church people are in proper exercise of their apostolate. But the multiple benefices of former days must not be allowed any longer. Neither bishops nor pastors should have elaborate living quarters. In fact, amid all the bells, costumes, and trinkets, the only *objet* of any importance is the bishop's cross.[20]

Religious orders, too, must show goodness and simplicity, and be useful to the faithful. Fauchet gives high marks to the Trappists and Carthusians for their continuing fervor. Seminary education must be pruned of its arbitrary strictness and promotion of puerile thought and religious routines. And the theology programs of the day only encourage the rush for degrees in order to secure a better position in the church. Exalted titles of all sorts should be dropped, beginning with *Monseigneur.* For all his radicalism, Fauchet was a defender of celibacy, consistent in that he believed celibates could be more at the service of the people, "since their love is not concentrated inside their house."[21]

The Political Dialogue

Fauchet focused on the everyday qualities of life, love, and truth in his journal *Bulletin de la Bouche de fer*, named for a letter box placed on the publication-office door of his political society.[22] His first address to the Confédération universelle des amis de la vérité presented what he took to be real religion to his political colleagues, beginning with a frank look at the problems caused by religion. Whereas religion should have softened intolerance, liberated thinking, strengthened virtue, and brought happiness, in fact religion has been divided against itself, tormented consciences, and been a source of great unhappiness. In reality, "there can be only one true religion, that which says to men, 'Love one another,' and which gives them the most gentle and powerful motives for accomplishing this unique duty. This religion exists; it is eternal as is the law of love; men, separated from one another by the laws of discord that rule empires, have not known it. It should be shown to them in its chaste nudity and in its pure truthfulness; and the human race, taken with its divine beauty, will adore it with one heart."[23]

In a second discourse published in *Bouche de fer*, Fauchet opens an enthusiastic dialogue with Freemasons, increasingly favored targets of clerical Catholicism. First he distinguishes between good and bad in masonic membership. At its best Freemasonry is an experience of a "living light" and "great fervor," even though for some it can lead to an unfortunately phony vision and unruly imagination. But Fauchet emphasizes the good: "The real composers of the ancient and new mysteries of the lodges are the sure friends of humanity, who aspire only to the happiness of a universal regeneration and who must reach for it by the worthy means of the height and beauty of their hopes." Nevertheless, he recognizes that the others are dangerous, not so much in their goals as in the means they choose: "Superstitious corruption, terrible destruction, and mighty ruins seem necessary to them in order to erect the temple of concord and harmony."[24] Evil men, who are "false interpreters of the masonic allegories, and who have loaded them with hateful symbols, and with horror-filled trials," are in the shadow of virtuous men, the only ones who count.[25]

Fauchet admires the Freemasons, finds their goals of universal religion and reorganization of society to be the same as his, and appreciates the friendship and belief in God that they preach. And so he owes them an explanation of his reasons for not joining: "Venerable brothers! Worthy friends of mankind! I have not wished to, nor ought I to have been, initiated into your mysteries, because the truth of them escapes me . . . but I know enough to be sure that none of you can deny the facts that lie at the base of your doctrinal traditions."[26] He could not follow them in their explanation of the great mysteries and in their secrecy, then; but he certainly gives his full support to their effort to improve the lives of people everywhere. By saying that they will be the "patrons of humanity everywhere on earth," he is clearly hoping for their worldwide success.[27]

Jean-Jacques Rousseau himself, "the great genius who has rendered such a great service to humanity," was not a nemesis for Claude Fauchet, who seeks a balance between the "social contract" and Christianity.[28] Love of all people, the creation of laws that benefit them, these were Rousseau's themes, but Fauchet finds that he is misused, no longer properly understood. Other great writers share his lot, but Rousseau least of all deserves this fate: "We could submit to the same test . . . Montesquieu, the weighty Mably, the eloquent Raynal, and all the profound legislative writers: but Rousseau suffices, for he has said in substance all that is best in the best authors who have spoken on law."[29] Of course, for Fauchet the gospel is the great message and the great text, because it gives human love its divine quality, and maintains a special type of equality among all peoples because it makes of them a human family under God: "It is the only religion in the entire world that has this ultimate basis." But it is a less ecumenical Fauchet, who says in the next sentence, "All the others are exclusive, hateful, and alien to our views of full concord, just as they are [alien] to the true well-being of men."[30]

In another discourse on the same subject, we find a different, even highly critical, view of Rousseau, noting that Voltaire, too, had major criticisms. Fauchet's respect for "the great man" stands firm, but, as for his ideas: "We will not adopt them because of the genius of his speech and our belief in his importance. We will examine them in their own right, with as much impartiality as if the author were unknown to us."[31] Fauchet's problems with Rousseau do not seem to come from his own immersion in the gospel, but from a very positive philosophy of revolutionary fraternity. He finds "inexact" the Rousseauian axiom, "Man is a loving being by nature and finds his happiness only in fraternity," and the conclusions Rousseau draws from it, that family is the only natural society and is such only to the extent that each individual enjoys full development, are "completely false."[32] On the contrary, says Fauchet, "man never ceases to relate to his fellows by natural means; and it is universal relationships out of nature that constitute the true unity of society." Otherwise, society could not exist and people would "vegetate, isolated in the forests."[33] He then proposes his own philosophical program to go beyond Rousseau, social philosophy with a Christian ethical base: "The whole series of principles of natural sociability, which do not stop at all with the family in society, as Rousseau neglected to say, but which, on the contrary, extend, always in the order of nature, to the city, to the nations, to neighboring peoples, to all men, to the university, and unto eternity."[34]

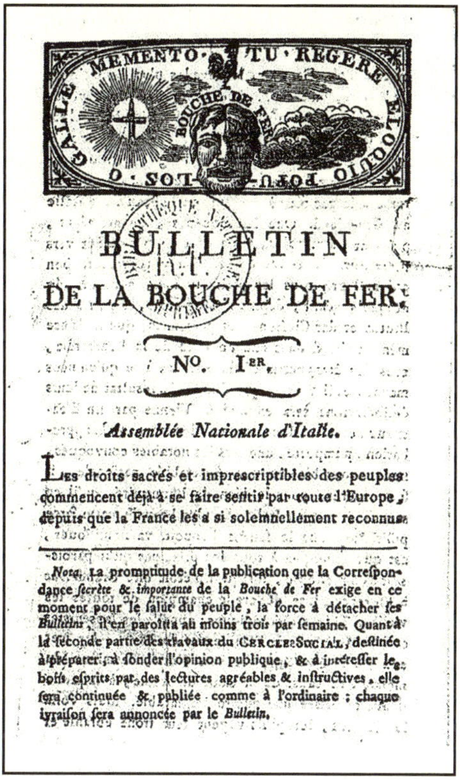
GALLE MEMENTO TU REGERE ELOQUIO POPULOS
BOUCHE DE FER

BULLETIN
DE LA BOUCHE DE FER.

No. Ier.

Assemblée Nationale d'Italie.

Les droits sacrés et imprescriptibles des peuples commencent déjà à se faire sentir par toute l'Europe, depuis que la France les a si solemnellement reconnus.

Nota. La promptitude de la publication que la Correspondance *secrète* & *importante* de la *Bouche de Fer* exige en ce moment pour le salut du peuple, la force à détacher ses *Bulletins*, il en paroîtra au moins trois par semaine. Quant à la seconde partie des travaux du CERCLE SOCIAL, destinée à préparer, à fonder l'opinion publique, & à intéresser les bons esprits par des lectures agréables & instructives, elle sera continuée & publiée comme à l'ordinaire; chaque livraison sera annoncée par le *Bulletin*.

Figure 10 An issue of the political journal edited by Fauchet, *La Bouche de fer*, or *Mouth of Iron*, quaintly titled to evoke the image of the letter drop at the publication office. Fauchet was thus in the forefront of the dialogue between churchmen who favored reform and political reformers of all stripes, even some of the most extreme.

Responding with positive warmth to the radical revolutionary Anacharsis Cloots, Fauchet appears to find a kindred spirit. In his writings live "the spirit of liberty and love of men" that is expressed with "a most proud and ardent eloquence." Fauchet tells Cloots that his "good opinion of me was correct; the present persuasion that is unfavorable to me is fortunately without basis, and your fairness will bring you back to your first viewpoint."[35] With Cloots, Fauchet plays the master diplomat, or the man of great openness. Certainly he is inclusive: "I love good Jansenists, good Quakers, good Protestants, good Masons, good men, and finally, all the truly good in nations, religions, viewpoints, and societies."[36] There is truth everywhere and he cherishes the truth. He explains, too, why he is a constitutional bishop: "You will find me always ready to use my feeble talents to work with others for the well-being of men."[37] Modestly, perhaps a little too modestly, he adds that others could do it better but that he will do his best.

Praise of Voltaire and his work here is a striking example of Fauchet's use of all that is good. Voltaire had great talent and worked for people, "despite his errors and pretensions." Fauchet's admiration was realistic: "As wonderful as he was, he was a man; and the men I admire the most I do not adore."[38] He dares to label Voltaire an "aristocrat" (in society and literature), because it is a simple historical fact, and so the statement cannot be offensive in any way. Assuming that he and Cloots are in cahoots on this, Fauchet criticizes Enlightenment intellectuals (probably because they were so little concerned for the people) and praises the Freemasons: "I am at as much of a remove as you could be from the Illuminés of Germany, in Prussia and elsewhere, who live by such cruel illusions."[39] If they are Freemasons, then they are disfiguring Freemasonry.

Fauchet repeats for Cloots his conviction that Christianity is a religion of total love, found in the gospel and nowhere else. It is only theologians who merit the antagonism to religion: "It is not the small and barbaric religion of the theologians that I profess."[40] He prefers the unbeliever to the theologian, because "the first can use natural rectitude in controlling sentiments, in a way different from the second who no longer listens to nature and sanctifies his fanaticism by his zeal."[41] This is why he can work things out with Cloots, a man of honest sentiment who goes by the natural law ("for lack of the gospel"), and who is incapable of any dissimulation. The fanatical theologian, however, twists the gospel for his own ends, and here Fauchet offers no explicit criticisms. Fauchet's "universal religion" embraces all people of goodwill and hopes for the repentance of others. It is a religion of kindness and goodness, and Fauchet is happy to proclaim in conclusion, "Noble Cloots, you have it deep in your heart."[42]

The Constitutional Bishop

Biographer Charrier was always ready to decry Fauchet's faults and see all opposition and dislike in a positive light. Thus his election as constitutional bishop was seen as a combination of default and self-promotion: others were not interested in the position, few people wanted Fauchet, but he pushed his candidacy just enough to get through. In fact, Claude Fauchet had a number of qualities (elsewhere noted by Charrier) that made him a proper candidate, even a very good one. He was one more constitutional intellectual who had a good preaching reputation and was politically engaged.

Passing through Lisieux, Caen, and Bayeux in taking charge of the diocese of Calvados, he met with a much more positive reception than had some of his colleagues in the constitutional episcopacy. There were many receptions: the official departmental reception, the municipal reception, and especially receptions in the clubs. By this time, Fauchet had worked his way into the good graces of the Jacobins as well. His political position was probably more stable than his ecclesiastical position. True, given his competence, the refractory priests were not in a position to degrade him; but there was formal opposition, including condemnation by the Old Regime bishop of the region. Even Charrier admits that Fauchet cut a fine figure at that time: "Attractive in appearance, manners that, for all their exuberance, did not exclude dignity; with an open and generous heart, he exercised a great power of seduction over those around him."[43] For all his intellectual and personal flash, Fauchet was still preoccupied with his image as a worker in the vineyard, dedicated to the improvement of everyday life for the simplest people.

At the beginning of his first pastoral letter, Fauchet reminds his people that they have a special relationship with him because they elected him: "Your will brought me up to the top rank of your pastors; it will put me down if I do not fulfill your goals." He claims to function at their beck and call and goes so far as to say that they represent for him "the voice of God"—in the elections.[44] Proper, then, to review the history of election in scripture and the early church. It was the election process that set St. Peter straight, and it would be the election process that would set straight the church of France. Fauchet gets a bit ahead of his argument here, because Peter, he has to admit, was appointed directly by Christ and mandated to strengthen others in the faith. But with a little spin, Fauchet gets a version of Peter, who is converting *to* the beliefs of the brethren and so strengthening them: "Brought back to the common faith of the brethren, did he not adhere to and confirm their beliefs?"[45] The role of the brethren in maintaining Peter in his high office is definitely clearer in later events (no spin needed here). The scripture story has Paul admonishing Peter for his insistence on observance of the Mosaic law. And, far from resisting, Peter had a special love and gratitude toward Paul from then on. "With what admiration, what modesty, what tenderness, he spoke of the teaching of his very dear brother Paul!" says Fauchet.[46] All this means, of course, that those exercising the Petrine Office—the popes—should be like Peter, who insisted that "pastors should form their minds and hearts at the good pleasure of their flock, and thereby become for all the faithful a model of wisdom!"[47]

Fauchet believes that the malaise in the church runs deep. But working with governments could keep churchmen more effective and honest: "Public order and common sense share the same space, and observation is necessary for any concerted and harmonious effort."[48] Churchmen have true authority and should be consulted, to be sure, but consulting the church produces fewer good results when its organization is faulty. One must be wary of the bishops. It is one thing to accept their divinely guided teaching: there they had to monitor themselves, "because the entire church would have rejected them, and the Holy Spirit would have inspired the truth in people's souls, to constrain the majority of pastors to the doctrinal infallibility they owe to the guidance of Jesus Christ."[49] But their organizational programs have been utterly selfish and self-serving—and unsuccessful. And here Fauchet takes off on Trent, a council that was more interested in correcting Protestants than in correcting abuses in the church, all of this due to "papal despotism and the aristocratic rule of the bishops."[50]

The National Assembly, then, is the means of correcting the chronic problems of overextended church authority: "The consent of the people, a consent always expressed in the old laws, is it lacking in the new decrees of the National Assembly, which is today bringing the clergy to its original form?"[51] In fact, it belongs both to the "essence of the church" and to the "substance of the nation" to work together for the preservation of "gospel truths."[52] And Fauchet urges the people to keep bishops in line. The bishops would never do it on their own, most recently showing their intransigence by stubborn resistance and even flight from the country. He further proposes that the people must be assured that the new constitutional episcopacy never sink to the ways of the Old Regime. Their consecration secures divine authority, but "it is from you, dearest brethren, from you who are the family of Jesus Christ and his faithful people, that they receive the right orientation in the use of this divine power."[53]

Claude Fauchet was elected to the new Legislative Assembly some months after the publication of his first pastoral letter. There, he took a strong stand against the refractories, although this antagonism may have been tied to a personal vendetta against the minister of the interior, Jean-Marie de Lessart, reputed to be sympathetic to the refractories.[54] He also praised the restraint of his Comité de surveillance (in Calvados) in contrast to a smaller comité in Marat's commune (in Paris). A contemporary reporter, knowing that

Fauchet could bring tough politics into church, was surprised to hear at Notre-Dame a "very mystical sermon that could as well have been preached in 1400 as in 1791."[55] To the chagrin of constitutional colleagues, he was still in favor of a lavish episcopal guard.[56] His pastoral letter of 1792, written one year after his installation as bishop, began with a clever résumé of the church–state ideas he had come to espouse across the years, beginning with the supremacy of the gospel as "the only religion of holy liberty."[57] It is true that the human passions have caused major harm, but they will never gain universal control, because they "will only make people seek refuge in the true religion."[58] Fauchet pairs republic and church works at every turn: "The more the pure light of reason is propagated in the human mind, the more evident will be the great principles of religion. The more the taste for republican virtues and universal fraternity win hearts, the more will the need for evangelical Catholicism make itself felt in all souls."[59] In the design of providence, the rule of reason will serve the gospel and the good of the world. But ultimately reason will fail, and then there will only be the gospel: "[The human race], feeling itself torn apart again by the terrible anarchy of the passions, and by the impotence of reason by itself, will turn toward heaven and find . . . the peace brought by virtue, the bond holding people together, and the happiness of the universe."[60] In government, then, let all support the rule of law.

Fauchet never doubted the evangelical advantages of a revolutionary government, and in the Convention he would pursue his alliance with the Jacobins in a final attack on the king—although a regicide he was not (see chap. 6). One of the earliest influences on his religious program, however, was Adrien Lamourette's theology of the church, which must now be seen in its setting.

Chapter Four

THE CHURCH OF ADRIEN LAMOURETTE AND HIS ALLIES

At the center of both religious and political action in the first years of the Revolution, Adrien-Antoine Lamourette was an inspiration and guide for the high-energy church–state activities of both Henri Grégoire and Claude Fauchet. He was also a bridge personality between the towering figure of the National Assembly, the comte de Mirabeau, and the church law scholar, Armand-Gaston Camus, advising Mirabeau on matters ecclesiastical and promoting the reforms of Camus. Appropriately elected and consecrated a constitutional bishop, Lamourette was subsequently elected to the Legislative Assembly, the setting for his dramatic call for political reconciliation, the "Kiss of Lamourette." The complexity of his personality and theological program has now received full treatment in the work of Caroline Chopelin-Blanc.[1]

The comte de Mirabeau, Honoré-Gabriel Riquetti, was not only the dominant aristocratic personage in the Constituent Assembly; he was the most authoritative personage there from any level of society. Had he lived, Mirabeau might have been the uncontested leader of the Revolution, which he would have channeled into a constitutional monarchy—the debate is still on, however, as to how far he was willing to go to save the monarchy. We can at least say that Lamourette's confidence in Mirabeau's apparent good faith promotion of the Constitutional Church was not fully justified, for Mirabeau was playing churchmen against one another, trying to gain time as he worked with King Louis to strengthen the monarchy.[2] He appeared to be a patron of the Constitutional Church, and he tried to advise the king himself in all areas of government at the same time, including religion. As soon as Mirabeau drafted Lamourette as his counselor on church–state affairs, the latter helped him with a speech, presented on 2 November 1789, against the privileges of the clergy and in favor of the seizure of ecclesiastical properties.[3] Later Lamourette abetted and advised Mirabeau for his speech in the Assembly on behalf of the establishment of the Constitutional Church. In turn, Mirabeau strongly supported Lamourette for the see of Lyon, traditionally the archdiocese of the primate of France—in dignity, though not authority and power, more important than the see of Paris: "Mirabeau was no stranger to the Lyon election. It was he who designated the candidate, saying that no one else was capable of filling the position. The zeal that he employed in this situation was a payment for services rendered."[4] And on 27 March 1791 Lamourette was consecrated bishop by Gobel in Notre-Dame Cathedral. Lamourette was an ardent proponent of theories on church authority worked out by the theologian and canon lawyer Gaston Camus, "who brings together a strict Christianity, a clear and precise mind, and the talent for discerning customs born of superstition and ignorance from those which follow the inviolable principles of the divine constitution of the church."[5] Camus's contribution to the structuring of the Civil Constitution was, if anything, more important than Lamourette's own writings and advice, and more vociferous than the speech style of Mirabeau![6] Across those 1790 discussions of the Civil Constitution of the Clergy, the voice of Camus, canon lawyer and dedicated lay Catholic, was instrumental in moving the debate forward in the Constituent Assembly.

The Reality of the Catholic Constitutional Church

Focusing on the challenges of the church's contemporary role in society, Lamourette developed a formal, balanced theology of the church from the top down: the role of the pope, as well as the prerogatives of the bishops as the successors of the apostles (no more beholden to the pope for their spiritual powers than the apostles were beholden to Peter). On a presumed scriptural basis and in the light of history and legal reasoning, the role and prerogatives of the French church become clear, and Lamourette was sure that they coordinated perfectly with the new revolutionary government. Given this theology, his talents, and his connections, Lamourette would have been a likely candidate for the office of constitutional bishop, even without the attention and backing of Mirabeau. A crabbed and crabby description of Lamourette's formal taking of office was published in the *Revue du Lyonnais*: "The bishop, surrounded by unbelieving magistrates and having on either

Figure 11 Adrien Lamourette in his bishop's attire. This image represents him as he was during the first years of the Revolution, when he was at the height of his influence, but it was actually published after his execution in 1794 during the Terror. As a central figure in the Legislative Assembly, he issued a call for reconciliation, the famous "Kiss of Lamourette." (Bibliothèque nationale de France)

side of him a Calvinist minister and a scandalous priest, preceded by the national guard, had less the air of a pastor entering his sheepfold, than the winner of an episcopal residence, who, braving all the decorum, begins by solemnizing the equality of all religions."[7]

A long pastoral instruction, really a small book, appeared at the beginning of Lamourette's short tenure as the constitutional bishop of Lyon.[8] It was a balanced and complete summary of the polity and theology of the Constitutional Church.[9]

A democratic Christianity would be the fulfillment of the mission the church has carried on for 1,700 years, the calling together of all peoples: "It is the only religious institution that contains within itself the principle of the union of all nations into one family and which manifests to the human race the true indissoluble lines of universal fraternity."[10] But Lamourette is swinging for the fence here. Not just some general fulfillment, some manifest destiny, this will be the church's greatest moment: "So we will see

Christianity acquire for the first time an existence in conformity with its nature, which is *to consummate everything in unity, to concentrate everything in charity*, and to overturn the walls and fortresses with which nations surround themselves in order to keep others out, and to construct human society on the model of the eternal and indivisible society of the divine persons."[11] Even the waywardness and destructiveness of revolution does not dampen Lamourette's enthusiasm, as he calls it "a circumstance that we must rank with the great miracles of providence: that in the revolution in this kingdom, the Christian religion resisted all the means of destruction with which its enemies suddenly found themselves so powerfully equipped."[12]

With so much good being accomplished, Lamourette cannot but be disappointed in the response of the pope to the possibility of the Constitutional Church, although he makes excuses for him. It is not the pope's personal fault that he "let himself be wrapped up in a coalition that was not worthy of the superiority of his rank, nor the seriousness of his duties, nor the wisdom of his administration."[13] And he simply gave in to foreign political pressure from other countries, all of which renders null and void the judgments he pronounces and the sentences that he hands down.[14] He does not have the "qualities necessary to judge us nor the power necessary to punish us."[15]

What could the pope have wanted to convey by this decision? Lamourette caricatures the papal decision-making process, on the premise that the Archbishop Boisgelin's *Exposition des principes* was *not* a compromise, but rather a reactionary, document. He begins by asking what his readers would think of a judge who wants more information from one of the parties to a dispute, and then, instead of an impartial judgment, simply accepts the viewpoint of that party. The pope listened to the conservative French bishops who simply wanted to reinforce their own authority. The problem is that the papacy has become such a worldly institution: "For inasmuch as the see of Peter has become a throne of power, and the vicar of Christ sees himself as a master of the world, who will set up for us a sure and unbreakable rule of behavior to help us distinguish a judgment of the [papal] court from an apostolic decision? Who will assure for us that in the pope, the errors, prejudices and pretensions of the prince will never obscure the judgment of the pontiff, and that he will never wrongfully use the condemnation of the church to support the injustice of arbitrary authority?"[16]

First, Lamourette takes on the *primacy* of the pope. According to the Catholic interpretation of scripture, Christ conferred a genuine primacy on the head of his church. Lamourette says that this has been the teaching of orthodox Christianity across the centuries. But the question more precisely is what this primacy consists in. Go to the moment when Peter and the other apostles were gathered together after Christ's ascension, when the apostles submitted themselves only to Peter's "superiority of inspection and surveillance, to an authority of admonition and exhortation that has nothing in common with the more full spiritual and divine jurisdiction."[17]

Second, the apostles themselves receive a special universal jurisdiction and mission. Lamourette quotes the gospel: "*I send you as the Father has sent me. Go forth on the earth; announce the gospel to every creature. Receive the Holy Spirit. Whose sins you shall forgive they are forgiven and whose sins you shall retain they are retained. And behold I am with you until the end of time.*" The mission and the jurisdiction were given by Christ himself *directly* to the apostles. There is no record that the apostles, before they set out on their mission, ever went to Peter "in order to receive an investiture other than that which had been given by Jesus Christ, or to search for an institution and a mission other than those which had been so formally and distinctly conferred at the very moment when their divine master imprinted on them the character of his eternal priesthood."[18]

Third, episcopal consecration is "indivisible and numerical": a bishop has full apostolic powers and has them as an individual. Lamourette is here insisting that the obvious spiritual powers of the individual bishop are not limited; in other words, that he possesses these powers as an individual relative to all the bishops, in the same way that an individual apostle possessed spiritual powers relative to the whole group of apostles. He has a universal mission, "such that always and everywhere a bishop is *instituted* and *sent* directly in virtue of the sacrament by which he was *ordained*."[19]

Fourth, apostolic succession consists in ordination, and the profession and transmission of the faith of the apostles: "This is to say that ordination and catholicity connect a bishop with the chain of pastors who have governed the church from the time of the apostles to their last successors."[20] The pope is nowhere directly involved in this chain of powers. But some of his promoters would place him there as if he, and not Christ, were the source of the episcopal office. So Lamourette complains, "They accuse us of interrupting the succession, only because we refuse to recognize in the visible head of the church, the source of our jurisdiction and the author of our mission, and because they would have it that all spiritual power is derived from him just as it derives from the invisible and supreme authority."[21]

Important consequences flow from these principles. The civil power is supposed to handle all that pertains to the external and political aspects of religion. In this sense, religion is a matter for civil administration the same as any other: "The state alone is the creator of the public existence of Christianity."[22] But the inner spiritual power of the priesthood can never be touched, changed, or removed by the temporal power. This comes directly from Christ by ordination and cannot be altered by any temporal regime, including the temporal ecclesiastical regime of the church. In this context, practices and customs pertaining to the layout of ecclesiastical regions and elections, and clerical influences of all kinds, are nothing more than customs; they are not rules. So, the doctrinal decision of the Roman court on the ecclesiastical constitution obviously goes against the early teaching of the holy apostolic see and all church teaching of the first centuries: "This judgment is heretical in that it concentrates in the pope all the spiritual power that Jesus Christ confided to his church, and attributes to him the dispensing of a jurisdiction that can only come from God alone by the institution of the sacrament of orders."[23] And so Lamourette has gone the limit: the pope's viewpoint is itself heretical.

Mirabeau and the Constitutional Church

Six months before Lamourette published the foregoing powerful and clear pastoral instruction, he was helping Mirabeau craft a powerful and clear promotion of the Constitutional Church. In the National Assembly, on 26 November 1790, Mirabeau followed an impassioned intervention on behalf of the Constitutional Church by Jean-Georges-Charles Voidel with a tempered speech that, nevertheless, contained strong praise of the church and strong criticism of the non-submissive Old Regime bishops and priests.[24]

In his discourse *Sur la Constitution civile du clergé*, Mirabeau accuses his antagonists of hiding religious hypocrisy behind a mask of piety and good faith. They pretend to mitigate and modify this constitution, but in fact are destroying religion itself. They at once betray public religion and ignore the people's will. In fact, they are plotting to overthrow the Civil Constitution: "No, Messieurs, what we resent is not that you bring temperament-based features and changes to the established Civil Constitution of the Clergy; but that you have stopped being rational and have renounced justice altogether, that you trample underfoot the faith of your fathers, and that you destroy a

Figure 12 The comte de Mirabeau, the principal legislator trying to hold together the Revolution and the monarchy, who depended on Adrien Lamourette for his speeches on church and state. Here we see a mythic representation of Mirabeau, crowned by Benjamin Franklin, being received with important figures of church–state history in the left background (Voltaire, Fénélon, Montesquieu, and Mably) and the great figures of classical history (Cicero and Demosthenes) in the right background. (Bibliothèque nationale de France)

religion whose destiny you had linked to that of the empire. Your fall into [such] irreverence would mark you with an odious character wherein you seemingly enlist people's piety in order to divide and conquer the legislators from whom France awaits regeneration."[25]

The bishops, Mirabeau says, pretend to wait on the pope's word, but they have already moved the pope in the direction they want. Their warnings about a schism are in themselves words of discord and revolt, inasmuch as they use religion to punish others and avenge themselves; they are the ones who are creating a schism. They say that the Civil Constitution goes against the rights of the church, but Mirabeau notes that, in the days of the Roman Empire, the church was nothing, and had to work out its spiritual prerogatives totally separate from the state. In those days, the church leaders simply wanted imperial authorities who would not be hostile or angry. Their only real support came from the people they served. How grateful the church fathers would have been if they had the support the French legislature was now giving the church.

Mirabeau has nothing but ecstatic praise for the Assembly's attention to religious reform: "This is the moment when you render [religion's] destiny inseparable from that of the nation, when you incorporate it into the existence of this great empire and when you set aside the most solid segment of the state's substance for the perpetuation of its government and its religion. This is the moment when you make [the church] gloriously take its place in the sublime division [of labor] in the loveliest kingdom of the universe, and when, planting the august sign of Christianity on the highest places of all of the departments of France, you confess before all the nations and across all the centuries that God is as necessary as liberty for the French people."[26] Conversely, Mirabeau has nothing but anger for the bishops who, in return, denounce these marvelous legislators for violating the rights of religion, stereotyping them as the persecutors of Christianity.

The recalcitrant bishops are the real intruders, because they willingly used a corrupt system to get ahead in the church. They are anxious about elections *now*, but whose voice was heard, whose rights were honored in all the Old Regime trickery? Theirs only. Furthermore, Mirabeau now wonders how bishops, if they are not bona fide citizens, could hold valid elections for the sake of (in place of) the citizenry. Why should they not become part of the new state, the new citizenry, in other words, part of the Constitutional Church? By regaining the respect of the people the bishops could even influence the elections that so concerned them.

Addressing himself directly to the bishops present at the session, Mirabeau asks them how they can remain passive when destructive anti-constitutionals are in action. He is simply scandalized that they do not encourage people to respect the new regime. What happens if priests who work with the government become discouraged? The hope of reaching the people lies with these priests: when it comes time to be rid of the "old Leaven," the people will not accept those other priests who support the old repressive ways.[27] The new Constitution will attract people, and civil leaders also, to those priests who are loyal to that Constitution. Mirabeau wants to inspire the bishops and priests to preempt the problems the state and church face, and so he would be ready and eager to sanction them if they fail to do their duty.

Then Mirabeau proposes a bill, in opposition to the bishops' *Exposition des principes de la Constitution civile du clergé*, which he takes to be "directly contrary to the liberties of the Gallican church and manifestly prejudicial to the authority of the constituent body."[28] In his heavy-handed first article, Mirabeau has the Assembly declare invalid (*déchu*) the election of any bishop who requests official approbation from the Holy See instead of sending a simple declaration of unity, and remove any metropolitan or bishop who would refuse to grant canonical confirmation to newly elected bishops or curés.[29] For Mirabeau, national politics determined the role of the church and not vice versa. The ministry of bishops and priests existed for the sake of citizenship, which meant that the pope, a bishop outside of France, should not interfere with the religious organization of the French state. Under the constitutional monarchy, a free people should be served by priests who are real citizens. Mirabeau proclaimed that the church government structures, if set up according to basic Christian tradition, coordinated perfectly with the church government structures as he understood them. The bishops are spiritual leaders, and the pope is of the same order as the bishops, with the further task of coordinating and inspiring. Nothing in church authority justifies territorial political jurisdiction, which means that the distribution and extent of anything beyond spiritual activities is a matter of government authority and popular election. And so Mirabeau, for the sake of the nation, proposed measures that would ensure the fairness of episcopal elections and would tightly control the number of priests ordained and their control over the lives of citizens. A bishop who would have recourse to outside authority (i.e., the pope) and a priest who would fail to support the national government should be refused permission to continue in the ministry.

Armand-Gaston Camus on Church Law

If Mirabeau in the Constituent Assembly, influenced by Lamourette, could take on recalcitrant bishops and priests, Armand-Gaston Camus, an influence on Lamourette, could take on a recalcitrant pope, making his points with a lawyer's rhetoric. In fact, Lamourette offered a grand-scale presentation of Camus in that 1791 *Instruction pastorale*. Camus compares the pope to an angry infant, who has heard all kinds of condemnations of a criminal, and uses the same language during his own games with friends: "Words that designate all the punishments trip from his tongue; as they come out of his mouth they are heaped on the head of someone whom his useless sentences and vain warnings would never injure."[30] Of course, this type of childish anger means nothing: the child has no right to judge, he does not have appropriate rank in society, and so "the name of the punishments can be fearsome, but a punishment spelled out in an invalid verdict has not the least shadow of a reality."[31] And so it is with the pope and the brief he issued: he does not have the power to censure here. In the primitive church, the pope's censure power was limited to the diocese of Rome, and now, centuries later, the pope certainly does not have the right to pronounce on the Gallican Church: "The special discipline of the church of France, the liberties of the Gallican church have taken away the possibility of a rendering a judgment in any given case, on his own account and from [distant] Rome, against the French bishops and priests."[32]

It is clear to Camus that the ways of the primitive church are revealed in the discipline of the African churches "in the era when this particular church used to edify the other churches by the holiness of its pastors. There it was forbidden in expressed terms to appeal abroad, that is to Rome under pain of being forbidden communion with all the African churches."[33] The pope was bishop of the capital city of the empire, but he did not have jurisdiction over other churches for this reason. In fact, the African bishops wrote to Pope Celestine, asking him not to accept into his jurisdiction those priests who were renegade from their own (African) dioceses. This was in keeping with the decrees of the Council of Nicaea, which "assigned the examination of the conduct of clerics and bishops to their metropolitan; prudence and justice had convinced the council fathers that all matters should be resolved in the place where they began."[34]

To be sure, there were instances in later history where Rome was brought into local controversies, but papal authority was strictly limited. From the time of the Councils of Constance and Basle, priority of judgment was always given to local church authorities. The Pragmatic Sanction, coming from the same period, confirms this, says Camus, citing the relevant article: "The pope or his legate [*a latere*] are not able to understand the ecclesiastical issues to begin with, nor exercise jurisdiction over the subjects of the king, and those staying in his kingdom, territories, lands, and seigneuries subject to him, whether by citation or delegation or any other way."[35]

Figure 13 Canon lawyer and Ecclesiastical Committee member Armand-Gaston Camus was a major representative of a special class of church–state expert—a canon lawyer, quite literally a lawyer, not a clergyman—whose expertise was in church law and the traditions that served as the setting for the development of this kind of law. Lamourette relied completely on the expertise of Camus, who, in effect, was one of the principal figures in the promotion of revolutionary church reform. (Bibliothèque nationale de France)

This means that the pope cannot say anything against the Constitutional Church. He has just piled up censures, suspensions, warnings of excommunication without the right to use any of them—an exercise in futility. "All these declarations are illusory, all these censures are invalid for lack of authority," according to Camus. "The pope has done nothing because he does not have the power."[36] The constitutional bishops are just not subject to the pope in these areas of church life. Ecclesiastical censures are possible, but only if the person pronouncing them has the power and the right: "So then, none of the persons named in the brief of 13 April 1791, or in any other similar brief, is bound by the censures it contains."[37]

The Catholics of France are in exactly the same situation now as they were in before the Revolution, "united and attached to the successor of St. Peter. All recognize the pope as the visible head of the church, as the center of unity, and it is impossible that there be a schism where this recognition exists."[38] The people need to know that the constitutionals are guaranteeing the presence of the church by working out an agreement with the government: submission to earthly political power combined with religious charity can only guarantee peace and serve the interests of religion. Needless squabbles weaken church influence. The arguments of Camus, in themselves and as cited by Lamourette, were constructed to justify a Catholicism for a new revolutionary era.

Legislator and Bishop

In September 1791, Lamourette was elected to the Legislative Assembly, where he acquired a reputation for moderation on most issues. But not as far as King Louis was concerned: it was Lamourette who made the motion that Louis be more isolated in his captivity. Otherwise, he voted against suppression of religious orders, and opposed all attempts to do away with ecclesiastical dress and to discount the church's laws on marriage.

Lamourette presented a dramatic pairing of his enthusiasms for church and for state in a sermon he was invited to preach to the local Paris soldiery at Notre-Dame, probably because of his prominence in the Legislative Assembly.[39] In the pulpit, he highlights the grandeur of the new state, which is built on "incorruptible and eternal foundations of liberty and equality."[40] Contrast the new state with the old one destined for destruction: "There it is, the wonderful empire that rebuilds itself with majesty on the ruins of all the abuses and all the disorders that for so long have pulled her toward the tomb."[41] In the Revolution the old-style kingdom of France was "swallowed up" with all those other kingdoms of history that human beings could no longer tolerate. He was not a monarchist, but a *constitutional* monarchist, and in a paroxysm of appreciation of the Constitution and Catholic Christianity, he says that "Christianity is even more eminently *constitutional* than the Constitution itself."[42] And as a good bishop, Lamourette concludes with the warning that the new irreligion could be an even worse danger than the old tyranny and that "there is no true liberty nor true security where vice does not have the restraint of remorse."[43]

As for the Kiss of Lamourette, that famous little scenario in the Legislative Assembly, we know that Lamourette himself was proud of it, because he published a full version of the proceedings the same year.[44] He was motivated, first of all, by the external threats to the new France, making political strength and basic unity all the more necessary: "Messieurs, you have only

Figure 14 The extravagant legislative drama that came to be called the Kiss of Lamourette, so called because Bishop Lamourette had melodramatically invited all members of the Legislative Assembly to stand and embrace one another as a symbol of working together on a government that would be a constitutional monarchy with republican values—a plea for both monarchy and equality. In the emotions of the moment, important political differences were forgotten, although subsequently a few monarchist legislators continued to oppose the Revolution and republican absolutists continued to work against the monarchy. (Bibliothèque nationale de France)

to take a moment here, beautiful and solemn, a moment more full and more useful for the wonderful people of whom you are the representatives than all your most memorable days and sessions. You have only to offer to France and to Europe a spectacle more fearful to all your enemies than all of the open cannon [*bouches d'airain*] that you have at your frontiers. Regarding the unity of the nation's representatives: this most wonderful reality holds fast only by a thread that you can break in an instant; and the most unfortunate of divisions derives from a most unfortunate misunderstanding; all the antagonisms that maintain it are reducible to one point and are summed up in one point."[45]

For Lamourette, the threats from within came from republicans who would destroy the monarchy, and those monarchists among the nobles who would set up two chambers, in order to divide and conquer the constitutionalists: "One section of the Assembly attributes to the other the seditious goal of overthrowing the monarchy and establishing the Republic; and the Republic attributes to the others the crime of wanting the destruction of constitutional equality, and of working to create two chambers; there is the disastrous home base of a disunity that will spread to the whole empire and become the basis of the reprehensible hopes of those who are operating the counterrevolution."[46] It was not exactly an embrace he proposed, certainly not a kiss, but a fraternal stand-up-and-be-counted: "Strike down, gentlemen, by a unified condemnation and by a last and irrevocable oath, strike down both the Republic and the two chambers; let us swear to eternal fraternity, let us condemn together, as one and the same body of free men, both the spirit of anarchy and the spirit of feudalism: and the moment when our domestic and foreign enemies will not be able to doubt that we want something fixed and precise, and that what we will, we will together; this will be the true moment of which it will be said that liberty triumphs and that France is saved."[47] And so, "I make the motion that the president say to the Assembly that those who reject and hate equally both the Republic and the two chambers rise to the feet."[48]

Lamourette's intervention was a resounding success. According to minutes of the day's event, all members of the Assembly jumped to their feet, cheered, threw their hats in the air: "You hear only one cry, 'Yes, we swear it.'" And "the left and the right came together in perfect unity, to make one body, truly united in its sole need to effect the public good. Members once distant and even sworn enemies suppressed all divisiveness in a powerful embrace." M. Matthieu Dumas embraced M. Albitte, M. Dubois-de-Bellegarde hugged M. Viénot-Vaublanc, MM. Merlin, Fauchet, Emmery put their arms around MM. Jaucourt, Ramond, Chéron-la-Bruyère, and Brissot embraced Robespierre! "The public in the galleries, whose acclamations had already been long resounding, rose and swore the same oath. One member cried out, 'The fatherland is saved!!'"[49] It was the same kind of euphoria that gripped the Assembly almost three years before, when on the night of 4 August 1789 the nobles renounced all their privileges, fraternally greeting and embracing all those present.

The reconciliation was ephemeral and Lamourette's theological achievements, derived in part from Gaston Camus and used by Mirabeau for his own purposes, were little help to the constitutional bishops. These men, later, had to assure pastoral care in a church that was surviving more than thriving.

Part Two

SURVIVAL, 1791–1795

If the first two years had been difficult and frustrating for the revolutionary priests and bishops, succeeding years proved even more so; everywhere reform-minded bishops and priests faced traditional political and Catholic resistance, even though the monarchist parties lost considerable influence over the course of 1791. Republican factions vied for influence and control of the increasingly chaotic Constituent Assembly, and the new Legislative Assembly comprised a critical mass of secularized and politicized legislators, who wanted to empty the constitutional monarchy as much as possible of its monarchical elements. The attempt of King Louis XVI and his family to escape the heavily republican atmosphere in June 1791 and live outside of France stiffened the legislators' resolve, even as the majority of them accepted the monarchical elements of the new Constitution. Matters were not helped by threats from the Prussian and Austrian monarchs, concerned for the safety of King Louis. Social tensions translated into political energies with serious potential for violence, such as the July 1791 massacre of anti-monarchists on the Champs de Mars. By the end of the year, the Legislative Assembly was contending with Louis over the status of nonconstitutional priests.

The Assembly and the king spent two-thirds of 1792 in ever-increasing competition, ending only with the suspension of the monarchy in August.

Already at the beginning of the year, lawmakers worked to ensure that France would dominate, or at least achieve parity, in the relationships with Austria and England. Domestically, a new public festival system was made yet more revolutionary by a national celebration in honor of liberty, equality, and fraternity. For a brief moment in July, it appeared that some reconciliation would be possible when Bishop Adrien Lamourette, in formal session, dramatically called out to his fellow legislators to combine constitutional monarchy with legislative independence, but several days later the "Fatherland in Danger" declaration reanimated all the old tensions, and a little over a month later crowds invaded the Tuileries Palace and ended the monarchy. The brilliant victory of the French forces at Valmy against foreign invasion in September 1792 occurred on the very day that the Legislative Assembly ceased to function, though not before one more central social and religious reform was enacted, the legalization of divorce.

Political leaders reworked the Legislative Assembly into a fully republican, temporary assembly called the Convention, the bloody prelude to which was a massacre of aristocrats and priests in central Paris in the first week of September 1792. The constitutional bishops elected to the Convention—Grégoire and Fauchet, yes, but also fourteen others—had to confront, in January 1793, the trial, condemnation, and execution of the king, followed by the radicalization of politics (the Committee of Public Safety set up in April) and the official establishment of the Terror in September, with Maximilien Robespierre as the driving force. But really from April through the end of the year the radicalization of revolutionary politics moved in tandem with action against the church and against churchmen: the Law of Maximum on wheat prices, the death penalty for hoarders, combined with the establishment of new festivals and a full revolutionary calendar. In the last three months of the year, Convention radicals assured the execution of Queen Marie Antoinette as well as leading Girondins, guaranteed indemnities to abdicating priests, permitted local prevention of Catholic worship, used Notre-Dame for a quasi-atheistic Feast of Reason, and finally closed all Parisian churches.

It was Robespierre who opposed the dechristianization campaign and promoted freedom of worship, a strange contradiction, because 1794 was his year to promote an alternative to traditional religion, Deism, with its official expression in the Feast of the Supreme Being, and his usual radical politics were in full effect with the omnipresent Terror. Robespierre's colleagues, assuming that his belief in his mission would push him to send them to the guillotine, overthrew him, and then moved on to ending the bizarre relationship of the revolutionary state to a persecuted, albeit subsidized, Constitutional Church.

Priests and Bishops

Chapter 5. The history of the first year of the Constitutional Church—officially beginning with the consecration of the new bishops in February 1791 but approved more than six months before—reveals a set of harassed bishops and a critical mass of priests whose lives and ministries were deeply troubled by the sabotage efforts of the refractory bishops and priests, and the overall chaos of the new era. They wrote to the central government committees from all parts of France: Expilly and Demasles, from the Finistère and the Morbihan in the north, Saurine from Landes in the south, Cazeneuve from the Hautes-Alpes in the west, the regions most troubled by refractories. During the Legislative Assembly's year of existence (from the beginning of October 1791 to the third week of September 1792), bishops Pierre Pontard of the Dordogne and Pierre-Anastase Torné of the Cher, seemingly out of nowhere, became national spokesmen for the Constitutional Church, almost as influential as Claude Fauchet. Their high-profile exposure as bishops favoring reform had gotten them into the Legislative Assembly in the first place, but their personalities and Assembly interventions pushed them to the fore among the twelve bishops there. Torné quickly descended into local political obsessions and Pontard, somewhat later, into idiosyncratic mysticism. Vast numbers of constitutional priests were on their own. The less that preaching and liturgical ministry gave meaning to their existence, the more they turned into ideologues in search of roles in the new political era, all this dramatically illustrated by their letters from 1791 to 1794. Their loyalties ran the gamut from Grégoire's dedication to Sieyès's expediency and beyond. They plumped for clerical marriage and for services in the vernacular, for Enlightenment culture and republican politics, and, at the extreme, the destruction of dogma, worship, and the organized church.

Chapter 6. Opposition between the king and his government had earlier come to a final showdown, more over the increasingly antireligious legislation than anything else. Political leaders reworked the Legislative Assembly into a fully republican, temporary assembly called the Convention. The bishops' assistants (episcopal vicars) elected to the Convention were often radicals who spent their legislative time trying to limit or finish off the Constitutional Church. François Chabot, a former Capuchin Franciscan, was one of Grégoire's vicars, and his polar opposite. A dramatic exception to the destructive-vicar norm was Yves-Marie Audrein, who made his mark on the Convention, and then later became a leading figure in the attempted revival of the Constitutional Church in the 1790s. Although only one bishop of the Convention, Jean-Baptiste Massieu of the Oise, became a terrorist, the accommodation to radical revolution by bishops Jean-Baptiste Saurine of the Landes and Antoine-Hubert Wandelaincourt of Haute-Marne, among others, and the promotion of radical revolution by bishops Léonard Gay-Vernon of Haute-Vienne and Massieu himself, among others, revealed itself in their political activity, and in the preaching and writing that accompanied it. Most of them had to know they were at the top of a government that as a whole was doing everything to destroy their ministry at home and restrict their rights as citizens and legislators. In these chaotic and perilous times, however, there was no sure recipe for ultimate survival. On the one hand, Fauchet and Lamourette were guillotined (October 1793 and January 1794, respectively); on the other, Grégoire survived to offer hope for revival in a set of pastoral reflections published in March 1795, as the Convention was entering its last months.

Chapter 7. Some priests became renowned agents of violence. Jacques Roux was a leader of the Enragés, a radical populist who even turned against the Convention, and Joseph Le Bon was a formal agent of the Terror on behalf of the Convention. Their personal and ideological mutation from agents of a religion of love to agents of violence was complex, but in some measure traceable, because they brought a spirit of violence to their political action and yet exhibited a dedication to truth and justice. The disintegration of priestly careers continued through 1794, not all of them disintegrating as revolutionary careers, of course. The government encouraged and received the formal renouncement of church service from substantial numbers of priests. Some of them abdicated (*abdicataires* was the French noun) only their official positions, but many went to great lengths—and rhetorical heights—in abdicating everything from priesthood to Christianity. They survived because they secured and publicized their antichurch credentials—their strident voices, if not their actions, in harmony with the destructiveness of Jacques Roux and Joseph Le Bon, neither of whom survived.

Chronology

1791

20–21 June	The king's flight from Paris to Varennes. Constituent Assembly suspends Louis XVI.
25 June	The king brought back to Paris.
11 July	Body of Voltaire, honored as forerunner of the Revolution, transferred to the Pantheon.
17 July	Massacre at the Champ de Mars of members of crowd demanding removal of the king.
27 August	Declaration of Pillnitz by kings of Prussia and Austria insisting on the prerogatives of King Louis.
12 September	Avignon, a papal enclave, formally attached to France.
1 October	Meeting of the Legislative Assembly.
29 November	Decree makes refractory priests "suspects."
19 December	Louis vetoes the decree against the refractory priests.

1792

25 January	Legislative Assembly issues an ultimatum to Austrian emperor, and ex-bishop Talleyrand arrives in London to attempt a rapprochement with England.
14 April	Law requiring all ecclesiastics to take a second oath, the Liberté–Egalité oath.
15 April	Festival of liberty, equality, and fraternity in honor of the Châteauvieux regiment proves to be a demonstration of strength by radical revolutionaries.
24 May	Jacques Roux demands the death penalty for hoarders.
27 May	New decree against refractory clergy: they are to be deported if denounced by twenty citizens or more.
7 July	"Kiss of Lamourette," result of a motion by Adrien Lamourette, briefly reconciles factions in Legislative Assembly.
11 July	Decree of "Fatherland in Danger."
10 August	Invasion of the Tuileries. The king and his family take refuge with the Legislative Assembly, which suspends the monarchy.

26 August	Law requiring deportation of refractory clergy who do not go into exile.
2–5 September	Prison massacres of nobles and priests.
20 September	French victory at Valmy. État civil laicized and divorce legalized in last decrees of the Legislative Assembly.
22 September	Republic proclaimed.

1793

21 January	Execution of the king after a series of votes for the death penalty, including those by some priest- and bishop-members of the Convention.
10 March	Failure of an Enragé insurrection with subsequent establishment of the revolutionary tribunal.
11 March	Revolt in the Vendée, specifically against conscription and generally against perceived irreligion of the government.
6 April	Committee of Public Safety established.
4 May	Law of Maximum on wheat and flour.
31 May–2 June	Expulsion of Girondins, although Claude Fauchet is not included.
24 June	Vote for a new Declaration of Rights and for the Constitution of 1793.
25 June	Manifesto of the Enragés presented to the Convention by Jacques Roux.
26 July	Death penalty against hoarders decreed.
10 August	Festival of the new Constitution.
5 September	Terror declared "order of the day" in the Convention.
29 September	Law of Maximum on prices and salaries; arrest of Lamourette.
5 October	Revolutionary calendar adopted, supplanting traditional Christian celebrations of Sundays and feast days.
16 October	Execution of the queen.
30–31 October	Condemnation and execution of the Girondin deputies, including Fauchet.
2 November	Convention offers indemnities to abdicating priests.
6 November	Recognition that communes can suspend Catholic worship.

10 November	Celebration of the Festival of Reason, incorporating the high altar of Notre-Dame Cathedral into the principal scenario.
21 November	Robespierre reproves the dechristianization campaign in the Jacobin club.
22 November	All Parisian churches closed by order of the Paris Commune; decree promising compensation to abdicating priests.
8 December	Convention under Robespierre's influence passes laws guaranteeing freedom of worship.

1794

10 February	Suicide of Jacques Roux.
7 May	Law instituting *fêtes décadaires* and cult of the Supreme Being.
8 June	Festival of the Supreme Being, with principal oration given by Robespierre.
10 June	Beginning of the Great Terror.
27 July	Fall of Robespierre.
18 September	Law terminating all subsidies to religion—in effect, the separation of church and state.
21 December	Grégoire's speech in favor of freedom of religious practice; debate on the *culte décadaire.*

Chapter Five

THE FAILED RELATIONSHIP OF REVOLUTIONARY CHURCH AND STATE

Coming just before the fall of the monarchy in August 1792, the Kiss of Lamourette was too little reconciliation too late—and it was only at the highest political level anyway. Across all of 1791, under both the Constituent and the Legislative Assemblies, reconciliation was at a premium. Constitutional bishops and priests had been complaining that the turbulence created by Old Regime bishops and refractory priests was a major problem in their home dioceses, and they pressed legislators for solutions to these conflicts. These were not the only complaints, but they were communicated to the highest levels of government.[1] The Legislative Assembly did provide a forum for Fauchet and several other bishops, but they had a relatively minor political impact. The evolution of their pastoral style is the more important story. The enthusiasm of influential constitutional priests also waned quickly, replaced by frustration with the retrograde theology and politics of the church, as they understood and interpreted it in public forums such as the review *La Feuille villageoise*.

Thwarted Bishops and Priests

Bishop Louis-Alexandre Expilly of the Finistère, one of the first two constitutional bishops consecrated in February 1791 by Talleyrand, was complaining vociferously about the refractories by the middle of the year to his friend Jean-Denis Lanjuinais, who presumably presented the letter to the Comité des recherches: "My friendship for you, my dear Lanjuinais, will put you in charge as lawyer. The deposed curés are not indicted for remaining in

Figure 15 Bishop Louis-Alexandre Expilly was one of the first two constitutional priests to be made a bishop. On 24 February 1791 he was consecrated by future renowned politician Charles-Maurice de Talleyrand, at that time a bishop and assisted by two Old Regime auxiliary bishops. Expilly was only the first in the line of newly consecrated bishops who found themselves little appreciated in their new dioceses. (Bibliothèque nationale de France)

their parishes and setting altar against altar in so doing."[2] Everything could go wrong if the authorities do not intervene and make the refractories leave their old parishes for good. Constitutionals have been waiting patiently for the National Assembly to make the proper move here, and would still like results. Expilly signs, adding, "Above all speed, again speed, and finally speed." He had already strained to make the new church arrangement and his new appointment "work." Writing a brief essay to Archbishop Champion de Cicé and a letter of "communion" to the pope, he tried to mediate between them and the restructured church. A few days after his own consecration, he assisted Jean-Baptiste Gobel of Paris in consecrating Jean-Baptiste Saurine.[3]

Saurine himself, the new bishop of the Landes, not only had problems with priests, but also with the old bishop, Msgr. De la Neufville, when he refused the latter permission to exercise episcopal ministry: "I forbid you, in my role as the legitimate bishop of the department of the Landes, and after having consulted my council, to exercise any episcopal function in my diocese, without my express signed permission. . . . I forbid you and any other bishop to wear the color or other exterior sign that would indicate the public exercise of episcopal authority, simply because I am the only one who has the right to do so in this diocese." Aware of his own episcopal obligations, Saurine would like to be conciliatory toward the old bishop. But M. Lalande, gendarme national of the Dax brigade, offered the following testimony about what happened when he delivered the letter to the old bishop: "I delivered to Monsieur La Neufville the relevant letter, with the request that he formally acknowledge receiving it, but he very good-naturedly refused, and after having read it, the said M. La Neufville responded that M. Saurine was an idiot, that he would not answer such impertinence, and that he would keep the letter for his own use at the proper time and place."[4] Saurine also was a consecrator of bishops, twenty-one of them, in fact. With a formidable intellect, training in law and Hebrew, and something of a schoolmaster's mien, he was not one to be intimidated. (On his prudence as a member of the Convention, however, see the following chapter.)

Bishop Ignace de Cazeneuve, consecrated bishop of Hautes-Alpes at the beginning of April by Gobel on the same day Saurine was consecrating two bishops in Bordeaux, reported the scheming of the Old Regime bishop, who continued to send official letters bearing his episcopal coat of arms. Cazeneuve said that such pretended authority on the part of a former bishop was expressly against the law, and that "such a step, as unwise as it is faulty, can only disturb public order and tranquility, trouble consciences, spoil the harmony that exists between the ministers of religion and the flocks that are confided to them."[5] It was clear that the Old Regime bishop was in cahoots with a troublesome curé, supposedly a constitutional, and this concerning a dispensation request by a local aristocrat. Taking into consideration the actions of both the bishop and the curé, Cazeneuve declared that he would begin a process against the curé, who was legally bound to obey him, and that he would denounce both the Old Regime bishop and the curé to the National Assembly.

In striking contrast to these concerns about Old Regime bishops, Charles Le Masle, consecrated bishop of the Morbihan in May, offered defenses of his old-fashioned parishioners. A curé for many years and of somewhat delicate health, his main goal was to "heal the wounds suffered in a department hit by fanaticism, which by misleading people with [false] religious ideas, looks to make them rebel against civil law." He wrote that these reconciliations were "the best reward for a patriotic bishop," but that his poor farmers and their families were in constant danger of being seduced by false propaganda. He needed the help of the Assembly in propagating his own love of the Constitution. This would include pardon and forbearance for those of his flock who had resisted thus far.[6] Some personalities are incapable of real revolution and can easily be convinced to resist the new government. Let the National Assembly realize that these people "have simply been the blind instruments of perverse men who seduced them and had the cowardice to lead them to the precipice without submitting themselves to the same danger." Let the National Assembly realize that the threat of death experienced by these has been enough to change them completely. Let the National Assembly realize, finally, that a pardon would do more for peace and tranquility than would harsh punishment.

Constitutional priests were, if anything, more anxious about local resistance than were the bishops—and small wonder, because in a very real sense they were on the front lines. A few of them managed to bring their problems to the attention of the Comité des recherches, and thus constitute a representative sample of the constitutionals. A letter signed "several priests recently elected as pastors" reported that the situation was seriously deteriorating in the Jura and that the dismissal of the refractories and the installation of the constitutionals must be done quickly. A decree to the following effect would help: that newly elected constitutional bishops be installed as quickly as possible; that installation precautions be taken; and that nonjurors be replaced immediately.[7] Much damage had already been done: "They have cruelly upset us and torn us apart for taking the oath; they treat us openly as schismatics and hold up to our faces the impossible requirements of retracting and imitating their conduct." A former canon from Luzarches (Seine-et-Oise) and a constitutional complained that his refractory colleagues continued to celebrate the office, and that he did not want to be held responsible for the continued meetings of the diocesan, presumably refractory, chapter.[8] He had to admit that he could not very well refuse to go to prayers, but that he refused to go to other meetings. The bottom line was that he believed the silver vessels—of which he provided an inventory—of the church should be put under lock and key. "I have the honor of noting for the gentlemen on the committee that it would be immediately useful to put under seal the silverware of the church of the former chapter of Luzarches, valued at ten to eleven thousand pounds."

Constitutionals felt they could do no right, whatever their contributions and talents. The curé of Courmenil (Orne) lists first his own religious and political contributions: "I am a patriot, I have been appointed chaplain of the federated national guard. . . . I have celebrated holy Mass on the altar of the fatherland in the midst of elaborate public ceremonies, I have been appointed mayor. . . . I have had 14 July celebrated in my parish with all possible dignity, and at each one of these ceremonies I have publicly pronounced the civic oath."[9] And with all of this he has to face up to a local conservatism: "I have seen the bad effects that the response to the administrators of the department of the Orne and the pamphlet attached to it have produced on the minds of the curés of the diocese, and through them on the people who are subject to them." The people do not want to give up their refractory curés, "the contagion is only too widespread already," and so woe betide anyone who replaces these curés. If these problems are not alleviated, the Constitution itself, for which he is ready to shed the last drop of his blood, will fail to take hold.

Old Regime bishops were as much of a problem for constitutional priests as they were for constitutional bishops. A colorful and graphic letter from priests of the district of Brioude (Haute-Loire) satirizes the non-juring bishops: "The ministers who have imitated them [the bishops] are the heroes of our religion, and we are the criminals, the Judases, the traitors of this religion." If the government does not punish them and make it clear to their congregations that disobedience and refusal to be part of the Constitutional Church are criminal actions, there will be no solution. The government should either release the constitutionals from their oath or make the refractories take the oath. Mirabeau has promised to help, and the constitutionals say that without his help "we will be forced to retract publicly, however angry it makes us to do so . . . but excusing ourselves because we could not do otherwise to avoid the harmful and cruel persecution that threatens us."[10]

Certainly the originality and persistence of a refractory priest could disturb a whole region. A grimly practical solution to the problem was sent in by a curé from Gisors (Eure), who requested that the refractories be kept a distance of two leagues from the parishes! He accused aristocrats of treating the old curés as former vassals, bribing them and turning them against constitutionals, whom the aristocrats consider excommunicated. They themselves no longer come to services and forbid their servants to do so. The refractories, supported by the aristocrats, promote schism by giving absolution only to those "who promise not to go to mass or confession to the new replacements," all of this with sad effect on the adults' Easter duty and the children's first communion.[11] *Les bons curés patriots* want to save and protect their people by their own ministry, but the government must help:

Figure 16 A caricature of resistance to the oath on the part of a curé, or parish priest. Some of those who took the oath did so without enthusiasm, and they were accordingly berated by those priests and members of the faithful who were genuinely committed to the new revolutionary government, still a constitutional monarchy at that time. (Bibliothèque nationale de France)

"Without that the loyal curés who provide replacements would not be able to win over the seriously indoctrinated parishioners and will be obliged to resign."

The Legislative Assembly and the Bishops

It was a fluid situation across those last months of the Constituent Assembly and the brief life of the Legislative Assembly, in session from 1 October 1791 through 20 September 1792 (the Lamourette "Kiss" occurred toward the end of this period). The interaction of the political factions became ever more competitive, with Deist sentiment prevalent throughout the Jacobin ranks, and even an atheist strain in the Girondin ranks. The Feuillants split from the Jacobins to maintain support of the constitutional monarchy, and the Cordeliers competed with them in the support of republicanism and insurrection. The principal religious problem facing the legislators came from the political and cultural division created by the two clergies, even though only the constitutionals had a voice in government. The bishop delegates to the Assembly were Eléonore Desbois de Rochefort, Claude Fauchet, Léonard Gay-Vernon, Marc-Antoine Huguet, Dominique Lacombe, Adrien Lamourette, Claude Le Coz, André Lefessier, Pierre Pontard, and Pierre-Anastase Torné; the duration and intensity of their interventions have recently been examined by Caroline Chopelin-Blanc.[12] Yann Fauchois, in his chronology of the legislative sessions, notes in particular the speeches of the bishops Pierre Pontard and Pierre-Anastase Torné.[13]

Little is recorded about the life and career of Pontard, other than his years as curé of Sarlat in the Dordogne, of which he became the constitutional bishop. With politics his only concern, he was a committed deputy to both the Legislative Assembly and the Convention. Torné was a man of much wider interests and accomplishments. Over sixty when he was elected to the Legislative Assembly, he had been a member of the Doctrinaires, a religious superior, a diocesan canon, a member of the Academy of Nancy, and early on a court preacher to Louis XV. Ambitious and authoritarian in the church and a committed Jacobin in politics, he was inveterately opposed to the ministry of the refractories and the work of the religious orders.

Some months before he headed off to the sessions of the Legislative Assembly, Pontard wrote a harsh and dramatic letter to the Old Regime bishop whom he succeeded.[14] Bishop Grossoles-Flamarens had apparently attacked the principle of public elections when he refused to recognize the election of Pontard, and Pontard considers this reprehensible. After all, what better way is there to know the will of God than in the course of such elections?[15] Pontard rails against everything that Grossoles-Flamarens had written about the Constitutional Church in a recent statement; several remarks in particular he considers heretical, especially the attack on the valid authority of the constitutional bishops and priests. Before the Council of Trent every priest heard confessions without any participation in authority other than his ordination. The Council of Trent decreed that priests who were not officially members of a given diocese could not hear confessions without the local bishop's permission, but this decree was never promulgated in France. Then Pontard gets down to the operative question, "who is bishop here?"—himself or Grossoles-Flamarens. The latter believed that only death, a canonically proper decision to relieve him of duties, or his

Figure 17 The Constituent Assembly was succeeded by the Legislative Assembly, with its new Constitution. Two weeks before the first meeting of this new legislature, King Louis, after his attempt to flee the country with his family—as much because of the Civic Constitution of the Clergy as for any other reason—appeared before one of the last sessions of the Constituent Assembly to swear an oath of fidelity to the nation and the law. From 1 October 1791 through 10 August 1792, revolutionary bishops and other legislators grew increasingly impatient with the church–state structure of the constitutional monarchy. (Bibliothèque nationale de France)

own resignation, accepted by the church, could remove him from office. In response, Pontard positions himself to indicate that Old Regime legitimacy has a weak base: "And by whom, my dear colleague, has this flock been confided to you? By a license and a bull, both of them daughters of the concordat, which is to say, from the most infamous agreement that has ever dishonored state and church. In order to find true canonical acts of institution, one must go back to the gospel and apostolic times."[16] Pontard responds that the church had been forced to accept the old hierarchy for want of other possibilities, but "it never approved your [canonical] institution; far from it, it has protested the horror of the Concordat, and has never withdrawn its protests." The church has been ill and has had to accept anyone: "You have only been considered to be bishop of Périgreux during the crisis of the sick [church], that is to say when the violence and despotism that gave birth to the Concordat held the people of France in this state of crisis, oppression, and mediocrity."[17] So he is saying that the Old Regime church was the sick offspring of an authorization mistake in church–state life. He puts a special twist on the gospel passage, *Qui autem intrat per ostium, pastor est ovium* ("He who enters by the door is the shepherd of the sheep," John 10:2), making the door of the sheepfold *confidence.* But how could the people have had confidence in him, when they had nothing to do with his appointment? Grossoles-Flamarens simply wrangled his way into the position. It was now to be an organizational decision by the government, and it was up to the government to maintain his position: "No one of you can succeed in his work without granting by way of anticipation the legitimacy of operation of the national assembly, which must make judgments about the suppression of a see or of its bishops as well as the retention of a bishop."[18]

Pontard turns in a dramatic performance, alternating between respect and insult. First, he accuses Grossoles-Flamarens of the worst horrors. He and those of his ilk are like a defeated and marauding army, "fleeing by a roundabout path, it cuts down, massacres, and destroys all it meets, all that opposes its passing through."[19] He hands over the pastoral instruction to Satan (whatever that is supposed to mean) and invites the faithful to pray for their wandering, perhaps lost bishops. Then the sudden turn: "I come back to you, Sir, to render homage to your goodness."[20] Grossoles-Flamarens would never have behaved this way on his own, but he has been misled. Pontard goes on and on about what a good pastor the old bishop has been: "You have loved, helped, and nourished the needy sheep of the fold that we confided to you."[21] Despite his virtuous acts, he does in fact—insult mode again—"victimize [his] sheep, exterminate their pastors, ravage and destroy the sheepfold." Now respect mode: "Such views would never have entered your head."

And so Pontard ends fraternally! You would think that he had been offering simple constructive criticism: "But the sharpness in my way of speaking changes nothing in the true feelings of charity that I have in your regard."[22] The diatribe ended, Pierre Pontard figuratively bows low and takes his leave in full Christian charity: "Your very humble and obedient servant."

In the midst of the Legislative Assembly discussion about severe sanctions for the refractories promoted by Fauchet, Pierre Pontard tried to sideline the whole affair. He told the Assembly that they have "wandered a great deal in speaking of religion and of sects." In an appropriately moral mode,

Pontard said that although humans are made in the image of God, God gave them the liberty to ignore this fact. The Assembly, then, should not be in the business of sorting out priests, religions, or sects, and reforming them. The matter at hand was the simple reestablishing of "public order."[23] Pontard responded to an address given by Condorcet, with special reflections on the dangers posed by religious fanatics, whom the Roman church administration loves to stir up (he gives the example of the condemnation of the Civil Constitution that was issued just as the people's resentment over change was at its greatest). Says Pontard, "What are we waiting for today? That all the powers unite against us? We must wait for Rome to sound out its condemnations, and I would like M. Condorcet to please add a sentence to warn the people that they ought to expect this misfortune"[24] The fact that Pontard was a millenarian—awaiting the imminent second coming of Christ and a new spiritual age where a structured church would be superfluous—came more to public notice during the Convention years.[25]

Bishop Torné's major discourse for the festival of the federation of 14 July 1791 came after the flight of the king on 20 June, and was certainly a register of his subsequent legislative orientation. Although his themes were nation, law, and king, he had most to say about the king. For all three themes, he exalts the role of religion, which had, he says, only a subordinate part to play in the Old Regime.[26] The nation of free citizens was nothing in the eyes of the old administration: "To dare to pronounce the name [of religion] in front of those who exercise some little bit of royal power, would have been to use the language of a troublemaker and risk punishment." As for the law, "instead of reaching toward the good of all, the will of only one person held down all the others, and most often sacrificed the general public to the privileged classes."[27] The monarchy, "eternal toy of the great powers of the state," is the cover-up for all the horrors perpetrated by the aristocracy.[28]

Torné wants to warn the legislature about the refractories. He knows that were it simply a doctrinal squabble, the government would have no interest. Their errors are dangerous and it is crucial to know exactly where the danger lies. Even so, once this religion is removed from public life, the government should not interfere. What goes on in silence, in secret, and in families is a private affair: "But be patient; natural sentiments that are stifled for the time being, or confused by *esprit de parti*, will soon regain their rule. Yes, peace will soon be reborn in families, because they are worn out by religious disputes, and have the desire for tranquility, the need to love, and the custom of living together."[29] He was aware that by highlighting the issue, he would himself be causing problems, but his solution was a simple one: send them elsewhere, away from Paris and the departmental capitals. "Let these citizens choose their dwelling place; and let us make sure above all that we do not add the madness of hunger to that of fanaticism."[30] What disturbs Torné most about the impending legislation is its blind impartiality: "It visits the same punishment on the contentious and the apathetic, the troublemaker and the good man, the leader and the laggard, the frantic and the wavering, the eager youth and the calm old man, on him whose refusal of the oath results from great vices and on him whose refusal of the oath comes from great virtues."[31] Simply for the satisfaction of preventing refractory religious services from taking place, legislators wanted to organize some extremely severe punishments. Why should refractory priests not be allowed to worship God on their own terms? "At the same time as we forbid them to celebrate the sacred mysteries, we allow pagans the mysteries of Isis and Osiris, Muslims the invocation of the prophet, and rabbis the offering of holocausts [*sic*]."[32]

Torné lists twenty features of religion to show that if people are left free, religious practice will serve the good of the state; he simply produces the standard catalog of arguments proper to eighteenth-century writers. Freedom weakens rebelliousness and tempers the "effervescence" of religion. Resistant factions within the French church would gradually lose their strength were they not forced to maintain a clandestine existence. And why make those poor Catholics who follow the refractories suffer? "Why force the refractories and their poor followers, principally in the countryside, to acquire their churches at great cost, rather than offer to alternate services with them in our churches?" Torné knows that his ideas of tolerance will seem strange after so many centuries of ingrained intolerance, but the people can be taught and gradually induced to practice tolerance and embody religion at its best. He wants to propose a series of measures to activate his proposals for learning and tolerance, believing that he is especially well placed to do this: "In matters of religious tolerance, the teaching of a bishop imbued with the true spirit of religion is not far from the teachings of philosophy; and pastoral zeal here accords perfectly with the moderation of the legislator."[33]

Bishop Torné mounted the tribune of the legislature on the fateful day of 10 August 1792 to urge the overthrow of the king and the end of the monarchy, thereby ensuring that there would be no republican voice more radical than that of a Catholic bishop. Beginning with the title "Strong measures necessary to save the fatherland," he disingenuously suggests reason and calm . . . because he has intransigent and harsh solutions to propose. The danger is that the nation is threatened from without by the kingdoms that are loyal to Louis for the sake of monarchy, and threatened from within by those who would descend to civil strife to overthrow the Constitution for the sake of loyalty to the king. The rumors have spread far and wide that Louis, left in place even after his attempted flight from the country, is now out to destroy the actual government: "In these confused circumstances, it is up to you, Messieurs, to solemnly declare if, as far as these different accusations are concerned, Louis XVI is guilty, innocent or suspect."[34] The word is that the king is directing a criminal conspiracy, and Torné is concerned lest a moderate and false constitutionality hold the legislature back from resolving the problem: "Would this not be the stupid carelessness of a sick person, who, after accusing his doctor of poisoning him, would, while the legal procedure is going on, continue to rely on him for a cure?"[35] The country wants a legislature that will judge the king, and legislators are saying that the Constitution will not let them do anything. The country wants a "national convention," says Torné. "If you judge yourselves incapable of saving the fatherland, you can, without doubt you must, announce to the nation this unfortunate inability, and ask it to save itself by means agreed upon in the popular assemblies."[36] He unremittingly pushes for intervention, because he is sure that the safety of the people requires it. If they should rise up against the legislature, it would be a result of the legislature's prior failure: "It would not at all then be a revolt of people against the law; but the revolt of the law against the people."[37] There must be a new legislature, then, that can more directly and fully represent the voice of the people.

Torné believes that the king has abdicated every duty and violated every trust. He does not omit here Louis's penchant for the refractories and the constitutional *rétractés*: "Although he did not officially oppose the oath, he placed under his aegis and gathered around himself the seditious priests who rejected or retracted the oath desired by the nation."[38] There is no choice, then. If the Constitution is too weak to defend the people against this royal criminal, the Constitution is at fault: "For every nation ready to lose its liberty because of the weakness of its particular Constitution, the only goal left for it is wholly contained in the words, 'The safety of the people is the highest law.'"[39] The king is the enemy of the nation; he and his family should be considered hostages of the nation, and his constitutional inviolability must give way before the military law that dictates the control of hostages. The first and basic move is to suspend the executive power of the king; then "a national convention can at once, if such is sovereign will, bring down Louis XVI and the entire dynasty, the monarch and the monarchy, and place above all these heads the unyielding standard of equality."[40]

The leading bishops of the Legislative Assembly, in and out of sessions, did everything they could to render the Republic acceptable to their parishioners and destroy the influence of Old Regime churchmen. They urged the legislature to support the particular apostolate of the Constitutional Church, and to the extent that they vaunted the Republic they attacked the king. But this apostolate of liturgy and preaching that would wed Christian community and a republic (or at least a constitutional monarchy) never had the time to coalesce. There was too much preoccupation with collective identity and too much confrontation for the bishops holding political office to develop their own side of the church–state relationship. And parish priests across these many months had their own issues to address.

Curés Transformed: A Symptom of Failure

Many constitutional parish priests were in major transition: they did not want to be curés in the traditional sense, and eventually did not want to be curés at all. A principal rallying point for constitutional priests using their traditional status as a power base for revolutionary thought was the popular journal *La Feuille villageoise*, intended for the simple people of the countryside and their guides. *La Feuille* was a strident promoter of revolutionary ideals in the practical life of peasants in the provinces, in its own words, "addressed each week to all the villages of France, to teach them the laws, the events, and the discoveries that interest every citizen."[41] Inasmuch as the form and outreach of *La Feuille* has already been definitively studied by Melvin Edelstein, I push on to view in further detail the ideas of the clergy: from the beginning, the paper cultivated the favor and attention of the patriotic country curés, and provided revolutionary priests with a forum for public expression.[42]

Where the people supported them, constitutional clergymen could write to the *Feuille* editors in high spirits. The curé of Septmonsel (Jura) said he was "a happy pastor of this canton, once a serf and today a free man." And he could only be grateful to the *Feuille*: "I thank you in the name of

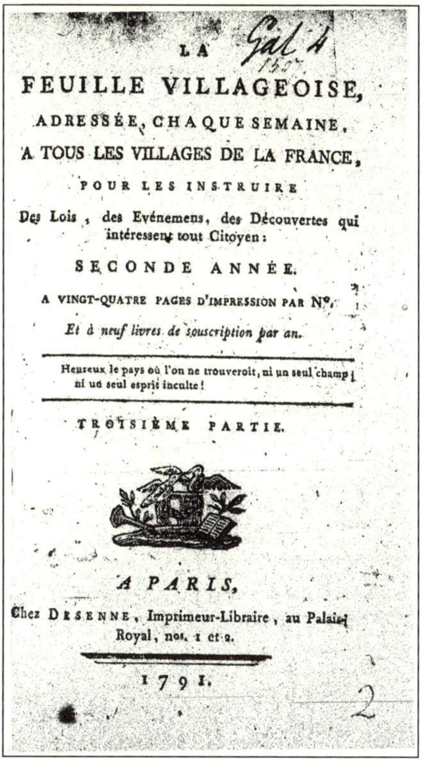
LA

FEUILLE VILLAGEOISE,

ADRESSÉE, CHAQUE SEMAINE,

A TOUS LES VILLAGES DE LA FRANCE,

POUR LES INSTRUIRE

Des Lois, des Evénemens, des Découvertes qui intéressent tout Citoyen:

SECONDE ANNÉE.

A VINGT-QUATRE PAGES D'IMPRESSION PAR N°.

Et à neuf livres de souscription par an.

Heureux le pays où l'on ne trouveroit, ni un seul champ, ni un seul esprit inculte!

TROISIÈME PARTIE.

A PARIS,

Chez DESENNE, Imprimeur-Libraire, au Palais-Royal, nos. 1 et 2.

1791.

Figure 18 Cover of an issue of *La Feuille villageoise* (*The Village Bulletin*). Parish priests subscribed to this paper to express their religious and revolutionary viewpoints, sharing their ideas with one another and, in general, staying abreast of the revolutionary possibilities for the countryside. They were really intermediaries between the government revolutionary forces and the simple people.

the docile inhabitants: they are like sheep as regards the law, reason, and religion. But they would be as indomitable as lions if they were to be attacked by the enemies of the fatherland."[43] Freedom for curé and people guaranteed an open learning situation. The government "watches out so that no one bothers his neighbor as he renders his own simple worship to the divinity," said Dupuis, curé of Droyes (Haute Marne).[44] Such emphasis on freedom and openness moved him to call for the personal reconciliation of Catholics and Protestants. And he asked *La Feuille* for help in combating peasant superstition: "Gentlemen, could you find some simple way to make fun of the foolish reverence that the villagers in several regions have for relics and the statues of saints that our collectors of legends have barely heard of. The relics and images that the monks were pleased to accumulate in their convents find refuge in parish churches, and they might receive homage that is close to idolatry."[45]

Reforms Needed

Priests should be united with the people as family men, and worship should be in the language of the people. All should find their proper place in a new era of republican values for church and state.

In the new era of freedom, priests and people turned once again to the continued discussion of the age-old problem of priestly celibacy, which was actually a Constitutional Church controversy since late 1790. It was Dupuis who broached the topic by somewhat disingenuously posing the question, "In the new order of things, can a curé marry and keep his position?" He said that he read "in a few news publications that priests had, in effect, gotten married, even in the capital." He said that he, too, would marry if his conscience so directed and, in some way, duty called: "I believe that celibacy has never helped and never will help the cause of good priests."[46] Writers returned to the subject of priestly marriage several times in subsequent months. The curé of Cabrières (Hérault) made a game of the hypocrisy of the priests who condemned clerical marriage at the same time that they themselves engaged in sexual practices: "The majority of my confreres marry; but those of the communion of Tartuffe, instead of imitating us, cry out in loud voices, even as they defile the marriage bed of the man next door."[47]

Parent, curé of Boisisse-la-Bertrand, plunged into extensive theorizing about marriage, starting with the argument that there was nothing spiritual about celibacy: "In vain do many of our bishops, in vain do all the theologians of the world set up in opposition to marriage the *interior, spiritual* discipline of the church; I will prove that the element of discipline which obliges priests to celibacy is *very external, very fleshly*, and that *without need of a council*, it cannot be too quickly proscribed by a government that is a friend of morals, and consequently of the population, and consequently of marriage."[48] With the estimate (too low, we know today) that there were about eighty thousand priests in France, he argued that forced celibacy impairs the effectiveness of priests and increases their potential for failure and misbehavior. Scripture supported him: "The spirit is willing but the flesh is weak," and again, "What begins by the spirit ends by the flesh." Worse, "in forcing them into celibacy, do you not condemn as many women to it?"[49] In sum, celibacy simply leads to debauchery and all kinds of evil.

Worship in the vernacular was of a piece with effective teaching. The curé of Salagnon (Isère) argued the party line that for religion to be authentic, people had to pray in their own language. A dead language goes completely against all reason and common sense: "If the founders of Christianity had come to tell the people to whom they were addressing themselves for the first time, 'We bring you a form of worship in which you will speak to God in a language you do not understand, and without knowing what you are saying, . . . the apostles would have been taken for imbeciles.'"[50] Couet, curé of Orville (Loiret), decried the Latin mumbo jumbo of his people, "shouting themselves hoarse in a Latin that they did not understand, without having prayed a single prayer."[51] Without eliminating Latin completely, he went about the business of liturgical reform. No more negative and long elements of the services for the dead, no more dry sermons; he substituted instead a prayer on moral themes, civil as well as religious.[52]

Replacing the Old Regime with a New Republic

Some clerical letters berated both the monarchy and a papacy they believed to be as bad as the monarchy. One curé noted that the papacy was more concerned about a king's allegiance to the papacy than a king's allegiance to his people. The "court of Rome" promoted wealth and learning, but not humility (reference here is made to the beggar-saint Benedict Joseph Labré): "It is at the Vatican that one finds the source of all the superstitions of Europe. This poisoned source will dry up when the people just laugh at the thunderbolts from Rome, the briefs and (papal) bulls of the old man of the seven mountains."[53] And Dupuis substituted the great revolutionary theorists for the old religious authority. Reading Rousseau, he had the sense that he was reading scripture: "This passage [from *Émile*] contained such a clear prediction of our immortal revolution, that the philosopher seemed to be inspired by the divinity." Rousseau seemed to know as much about the future revolution as did the major Old Testament prophets about the future of the "fanatic" Hebrew people.[54]

Across 1793 and 1794, the curés were increasingly vociferous in their defense of the Republic, with, as usual, civic and moral responsibility at the center of their message. The good pastor should himself be an ideal republican; he should assume the same role in civil society that he had assumed in religious society, the two being completely amalgamated. One priest held it as his "first duty as republican, mayor, and curé" to teach hatred of royalty on the feast of the patron saint of his parish. "As pastor and as a republican I reconcile (without difficulty) the moral teaching of our religion with the principles of republicanism. By the way, all our *catholic* priests would do well to do the same."[55] He included, and the editors duly printed, a long, nine-page quotation from the Book of Kings, sure proof that kings were a moral evil.

The hearts of these curés were in radical revolution, not in the conservation of ecclesiastical forms. When radical revolution no longer left any room for traditional religion, the curés renounced traditional religion, not only in form and expression, but in substance too. In spring 1794, Parent held forth on real religion, as opposed to the religion of priests, with its combination of "morality, dogmas, discipline, rituals, observances, practices, ceremonies." Priestly religion was self-serving and hypocritical. Despite some good deeds, they are "obliged to say, *Do what we say and not what we do.* And that, in fact, was the best morality they could teach."[56] Parent continued, swinging in every direction, arguing that religion leads to fanaticism and war: "What is more absurd than their dogmas? What is more ridiculous than their disciplines? And, nevertheless, that is what they hold to most. The so-called wars of religion were not for the sake of morality, but for dogmas, practices, and observances. The morality of Calvinists and Lutherans is absolutely the same as that of Catholics. Why, then, for such a long time have they flooded Europe with blood and carnage."[57] And what was at stake in all this, according to Parent? Terminology, tiny points of dogma, slight differences in moral teaching, the whole religion business that was really "no more that the tales of Bluebeard."[58] Parent wanted a religion of and for the people: "The people must be enlightened, instructed, virtuous, friends of the truth. . . . One confuses often the word *religion* with the word *worship.* We do need a religion and popular worship, or rather a religion of truth, of virtue, and of law."[59] Then the punch line: "Priestly worship; no, *we no longer have any need for priests.*" His is a religion of reason, good behavior, and following the law. With a quote from two patriotic songs, he triumphantly concluded, "This is my religion. Soon without doubt it will be [the religion] of all the French and, subsequently, of the universe"—this moderated perhaps by his final words, "At least that is what I hope for and desire."[60]

Long restrained, longtime posing, the principal curé ideologues could not restrain themselves. And so Dupuis, now also ex-curé, after his long struggle to live, how shall we say it?—*side by side* with basic Catholic teachings—now attacks them as *absurdities*: "Original sin, one God in three persons, the real presence of a God in the bread one eats, unending torment in the other life. None of this could be the true religion." Catholicism has been "a work of superstition and imposture like all the others."[61] *Philosophy*, with its exploration of real causes and effects, had to be, then, the great ideology, the great savior: "It does not forget that understanding [*indulgence*] is as necessary to the philosopher as intolerance is essential to the priest."[62]

The clergy of *La Feuille villageoise* began ministries of active engagement in the new political, social, and cultural life of the nation. But their church identity and activity was gradually swallowed up in the politics of radical revolution. With the fall of the monarchy, they attacked both monarchy and papacy while elevating Rousseau and the Republic; they attacked the worldliness of the refractories while they praised the dedication of the revolutionary clergy. They took on justification of the secular republic, secular ideology, and secular living as a moral responsibility, promoting these secularisms in the name of the gospel. Those who held out as priests the longest believed that the country people needed their priests and that a human ministry of love and tolerance justified the maintenance of the old identity. In the end, they equated standard belief with superstition and considered priesthood to be an aberration, views that thwarted bishops and priests nationwide seldom promoted in 1791–92, but embraced in greater numbers during the Convention years.

Chapter Six

THE TRAGIC CONVENTION YEARS

The Convention was a freak of political nature to begin with, a temporary solution to the dismantled constitutional monarchy. The Legislative Assembly had presupposed a monarch as the executive branch of government. With Louis XVI definitively repudiated in August 1792, legislators provided for a temporary Assembly to run the country until a new, finished government structure could be developed and put in place; they chose the label *Convention* in honor of the American Continental Congress.

Thirty to forty thousand priests left France as the Convention was getting established, but the Girondins organized several new departments with the provision for a bishop of each region even so; this, according to Jean Leflon, was the result of "the wish to exclude the non-patriotic clergy, and the need to give satisfaction to those areas of the population who valued their worship."[1] Otherwise there was the cessation of all support of church functionaries, restrictions on processions and other exterior ceremonies, and, most important, the secularization of the marriage contract. Grégoire himself could approve these measures as strictly civil law. But the laws on divorce in particular caused churchmen to scramble for a religious response: they justified it for non-Catholics, who were not obligated to support the church's stand. The ploy did not work, because divorced Catholics claimed the right to be married in church and receive the formal nuptial blessing. Government officials then insisted that priests announce the banns of marriage for those formerly divorced and preside at the marriages of other priests, threatening deportation for anyone who would refuse. All this was too strict for Robespierre himself: "Do you want to create a new generation of refractories?" he asked.[2]

Complex in his religious orientation, Robespierre was opposed to any measures that would deprive the people of traditional religious consolations before more enlightened ways could be learned. It would appear, however, that he was willing to go as far as he could to neutralize clerical influence. He spearheaded the attempt to set up a national religion in the mode of Jean-Jacques Rousseau's "civil religion," with any and every Catholic church a possible venue for the services. A central figure of the Convention, of course, Robespierre was also the central civil–religious figure. Albert Mathiez years ago insisted that Robespierre wanted only to guarantee the unity and stability of the Republic, that he preoccupied himself with religion only inasmuch as he needed it to bring off his political program.[3] But, in fact, his sermon preached in praise of and on behalf of the Supreme Being suggests a preacher who repackaged both Rousseau and Christianity. The setting for the ceremony is well known today because of the numerous reproductions of that gathering on the Champs de Mars, near the great old École militaire in central Paris. The terrain had been changed from flat fields to hills and plateaus, replanted trees, ad hoc altars, great columns, and classical statues. The liturgy was ornamented sufficiently to appeal to a population accustomed to rich religious liturgies.

The Convention did not formally rebuke the dechristianization measures, although it counseled prudence. It seemed to support the measures by offering an indemnity on 2 November 1793 to priests who wished to abdicate, which could mean anything from token resignation to renunciation of religious faith, and by passing on 6 November a measure authorizing individual communes to close their churches if they wished. Yet many people insisted on the old ways. The preceding year had ended with numerous celebrations of midnight Mass, even though the churches were supposed to remain closed. In the west of France, resistance stiffened, as peasants loyal to the monarchy fought against conscription into revolutionary armies and on behalf of the maintenance of Catholic worship. Balancing the ledger here was Jacques-René Hébert's periodical *Père Duchesne*, eulogizing and promoting the good-hearted, dechristianized peasant. Jean-Paul Marat would have it that the constitutionals could not be trusted any more than the refractories: "Jacobins, I will speak a truth to you; you do not know your most mortal enemies; they are the constitutional priests; they are those who in the campaigns protest the most against anarchists, troublemakers, the canton system, robespierrism, and jacobinism. . . . Say it openly: these priests are our enemies."[4] Dechristianization, with or without a Deism substitute, intensified with the new calendar year, because of the initiatives of the *représentants en mission*, with ex-Oratorian Joseph Fouché the front-runner. When the movement regained Paris, Bishop Gobel was pressed to abdicate. Roused from sleep, he insisted on convoking his council, which voted on behalf of his abdication.

Then came the shining moment of Henri Grégoire. Standing before the Convention, having been preceded by abjuring priests, Protestant ministers, and Gobel himself, he declared, "As for myself, Catholic by conviction and sentiment, priest by choice, I have been designated by the people to be their bishop. But it is not from them or from you that I hold my commission. I consented to bear the burden of the episcopate at the time when it was surrounded by difficulties: they harassed me to accept it. They harass me now to submit an abdication, which they will not get from me; I remain a bishop to continue my work; I invoke [the principle of] religious freedom."[5]

There had been nothing that he or the other bishops of the Convention could do to prevent the rapid slide into violent politics. They were, in the main, studious types and, with some exceptions, kept a low profile. In any case, they were more than indifferent members of the clergy, politically and religiously swayed by the latest appeals of colleagues and communities. They had genuinely engaged themselves in the political revolution of 1789 and the following years. Membership in the Convention was a major step in their new episcopal careers, with the January trial of the king and the beginning of the Terror, in September again, one year after the massacres of 1792. To accommodate all of this, the bishops had to resolve the contradiction between a ministry of peace and violent political reform. If they wished to promote revolution, they had to pass with some degree of rationality from active Christian ministry to terrorist or terror-supporting activity. Accommodation to or promotion of revolution are the only two choices if the options are broadly set. In fact, the sixteen bishops who were elected to the Convention, or the priests elected to the Convention who were subsequently consecrated constitutional bishops, ran the gamut from simple, genuine accommodation through totally engaged and vociferous promotion. As the constitutional bishops struggled to position themselves in revolutionary politics, so, too, the priests of the Convention positioned themselves politically and religiously, most often as engaged revolutionaries.

Radical Convention Priests

The episcopal vicars, the bishops' chief assistants who were delegates to the Convention, proved a troublesome lot. Ruth Graham remarked long ago on the elevated number of radicals and terrorists that emerged from among the episcopal vicars who had been elected to the Convention. Their collective profile is not at all as balanced as the accommodating and promoting bishops themselves. Three of the vicars, Jacques Goyré-Laplanche, Jean-Baptiste Monestier, and Philibert Simond, repudiated all church connections and, as agents of the government, persecuted their priestly colleagues.[6] None, however, achieved the notoriety of François Chabot, vicar for the bishop of Loir-et-Cher, Henri Grégoire, of all people![7] Undoubtedly Grégoire was overimpressed by Chabot's personal and administrative bravado. Years later, in his *Mémoires*, recalling "the Capuchin Chabot whose ways and conduct people so touted, and whose talents I can only praise," he wrote, "May God grant that his tragic death expiate his mistakes."[8] Chabot was an intense, self-absorbed ideologue who manipulated everyone within his parameters: an outstanding radical and abettor of terrorism.

In complete contrast to his destructive colleagues, Yves-Marie Audrein, an episcopal vicar from the diocese of the Morbihan, made his mark as a dedicated, spiritual, and intellectual constitutional priest. No single clergymen intervened in Convention affairs more than did Audrein, and he was rewarded for the vigor of his religion-oriented speeches and pamphlets by election to the episcopate himself, in 1798, long after the Convention had disappeared.

The Constitutional Vigor of Yves-Marie Audrein

Audrein began his career with fourteen years at Quimper and then a stint at Louis-le-Grand in Paris, where both Robespierre and Camille Desmoulins were his students. His preaching and his political speeches both contributed to his reputation. He was vicar general for the bishop of the Morbihan and deputy to the Legislative Assembly from the same region. An enthusiastic supporter of the oath, he also supported teachers who belonged to recognized religious congregations and condemned the refractory clergy. He tried to save priests during the September Massacres, but he voted conditionally for the death of the king in the Convention.[9]

Back in 1791, Audrein eloquently promoted the Constitutional Church.[10] On the occasion of renewing his oath to the Constitution, he compared the constitutionals to the Maccabees, following the law of God, instead of that of a foreign king: "The same submission to the laws decreed by our august representatives and sanctioned by the best of kings, my colleagues and I have judged the best way of commending ourselves to you."[11] He protests his outrage against the pope's condemnation ("if he was the author of it"), which compared the constitutional reform to the Anglican heresy: "How could he, then, by the most disgusting of deceptions, . . . how could he shamelessly support, and convince weak souls of the idea that the National Assembly did the same thing as the parliament of Henry VIII?"[12] Further, Audrein cannot fathom why the refractories deny the actual validity of the sacramental action of the constitutionals, as if "the unlimited power of the words of consecration in the Mass depend on the priest and not on Jesus Christ."[13] That they are talking theological nonsense is clear when they refuse validity to the baptisms performed by constitutional priests: "Dare they say that baptism, the only one of the seven sacraments that every person in the universe can confer, that baptism administered by a constitutional priest is invalid? Or to go even further and threaten with anathema the resistance that we offer to a teaching that is so foolish, criminal, and insulting to the divinity!"[14] And so Audrein responds in kind: what we have here is "the infernal plot hatched by the enemies of our liberty to destroy the constitution." He labels the anti-constitutionals with a variety of epithets from scripture and elsewhere: "A thousand times blind, a thousand times insensate, they do not even know enough to cover themselves with sheep's clothing. . . . their lips form lies, their eyes radiate vengeance."[15] According to Audrein, they are responsible for the shedding of the blood of their brothers.

Writing just before the opening of the Convention, with the country at war, Audrein said that revolutionary army victories were a sign of God's great design.[16] And woe betide those who oppose: "Here at your gates, in your midst, stand the armies of France: accept peace or you will be lost! At the sight of all this would not anyone exclaim that here, in a certain sense, there is a master plan."[17] He takes a shot at all the countries that are now opposing France. Britain was, of course, "the perfidious island" (he has just finished a footnote on William Pitt): "We know that Pitt, unable even with financial trickery, to bring about the destruction of France, first tried to light the flares of fanaticism and ended by proscribing the very idea of God."[18] And so, he threatens Britain, "more perfidious than Carthage,"

Figure 19 An episcopal vicar of the constitutional bishop of the department of the Morbihan, Yves-Marie Audrein was an outstanding counterexample to the stereotype of the radical and destructive Convention vicar. In this bizarre and inconsistent caricature of a Jacobin "procession" of aristocrats, politicians, and clergy, Audrein is the figure labeled "14," and if the label is accurate, this is the only image we have of him. At the time of the publication of the image (1792 or 1794), he was either a member of the Legislative Assembly or the Convention. (Bibliothèque nationale de France)

with a violent religious justice: "Even unto the last generation, if the spirit of vengeance does not make you soon disappear from the height of the earth's peoples, hating your name will become a religious act."[19] And the regions on the other side of the Rhine? "Glorious *Rhine*, it is no longer in the name of a court that we will wreak vengeance on your tyrants. Free men will brave your waves, and beyond your banks they will henceforth ensconce their theater of glory."[20] The other side of the Pyrénées? "Ancient Pyrénées, unto the sorrow of peoples you once served the fanaticism of kings. Expiate your crime; serve the cause of liberty rather than that of despotism." The other side of the Alps? "Proud Alps, thus far a fatal destiny for the courage of the French! Your snows and winters, your impassible frontiers, hunger, thirst, everything will be overcome: redoubtable virgin territory still, despite the wear of time. We must free everything within your proud slopes."[21] Holland? "Great floods of Holland, you come to a halt before the heroes of Jemappe! And if others would follow up on your rage, the intrepid republican spirit will force them into submission. The traces of liberty in your land will be animated by the armies of France."[22]

In the Convention sessions and committee meetings, Audrein could move quickly to the attack and occasionally make a scene, as when Jacob Dupont was repeating once again the banal theme that the gods of humankind are nature and reason. "Cannot stand any more of this" ("On n'y tient plus"), said Audrein, and walked out.[23] He set his sights on Boissy D'Anglas during the Convention discussions of freedom of worship: "What here, Boissy! At the very moment when this beneficent religion is to appear at the tribune, olive branch in hand, passing out everywhere the balm of consolation, opening up consciences and bringing all the French people into the bosom of the republic, you seize the moment to artfully display destructive principles, and cause [religion] to be insulted by its cruelest enemies!"[24] Boissy would eradicate religion from national life, it would appear, permitting only a casual leftover cult. Audrein believed that religion was in an unfortunate state at the court, that "it needed to breathe the pure air of the Republic," and that now, "a stranger to foreign affairs and completely occupied with establishing happiness in the soul of a free people, it deserves public veneration more than ever."[25]

Boissy was presenting himself as indifferent to religion when he was actually being destructive. Religion, of course, is the great good of humankind: "While you are saying that you will not do anything in this matter, you attribute to it crimes of commission and omission. But what does it have in common with the cruelty of kings, that religion which is more gentle still than humanity itself?"[26] Accusing Boissy of promoting a shadow religion, Audrein will have none of it: "You give to the church for ministers men who are isolated. Without leaders and without counsel, delivered up to their own ignorance, wandering aimlessly, condemned to the shadows, strangers even to those whom they would lead to happiness! By doing things this way, are you not really voting for a death penalty?"[27] And he rises to high rhetorical passion, if not violence: "My soul rises in wrath, I quake with shame as I highlight such foolishness." Boissy had said that "religion will yield in the face of reason, *when it will be supported and directed by the government itself,*" and Audrein rejects Boissy's attempt to associate the government with his own philosophy: "No Boissy, no, I swear to you supported by the wisdom of three committees, you have in no way been authorized by them to speak in this fashion."[28]

During the last months of the Convention, Audrein appealed for freedom of worship for both the people and would-be philosophers. The regular citizens should let all know their profound appreciation for the church: "People of France, good people of the countryside, make yourself heard to your representatives! Give them a sense of how much you need your religion, and of how pleased you would be if they give you the use of your churches!"[29] He would have it that the intellectuals and philosophers among the constitutionals are a special crew—open-minded or forward-looking enough to believe in the new Republic. "Expect to share the fate of this *poor abbé Audrein*, for whom it is a pleasure to harass *our good philosophers*; but ought I to add that we need to follow Seneca and scorn the contempt of foolish men: . . . let us speak, even for those who do not want to listen to us; let us write for those who care not to read us."[30] Of course, religion is not just a matter of philosophy: "Woe to him who seeks the motivation for such a decision in his head and not in his heart."[31] On the other side, the pure thinkers often have a profound aversion to religion. "I have seen fine men tremble with anger when they hear tell of the churches, such is the terrible impression that our atheistic system has left us!"[32] And yet, he hopes to appeal to them on their own terms: "Should I not say to them, 'Where it is a matter of public tranquility and the happiness of your country, and you are dominated by ill humor, prejudice controls you. You are not thinking of the people, nor of their desires! You decide against them! And you should live only for them! What a frightful abuse of power!'"[33] Because with the repression of "this divine religion, streams of blood flow on all sides. Should not the possible loss of France be motive enough to make them change their ways?"[34]

More like a preacher than a philosopher, he keeps at this theme of the deep religious needs and desires of the people. Do not be taken in by ideologues, in love with their own abstract principles. The average citizen counts: "Certainly if in the present discussion, the desires of twenty million eight hundred thousand French, manifested in so many ways, were to have no apparent weight, you would not dare, I think, say that the law is the expression of the general will."[35] He evokes the people's needs, their tribulations, and again, their wish to have their churches back: "Return them, return them to my old people, and let their dying eyes see there again their victim God return them to those weeping mothers who go there to forget their sorrow and complete their offering!"[36]

He concludes with a profession of faith, insisting that he will obey whatever laws are legislated, but evoking the constitutional clergy, who are just like him: "They are part of that crowd of sorely vexed priest patriots. And our conspirators well know that they will find among these men noble defenders of the Revolution."[37] These are the real priests of France, and the government needs to recognize that fact: "Give to these priests the backing that will serve so well the public peace. Call them to your aid; and count on their success. Learn to make them your friends and you will have at your disposal the most powerful of influences for the public good, that of conscience."[38] There is a double standard—everyone has freedom of religion and expression, but not the priests. "Faults are only personal things; error is not a crime. Except where priests are concerned! Then there is another standard, another measure. They are all supposed to be fanatic, and so they all ought to be punished."[39]

Sometimes contentious and sometimes conciliatory, Yves-Marie Audrein came to lament the death of the king. He was as convinced as was Grégoire of Catholic and republican truth, but did not have the strong, rounded personality of Grégoire. His biographer, Hémon, in 1903 could not get beyond the problem that he was not a major thinker, in effect a continuing intellectual influence.[40] But he was a substantial intellectual in his day. More important, he was a dedicated churchman, in total contrast to the destructive Chabot and the majority of the other episcopal vicars who floated about the Convention.

The Revolutionary Violence of François Chabot

Chabot had been remembered as a well-behaved, extremely religious youth. Entering into the clerical state (tonsure) in 1772, he joined the Capuchins at Rodez. Much attracted to logic, mathematics, and philosophy, he read voluminously from the very philosophical works that were forbidden to his students. Devotion to duty was evident even in his early days as a mathematics teacher, preceded by extensive formation and practice, in a number of courses over three years with the Capuchins. He tells how he once spent thirty-six hours without interruption to solve a problem, all of this paying off in a successful teaching career in math and finance.[41]

The erosion of his pious convictions eventually affected his preaching, and by 1788 he was forbidden to preach in the diocese of Rodez. This, undoubtedly, contributed to his radicalism, and so when the Civil Constitution of the Clergy went into effect, he abandoned his convent and became a clerical free agent who was accepted into Grégoire's administration. He was elected to the Legislative Assembly; he sat with the far left and attracted attention by his relaxed, some would say sloppy, ways: neck uncovered and shirt open. With the advent of the king's trial, he voted against appeal to the people and for execution.[42]

Chabot got back to the Convention in time to take part in the persecution of the Girondins, offering quasi-data and easy stories that contributed greatly to their fall. He likewise mounted major attacks on the general membership of his fellow constitutionals! "I have a truth to tell you: you do not know who your mortal enemies are. They are the constitutional priests, who yell the most during campaigns about anarchists, troublemakers, dantonism, robespierrism, and jacobinism. They would like to establish a priestly throne on the ruins of liberty."[43] As a member of the Comité de sûreté générale, he was noted for his denunciations of colleagues. But he attacked everybody, even the redoubtable Committee of Public Safety. Cambon was a fool; Guyton-Morveau was "a Quaker who was always quaking." The next Committee had only three patriots; the Comité des finances was counterrevolutionary. And on the other side, the Enragés he called animals.[44] Chabot's negativity was too much even for Robespierre himself. He lasted only a few days after he was sent to quell disorders at Amiens. And it was Joseph Le Bon who replaced him at that point. Albert Mathiez considers the Chabot affair to be a key to the politics of the Terror:[45] "The denunciation of the boastful and corrupt Capuchin gave substance to the suspicions that hovered over the members of the Mountain (the radical Jacobins in the Convention), sharpened their distrust of one another, and led them to destroy one another." Still and all, Norman Hampson has insisted that "Chabot did expose *something*, even if he did not know what it was, and his 'revelations' played an important part in determining the mysterious policies of the Terror, even if not quite in the way he intended."[46]

Marriage into a well-placed business family brought him considerable wealth; not a small amount of his political and legal shenanigans had to do with money and investing. His brothers-in-law provided him with food and lodging for five years, as well as four thousand livres a year for other expenses, which Chabot defended with a smoke-screen explanation of the

Figure 20 François Chabot was one of Grégoire's episcopal vicars when he was elected to the Convention. Pictured here as half Franciscan priest and half revolutionary leader, his corruption in public and private life was so extensive that he was considered to be immoral even by the standards of secular revolutionaries. (Bibliothèque nationale de France)

money: "They [his brothers-in-law] gave us the right to remove it from their house, and then they obliged us to hand over this dowry in assignats or in émigré properties." Furthermore, "they set us up in a community of goods with my wife, and they desire that our marriage, and the share that would come to each of the children, be completely in conformity with the laws of the French Republic." None of this prevented him, when he approached the Convention podium to renounce his priesthood, from saying that he remained an episcopal vicar because "my wife and I needed to earn a living."[47]

Chabot was one of those ex-celibates who would wax eloquent on the beauty and joys of sex if given the slightest encouragement: "I have been accused of loving women. Yes, yes, I love them, and I say, moreover, woe to the man who does not. He resists the holiest, gentlest, and most sacred attraction of nature, and he will never be a good republican. To have virtue, one must follow the laws that nature has engraved in the hearts of all men; and the laws of human reproduction follow right after that of self-preservation, or rather it is only its supplement."[48] Sex is the key to all the other virtues, but religious fanaticism has tried to repress it, in vain: "Such fanaticism has not changed [human beings], and their need for [sex] has been increased by their inability to satisfy it." And on he goes: "Oh infinite wisdom of our God! It pleases you to confound human prudence by turning against us the means we believe proper to deliver us from the taunts of our enemies, because you reserve for yourself the responsibility of confounding them when you wish and by those very means that their madness invents against us."[49]

In the end the Revolution surpassed Chabot's fondest expectations in three areas in particular: "Royalty dead before the king, fanaticism dead before the priests, and the assignats turned into legal tender." He hoped that the clergy would eventually become extinct—no new priests and no new religious. Unfortunately, the king was such a problem that he had to be removed completely: "I believed the king to be a democrat in good faith, so I voted to bury the throne with him, but I also wanted to ensure that the government operation could always go on without him."[50] And so, he who abetted the September Massacres in 1792 and contributed to the testimonies against leading Girondins in 1793, was himself guillotined on 4 April 1794, the same day as Danton, Desmoulins, Hérault de Seychelles, and Fabre d'Eglantine. It would be difficult to find in the annals of the French Revolution a more extreme example of both priestly and political corruption.

The Convention Bishops

True, the great moment for the Constitutional Church was Bishop Henri Grégoire's solemn proclamation of his fidelity to the Christian faith and his priesthood. There were outstandingly low moments, too, as certain bishops formally or informally abjured their calling during the Terror. Across the Convention years (1792–95), in and out of the formal Convention assemblies, the constitutional bishops either accommodated themselves to the radical revolution or promoted it—two basic styles then, with variants in between. The accommodators intervened very little in the legislative discussions; the promoters intervened more often after they had renounced the episcopacy and begun the tasks assigned them as members of the Convention. Representative expressions of their political and priestly attitudes can best be found in pastoral letters and occasional essays, issued before and during the Convention years. The number of bishops seated at the Convention's opening on 21 September 1792 was actually sixteen, although two important lists put the number at seventeen: Jules Guiffrey in 1889 and Paul Pisani in 1907. August Kuscinski's old standard dictionary of delegates to the Convention correctly puts the number at sixteen: Saurine and Wandelaincourt, who are presented here as accommodators; Massieu and Gay-Vernon, who are presented here as promoters; and Grégoire, Thibault, and Fauchet, whose revolutionary credentials have already been established. Cazeneuve, Huguet, Marbos, and Sanadon, though active in the Convention, published so little that they will not be considered here, nor will Lalande, Séguin, Villars, and Lindet, few if any of whose representative publications coincide with the Convention years. Royer, bishop of Ain under the Convention, will be presented in chapter 12 in his later capacity as bishop of Paris. Torné, although elected to the Convention, resigned before the first session.[51]

Accommodating Revolution: Saurine and Wandelaincourt

Although among the leading accommodators, Bishop Jean-Baptiste-Pierre Saurine little favored republican government, he advertised religion as a support of and complement to the law-and-order values of government. It was clear that he saw himself caught between two extremes: those willing to destroy the government, and those willing to destroy any opposition to the government, loyal or otherwise. In effect, he was a lawyer—for this was his original training—who defended the Gallican moral balance. Bishop Antoine-Hubert Wandelaincourt, analyzing the forms of church organization and education, touted church as the educator of an evolving society.

Saurine, though intervening minimally in the Convention, was among the most enduring of the constitutional bishops, ending his career years later as bishop of Strasbourg under the Concordat. During the Convention years, he was more interested in making the people active in the church and less interested in putting down the aristocracy, more interested in ecclesiastical renewal and less interested in a new government. Study of Hebrew

Figure 21 Bishop Saurine was an intellectually powerful but politically prudent member of the Convention. The engraving dates from his appointment, when still a priest, to the Estates General and Constituent Assembly. Looking back on those years, he gave vent to his anger over the death, destruction, and suppression of religion that issued from the Convention decrees. (Bibliothèque nationale de France)

had gained him a reputation as a savant, and the acquisition of a law degree enabled him to take part in the Parlement of Paris. He served as a delegate to the Estates General and was a member of the Constituent Assembly. Given his alacrity and enthusiasm in taking the oath, he was a natural choice as constitutional bishop. When he was elected bishop of the Landes, he quickly set himself to reorganization of the diocese, defense of the Constitutional Church, and explanation of papal error. In the Convention he was a moderate, courageously opposing the execution of the king. During the trial of Louis XVI, he voted for an appeal to the people, and then for imprisonment until the return of peace, followed by a reprieve. No false hero, he was practical about imprisonment: "I do not fear any court, but I have to fear the prisons where cutthroats threaten each day to use their daggers. No one can object if I make use of my natural rights and yield to the duty [these rights] impose to avoid such dangers."[52] He wanted this made public to the Convention, and it did get him off.[53] He was imprisoned, however, in May 1793 for protesting the expulsion of the Girondins, and was not released until the fall of Robespierre. His last service to the Convention was on the Comité d'instruction publique.[54]

Looking back on the Convention tragedy, Saurine insisted that government needs the support of religion: "The power of [government] is limited to punishing actions without really serving as a barrier to the passions."[55] Then, in a pastoral letter of seventy-two pages, written less than a year after the fall of Robespierre, Saurine described the challenge of living morally amid chaos and proposes a simple goal: "Nobody is ignorant of the horrible tyranny that weighed upon us, the torrents of innocent blood that was shed, those cruel persecutions that brought mourning and tears to families and [whole] cities, the calamities that ravaged town and countryside, the impious actions that destroyed the holy places, the unknown horrors out of the past that have besmirched our own history."[56] No more sweet talk about the revolutionary government: the damage has been extensive, and the danger is still real: "Having just escaped the chains of tyranny, we walk on the edge of a new precipice; we struggle against what remains of the anarchy that has rent us asunder and does so still."[57] He is caught between those who would overthrow the government and those who would defend the Republic by any means, "crushing all those they suspect of being its enemies, and taking over their property."[58] His ideal people, obviously, are all law and order, looking only to the common well-being, "peace, tranquility, and the common good."[59]

Antoine-Hubert Wandelaincourt was a good centrist figure, who appears to have worked hard at first to establish the meaning of the Constitutional Church and win over the clergy. His treatises cover morality, education, and government, with special attention paid to Christianity. At first an administrator of a *collège* at Verdun, then a tutor in an aristocratic family, he was a curé in the diocese of Châlons from 1784 onward. A committed constitutional, he was elected to be constitutional bishop of Haute-Marne when Gobel passed up this and another see in order to go to Paris. In the Convention he sided with the moderates, declining to condemn the king, because of his priestly "gentle ways," but he was willing to vote on the case: "Although I recused myself as judge, I must nonetheless look out for the welfare of the Republic. [Inasmuch] as no banished king has a successor, I am for banishment."[60] These "ways" eventually got him into prison.

In *Éléments de morale; ou, Devoirs de l'homme et du citoyen*, written in 1793, Wandelaincourt presents a classical dialogue between child and teacher, the *student* (*enfant*) and the *master.*[61] Standards for reason and equilibrium may seem abstract, but they are vital to human life and development: "Reason teaches us that only those people are happy who are beyond the reach of dread, sorrow, sensuousness, and the futile joys of this world."[62] Pleasure has its place, not to degrade humans into brutish sensuality, but to free them from the pain caused by their own failures and the fickleness of others. And in his *Plan d'éducation publique*, a text submitted for inclusion in the Convention records, he continues the mission of education that he had begun as a seminary professor.[63] The basic principle is that "the most flourishing and the happiest states have always been those whose young people have received the best education."[64] Without education comes vice, as is evidenced by the combination of gross ignorance and destruction seen in earlier centuries. Education, then, is of primary interest to governments, to advance the government's own reputation and the happiness of its people. And, finally, the bottom line of essential values: "a uniform discipline," "love of the fatherland," "respect for laws," "appreciation of the rules of the place where they must live."[65] He highlights the parents' primary role in education, on the simple assumption that neither justice nor generosity makes sense unless one believes in God: "What human motive (for the atheist has no other) could determine me to work to the general good instead of my individual interest, and to sacrifice my life for the fatherland?"[66] Wandelaincourt is absolutely wedded to the idea that without belief in God and fear of sanctions there would be no morality, quite cavalierly denying that an atheist could possibly believe in self-sacrificing generosity for the fatherland or for anything else. The atheist considers generosity an aberration, because to sacrifice oneself for no personal gain is to go against human nature. Here Wandelaincourt has the usual Rousseauian (and Voltairian) arguments to deflate: "It is not true that Christianity extinguishes the warrior virtues. Is it not simple, active, painstaking moral acts that prepare the way for them?"[67]

On the new government constitution itself, Wandelaincourt's observations are philosophical and vague, a discreet bishop pushing rationality and peace on the Convention.[68] True to traditional Augustinian theology, he can only justify a defensive war, and so must explain one of Montesquieu's formulations: "When Montesquieu permits an offensive war, it is easy to see that in the case of which he speaks, it is really a defensive war. The right to bear arms derives from the necessity of defending from oppression, *the diverse nations seek the most good for themselves in peacetime, and in war the least evil possible without harming their true interests.*"[69] General human law (not national laws, which Montesquieu shows to be only locally appropriate) is as invariable as the laws of nature. And he has a balanced attitude on penalties and censors. Countries need both in moderation. For penalties, he would not have people accustom themselves to execution, but admits that "on one hand, unpunished crimes are the ruin of republics."[70] The important thing is that laws not be made up to defend party or caste interest.

Promoting Revolution: Massieu and Gay-Vernon

First a tutor and professor at the University of Nancy, Jean-Baptiste Massieu became curé of Cergy (Val d'Oise). Elected to the Estates General from the *bailliage* of Senlis, he was a member of the Comité ecclésiastique, defending such measures as a marriage blessing for the divorced and for priests, and the suppression of religious congregations. After having actively sought the see of Versailles, he accepted election as constitutional bishop of the Oise.

Though written after the "Fatherland in Danger" declaration, Massieu's letter of July 1792 contained a surprisingly large dose of spiritual admonition, centered around a vital quote from Psalm 126: "But if the Lord does not defend it, those who watch over it labor in vain."[71] This was the bishop who within months would make his transition from spiritual and political vigilance to violence. Massieu has the Republic at the center of his theological world. He develops the themes of God's goodness and protectiveness at some length. The Republic is the gift of God and the vehicle of God's will in history: "He has until the present day visibly favored all the true friends of peace and brotherly equality who constitute our political laws, and harmonize them with the eternal laws of wisdom and with those he has dictated himself through the lips of the divine Legislators who come from him [*sorti de son sein*]."[72] And it must have given the legislators in the Assembly a boost to hear that the prophets and evangelists, too, were "legislators." Old aristocratic and royalist types obviously have their own interests to defend and insist on rights that no just law would support. This puts them in a strong position to take advantage of a people who are dedicated to liberty—but this people, of course, will break any new bonds of slavery.

Massieu then plays out the theme—an obsession of the most militant Jacobins—of danger from within, seeing counterrevolution as rank immorality: "At the heart of the empire, a whole group of false brethren, slaves

Figure 22 Bishop Massieu sketched as a mild, almost angelic-looking priest. As a bishop, he passed from a mild promoter of moderation to an ardent promoter of the Terror. In fact, by the time he was elected to the Convention he was poised to reject his priestly and episcopal vocation and pursue his fellow legislators' most extreme goals. (Bibliothèque nationale de France)

of the most despicable vices, pride and greed, rejoice in the evils that have come upon the fatherland, and never cease to protect and nourish them."[73] Again, these scoundrels are totally selfish, totally bad-willed. Of course, then, he can make his full negative judgments about these people: "In the vain hope that there will be . . . rejoicing and prosperity for them alone, they hatch their bloody plots."[74] God ensures the safety of his people—the French and the rest of the universe. "The creator of the human race will not permit [the nation] to become the prey of a few ambitious people. The cause of the French is the cause of the universe, because they want only the reign of justice and law."[75] And, of course, God is on the republican side: "The God of armies will fight for France," "the selfless nation and champion of truth and right," "which desired to arm itself only one last time for the sake of humanity: already it has inspired in an innumerable multitude of generous citizens the firm resolve to die, if necessary, for the law and the fatherland."[76] Well, all right, there is a certain morality required for God to be always on our side. So Massieu concludes as he began, with the surprising witness to the action of God: "But our vigils, our efforts, our resolutions, our courage, are nothing without the blessings of the all-powerful master of nations and empires. . . . Let us make our cause always worthy of his paternal attention by our uprightness of heart and purity of intention."[77]

In December 1792, Massieu was still clear about his priesthood—"I am a minister of religion"—even as he voted against the motion to require weekly public readings of the Convention documents; but in August he wrote to express his "genuine assent" to "the just vengeance of the laws concerning the evil foreigner [Marie Antoinette]."[78] At the trial of Louis XVI, Massieu had voted against the appeal to the people and for execution without reprieve. Within a year, in November 1793, he submitted his abdication of priesthood with the following words: "I give up a position that I had accepted only to fight against the plague of fanaticism, which the wise and courageous decrees of the Convention have definitively overcome. My feeble efforts become useless here, and I want to remove any suspicion that I fight under dishonorable standards."[79] He was sent as a *commissaire* of the Convention to the Departments of the Marne and the Ardennes, where he helped to organize the labor force. He followed through on the style of his condemnation of the king and his abdication language with an enthusiastic report of the revolutionary festivals celebrated in Reims Cathedral. Whereas the cathedral had been earlier used for "the most absurd ceremonies of fanaticism and despotism . . . the new inauguration has certainly expiated the rank dishonor that the ridiculous and vile anointing of our tyrants conferred on this temple every time that ignorance and stupidity provided a new master for France."[80]

After his marriage to the daughter of the mayor of Givet, Massieu continued to survey army loyalty there and then presided at the celebration of the Feast of Reason. He saw to the arrest of priests, and worked with another ex-constitutional priest, Louis-Félix Roux, a member of the Convention, but no relation to the Enragé priest Jacques Roux. Companions in contentiousness, some of their shifty dealings displeased the Committee of Public Safety. After the two of them had gone to the dedication of the Temple of Reason at Sedan, they had a falling out. Collot-Herbois tried to reestablish calm by reprimanding them both. He was outspoken in his criticism of the trial of Marat; that there should even be such a trial wounded his sensibilities. Despite his good work to set up the Terror, he was arrested because he had presumably squandered vital supplies. Then he took part in the movement of the Givet garrison against the Austrians, and applauded the Convention decree that reduced the bishops' stipends to 6,000 livres. In the Committee on Public Instruction, he advocated the use of old parish rectories and a proper salary for *instituteurs*, and subsidies to artists. After the fall of Robespierre, he remained attached to the Mountain.[81]

Bishop Léonard Gay-Vernon vigorously proclaimed that republicanism was Christianity and that Christianity was republicanism. With equal vigor he attacked the Old Regime, preaching instead an open Catholicism with a secular moral cast to it. Priest along with two of his brothers, Gay-Vernon was curé and then mayor of Compreignac. He was elected constitutional bishop of Haute-Vienne, and deputy to the Legislative Assembly. Writing just after the execution of the king, Gay-Vernon wanted to be more intimate and pastoral in his letter to priests and people of his department, but he immediately moves into the language of republican extremism when he lists the misdeeds of churchmen and counterrevolutionaries.[82] The clergy are often recalcitrant, but the nobles were so bad that they were the instruments of their own undoing. The king, to whom he showed no mercy during the trial, was the worst. "It was necessary for the last Louis to pile up every crime and treachery to lead the French to a republican system," and he is to blame for the invasion by the other monarchies.[83]

In a paroxysm of invective worthy of a speech to the Convention, Gay-Vernon totally transforms his pastoral talk into an attack on "court monies, deftness of intrigue, audacity of assassins, fears spread throughout the departments, a system of appeal to the people so cleverly conceived to flatter and confound them, the menace of a faction created to control the weak, the terrible invectives spewed out at the good people of Paris, and the clamor of a gang of journalists bribed to lie [*vendus aux mensonges*]."[84] But he calms down to a quasi-episcopal finale, because religion (i.e., rational religion) can still be a force for good: "an arch cast toward liberty that nothing can impede, an invisible force that turns the thoughts of the wicked against themselves, and brings out of the midst of dangers the greatest security."[85] Gay-Vernon begins his presentation to the clergy with a strong backing of the Convention and its legislation. He promotes equal reverence for Convention and church, it would appear, because the republican ideal is operative in both settings: "The Church is a perfect Republic."[86] Republicanism is, then, the ultimate goal of Constitution and Convention, to which people owe trust and obedience. He attributes a role of mediation to the Convention that is normally assigned to the church. The church—in its ministers—has its own realm and should not tell the government how to run the country.

Although unwilling to make either religion or philosophy normative, Gay-Vernon believes that they state the ideal. In fact, he appears to value the church ideal because it seconds the philosophical ideal. In ancient times the church was willing to let the state regulate marriage as an institution. Why cannot the church operate the same way today, offering guidance rather than rules? Only the marriage blessing should be held in reserve: "If the faithful, after having divorced, request the nuptial blessing, make it clear to them, my dear colleagues, that as simple ministers of the church, we must be in conformity with its laws . . . and with the perfection and holiness of its customs."[87] This was the way of the philosophical schools of the ancient world. His passion is, then, purity and regeneration: "As republicans and Catholics, we must . . . let subsist only what nourishes piety toward God in everyone's heart, only what nourishes love of neighbor, dedication to duty, respect for law; let subsist only what can move men to work, stimulate their industry, regenerate them, and perfect their physical and moral well-being."[88] The Old Regime clergy kept people ignorant, and tolerated their superstition in order to control them.

In the Convention, Gay-Vernon was a member of the Comité de division and seated himself with the Jacobin Mountain. His interventions were minor—for example, reading a report on a local official who invited his people to disregard the Convention decrees.[89] During the trial of the king he had voted against appeal to the people, and for death. He abdicated with no particular antagonism to the old ways, but cited the consistency of his freedom- and reason-promoting ministry: as priest, he had encouraged his parishioners to request a new curé if they became dissatisfied with him, and as bishop he immediately handed in his pectoral cross when Torné demanded the abolition of clerical dress in the Legislative Assembly.[90] Subsequently, he backed legislation requiring that all teachers be married or widowed (thereby eliminating priests and nuns). At one time supporting Robespierre, he came to condemn his memory. When criticized as a former priest, he said he honestly fulfilled these duties when they were his.[91] Though he railed against celibacy, there is no evidence that he married.

Convention-Era Outcomes: Fauchet, Lamourette, and Grégoire

Claude Fauchet, although a Girondin, had been cultivating his relationship with the Jacobins when François Chabot began to harass him. According to Chabot, Fauchet had intrigued with Madame de Staël to put ex–minister of war Louis-Marie de Narbonne into a controlling triumvirate should the Constitution fail. Later, other Jacobins accused him of trying to obtain a passport for Narbonne, should their political intriguing backfire. But Fauchet had loaded the Jacobins with compliments; it was Robespierre he criticized: "The Jacobins of Paris at the beginning of the Legislative Assembly were not numerous, but in strength and wisdom they were attached to valid principles; all the solid patriots of the new national legislature made it their duty to work together to fight in the breach the strongest party, the Feuillants. They obviously took no liberties; prudence and strength characterized their deliberations." The compliments were limited to the early days, when he, Pétion, and Brissot presided, and "Robespierre was absent," having gone to his home region "to parade his arrogance." He was far from the strong man of the club when he came back, "but [catered] to the inert mass of colleagues, who submitted to the first blowhard who, wanting to take charge, put some tenacity in his operation." Then, "he won over the galleries by his cowardly groveling before the people that composed them, and by his continual publicizing of his own dedication and endless censuring of those who did not blindly embrace his opinions."[92]

Fauchet raged against the evils of the monarch in a discourse surprisingly angry and vengeful for someone who had enjoyed some years as a favored preacher at court: "He merited more than death. Eternal justice condemns the fallen tyrant to a long suffering in life, in the midst of a free people." He lambastes the "huge and last crimes of the hereditary tyranny," which he calls "that ancient plague of the nations." In this matter, he demands from the Convention "an impassive calm in the solemn judgment," because "the nation must rise to the full height of its wisdom in order to judge him impartially."[93] Calling Louis "the kind of man who devours others," he turns this antimonarchist ranting into a demand for life imprisonment. It would be a lesson for the rest of the world and for Louis himself: "There is no law that can get at his crimes; but nature avenges itself against us because of the powerlessness of our legislation; she inflicts on him a punishment worse than death: she prolongs his existence; she lets him be the laughing stock of the universe, as on a scaffold of ignominy. He will unceasingly witness, what torture! the adverse effects of his crimes, the noble and immortal and everlasting vengeance of the great-souled nation he wanted to shove down into the horrors of slavery."[94]

Fauchet wanted it both ways: to see himself as a quintessential republican *and* as a Catholic bishop who could not stain his hands with the blood of others. In the last issue (June 1793) of his review, *Journal des Amis*, he wrote that other constitutionals in the Convention had voted for the death of the king, whereas he, for all his strong language, had stood for effective punishment only. When this brought him quickly into conflict with Jacobin extremists, he reacted forcefully to the virulent Montagnard attack against the Girondins and himself: "Anarchy hurries to multiply its victims. I have been designated for its two-edged sword; I bless providence that has called me to so glorious an end; I hope that the blood of the martyrs of liberty, truth, and justice will be useful to the fatherland. The reign of the truly depraved can last only an instant; it self-destructs."[95]

Addressing himself to his flock in Calvados, he concludes in an episcopal blaze of glory: "And you, dear faithful, hear, perhaps for the last time, the voice of a pontiff who has not had the time to show you all his devotion and all his love, but who has not ceased to carry you in his heart, and who wanted to consecrate his entire life to loving and serving you."[96] The final admonition to faithfulness: "Do not abandon the faith of your fathers and the dear religion which is nothing other than liberty in its heavenly purity, fraternity in its evangelical perfection, virtue in its divine beauty, happiness even across persecutions and the anguish of death."[97] It is clear that he sees his own life and preaching as a martyrdom: "Death! I see the threat to my own head. O my brethren, O my friends, I await it only with serenity and with true joy. My only fear, I manifested it often in these days of persecution and it is in the depth of my soul, my only fear is that I will be judged unworthy by the Sovereign Master of our destinies, of so beautiful a death. To die for justice, for truth, for law, for religion, for the happiness of men, what a blessed death!"[98] The more his own death is in the likeness of Christ, the more he will channel the redemptive effect of that death: "I belong to God, I belong to the fatherland, I belong to the church, I belong to you, dear fellow citizens, dear members of the faithful; but I will always be such; my blood will be of more value than my voice, my death will be of more use than my life."[99]

Within the year, after a brief stay in the Conciergerie, Fauchet was guillotined, with his last days remembered by the comte Jean-Claude Beugnot. As others were disappearing, Beugnot could only hope that Fauchet, along with Ducos and Fonfrède, would survive. Evidence was that Fauchet had sent for his breviary, which somehow had escaped notice as he moved about. Beugnot and his companions "presumed that perhaps in these final moments some of the victims had been troubled by religious concerns, and that Fauchet stayed with them to offer some consolation."[100] Beugnot gives himself over to a eulogy that, he believes, even anti-Christian philosophers would support. Fauchet's political career naturally gives him pause, but otherwise he finds the bishop of Calvados to be a worthy prelate: "Raised in a Catholic culture and nourished in its schools, his mind was confounded early on by all the prophecies, miracles, and glamor. Destined himself to preach this religion, his own tastes confirmed him in it, and since it is not easy to stop once started, he almost turned into a prophet himself. The bishop's residence in Calvados distracted him from the reveries of the Cercle social, and he ended up a priest of good faith. At a time when men have neither the need nor the intention to take on these matters, he proclaimed his firm beliefs and brought his conduct in harmony with his principles."[101] Given his political intensity, Fauchet often had to protest the priority of his religious ministry, says Beugnot, who believed that "every day he piously read his breviary, read holy scripture, and declaimed [*sic*] a chapter of the *Imitation*."[102]

Beugnot noted also Fauchet's predilection for the Book of Revelation: "The book of scripture for which he had the greatest liking was the Apocalypse. He maintained that it was the French Revolution in particular that St. John had seen on the isle of Patmos, and he acknowledged that until the period of the taking of the Bastille he found it difficult to understand, but that, ever since that time, the explanation flowed of its own accord."[103] The tragedies of the revolutionary era were the clear manifestation of the trials and tribulations of the end days. Of this, Fauchet was even able to convince unbelievers. "He found in the Apocalypse the birth, the progress, and the triumphs of the Jacobins, the reign of Robespierre, the noyades of Carrier, the fusillades of Collot and even the carmagnoles of Barère. He often made such striking connections and developed them with such eloquence that he moved the cold materialist [Armand] Gensonné, and [Jacques] Brissot was astounded by them."[104] In the end, though, Fauchet avoided the millenarian extremes of Pontard.[105]

Beugnot shared the same cell as Adrien Lamourette in those last days, writing in his memoirs that "the constitutional bishop of Lyon" was a pleasant and kind cell mate, "an educated man, a fine orator, and at the beginning of the Revolution, one of the most distinguished priests of the Oratory."[106] Lamourette had been a Vincentian, not an Oratorian, so Beugnot's memory was playing tricks, perhaps because members of the Congregation of the Oratory had been among the most ardent revolutionaries. He does remember details of Lamourette's heroism during the siege of Lyon, "when he brought spiritual aid to his flock across bullets and grapeshot."[107] In the Conciergerie he offered ministry and consolation: "I never saw anyone move so far into Christian stoicism. We saw him fulfill regularly and without affectation, the duties of a priest."[108] He and Father Émery, the simple but charismatic priest who was the best known of the refractories, worked together: "Although a constitutional bishop and consequently much opposed, to all appearances, to Monsieur Émery, the ex-superior of Saint-Sulpice, also placed in our destitute company, he was half occupied in the good works of this fine man."[109] If Beugnot's memory served him right, then the story that Émery brought Lamourette around to retracting his oath in the end was true: "He charged me with the task of publishing his retraction of the oath he had sworn to the Civil Constitution of the Clergy."[110]

Two anecdotes count here: Lamourette calming Beugnot's fears and steadying his resolve, and Lamourette at the center of a suicide drama with Clavières, ex–minister of the interior: "One hour after we had gone to bed and fallen asleep, I was awakened by the cry of Lamourette: 'Clavières! Ah! Poor man! What have you done?' and I heard then two equally horrible sounds: the groaning of a man who was dying and the sound of his blood, which was dropping from his bed onto the stone floor. . . . The two priests fell to their knees and invited us to do the same to ask God's grace for the unfortunate man who was dying before our eyes."[111]

Lamourette, for his part, was completely resigned to his fate: "When Lamourette was led to the tribunal, he admitted that everything he was accused of was the most sacred duty of his state in life, confessed his faith, made the sign of the cross, and awaited his judgment."[112] He was guillotined in January 1794, ten days short of the one-year anniversary of the execution of King Louis XVI. While in prison he "retracted" his oath in favor of the Constitution and repented his membership in the constitutional clergy, all of which the refractory clergy considered their victory.[113]

But it is not clear that Lamourette was as enthusiastic a retractor as he was a promoter of the Constitutional Church. What we have here is more a general, and long-winded, confession of his sinfulness: "On the point of being judged by men for having tried to oppose the disorders of the spirit of anarchy and license, and probably on the point of being judged by God's tribunal for my sins and all the faults of my life, for which I sincerely and humbly ask his pardon, and for which I firmly hope in his great mercy, because of the satisfactions and infinite merits of Jesus Christ, our Savior."[114] It is clear that he regrets having contributed to controversy and confusion:

> I declare that I repent with all my heart all that I have said, done, and written that tended to support the principles in accordance with

which they have made those changes in France which became so harmful to religion and so to the true happiness of the French. . . . I demand pardon of God and of the true children of the church for having cooperated in making these deplorable changes by an oath that the Holy See has condemned. . . . I beg pardon of God for having accepted episcopal consecration, of which I was unworthy, and of the church for having filled a see that was not vacant, for having violated the sacred laws of the discipline and underrated the authority and superiority of the sovereign pontiff and of the Holy See.

Written in the Conciergerie de Paris, 7 January, the year of Our Lord 1794. Signed, Adrien Lamourette[115]

Certainly a formal retraction—with nuances. The government has gone bad and this moves him to recognize that working with the government has been a mistake. Of course, he says what he has to say relative to Rome. He regrets having gone along with the changes that have become so harmful. In other words, he did not like the way things turned out.

Henri Grégoire had always believed that the gospel itself was liberation, and in the worst days of the Convention, he would remember the Tennis Court Oath, and so be restimulated to suffer the more: "Touched by this image, and hurt by the contrast offered by events that followed, I wept burning tears of joy and despair."[116] Out of these shadows came the revolutionary calendar, replacing the old Christian feasts, replacing even Sunday itself by a special "décadi" celebration at the beginning of a ten-day week. When Grégoire asked Gilbert Romme why he had created the revolutionary calendar, Romme "admitted to me," wrote Grégoire, that he did so "in order to *destroy Sunday.*" The priest retorted, "Sunday existed before you and it will exist after you." Grégoire watched radical anticlericalism and destructive projects come to the proposal stage. The old intellectual academies were destroyed; intellectuals were put in prison or fled into hiding; great architecture and monuments were threatened with destruction.

In a pastoral letter written as the Convention was entering its last months, he eloquently presented and lamented the great and awful drama that had taken place: "Brethren, it has been a long time since you heard the voice of your bishop; across the distance that separates us, my tender words are hardly an adequate witness to my affection."[117] Times have been terrible and it does no good to cover this up: "Tyranny has stifled our ideas; it forbids publishers from publishing them; and has ended the dissemination of the results of a free press." Surveillance was constant: "The secrecy of letters was violated, correspondence was intercepted: to write someone was to needlessly compromise one's liberty, even one's life, in the course of that frightful year." It was a year of death and destruction, "where blood, even that of the just, flowed everywhere, when France was covered with victims, of which a great number had been killed, covered with executioners, of which the great number are still living." The church could not have been in a worse state: "With whom could we correspond, anyway, when in the middle of this scandalous defection, and deprived of dependable information, I did not know who the people were that remained faithful."[118]

Despite everything, though, he still tries to inculcate loyalty to the Republic, even to the post-Thermidorian Convention: "When, in order to respond to my obligations and my heart's call, I visited your parishes, with what care did I inculcate in you the hate of despotism. The gospel, I said to you, proclaims to us that we are brothers. The gospel consecrates the principle of equality and fraternity. Repeat your protestations of fidelity to the Republic and attachment to the National Convention. Do not allow in your religious assemblies the impure alloy of men who want people to regret the passing of the wretched royal regime. One who does not love the Republic is a bad citizen and consequently a bad Christian."[119] And a bit of personal history, finally. He has been bishop of Blois for four years and feels the demands of the apostolate: "If, despite the multiple signs of witness to your goodwill, trials have followed me everywhere, and if in my apostolic labors, I contracted an illness that will accompany me to the tomb, what does it matter, provided that religion flourishes and that the Republic grows strong and that those truths of which I was the voice bear fruit in your hearts?"[120]

The Convention years were blighted by the Terror with its fake trials, settling of political scores, and summary executions; some of the politically engaged priests and bishops participated in the violence. Outcomes included martyrdom (Fauchet and Lamourette) and a reinvigorated priestly apostolate (Grégoire), which provided a counterweight to two priests who engaged with the extreme Convention violence, one as an Enragé in the Paris Commune and the other as a *réspresentant en mission* in the Somme—ultimate renegades, then, if the charity requirements of the Catholic priestly tradition are the criteria judging priests and bishops.[121]

Chapter Seven

TERRORISTS AND ABDICATORS

Ultimate Renegades

Two leading clerical promoters of violence under the Legislative Assembly carried their work to term under the Convention, renouncing their priesthood along the way: Jacques Roux, as a member of the General Council of the Paris Commune, and Joseph Le Bon, as *représentant en mission* in the Somme and Pas-de-Calais, represent the nadir of priestly degeneration that was reached by the end of the Convention years. Not that it had to be that way. John McManners, the most even-handed of historians and Anglican priests, wrote some years ago, "When the full story of the *curés rouges* and the *sans-culotte* monks is written, more true idealists may be found in their ranks than has been imagined—men whose former religious vocation had left them with a dream of an egalitarian, regenerated society arising from the Terror."[1]

Roux and Le Bon were idealists, both were teachers in the beginning, and both were articulate and competent in their teaching positions. But they also had violent character traits that accorded poorly with their roles as priests and teachers. As seminarians and young priests, their characters were molded by a combination of serious moral commitment and self-regarding extremism. Their extremism emerged when nurtured—or triggered—by personal or social dramas. Jacques Roux became the archetypical Enragé, a man elevated to chronic anger by his passion for social equality, and the best-known member of the extremist revolutionary group so labeled.[2] His uncompromising professor–priest personality mutated into an uncompromising advocate of the poor, so extreme that even Robespierre thought he was a real liability, an "ultra-revolutionary." Joseph Le Bon was a moralistic professor who came to promote a revolutionary ethic for daily life and for politics. This mutation from rigid religious morality to uncompromising revolutionary morality produced a formal representative of the Terror. Whereas Roux was a demagogue and agitator, Le Bon was a purebred law-and-order man; both of them, in their character traits and discourse, represented two specific styles of moralizing revolutionary violence that developed out of the Constitutional Church apostolates.

Other moralizing revolutionaries renounced priesthood and took on other social roles without physical violence, for the most part. But their verbal violence, and the effect that had on the vestiges of the old Constitutional Church apostolate, made them revolutionary counterparts of Roux and Le Bon. Whatever their contributions to French town and countryside in 1793–94, they were renegades to the church that had formed them.

Jacques Roux, the Enragé

While Roux was still a seminarian in Angoulême, a new teaching position opened up at his *collège*, Saint-Louis, run by the Vincentians. The school admitted not only seminarians but also regular students, making it necessary to offer courses in philosophy and physics. The setup required a professor who would be "a layperson residing at the seminary." At the age of twenty, Jacques Roux, then only tonsured, was given the job. His teachers and the bishop himself praised his cleverness and appreciated his rigorous disciplinary style, because he could so easily reject children of lesser talent, even if they came from families who had received him in their homes with great kindness. Years later, Roux insisted that his ways were just—and all the more satisfying perhaps—because the families were aristocratic. After ordination, he served briefly as assistant in a number of parish churches.

No doubt the uncompromising Roux had a mean and vicious streak: witness his 1783 attack on "the stench-laden aristocrat Souchet, driven from her department for concubinage and working in Paris as a prostitute, even though she looked barely human, a tigress who carries on her forehead the imprint of all her crimes, in order to get back at me for not having admitted into philosophy class fifteen years ago, a number of her close relatives, who had the jawbones of an ass and the vices of her family."[3] Obviously no stranger to verbal violence, Roux was no stranger either to physical violence. The most bizarre incident during his teaching years was the murder of one of the students, the so-called Affaire Mioulle.[4] The young man was carrying on with some of his friends one evening, noisily and perhaps destructively. When they all got to throwing rocks at the seminary windowpanes, gunshots came from within the building, and poor Mioulle was killed. Although the cook, Frère Ancelet (his family name), was clearly the triggerman, suspicion fell upon Jacques Roux as the instigator, something he never admitted to, then or later. But if he *was* involved, this was the beginning of real violence, careless and damned-be-the-consequences violence, giving him a reputation that followed across several church assignments in his diocese.

Coming to Paris after parish work in Angoulême and Saintonge, he took the oath to the Civil Constitution with great liveliness at Saint-Sulpice, where he had obtained the post of an assistant. Saint-Sulpice had a large number of random assistants moving in and out, and we do not really know how Roux managed to secure this position, which, of course, got him out of the provinces and into the capital. He had a reputation as a preacher to the sans-culottes, saying of himself that he "concerned himself principally with the care of the poor, and his door was always open to the poor hapless people."[5] He then fully established himself in the Gravilliers section of Paris, hotbed of sans-culottism, by "serving" in the parish of Saint-Nicholas-des-Champs. R. B. Rose praises Roux for his dedication to his section and his parishioners, emphasizing that Roux would go about his parish neighborhood to look after his people until the end, but I am afraid that the full sources and categories provided by a leading Roux scholar, the German Walter Markov, do not allow for a generally sympathetic portrayal of Roux the priest.[6]

From Religious to Revolutionary Sermons

A review of the principal sermons published after he came to Paris shows that Jacques Roux had a number of formally religious "reflexes" in his preaching and general behavior. Even in 1790, he was still combining a language of Christian faith, hope, and charity with his revolutionary discourse. However much anger, hatred, and ideological fanaticism vitiated any religious expression, he still purported to be preaching the Christian message. Furthermore, the stated scheduling, location, and audience of his talks were often improbable (read here fictitious). In "Le Triomphe des braves Parisiens sur les ennemis du bien public" (1790), Roux piously announces, "The destiny of all men is in the hands of God; the destiny of all empires is determined by divine providence."[7] He evokes the power of Parisian patriotism, putting down the enemies of the state, and thereby abetting the divine power that has seized hold of the government and is now guiding it to new heights. Parisians are aiding God in the management of a renewed monarchy. For Roux, then, there is still God, and still the monarchy, and still the chosen people of France: "The grace of God openly acts upon us, and the moment fixed by the decrees of eternal wisdom to eradicate abuses, reform morals, and bring about both the humiliation of the wicked and the triumph of the good, is upon us. . . . France has become the vessel of election into which [eternal wisdom] indulgently pours his singular favors."[8]

Roux sees Louis XVI as part of the divine plan in what was still the language of the day, Louis having ingratiated himself with many revolutionaries by his loyalty to the Constitution in 1790: "It was nonetheless reserved for the century of Louis XVI, that monarch of goodness, justice, and peace, to bring about a bright new day." Louis gets good marks because he worked with the revolutionary agenda, "declaring that he would reign only by law, and by this act of submission, worthy of his goodness, attracting the attention of all of Europe." Roux then asks, "Who could watch without admiration, and fear, the most flourishing empire of this vast universe shaken in its very foundations, rise up, nevertheless, in the midst of its ruins with splendor and majesty?"[9]

Paeans of praise, then, for the intrepid citizens of France, including the women who fought alongside their men. The people will guide their king and the king his people, preserving the old family unity: "By this more intimate union of ruler with subject, or a father with his children; because of the wonderful accord of zeal, confidence, fidelity, strength . . . plots and perverted policies have failed, necessarily, in face of the altar of the fatherland."[10] Now are the enemies of both reduced to impotence and rage.

Roux can even arouse himself to ardent prayer: "O you who have breathed life into the sacred fire that makes the earth fruitful, develop, O my God, the seed of this liberty that you happily have placed in the heart of man, when you shaped with your hands the earth of which he is made."[11] But he addresses himself to a personified liberty in virtually the same way: "LIBERTY, the soul, the intelligence, the voice, the harmony of the whole universe . . . LIBERTY, daughter of heaven, mother of nature." This liberty is entreated to renew the land, "bloated [*engraisée*] with the bodies of the dead and more than watered—flooded—by our blood."[12] No contradiction here between theistic faith and patriotic virtue. Liberty resides with God, where it can "unfurl from the heights of heaven . . . its glorious standards, a sure sign of happiness and peace."[13]

It was a remarkable 1790 mix of Catholic Christian and philosophical revolutionary symbols: the Constitution that "all the peoples of Europe regard as the morning star that enlightens all who sit in the darkness and shadow of death"; a regenerated empire that will hang suspended between heaven and earth, time and eternity; and the Holy Eucharist, "in the name of the host pure and without stain that will be immolated at the foot of those altars still red and warm [*fumant*] with the blood of Jesus Christ."[14] In fact, the sacred host is evoked as the inspiration to shield the king from the sight of disorder and division. Yes, at this point Father Jacques Roux was counseling prudence, lest the happiness of the day become a memory, and violence profane the sacred name of liberty. Roux reveres "humanity" as the place where religion and virtue abide.

Roux talks his way back and forth across the borderline between hatred somehow compatible with clerical preaching and fanaticism that would make the terrorist. We see him vacillating between the two in the sermon he composed after the supposed assassination of the supposed curé of the supposed parish at Massigny, "L'Apôtre martyr de la Révolution; ou, Discours d'un curé patriote, qui vient d'être assassiné par dix-huit aristocrates" (1791), a long piece with only the minimal requisite mention of God.[15] There is something shadowy in this account, published in order to rally public opinion in favor of a curé of Massigny in the Aude, nominated by the electors of Languedoc and consequently murdered. Roux biographers Maurice Dommanget and Albert Mathiez were unable to find any record of Jacques Roux in Massigny, no record even of a parish (much less a curé) for this period.[16] The text for the sermon was "He has cast the mighty from their thrones and has exalted the humble" (Luke 1:52).

Alongside his regular references to God and prayer, Roux personifies the great patriotic virtues, giving them a kind of spiritual existence on their own: "Love of the fatherland, gentle hope of the liberty that has such great power. . . . Noble and holy liberty to whom alone it belongs to unmake abuses and regenerate morality, give wings of fire to my thoughts."[17] Here he can praise the Revolution without recourse to divine providence; here he cites, rather, "a chain of events that will make this age the most valuable in history and the most loved by future generations."[18] The inspiration of the French has been a "voice," which has not been a supernatural one, but which Roux seems to equate with the "unshakeable courage with which the capital city has thrown off the yoke of slavery and raised the standard of liberty."[19] He honors, too, the spirits of the great French geniuses in the arts and sciences.

As for the throne, he still values the modern French monarchy as protection against the return of ancient violence (he goes back to Abel and Joseph of the Old Testament) and tyrannies: "This fair kingdom was in the days of the [Catholic] League the victim of impassioned factions, the great *Henri* knew how to get rid of them; *Louis* was *alone* against all of Europe and was not taken aback."[20] Before the times of fulfillment, however, come the storms: "Were not the greatest days of Greece and Athens preceded by turmoil? Was not publication of the *Old Law* on Mount Sinai accomplished in the midst of thunder and lightning?"[21] In fact, Roux has to strain to accept the king, who only fits in as a well-controlled part of the nation; they are celebrating "*the anniversary of the fall of despotism*," when "*the monarch and the nation under a vault of steel impenetrable to any human power*, bent their knees before the law and the sound of earthshaking cannons, and came to adore the book of the Constitution, the star of common happiness!"[22]

As Paris moved toward violence in 1792, Jacques Roux was at the center of the action. He was still talking God and love in his "sermons" but damning day-to-day Catholicism—of which he was still a part. This presentation, "Discours sur les moyens de sauver la France et la Liberté"—presumably given at Notre-Dame, though that would have been unlikely—goes on for thirty pages in its modern edition.[23] He first signals religious fanaticism, betrayal by political leaders, and disobedience to the law as principal causes of civil strife in the land. But by "religious fanaticism" he means "priestly hypocrisy." Religion itself he calls "the daughter of heaven, the mother of nature, and of virtue," but in the hands of the priestly "race of hypocrites" it has become "a science of lying, trickery, and perfidious acts: a terrible instrument for sacrificing up men to God the creator of men, in order to bless and sanctify major crimes."[24] Roux rises to championship-level invective against priests who "drink from golden cups the blood of the people." He castigates them as "maddened" (*furieux*) and "stupidly atrocious," listing their murderous exploits across the centuries: "They lit the execution fires of Malabar and of the Inquisition, authorized the madness of the Crusades, the massacres in the Cevennes, the atrocities of St. Bartholomew, and all the sacrilegious campaigns of tyrants against their people."[25] No doubt the abbé Jacques had a problem with his sacerdotal Catholic Church. It represented the heritage of the Druids, he thought, whereas he and his like-minded compatriots were "avid to succeed the apostles and not the Druids, glorying in their evangelical mission, and raising up on the debris of Roman [papal] tyranny, the altar of liberty."[26] He wants the wealth hoarded by the church to circulate in society, for, "despite of the anger of the Vatican," he preaches liberty, equality, and fraternity. "Fatherland, conscience, and God" are his religion, a holy religion that will "force the pride of the [priestly] incense pot, like that of the diadem, to bow before the scepter of the people."[27] As France was invaded by foreign armies, Roux—as did many in his cohort—blamed the king.

From Revolution to Regicide

In his "Discours sur le jugement de Louis-le-dernier, sur la poursuite des agioteurs, des accapareurs et des traîtres," Roux's targets are investors, speculators, and price-fixers of all kinds, but no one more that the embodiment of both commercial and political power, King Louis XVI.[28] Little more than a year after his beautiful evocation of a king united to his people in love, harmony, and service, Roux wanted to "teach to all the peoples of the earth that crime leads tyrants to the scaffold." He said, "Liberty will be only a useless phantom, if you do not turn the explosive force of equality against the dethroned [royal] monster, who is the rallying point of counterrevolutionaries, and who conspires while in prison against the freedom of the people."[29] It is clear that the good abbé is ready for regicide, as he speaks to his fellow Assembly members (Section de l'Observatoire) on the day they are transferring their meeting place to the former church of the Ursulines: "If they are not slaves of those stupid adorers of the monster king's crimes, and if they have not received in advance filthy lucre [*un or corrupteur*] for absolving him, let them hasten to vote for the death of the traitor and perjurer, Louis."[30] Roux is simply—how shall we put it?—raging. He admits that the constituents and he himself were once willing to have a king, but "in their admiring servility" they never meant to justify a monarchical power that killed off its peoples: "Kings reinforce their despotism by the unjust shedding of the people's blood; it is time that the people's freedom be consolidated by the legal shedding of the impure blood of kings."[31] Roux lists the good historical precedents for bumping off rulers. England got rid of Charles Stuart; Rome, the sons of Brutus; and in French history both a descendant of Clovis and a descendant of Charlemagne were deposed. Why would not the French nation, "looking along the ravaged banks of the Meuse and the Moselle, on the heaps of bodies, the cities reduced to ashes" and "hearing the cries of fathers, mothers, and children in tears," firmly judge a king who was captured with a weapon in his hand on the tenth of August?[32] On that day they gained the right to destroy him.

By the beginning of 1793, Roux had so ingratiated himself with the sans-culottes and the Paris Commune that as a member of the General Council of the Commune, he was asked to accompany the king to the guillotine. He did not go as a priest, of course; the king had his own confessor. As Roux himself reported it,

> We were transported to the Temple; there we announced to the tyrant that the hour of execution had arrived.
>
> He asked for several minutes alone with his confessor. He wanted us to deliver a parcel for him, but we remarked that we were only deputed to conduct him to the scaffold. He answered, "That is true." He then gave the parcel to one of our colleagues to bring it to his family, and asked that Cléry, his valet, serve now the queen; in his hurry, he said, "My wife." He further asked that his former servants at Versailles not be forgotten. Then he said to Santerre [commander of the National Guard], "Let us proceed." He crossed the courtyard on foot and got into the second coach. During the trip there reigned a profound silence.
>
> There were no mishaps. We headed up to the navy offices to arrange the official report on the execution. We never took our eyes off Capet until he arrived at the guillotine. It was exactly ten minutes after ten, he had taken three minutes to get out of the coach; he wanted to speak to the people. Santerre was opposed to it; and [the king's] head fell. Citizens present then dipped their pikes or their handkerchiefs in his blood.[33]

That was it: cold-blooded but no indication of any other special perversion. Other stories circulated to the effect that Roux refused the king's request with one or another cheeky or callous response, or that he dipped his handkerchief in the king's blood or delivered a kick to his dead body. Most unlikely. It is true, however, that he later wrote, "I had the honor of bringing the last king of the French to the scaffold."[34] And the irony of a priest

Figure 23 The priest Jacques Roux is the second figure on the left in this image of the king saying farewell to the queen and his children. He was there as an official representative of the guard that had arrived to bring Louis to the guillotine. In all likelihood, Roux believed that helping escort the king to his death was a fitting role for a revolutionary champion of the people.

accompanying a man to execution to ensure, in some formal way, that the sentence be carried out, was not lost on his contemporaries.

Roux's behavior and attitude during the king's execution resulted from a combination of revolutionary concern for the poor and his own destructive and malicious personality. Amazingly, later in the same year, he was treating the Convention to the same behavior and attitudes that he had shown the king, in his *Manifeste des Enragés* (as Albert Mathiez has labeled it). Here Roux harangued speculators and business monopolies as a worse blight than the aristocrats. According to Roux, the income of the workers had declined: "Liberty is only a phantom when one class of men can starve another with impunity. Liberty is only a phantom when the rich have a monopoly on, and the right of life and death over, their fellow men. The Republic is only a phantom when counterrevolution day after day lives off the vital supplies that three-quarters of the population would have to shed tears to obtain."[35] But then he turns on the Convention members, comparing them to the Old Regime, telling them that the poor in England (an enemy) now have it better than the poor French do. All the sordid, selfish economic types can be found among the Convention representatives, he says. Even the Jacobins of the Mountain risk ending their careers "in ignominy" if they neglect reform.

Then Jacques Roux, priest and revolutionary, reiterates all his contempt for his old profession, blaming it for the nation's problems and his own personal problems: "Though a fatal destiny linked me to the priesthood, I renounce the errors of this state with all my heart. . . . I only exercised it in order to have the opportunity to recognize and unmask the crimes of priests. I would like to be in a position to make up for the evils that they have done to humanity by shedding my own blood. Let error, hypocrisy, ambition, and injustice disappear from the surface of the earth forever."[36] At the end of this piece we read the words of a man who, while preaching hatred, proclaims the beauty of peace and love. In one set of lines he says, "Let the French, conquerors of the Rhine and the Pyrénées, from the Alps to the Ocean, crush with thunderous power the coalition army of tyrants; let traitors, plotters, and public leeches die under the sword of national vengeance." Without a break he says, "Let liberty in fast flight conquer the world; let the olive branch, symbol of peace, quickly take the place of the bloody flags of victory; let abundance and happiness reign in the heart of our once suffering fatherland." Too kindly? Next words: "Let tyrants and fanaticism perish!" with a final salute to the recently excoriated Mountain: "Long live the French Republic and the Mountain, health and prosperity to all those who inflamed our hearts with the sacred fire of liberty and virtue."[37]

Brought to judgment, Roux attempted to kill himself with a small knife in the presence of the tribunal, and was brought subsequently to the prison infirmary. Several weeks later in prison he went to work on himself with another knife, this time with success. To all appearances, his violent life and violent death had betrayed those exalted ideas and passionate words that might have, in themselves, promoted the lot of the poor with great effectiveness.[38] He not only followed in the way of the Terror promoters, purveyors, and agents, he led the way—yea even, in his antagonism to the government, striking out in new directions.

Joseph Le Bon: The Terror Agent

There is a charming story to be told about Joseph Le Bon, the priest, recounted by the ever understanding John McManners. Encountering the refractory curé whom he was replacing, Le Bon said, "You are a priest just as I am, my dear Sir. It matters little to the Supreme Being that we do not agree over words, provided we both strive to glorify Him by our conduct."[39] Of the priests turned terrorists, none achieved more notoriety than did Joseph Le Bon. After a short career as a teacher with the Oratorians, he left the congregation to be a constitutional vicar, then (in Pas-de-Calais) a curé. After abandoning the priesthood he was elected mayor of Arras, the city where he was born in 1765. His father was legal officer (*huissier*) and then employee of the local city government. Le Bon received his early education at the Oratorian *collège* in Arras. An early biography reports that fellow students and faculty found him to be, well, today we would say "complex": "He stood out in those early years for his mood swings [*inégalité d'humeur*]: sometimes quiet and recollected as a Carthusian, he barely allowed himself a smile; sometimes passing to the opposite extreme, he broke into bizarre gaiety and dissipation. You would also notice something acrimonious, haughty, and malevolent."[40] But he was a good student: well spoken, and of superior intelligence and good taste. Some thought he was a bit frail, and, if not a coward, at least not much of a fighter. After finishing his studies at the *collège*, he entered the Oratorian Novitiate and was then sent to teach at Beaune. His superiors were satisfied by his spiritual progress and impressed by his intellectual abilities. When he began teaching for the Oratorians he was a major success with his students, a teacher genuinely concerned about their moral and intellectual progress, but one who needed their affection and approval at the same time.

From Community Life to Constitutional Ministry

As a member of the community, he had a choice of remaining a "lay" teacher or becoming a priest. When he was ordained deacon he wrote, "There is no need for me to recommend myself to your prayers; you know how necessary they are for me, distracted more than anything as I am, by so many needs and so much work."[41] Biographers believe that he may not have had sufficient time to prepare his theological studies, and he may have been overly taken with the secular philosophies of the day, but we have no hard evidence of anything out of the ordinary.

Joseph Le Bon was a priest made for revolution: ordained right after Christmas in 1789 by Talleyrand himself, he was filled with such enthusiasm for Christian mission that he wanted to preach in distant lands—that is, to be a classical foreign missionary. At first critical of the new political assemblies, making light fun of their cruder members, he came rather quickly to revolution himself. The question is whether his anger at superiors and colleagues turned him from religious missionary into secular missionary. One troubling incident may have been the turning point.

In May 1790, the school community was celebrating a prelude to the 14 July commemoration. After Mass, several of the students decided to run off to Dijon for more festivities. Le Bon was held responsible for kindling their enthusiasm and was dispatched to bring them back. Whatever the mode of exchange between Le Bon and his superiors, and however deep may have been his earlier antagonism, he certainly turned a minor crisis into a major drama. Back at the school, he tore up his Oratorian garb and declared that he belonged to the community no longer. The act was not definitive, however, with both Le Bon and his superiors working on a more serious, definitive decision.[42] This was, of course, the year of the Constituent Assembly debates on the Civil Constitution of the Clergy.

Earlier, however, he was genuinely pious, writing in June 1789 that "it [shows] not love of God, but love of self, if we abandon him when he wishes to purify our love by depriving us of everything other than himself. . . . The God of love, to whose glory I have sacrificed my life, visits his servant in his tribulations, and in the hidden depths [*au fond de la retraite*] where he pours into souls torrents of the ineffable consolations of virtue."[43] In his everyday life, Le Bon considered himself the victim of his own dedication and attachment to his students, and complained of the rejection he suffered. There are letters across 1788–90 to friends where Le Bon signed himself "Priest of Jesus Christ," and he would not hesitate to give spiritual advice.[44]

The oath of loyalty demanded by the Civil Constitution of the Clergy was not a problem for Le Bon; rather, it presented a new set of opportunities. He was invited to preach in place of refractory Josephites at Châlons-sur-Marne; and then the constitutional bishop of the Côte-d'Or, Jean-Baptiste Volfius, invited him to serve as a parish assistant in the city of Dijon. After looking at several possibilities, and hoping to be chosen curé of a small parish in Beaune, he finally agreed to be curé of Neuville-Vitasse, a town back north near his native Arras. And still there was no peace. Family members, especially his mother, were saddened by his choice of the constitutionals; in addition, the old refractory curé of the new parish was opposed to takeover by a constitutional. Le Bon was sympathetic to both family and curé. He monitored with great anxiety the deteriorating mental health of his mother, and he offered the refractory curé the right to continue to say Mass and see parishioners: "I do not in any way think I have the right to grant or refuse M. Le Bas the right to say Mass; however, this churchman seems to be so decent that I cannot keep myself from granting his request." He urged his people to accept one another, to be open-minded, and to know that God was little concerned with the petty theological and administrative differences now stirring up antagonisms: "Let them remember that people are entitled to their own viewpoints; that we cannot force anyone's belief; that persuasion, not force, brings people to truth."[45]

Little inclined to parish work, he stayed in his room, reading and writing, never seeming to mind that few parishioners attended Mass and few children attended catechism. And when it came time for first communion, he gave relaxed instruction, made no demands on the children, then, later on the day of the celebration itself, took the young people after Vespers to the town cabaret, where he bought each of them a beer. Currying favor with the young had been his habit for a long time, but the cabaret episode was carefully noted.[46] The report was that the villagers distanced themselves from him after that.

Rough in looks (his face had always been marked by chicken pox), strained in his relationships, he nevertheless had a certain eloquence and tried to balance his excitability with the appearance at least of impassibility: "He had at that time the severe look of the teacher"[47] His biographer suggests that Le Bon crossed another threshold here into total political involvement. Seeing church moral teaching as an inferior version of, perhaps only a transition to, the morality of reason, and seeing the church teachings on the one and triune God as rough versions of the religion of the Supreme Being, he believed that the old religious culture would be quickly sloughed off. He criticized the former curé's coldness with the parishioners, he would toss antiaristocratic slogans into his religious teaching, and he got rid of his soutane about the same time as he affected the wearing of a (partial) wig.

From Constitutional Ministry to the Terror

Living not far from Arras, it was inevitable that Le Bon would meet Maximilien Robespierre. When they dined together one day, witnesses remarked that the two seemed to inspire each other to violence. Robespierre's younger brother was there, too, and is said to have tried to introduce some moderation: "He wore himself out trying to calm them and get them to think about something else."[48] But Joseph Le Bon was emerging as a successful public figure. He became a member of the local Société des amis de la Constitution, and proceeded to impress the membership with his superior vision. His star rose quickly, and after election to the local Directory, he was finally chosen to be the mayor of Arras. When the king was finally ousted in August 1792, he quickly got rid of all in the administration whom he took to be "gangrenous."[49] These activities as well as his antagonism to the old church made his consequent abdication of priesthood inevitable.

Elected to the Convention, Le Bon was sent as a *représentant en mission* to Aire, a city in Pas-de-Calais with orders to preempt a federalist movement and root out anything that suggested resistance. "The Committee for Public Safety reports that the counterrevolutionary movement is growing in the city of Aire and other areas of Pas-de-Calais; and that attempts have just been made to put a federalist system in place," said a dispatch. "Decree that citizen Le Bon will be transported immediately to the department to suppress this dangerous plot by effective and active measures. Robespierre, B. Barère, Collot-d'Herbois, Billaud-Varennes, C.-A. Prieur, Carnot."[50] Le Bon then immediately set out to rectify the situation there.[51] Not only did he do his dispatchers proud, but Le Bon attempted to arrange the separation of children from their mothers in order to reeducate them in a "school for equality [*maison d'égalité*], and this after he had already sequestered the "aristocratic and fanatic mothers."[52] This was of a piece with the more fanatic Jacobin ideas as old as Sparta, of education by the state for the state.

Le Bon took well to the authority and dignity of his new duties. When a column of the Armée du Nord passed through Arras, he received them in full mayoral costume: a Henry IV–style hat surmounted by a tricolor panache on his head, a trailing sash around him, and armed with ceremonial saber. He said, "Who would have believed that I would come back here as a representative of the people, invested with unlimited powers! How are aristocrats doing now? And how is our municipality doing now?"[53] On a

Figure 24 A wildly dramatic view of the priest Joseph Le Bon as a bloodthirsty executioner. He is pictured standing on a pile of bodies between the guillotines of Arras and Cambrai. Shirtless, he is drinking blood from one chalice as he holds another up to gather blood gushing from the trunk of a recently guillotined victim. Condemned men, women, and children stand on the left, imploring heaven for help.

different note, he said that he was happy not to see any more of those little wooden statues of saints that earlier had been popular in the region, because all that was superstition for him and his cohorts. He could have mercy on simple criminal misdemeanors. It was the political nonconformists that he was after, reportedly examining fifty thousand letters of sedition and imprisoning a large number of refractory priests.

When both Joseph Le Bon and his wife were in prison, he pushed her to stand fast, of course. But he above all wanted to justify their sacrifice together, he being the one responsible for their imprisonment: "Will we say, because of our troubles, that virtue is a chimera, and that we were wrong to hold ourselves to it? This blasphemy will never enter my heart." With this focus on his own heart and on himself, he says further that he was never a "slave" to riches nor to pride nor to debauchery nor to hate! To be sure, he hated the enemies of France and of the Revolution. And his only crime was the pursuit of villains.[54] She, then, shares the lot of those other women whose husbands worked wholeheartedly for the Revolution. If she should share his lot, she can console herself by their example.[55] On this marriage, and on the marriages of some other former priests, McManners writes, "The passionate allegiance of some of these ecclesiastics to the Revolution, and certain excesses of the dechristianization policies were conditioned by their feelings of sexual release and their gratitude for domestic felicity."[56]

Joseph Le Bon was guillotined at Amiens in 1795.

The *Abdicataires* of 1793–1794

The Convention had been menacing the priests for *incivisme*, lack of *esprit public*, and legislators put together an attractive "retirement" package for all priests, radical or not. They would be immune to public suspicion and legal action against them, and they would receive a pension, *provided* they removed ecclesiastical garb, ceased priestly functions, renounced priesthood itself, and married. Within a few months, the majority of the publicly functioning clergy gave up their clerical functions, in one way or another.[57] Some priests resigned their parishes and the celebration of worship services. Others carefully restricted themselves to abdicating their "function" of priesthood. The formula urged on most of them required the renunciation of the "state" of being a priest, with the handing over of the documents and letters witnessing to their ordinations. Whatever formula they used, however, priests could still hedge their bets. Bernard Plongeron has said of the Paris priests that if this were not a unified action, it was at least a common way of thinking: "Let us sign our abdication, give all the evidence required to prove our patriotism, and continue with the least possible upset our pastoral work, free from continuing persecution."[58] But, in fact, an outspoken minority (developed personal expression is found only in a minority of dossiers) wanted freedom from the old religious constraints, a new status in republican society, and some kind of monetary compensation (the silent majority were not averse to severance pay either). The bishop of Paris himself could not pass up the apparent advantages, and abdicated before the assembled Convention legislators.

Revolutionary Credentials

Abdicating priests flaunted what they took to be their outstanding revolutionary credentials. François Beulazet, an episcopal vicar of Strasbourg,

Map 2 Estimated number of abdicating priests, 1793–1794

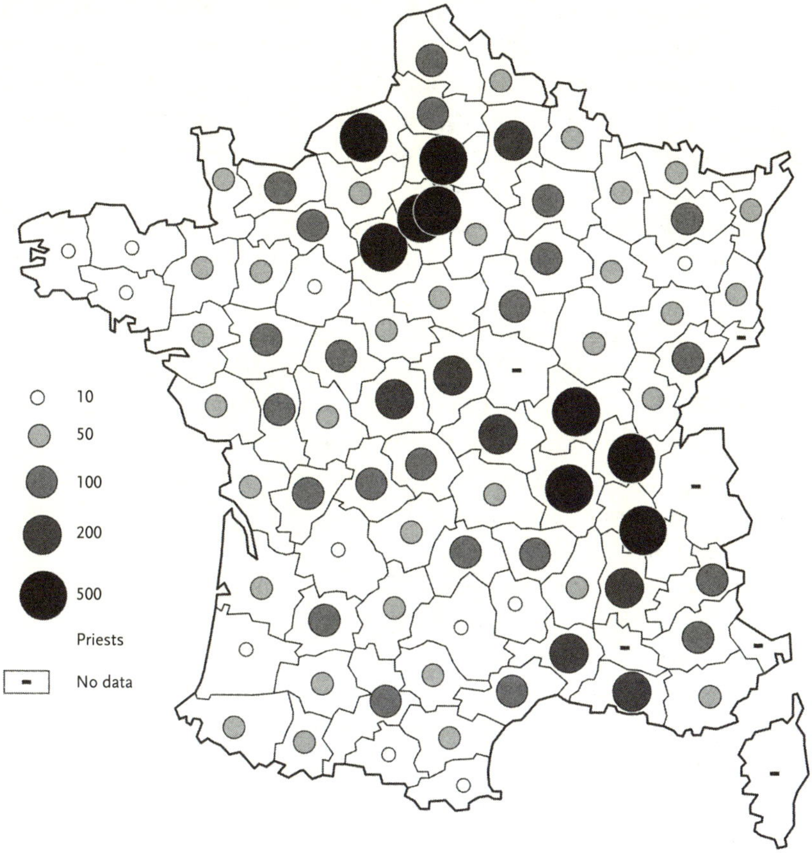

Statistics on the number of active priests who renounced their priestly functions in the individual departments of France across the year II of the revolutionary calendar. Somewhere between fourteen and twenty thousand priests abdicated, so the map should perhaps be interpreted as an indication of percentages, rather than absolute numbers.

was a model of self-promotion: he had been "first" in everything: "First priest of the former province of Alsace to be decorated with the national cocarde and first in line for the oath; first to surrender his silver rings and pay his patriotic dues; creator of the Société populaire de Belfort; first in Strasbourg to point from the pulpit to the veil of hypocrisy which covered up superstition and fanaticism in this city."[59] Such dedication put him in real danger. Once, celebrating the liturgy at the Alsatian city of Saverne, he barely escaped assassination by men furious at his favoritism of constitutionals and his restoration of a languishing patriotic (revolutionary) society.[60] Louis Courtonne was another who considered his accomplishments eminently noteworthy, in fact worthy of emulation: "Legislators. I want and call for revolution, my principles march on ahead of it; the revolution has only to develop these principles with greater force." Wanting an even more dramatic witness than his marriage, he "abjured publicly and voluntarily the charlatanism of a dishonest profession." He also needed government help as sequel to this public submission to the truth in order to care for his old mother, a task already of eight years' standing and for which he did not really have the money.[61] Another curé played the republican game, to the point of changing his name: "I want to be called, instead of Claude-Damas Gillard, Brutus Mucius Scaevola Gillard. Tell me, citizen legislators, when you send me the acceptance of my papers, if you accept my change of name, my zeal, and my love."[62] Dropping Christian names and picking up classical Roman names, pagan heroes instead of Christian saints, was very much the fashion by 1794.

Jacobin and *sans-culotte* were key self-labels. A former vicar in Saône-et-Loire vaunted his campaign against the principal rivals of the Jacobins, the Brissotins (who evolved into the Girondins), as they tried to corrupt those poor, dedicated sans-culottes.[63] He finally had to flee the town, thereby attracting the praise and notice of his fellow Jacobins. There followed a number of assignments: leading a detachment of two hundred men to General Nicolas at Clermont, searching out men who had gone into hiding, such as municipal officers who had fraternized with the Lyonnais and those who had run to help the Muscadins.[64] He was, in effect, the leader on guard duty, carting away the ideologically impure or recalcitrant. A Convention deputy from the Yonne, Alexandre Paintandre, wrote, "I was the first priest chosen by the electors from the district of Tonnerre, because I was known for my patriotism; and I have never given the lie to the favorable opinion that the electors formed about me."[65] And a onetime Franciscan assured the local tribunal that both he and his parents were always revolutionaries at heart: "Born poor of sans-culottes parents, but raised with their prejudices, I pronounced my vows in the order of Minims when I was seventeen." Leaving the order, he then filled the more patriotic position of military chaplain. So, they were faithful churchgoers and he became a priest, but they were all sans-culottes nevertheless.[66]

Attacks on Old Regime Religion and Society

This parading of revolutionary devotion and activity was accompanied by, and sometimes simply degenerated into, attacks on the old clerical and religious ways. Paintandre wrote that he could not really admit to hypocrisy because of his lifelong aversion to it. Given the evils of clerical religion, honesty is the only salvation for a cleric: "I know that any priest who holds to the teachings of the Roman Church can only be a knave, but he who has a few philosophical notions, who checks into the eternal laws of reason and truth could not be fooled by the gross errors of this lie-filled religion."[67] And so it went for these abdicators. For one, the aristocracy was a blight on human existence, but religious fanaticism was "of all the heads of the hydra, the most deadly for the people." It could be said that religion so channels fear and distorts the conscience that healthy citizenship becomes impossible.[68] For another, ordination was a sort of original sin; he, accordingly, wanted to "obliterate the original and impure stain of my ordination, renouncing the works of the demon of fanaticism and superstition."[69] Abdication was the occasion to cover priesthood with insults: "No more priests, the public good requires it; consequently, no more priestly papers. I surrender to you my own. Holding charlatanism in horror, why would I need the papers of a charlatan?"[70] But here, abdication did not preclude the proud inclusion of a homily to celebrate the marriage of a colleague.[71] So, the laws of nature are real religion, whose emissaries should give their all to the "extinction of fanaticism."[72]

Sheer nastiness suffused some texts, such as the testimony that began, "It is at the foot of the Mountain, which has hurled thunderbolts at the foul tyrant and his lascivious spouse and their vile servants, that I come before you to declare that I renounce forever the exercise of Catholic worship."[73] At times, nastiness is matched with at least minor eloquence. An Oratorian wrote the following: "I have always combated and detested priests. Do not suffer it to happen that these profoundly perverse men any longer oblige a simple and good people to prostrate themselves before a piece of bread, out of which their insolent pride would effect the creation of a god. Do not suffer it to happen that these priests, abusing the secret of confession, any longer divide families, cause blood to flow, overturn empires, and govern in any way they choose the human race."[74] At times the nastiness is simply sarcasm gone awry, as in one Benedictine's evocation of ordination day: "In

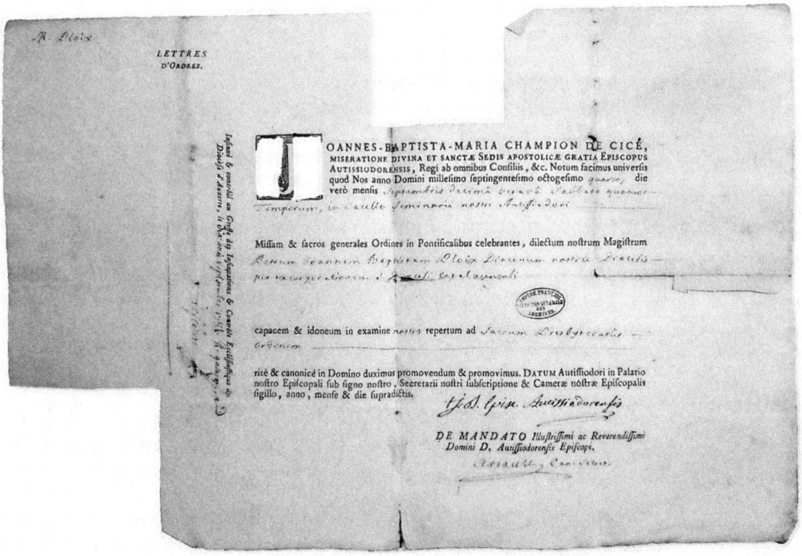
LETTRES D'ORDRES.

JOANNES-BAPTISTA-MARIA CHAMPION DE CICÉ, MISERATIONE DIVINA ET SANCTÆ SEDIS APOSTOLICÆ GRATIA EPISCOPUS AUTISSIODORENSIS, Regi ab omnibus Consiliis, &c. Notum facimus universis quod Nos anno Domini millesimo septingentesimo octogesimo quarto, die verò mensis

Missam & sacros generales Ordines in Pontificalibus celebrantes, dilectum nostrum Magistrum

capacem & idoneum in examine nostro repertum ad

ritè & canonicè in Domino duximus promovendum & promovimus. DATUM Autissiodori in Palatio nostro Episcopali sub signo nostro, Secretarii nostri subscriptione & Cameræ nostræ Episcopalis sigillo, anno, mense & die supradictis.

DE MANDATO Illustrissimi ac Reverendissimi Domini D. Autissiodorensis Episcopi.

Figure 25 A priest's formal ordination papers were kept across the years as he moved from one assignment to another. The above document was surrendered by one of the abdicating priests as a formal renunciation of the priestly vocation. This was always done so that the civil authorities would have the proof they required before granting any of the rewards or privileges promised. Authorities could not be sure that an "abdication" agreement was anything more than a promise to cease all public functioning.

1772, because of my destiny, I was forced to appear before a man who was dressed as a woman. This man said a few words that I never understood and put some kind of drug on my fingers. . . . After that they told me that I was a priest." And after this ham-fisted description of vestments and anointing, he begged his witnesses not to "regard [him] as one of those Druids who have tormented our Republic by their infamous maneuvers."[75]

The self-justifying mode was most prominent when one's own marriage was at issue. The foolishness of the old religion, the misbehavior of colleagues, and the opposition of families motivated these priests to strong promotion of the married state. One priest had been married for years: "I heard the gentle voice of nature. I secretly married a girl of my age, whose virtue and charm have been my greatest happiness for twenty-two years." Betrayed by a clerical colleague with government connections, he was carried off like a criminal, held in a Franciscan convent for two years, and treated with the cruelty bred of "the Inquisition and monastic callousness."[76] Another explained the difficulties of arranging marriage in the old social context. His fiancée was still slightly underage, but more importantly the father, "still attached to the old prejudices . . . could not bring himself to envisage his daughter with a priest."[77] A priest who had worked under Claude Fauchet reported with obvious satisfaction and, I do believe, a smile, his move from the tradition of celibacy to the new civil celebration of marriage: "From the moment that the law allowed priests to choose a companion, I forgot about the existence of pope and councils, I heard the voice of nature, and I exchanged an old breviary for a young Républicaine."[78]

Praise of Reason

Positive eloquence was saved for the Revolution and for reason. A former vicar at Notre-Dame Cathedral said that under the Old Regime he was persecuted for his views and values. If only his colleagues would abdicate also, they would contribute to this "triumph of liberty, reason, and truth."[79] Far more eloquent was a curé from Calvados, who combined an earnest prayer to reason with a few choice labels for the old religious symbols: "Divine Reason, receive my homage. I have always offered you true worship in the secrecy of my heart, and may it today be as bright as the light. I make my offering on the altar just put in place for the people most worthy of you. Free at last, rejoicing with my whole being, I depose upon [the altar] the ridiculous baubles, the absurdities that have hung on my neck until this moment."[80] A handsomely written letter, seven pages long and bound with a decorative ribbon, made the French nation a model of this worship of reason: "Soon the altars raised in honor of the new divinity [Supreme Being] will radiate out from the center to the whole Republic. Soon all foreign nations for whom the French serve as a model and guide *with good reason*, will abjure their prejudices and errors in the sanctuaries of the new temples and sing with us timeless hymns to the glory of liberty and equality."[81] Jean-Baptiste Géruzez, notable as a leading and fluent letter writer to *La Feuille Villageoise*, drummed up his standard praise of philosophy. In effect he gave a little sermon to the Assembly members: "Legislators, you have received of its [philosophy's] fullness, and its life-giving spirit is hovering over you." If everything these legislators do is channeled to the promotion of reason, they will be able to say, "The blind see; the deaf hear; the crippled walk; the dead come back to life; and the gospel of liberty and equality is proclaimed to the sans-culottes."[82]

In the light of reason, priestly activity would have been a waste of time: "A priest at twenty-four, I was named curé of three huge parishes . . . in the department of Deux-Sèvres, where I vegetated for thirty-six years."[83] This from an episcopal vicar of the department, who at seventy-one years old (the documentation of his ordinations and other clerical dignities was surely one of the most extensive submitted) simply and calmly stated that he had always promoted the Revolution. The old life was often lived against every inclination, said another, typical of the former priests who were only too grateful to the revolutionary government, "wise and benevolent," that made it possible for those "not infatuated by fanaticism to abdicate forever both the functions of ministry and the priestly character."[84]

The Making of an Abdicataire

Sixty-two-year-old Father Pasquer bemoaned and berated his socially insular and narrow education: "At sixteen, without experience of the world, never having been out of the sight of the church bell tower of my village, and having been educated only by pedants and others as untrained as myself, I was urged to cast myself into an order of fanatic friars [*mendiants*], then a standard resource for children of the lower middle class who like myself were born without means."[85] Religious education only filled his head with worse things, though after ordination he was happy to be a priest: "At the age of twenty-four, having my head stuffed with theological mumbo jumbo [*fatras théologique*] and the decisions of the casuists [*faiseurs de conscience*], I took orders with the best faith in the world, and with the satisfaction that a young priest feels when his conscience tells him that it is right to work in the vineyard of the Lord."[86]

But wider learning caused him to relativize religion: "At thirty years old, instructed by my own readings and by the trips that put me in a situation where I could study the world and above all the genius and the manners of the ministers of the principal sects which divided it, I came to recognize that all religions are only institutions invented by ambitious men to make others over into servitude, and that their dogmas are the workings of a delirious mind. Their various cults, methodical juggling acts with a seriousness and pomp that impress the vulgar crowd; all this can briefly amuse a philosopher, who, quickly angered by the charlatanism of the priests, steps back deploring the evils produced when they [the priests] take advantage of the credulity of weak mortals."[87]

With eloquence, originality, and a certain creative irritability, Father Pasquer set down the whole gamut of complaints in the abdicator repertory: resentment of formation and education, denunciation of credulity and the dishonesty of churchmen, contempt for the biblical tradition and Catholic teaching, personal satisfaction upon returning to normal life where the only rule is the rule of reason.

Outspoken abdicating priests—and I have highlighted the outspoken minority—made great drama of their revolutionary lives, showing how each contribution to the movement automatically gained them credentials as bona fide revolutionaries, some reaching for the *Jacobin* and *sans-culotte* labels. Many of them could not prevent themselves from attacking their old ways of life, the Old Regime priestly careers, and the old Catholic religion that they had come to see as decadent and damaging to its adherents: parents were to blame and marriage was the solution. Whether intellectual or not, they voiced a standardized praise of reason that was the lowest common denominator of Enlightenment philosophies. It would appear that convinced *abdicataires* wanted to remove the constraints of the priestly status and function for the sake of a better life for themselves and, often enough, better service to others in such careers as teaching and publishing. They survived; some of them even flourished; but by definition, the convinced *abdicataires* were no longer in the service of the church. So, if there was ever to be a revival of Catholic Christianity in post-Terror France, it would have to come from the priests and bishops who worked to structure a new version of the Constitutional Church.

Part Three

REVIVAL, 1795–1802

It was not until February 1795 that the post-Thermidorian Convention restored freedom of worship and more formally declared the separation of church and state, presaged by the earlier termination of subsidies to the church. Churchmen could not reopen their parishes at will, because they had to formally declare their submission to the Republic. The government had its own problems, with armed royalists who landed on the Breton coast (Quiberon), with groups of still active sans-culottes, and with a reactionary middle class that vainly tried (until dispersed by Napoleon in October 1795 with his famous "whiff of grapeshot") to prevent the meeting of the Directory, successor to the Convention and established by the Constitution of the Year III.

Although Notre-Dame Cathedral reopened in September 1795, there were major government lapses into the old suppression of refractories, and even of the former constitutionals. Now reconstituted by religiously charismatic and shrewdly political bishops, on the one hand, and an engaged team of former constitutional priests (the so-called presbytery) on the other, the French Catholic Church had to be rebuilt from the ground up. The bishops produced two encyclicals in 1795, one before and one after the reopening of Notre-Dame. And the clergy had to contend all along with the schizophrenic Directory government. Set up to preclude a bloody reprise of the

Robespierre–Terror years, agitated alternately by Jacobin and royalist politicians, the Directory authorities at first gave the constitutional bishops and priests something of a free hand in their apostolate—Catholic legislators who demanded greater religious freedom were among the deputies—but also demanded of everyone an oath declaring hatred of royalty. Doggedly, the legislators voted measures to continue the Convention-era programs across the Directory years, supporting further development of the revolutionary festival system, and encouraging the Deistic religion-substitute known at "Theophilanthropy." Their real preoccupation was the success of the French armies advancing into the German and Italian states. The victories of General Bonaparte in Italy, making possible the establishment of revolutionary republics, were followed by a march northward that brought the Austrian government to the negotiating table. At the same time Napoleon arranged for the troops at home to support a virtual coup by the leftist leaders of the Directory in September 1797. There were further "coups" in 1798 and 1799, the first to purify the legislature of far-left members and the second to secure greater legislative control of the committee of directors, and these had ripple effects on priestly life. Refractories again had to endure deportation and death.

With a series of adroit political and military maneuvers by Sieyès and Bonaparte, the Consulate was established. Only then was the old Deist festival system dismantled—though not all at once, for Napoleon wanted to take measure of the religious tensions of the day. When the Concordat between Napoleon's government and the papal administration was finally promulgated in April 1802, the organizational revival of the Constitutional Church was definitely over, and the ex-constitutionals could only hope that the time-honored principles of Gallicanism would live on in the attitudes and style of a critical mass of the bishops and priests of France.

Priests and Bishops

Chapter 8. A handful of bishops and a dispersed network of priests worked to remake the old Constitutional Church, none more than the shrewd and talented Augustin Clément, an aristocrat who had promoted Jansenist ideas and programs since before his ordination fifty years earlier. It was he who initiated the meeting that brought leading constitutional bishops together in Paris at the end of 1794. Together they tried to build an organization with a mass of usable parts left over from the earlier experiment: in effect, the bishops and priests who still believed in and wanted a specifically French Catholic—that is, Gallican—Church. This was a *new* Constitutional Church, a successor to the old one that had official government status from 1791 to 1794. Paris was, of course, the locus of the most determined effort of the United Bishops, formed around Grégoire and Clément; they produced two encyclicals in 1795—in March and in December—restoring Catholic life and Gallican Church discipline on the one hand, and reworking the relationship of this church to the state on the other. Naturally, the dissemination of these encyclicals was very limited, not an even match for the subsequent promotion of civil religion by the Directory government. The revolutionary calendar with its festivals and ten-day weeks, each culminating in a décadi celebration, was maintained, and the best the constitutional clergy could do was to promote the complementarity of the separate, not exactly parallel, calendars.

Chapter 9. Claude Le Coz and Jean-Baptiste Royer, dedicated and intelligent bishops, became, in spite of themselves, principal players (if not counterplayers) in the councils organized by the United Bishops. Le Coz encouraged the common efforts of Catholic church and republican government. He was not convinced of the timeliness of the 1797 Council at which he presided, but he kept order and assured dissemination of discussions and decrees on marriage, education, the liturgy, internal organization (the ever-controversial election of bishops), and a viable church–state arrangement. After the council, he supported reform efforts and traditional moral authority, defending the marriage bond, celibacy, and the dignity of the pope. Always a backer of Grégoire, he nevertheless constructed his own unique apostolate.

Chapter 10. Royer became bishop of Paris almost by default, although he had made worthwhile contributions to the constitutional apostolate as bishop of the Ain and by helping to reestablish a major Paris parish. In Paris, he had to face criticism from the United Bishops and the antagonism of some of his priests. At the turn of the century, a principal consolation was the success of Napoleon, the victories of his armies, and the stable benevolence of his government. At the Council of 1801, Royer was reluctant to preside. He had to agree to the council, of course, because it was held in Paris, but he remained in the shadow of the United Bishops, as Grégoire and Le Coz tried to steer the soon-to-be-superfluous council toward the challenges of church staffing and political negotiating.

Chapter 11. Napoleon had already decided on a solution to the chronic religious tensions in France: he would have his representatives, clerical and secular, negotiate an arrangement with the pope, a concordat between the church and the French state. Napoleon and the pope together required the resignation of all bishops, non-constitutional and constitutional, to the consternation of many of them. Throughout 1801, the government required departmental surveys of priests and bishops who could best serve the new church. Constitutionals had to face a cold welcome: without Napoleon's insistence, the pope would never have accepted them, and without the pope's acquiescence, the people—over the years more and more anti-constitutional—would have ultimately withdrawn substantial support. When the Catholic church of the Concordat between Napoleon's government and the papal administration was finally promulgated, in April 1802 (signed in July of the preceding year), the old Rome-loyal bishops and priests dominated. Those who had served in the constitutional churches throughout the revolutionary decade had to reintegrate themselves into post-Concordat church life, either as priests or as laymen, and were often obliged to ask for special dispensations to do so. The restored church was more papal Roman Catholic and less Gallican Roman Catholic.

Chapter 12. Priests who were able to serve in the new church initially hoped for acceptance of their priestly apostolates as they had tried to exercise them in the preceding six years. Twelve of the former constitutional bishops had been assigned to new dioceses, and the official journal of the constitutionals, *Annales de la religion*, continued to appear. However, the pages of the final years of the journal reveal frustration with demands for renunciation of the very ideas and efforts they believed necessary for the flourishing of Catholicism in France. In a series of vignettes, reviews, and complaints, former constitutional priests reported their efforts and their hopes that the time-honored principles of Gallicanism would live on in the attitudes and style of a critical mass of the bishops and priests of France. Many never repudiated the spiritual lives and the reforming ministries of the revolutionary years. But vindication of these lives and ministries they were not to see.

Chronology

1795

17 February	Restoration of freedom of worship.
21 February	Decree on the separation of church and state.
15 March	Encyclical sent out to all constitutional clergy by the United Bishops.
30 May	Declaration requiring submission to laws of the Republic in order to reclaim the use of churches.
21 July	Defeat of the royalists at Quiberon on the Brittany coast.
6 September	Banishment of priests who returned from exile.
8 September	Ceremony formally reopening the Notre-Dame Cathedral in Paris.
23 September	Proclamation of the Constitution of the Year III.
29 September	Laws regulating parish structures and priestly loyalty.
5 October	Bonaparte crushes royalist insurrection in Paris.
25 October	Reapplication of 1792 and 1793 laws against priests subject to deportation.
3 November	Official beginning of the Directory government.
13 December	Second encyclical of the United Bishops.

1796

19 February	End of assignats, originally issued using nationalized church property as collateral.
11 April	Law against bell ringing and all other public calls to worship.
5 July	Draft of a papal letter authorizing submission to the Republic revealed.
4 December	Weakening of anticlerical legislation.

1797

15 January	First Theophilanthropist ceremony in Paris.
March–April	Elections bringing many pro-Catholic moderate and right-wing deputies to power.
17 June	Speech of Camille Jordan, monarchist legislator, demanding freedom of religious practice and bell ringing.

15 August	Opening of the first National Council of the Constitutional Church.
24 August	Repeal of 1792 and 1793 laws against non-juring and deportable priests.
4 September	Coup of Fructidor, with Directory leaders countermanding the seating of monarchists elected to the rightest legislature.
5 September	Law imposing on practicing clergy the oath of "hatred of royalty and anarchy, of attachment and loyalty to the Republic and to the Constitution of the Year III."
12 November	Closing of the first National Council.
15 December	Grégoire complains in the legislature against republican calendar and institutions.

1798

3 April	Decree making republican calendar and festivals obligatory for markets, spectacles, fairs, and so forth.
11 May	Coup of Floréal, wherein the two legislatures invalidate the elections of Jacobin legislators, but also of some royalists.
5 July	Law forbidding publication of the *Annales de la religion*, which then appeared temporarily under a new title.
4 August	Law requiring the closing of public offices and schools on the décadi.
9 September	Law requiring that all public date references be in accord with the republican calendar.

1799

18 June	Coup of Prairial, wherein the two legislatures reshuffle the Directory membership to make it more submissive to the legislators.
1 August	Restrictions on liberty of the press lifted.
29 August	Death of Pius VI at Valence.
10 November	Coup of Brumaire, putting Consulate in place with Napoleon as first consul.
29 November	Abrogation of deportation laws against the refractories.

23 December	Law suppressing the festivals except 14 July and 22 September.
25 December	Constitution of the Year VIII in force.
28 December	Law allowing unsold churches to be used for worship.

1800

14 March	Election of Pius VII.
26 July	Law ending obligatory celebration of the décadi.
23 September	Feast of premier Vendémiaire, celebrating the union of past and present glory, followed by an audience of various delegations with Napoleon, during which Napoleon takes note of the constitutional–refractory antagonism.

1801

29 June	Opening of the second National Council.
15–16 July	Signing of the Concordat.
16 August	Closing of the second National Council.

1802

8 April	Organic Articles added to the Concordat, giving the government control of the publication of papal decrees and of legal cases concerning ecclesiastics.
9 April	Official reception of Cardinal Caprara, whose legation had reconciliation of priests as a principal duty.
11 April	Official notification of nomination sent to eight of the twelve ex-constitutional bishops who were ultimately nominated to the concordatory church; amnesty decreed for the émigrés, priests, and all others.
18 April	Promulgation of the Concordat.
29 July	Nomination of Joseph Fesch, former constitutional priest and uncle of Napoleon, as archbishop of Lyon.

Chapter Eight

THE NEW CONSTITUTIONAL FRENCH CHURCH

Henri Grégoire and the strongest constitutional bishops reorganized the French church according to the principles they had been preaching all along. Augustin Clément, that hardworking old maverick of an ultra-Jansenist, invited the bishops to his Paris residence for the express purpose of renewing the Constitutional Church under a strong episcopate.[1] "United Bishops" (*Evêques réunis*) was what these constitutional leaders called themselves, and *Annales de la religion* (issued from 1795 to 1804) was their official journal, a veritable summa of their accomplishments and hopes. Among the principal collaborators were Grégoire himself; Jean-Pierre Saurine, constitutional bishop of Landes (after Napoleon's Concordat with the Church, bishop of Strasbourg); Claude Le Coz, constitutional bishop of Ille-et-Vilaine (after the Concordat, archbishop of Besançon); Jean-Baptiste Royer, constitutional bishop of the Ain (and later, of Paris); and Eléonore-Marie Desbois de Rochefort, constitutional bishop of the Somme.[2] The editor was Noël Castera de Larrière, a theologian who earlier was a principal contributor to and then editor of the leading Jansenist journal, *Nouvelles ecclésiastiques.* The United Bishops were not the parish priests of Paris, of course, and therein lay a problem. The pastors of the old functioning constitutional parishes, though not hostile, were wary of any attempts to redo the Paris ministry, especially the cathedral ministry, without their full participation. They organized themselves into a presbytery, a daring 1790 idea whose time had come, they thought, in a limited partnership with the United Bishops, about the same time as Royer, the bishop of Ain, was finishing his fill-in work replacing the curé of the parish of Saint-Médard. As one of their first official acts, the priests of the presbytery then chose one of their number as the new curé of Saint-Médard, officially reopened 20 April 1795.[3]

Desbois de Rochefort guaranteed not only the publication of *Annales*, but also the establishment of the constitutionals' publication center, the Imprimérie chrétienne, on the rue Saint-Jacques. He was an enthusiastic, though not pastorally successful, bishop: he preferred to write and edit on behalf of the church rather than go to Amiens to face the pastoral challenge and the interpersonal conflicts of his diocese. He went there occasionally and even tried his hand at a diocesan synod. He was present at the two Constitutional Church councils of 1797 and 1801, where the United Bishops tried to assert their authority over all constitutional priests, some of whom believed that they had their own distinct authority. Across these years he, in effect, put his entire fortune at the disposal of Grégoire.

Le Coz and Royer operated somewhat apart from the core of the United Bishops, for opposite reasons. Le Coz had a vast agenda he seemed unwilling to leave to anyone else, and Royer was reluctant to force a strong or peculiar stand on anyone else. In the end, he was made bishop of Paris for this very reason—a compromise candidate, in other words. Desbois de Rochefort, with his high administrative profile, actually had a low ideological profile. But by holding together the *Annales de la religion*, he ensured that the United Bishops could always see their theology and programs in print. They wrote up precisely and concretely in *Annales* points and programs (which sometimes had only a shadowy existence).

The United Bishops saw themselves as the authentic leadership of the Catholic Church in France, representing a purer form of Catholicism than the exaggerated papal version promoted in France and in Rome itself. They believed that they could be loyal to Rome without catering to the papal entourage (who had the pope overplaying his own prerogatives). And the government promulgated laws facilitating the reestablishment of religious practice and the free reorganizing of religious administration. Churches and chapels were reopened, although services continued to be monitored by police, and the government was obliged to stay out of church affairs. Not long before this, the *Courrier de l'égalité* reported, "Yesterday, Sunday, there were two kinds of lines: a line at the Mass and a line at the bakery entrance," all of this culminating in the great filled-church celebrations of Christmas 1794.[4] But the United Bishops, finding themselves short of clergy, faithful, and government support, issued two encyclicals, in March and December 1795, looking toward a Council of the Constitutional Church to be held in 1797. Along the way, as the primary liturgists of the nation, they meant to direct public celebrations so they could lead toward real worship, rather

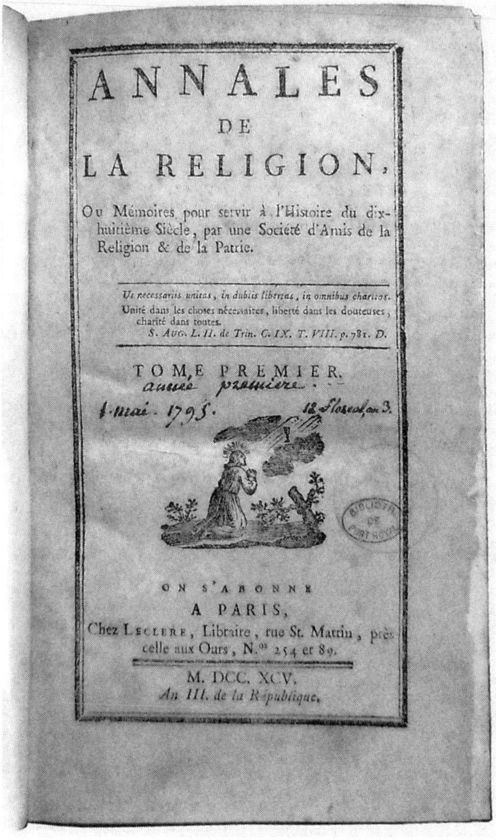
ANNALES
DE
LA RELIGION,
Ou Mémoires pour servir à l'Histoire du dix-huitième Siècle, par une Société d'Amis de la Religion & de la Patrie.

Ut necessariis unitas, in dubiis libertas, in omnibus charitas.
Unité dans les choses nécessaires, liberté dans les douteuses, charité dans toutes.
S. AUG. L. II. de Trin. C. IX. T. VIII. p. 781. D.

TOME PREMIER.
année première.
1 mai. 1795. 12 floréal an 3.

ON S'ABONNE
A PARIS,
Chez LECLERE, Libraire, rue St. Martin, près celle aux Ours, N.os 254 et 89.
M. DCC. XCV.
An III. de la République.

Figure 26 Annales de la religion, the journal of the United Bishops, consisting of leading bishops of the former Constitutional Church who wished to continue the French Catholicism that had been reformed in coordination with the revolutionary government—but who, with the end of the Convention, had no official status because of the separation of church and state. This publication helped center and interpret the restructuring efforts of this new version of the Constitutional Church.

than away from it. Revolutionary festivals had been introduced as early as 1790, had been systematized under the Convention, and were doggedly promoted under the Directory. According to the new revolutionary calendar, the entire year was divided into weeks of ten days each, thereby impeding the Christian celebration of Sunday, the first day of a seven-day week.

Damage Control: The First Encyclical Letter

In their first encyclical letter, in March 1795, the bishops stress the disastrous state of the church, and their post-Terror apostolate to repair the damage. They try to rally all priests and all lay Catholics by reestablishing their own episcopal authority. Their goal was a Gallican church that could work with the French government. Principles were promoted for reconciling priests, for administering dioceses, and for assuring the priority of worship.[5]

"Of all the persecutions that have afflicted the Gallican Church since the beginning . . . none perhaps has brought together so much treachery, violence, and cruelty as the last one": they believe themselves to be the special victims of the disaster, hoping that the "cowards and false-hearted men" who have betrayed Christianity will give over their days to a repentance as public as their destructiveness.[6] On the other hand, priests who remained faithful amid the dangers, the threats of prison and the chaos all about them, should give the church new hope. Now, priests are needed to "preach out with new confidence the saving divine word."[7] Out comes all their antagonism toward the Revolution with all of its horrors in a collage of scripture references: "The vineyard of the Lord has been laid waste. A small number of corrupt men . . . have given the bodies of God's servants as prey to the birds of the air. They have caused blood to flow like water all around Jerusalem, and they have permitted no one to bury them." All revolutionary destructiveness was considered sacrilegious, of course: "How many acts of impiety have they committed in the sanctuary! They have gloried in insulting God amid solemn prayers. They have beaten down the doors of the holy place, they have profaned and thrown to the ground the tabernacle of his holy name. They have conspired among themselves and said in one voice, 'Let us end and abolish from the land the festivals dedicated to the All-Powerful.'"[8]

Coming back to the "let us pardon them" mode, they then continue in a "we sinners" mode, recognizing that God permitted the attacks on a Christianity already profaned by the irreverence and lip service of its members. But now there seems to be a window of opportunity: if the persecution is not over, it has at least slowed down, and there is the beginning of freedom of religion: "Religion appears to emerge from the tomb and rise up amid ruins."[9]

Restoration of Discipline

The United Bishops write to rally *all* the bishops, who, humble and aware of their own guilt, must enter the sanctuary to purify it. And now begins the theme of pure, early Christianity: "The religion of Jesus Christ was brought to our ancestors by the first apostles. It is incorruptible, unchangeable in faith and morals: whatever it teaches, it has taught from its beginnings and will teach unto the consummation of the world."[10] This is more than you can say for the rules and customs distorted beyond recognition. Pure French Christianity, the Gallican Church, with its respect for the earliest tradition, has fallen on hard times, confronting a classic dilemma in its reform efforts: "The majority of those who can remedy [the church's problems] are insensitive to them; those who are sensitive to them cannot remedy them."[11] But God has given France another chance, and the new version of the old Constitutional Church is *it*. The ancient discipline can be restored, and the political challenge can be met. In response to the confused church–state relationship, the bishops want justice and protection from the government, and would themselves expect to offer submission and loyalty to the government. Love of God and country will get them through: "For we are children of the light and not children of darkness, and only he who does evil hates the light."[12]

The perversions of discipline belong to the medieval period, with its barbarism and False Decretals, and to modern times.[13] And they need to escape back to the real sources of church tradition: "Faithful to the wishes of the councils, we will bring order and discipline and uniformity to administration, prayers, and teaching, which is so well suited to the unity of the church, and harks back to the oldest forms in the first centuries. They presented a moving spectacle to those who 'adore God in spirit and truth.'"[14] The United Bishops are particularly concerned lest the constitutional bishops, randomly surviving and in isolation, lose homogeneity and common effort. Innovations and precipitate action will lead to anarchy within, and fuel calumny from without.

Together in Paris, the United Bishops are obviously trying to seize the moment. Recognizing the chance nature of all this, they are able to cite an important precedent in church history: "We would even have been able without temerity to give to our assembly a name used all across antiquity, when they labeled as COUNCILS those gatherings of bishops who sometimes in Constantinople or in other key cities, concerned themselves with the problems of religion."[15] They give here a reference to the old text of Thomassin, *Discipline ecclésiastique*, which dignifies the more important ecclesiastical gatherings with the label "council." And it looks as if this is supposed to be a plain and simple church enterprise in the face of special difficulties: prudence and Christian charity should smooth them away. The bishops are not trying to make this up whole cloth, but to pull together what remains. They count on their fellow bishops to advise them, to anticipate problems in their own dioceses, and to both rectify and improve what they, the United Bishops, are presenting. Finally, they are ready for their formal declaration:

> We the bishops of France, gathered in Paris and assembled in the name of Jesus Christ, after having invoked the Holy Spirit, consulted the most authentic and respectable sources [*monuments*] of the faith and discipline of the church, and having called together around us the priests and faithful worthy of commendation by their piety and their wisdom, we make a declaration of our faith and sentiments before the universal church, and we submit to the wisdom of our brothers, the bishops residing in their respective dioceses, and we address to the presbyteries of the churches with no bishop [*veuves*] temporary rules of discipline that seem to us applicable to the Gallican church needs at the end of a [period of] persecution and at a period of the reestablishment of Catholic worship.[16]

Fundamentals of Gallicanism

"Our Faith and Our Sentiments" follows, a numbered list that puts in order the fundamentals of their Gallicanism.[17] The faithful and their pastors, united in faith and in participation in the sacraments, form one body, of which Christ is the invisible head and the pope the visible head, but the bishops make it abundantly clear that they have no absolute dependence on the pope: "The bishops, the successors of the apostles, receive from Jesus Christ, by [episcopal] consecration, their power and their authority."[18] Taking off from Paul to the Romans 10:15, "No one should preach if he is not sent," they cite the Council of Nicaea: "The bishop must be constituted by all the bishops of the province, but if that is too difficult because of urgent necessity or great distance, three of them together in the same place will impose hands on the condition that all consent to it, and make this known in writing. The confirmation of what is done in each province must be given by the metropolitan bishop."[19] They cite, too, the Council of Trent, which confirmed the establishment by divine authority of bishops, priests, and other ministers, carefully noting that "the bishops are superior to the priests."[20] Priests, presbyters, were a fundamental challenge for the United Bishops: "We expressly condemn presbyterianism." "Pastors of the second order," the priests are "associated" with the bishops in the mission of pastoring, teaching, and governing.

Post-persecution Policies

Turning their attention to government, the bishops write, "Religion commands us to obey the ruling powers: following the example of the first Christians and the faithful of all eras, we make it our duty to be submissive to the laws of the Republic, to pray for it, to concern ourselves with its prosperity, to respect its magistrate, and to encourage the same sentiments in the faithful confided to our care."[21] And here marriage and divorce law is the first political challenge. They recognize the civil effects of political authority, but inasmuch as the church does not permit divorce, her priests are forbidden to give the nuptial blessing to divorced Catholics. Labeling celibacy as the "ancient, constant, and universal discipline" of the church, they forbid the exercise of ministry to all priests "who marry after their ordination." The possibility of priesthood is open to widowers and those who have no further marital obligation.

There is a long list of regulations to set straight what is confused and also to legislate organizational policy. It begins with a wonderful lineup of the difficulties the priests have gotten themselves into, all of them serious enough to preclude any return to active priestly duty. The bishops deal with the clergy, beginning with those who have renounced their faith, and including abdicators, those who married, and those who even persecuted the church.[22] They follow the precedents laid down in the *De Lapsis* of St. Cyprian, chapter 19, of the Council of Nicaea, the Councils of Elvira, Arles, and Ancyra, and the canons of Peter of Alexandria; in particular, they promote the principles established by the late medieval theologian Jean Gerson in their own context. Speaking of the Avignon schism (two popes, one at Avignon and the other at Rome), Gerson had said that schisms occur not only between church members and church authorities, but also among church members themselves. Here, then, were all the things that the refractories and traditional Catholics were doing to the constitutionals. What a scandal when church members regard those who take the other side in a controversy or remain neutral as excommunicated, the very thing that the refractories had been doing to them. When constitutionals were in full exercise of their ministry, the refractories most degraded them: "There is a recklessness, a scandal that reeks of heresy, to claim that the sacraments of the church . . . have no efficacy, that children are not baptized, that priests are not really priests, that they cannot consecrate . . . that it is not permitted to hear their Masses or to receive the sacraments from them."[23]

Reorganizing Dioceses

The bishops establish the ecclesiastical jurisdictions in accord with the new regional layout (for bishops) and the old parish layout (for curés). Ten of the dioceses will have priority over others in their region, with each of the ten bishops called a metropolitan. Other bishops will be subordinated to the local metropolitans. In any case, the sole appropriate way to choose a bishop is by election, and this in conformity with the rules that have come down from the primitive church, insist the United Bishops (this, as we know, being a major issue for them). Elections were at the center of the dispute about the acceptability of the Civil Constitution. Until the election, the see will be surveyed by the metropolitan and nearby bishops. Also in conformity with ancient tradition, the bishop should have two advisory boards, one composed of "pastors of the second order" (the United Bishops' pointed way of referring to priests), and the other composed of curés of the see city and the priests associated with the bishop in the governing of the diocese. The so-called presbytery can have fewer members than was customary in the early church, but they must be of irreproachable moral quality. And here the United Bishops had to be careful, because the presbytery of Paris in particular was virtually a separate power base.

All bishops are obligated to pastoral letters and visits. They should not ordain in haste or accept anyone younger than the prescribed age. They should ensure that the priests they already have are in good standing and provide them with a letter of commendation. Priests are to concentrate on scripture, preaching, and catechizing; they must teach the faithful reverence for the liturgy and the importance of baptism for their children. Lengthy advice is given on confession and reconciliation in this time of wickedness. The Terror may be over, but the bishops are still picking up the pieces: "One of the deepest wounds that the church has suffered is the relaxing of morals resulting in the case with which many priests reconcile sinners and admit them to participation in the sacraments. Pastors will recall here the maxims of the Council of Trent on justification and satisfaction, and the advice of St. Charles Borromeo to confessors."[24] Sound pastoral advice—the penances demanded should heal by attacking the cause of the sin, giving the faithful every confidence that real penitential acts (as prescribed by the canons of old) will lead to a change of life.

Good morals, then, are what the church has to offer society and government. The marriage blessing can be given to those who have been married civilly when they had no access to a priest. Sacraments and ceremonies are for church members only, however; all regular services should be in the church, and exceptional or special ceremonies should have the permission of the bishop. But the priority is to reestablish parish worship. In total contrast to the Old Regime, the bishops forbid the acceptance of money for offering prayers and celebrating Mass. Such selflessness would encourage the piety of the faithful, which is the basis for the improvement of worship, although the bishops' demands would appear to have a Jansenist tinge: simplified and clean churches with men and women segregated from one another, veneration of authentic relics only, and no frivolous ornamentation. Nothing less than exemplary behavior will work in these difficult times: "We exhort churchmen to gain respect by a simplicity and moderation that proclaims in all things the domination of the soul over the passions, following the counsel of the Apostle: 'Let your modesty be known to all the world,' to safeguard their reputation, because here the slightest blemish redounds on the priesthood in general, and to avoid and repair the smallest of scandals."[25] All this in imitation of the crucified Christ, model of the priesthood.[26]

Republican Christianity: The Second Encyclical Letter

Reorganization of the church, the priority of the first encyclical, was still on the agenda in the second encyclical letter, but the United Bishops now lay plans for the upcoming council and give much more attention to the specifically republican character of this Christianity.[27] Issued at the end of 1795, the encyclical's immediate goal is preparation for the urgently needed national meeting—or council—of church authorities, who, they proclaim, will eschew the arbitrary and the political, and return to the laws and church government of the great and successful Christian centuries. This may even be a season of opportunity, because the church flourished after its great trials in the first centuries of its existence: "Rid of every hindrance and servitude, based on the promises of Jesus Christ and the virtues of the pastors and faithful, it is still possible even so, following the designs of God, to make up quite well for the losses sustained by religion."[28] The old "servitude" is probably the Old Regime. It is striking that the constitutional bishops' first, and only, major heading is "The government of the Christian republic is entirely spiritual; it is based on revelation and tradition. Its distinctive character is charity. The obedience it requires is in conformity with reason."[29] "Christian republic," then, is their name for the *church*. Their central topic would be the basic defense of the role of the people in running the church: electing the bishops and priests who would both service and govern them.

Council Values

The bishops make a special plea for ecumenical councils, listing first the many crises that have come upon the church in the years since Trent closed more than two centuries before (1563). During this time, the church has defended itself against fearsome attacks on faith and morality, and has held firm. But the bishops want an ecumenical church in the full sense of the word: a church in which all the Christian churches are reunited. "An ecumenical council would reattach to the tree of Catholicism the many branches that Rome has separated from it, raise up the national churches that it [Rome] holds in oppression; perhaps it would succeed in realizing the project presented by the Sorbonne to Czar Peter, for the reunion of the Greek church; that of Bossuet for the reunion of the Protestant churches, that of Clement XIV, for the reunion of the Anglican church."[30] Even as the bishops reopen the whole issue of ecumenism, their immediate goal is this National Council, which they promote with one more rehearsal of the suffering of the church of France: the injustice and calumny, the wreckage around them, the contradictions, and the anguish. They would hope to reconcile the ecclesiastical forces in France and in Europe, such that they could even depend on them for help: "[A National Council] alone will have the fullness of authority and the breadth of wisdom and learning that will console the church of France; it will be pleasing to us to hold together in it all the pastoral efforts of those dioceses, whose political existence has just been joined to ours in the new order of things."[31] And they would also hope for understanding, counsel, and a fruitful exchange.

Election Challenges

Elections, the touchstone of the Constitutional Church, get an entire chapter in this second encyclical. The United Bishops deal with elections at every level and insist that elections are the "original and inalienable right of parishes and dioceses."[32] Certainly, they had in mind the organizational impasse that the French church had reached, with all the evils attendant upon an exclusively aristocratic hierarchy. Birth and wealth have no special rights in the church, which recognizes no titles other than wisdom and virtue. After the death of Christ, the apostles themselves were elected. That they decided to "leave to chance the choice between two disciples judged by the assembly to be equally worthy of filling the apostolic church shows on one hand the difficulties and the responsibility attached to elections, and condemns on the other hand the pride of those who wish to lay exclusive claim to the right of appointing to ecclesiastical offices."[33] In the context of fasting, prayer, and sacrifice they achieved elections that were the "models" for future generations: "It is to elections that religion has owed that multitude of illustrious men that the first centuries saw at the head of the different churches."[34]

Bishops are to be elected by both priests and people. It is not surprising that the United Bishops, who are themselves at issue here, would attend closely to this function. On that tricky relationship of bishops and their priests they say, "In the priest assemblies, surrounded by confreres *as if by a crown*," and the episcopal character which distinguishes him, should really be a sign of renouncement and humility.[35] Obviously trying to go carefully, then, the United Bishops posit a humble bishop who is completely at one with his priests: "Far removed from disputes, an opponent of domination and display, he presents his viewpoint, collects zealously others' insights."[36] The great bishops, St. Ignatius of Antioch and St. Cyprian of Carthage, made no major decisions without consulting their priests. As for the episcopal election proceedings themselves, the voters are the clergy and people, every Catholic over the age of twenty-one can vote, and if a vote is questioned the entire group can decide. The people of a parish region, of course, elect the curé, who is introduced here as a man for the people, a citizen! "Christianity has given to humankind the gift of the sublime institution of pastors. This class of citizen priests is spread out across the land of France; they live in the midst of men, without any family other than their parishioners, to the happiness of whom they dedicate their existence."[37]

In conclusion, the bishops want to admit their own faults. They ask for enlightenment and constructive criticism, and submit their views to the whole church. They need to fight on and repair damage at the same time, "such as the Israelites who with one hand held the sword to drive back the enemy and with the other repaired the ruins of the sanctuary."[38] It is clear that they are trying to establish themselves as *the* Catholic Church in France, by this final combination of reconciliation and condemnation: "Convinced that there must be among Christians a perfect unity, a compassionate charity, and fraternal friendship, . . . we declare as we did in our first encyclical that, pained beyond words by the troubles that afflict the church, we put ourselves at an infinite distance from all schism, whether general or partial."[39] Condemning those who deny the validity of their ministry of baptism, they are still ready to forgive past actions for the sake of peace and truth, and make their final submission to the will of God: "God who is rich in mercy, receive the dedication of our hearts, the feeble homage of our love for peace and truth."[40] In sum, the United Bishops saw their Republic through Gallican eyes and the Gallican (Catholic) Church through republican eyes. This was the direction of their leading thinkers from the beginning of the Revolution. It all came down to a reformed Catholic Church based on earliest tradition and a government based on the essential human freedoms that had been guaranteed, then betrayed, and now guaranteed anew by the new government.

A Constant Challenge: Republican Civil Religion

Bloody and violent dechristianization was over when the bishops issued the encyclicals, but the revolutionary culture that had been shaped to replace Christian culture was still in place. In place of the calendar of Christian celebrations from Christmas through the feast days of local saints, the revolutionary calendar substituted a cycle of festivals celebrating the stages of life and events of the Revolution. Moving beyond the encyclicals to deal with the festivals across the second half of the revolutionary decade in *Annales de la religion*, the constitutional bishops and priests tried to find a place for the new government festivals at the same time as they defended Catholic worship against attacks of moral inefficacy and superstition. With the décadi (the day of rest every tenth day) as the principal test case, they tried to specify the role of civil and religious celebrations. Originally adopted back in October 1793 and gradually expanded, the revolutionary calendar was reinforced several times throughout 1797 by the Directory. Instead of the weekly celebration of Sunday, the calendar based on the metric system provided for the décadi. Instead of dating everything from the birth of Christ, the birth of the Revolution with the first sitting of the Convention became Year One.[41]

Real Religion

A defense of Catholic ceremonies more clearly emerged in the *Annales de la religion* response to the interpretation of the religious celebrations offered by Directory member Louis-Marie de La Revellière-Lépeaux. The *Annales* author said that Catholic liturgies inculcate values, whereas civil liturgies are cheap and vulgar or lifeless. He sarcastically agreed with La Revellière-Lépeaux on the cheapness and vulgarity of the civil liturgies of marriage and death in particular, while making his own attack on the Deist society promoted by La Revellière-Lépeaux: "There has existed at Paris for some time now a new religious establishment, under the name of Société des Théophilanthropistes, that is to say, friends of God and of men. It appears that it is an attempt of modern philosophy to give some consistency to Deism, by the appearances of a periodic reunion of its partisans for a type of public worship."[42] The author called such worship ineffective and lifeless, citing Voltaire's report on the small numbers attracted by a similar cult promoted in England by Isaac Newton.

The differences between religious and civil festivals were carefully noted: "The civil festivals and the religious festivals have different aims; the former must gather the citizens, whatever their belief, to be instructed in the laws, to recall deeds honorable for the fatherland, to praise them, etc.; games for the amusement of citizens are an added attraction."[43] In the religious feasts "the citizen gives himself over to acts of cult; the offering of sacrifice, prayer, and recollection absorb his thought."[44] Indeed, the religious and civil festivals, because of their different qualities, should be separated from each other, "lest one thwart the other."[45] Objections were raised against any forced combination of festivals, or transferal and absorption of the religious by the civil festivals. What was to be gained? Catholics would still celebrate Sundays even as they celebrated the décadi. Jews and Muslims, who have their own sacred days, would also oppose the décadi. In effect, only a small number of compliant Catholics could be won over. The bishops concluded, "Politics itself ought then to oppose the transferal . . . the new calendar will gain nothing from a transferal so partial and so small."[46]

Figure 27 The French calendar promulgated by the revolutionary government commemorated the dramatic events of the new political era and was structured according to the metric system. The new calendar began with the founding of the French Republic, 22 September 1792 (called 1 vendémiaire, l'an 1), although it was not really put in place until a year later. Thus each 22 (or occasionally 23 or 24) September, a new year of twelve months of thirty days each began. Each month was named in accordance with the primary feature of climate and farming particular to that month (e.g., Fructidor was a month of growth in nature and Thermidor was the hot month). (Bibliothèque nationale de France)

Resolution of the Problem

The *complementary* features of the religious and civil festivals were clarified and simplified in a catechism prepared for use in the Ligurian Republic of North Italy (a satellite of France since working to change its constitution in May–June 1797); quotations appeared in *Annales de la religion*. The question: "What is the object of the civil festivals?" The answer: "To reunite the people and to arouse in their hearts by means of an honest pleasure, sentiments of concord, equality and liberty, love of the fatherland, desire for glory, and, in a word, to excite them to virtuous and magnanimous actions."[47] The question: "What is the object of the religious festivals?" The answer: "Some have the object of recalling for us the memory of the most august mysteries of religion, and others have the object of stirring us to the practice of the virtues that distinguish Christian heroes. By this one can see clearly the distinction between patriotic festivals and religious festivals."[48]

Civil celebrations were not in and of themselves a danger. The constitutional clergy invited the people to submit to the laws requiring festival celebration precisely because these laws would not harm religion. Were it not for those who would use the civil celebrations to harm religion, "we would only have spoken of them to invite the faithful and Catholic pastors to submit themselves to them."[49] The constitutionals were not fundamentally opposed to the *fêtes décadaires* and the republican calendar, and said they were calumniated in this regard. The government has the right to festivals, whatever the religion of the state, as the church has a right to its own festivals:[50] "The church has in its feasts a goal independent of what can be established in society; it can, then, choose days independent of the civil sector. All that one can require of it is that it not trouble the social order."[51] The constitutionals were not against the union of civil and religious domains in the abstract; such was simply not the situation in France: "We have already said and proved that the social and religious orders are essentially distinct and independent. Happy the people in whom they are allied and united, but this union is not essential to one or the other."[52] Dechristianizers were especially out of line, because extant laws ruled out any religious interpretation of the civil festivals: "Men who are the enemies of religion, and who wanted to give these festivals the form of worship, would have wished to profit from [the festivals] to make real the phantom of civil religion. . . . The law has carefully ruled out everything that could have the color or the appearance or the semblance of worship."[53]

The Décadi in Particular

The institution of the *fêtes décadaires* was the principal worry of Desbois de Rochefort, because freedom of worship would be seriously limited. That the décadi should be a day of rest was acceptable, but if Jews and Christians were to be prevented from properly celebrating their own Sabbaths, 95 percent of the nation would be offended. Ending on a positive note, the author assumed for the legislators the best of intentions, or at least tried to steer their intentions in his direction: "We do not believe that such a plan [to restrict religious freedom] could enter into the thought of the legislators; . . . they do not have the jealous eye of the inquisitor who is offended by usages that are different from his own."[54] In fact, though, Henri Grégoire and the United Bishops knew they would be damned if they did, and damned if they did not cooperate with the décadi. Should they agree to transfer the religious festivals to the days of civil celebration, they could be accused of trying to take them over. People determined to persecute them would say, "Do you see those priests who by transferring their services to a décadi wanted to seize hold of the civil festivals to turn people away from celebrating them?"[55] In self-defense the bishops proclaimed their commitment to state as well as church ("[we] who have suffered so much to defend religion and Republic; to defend one and the other we are always ready to pour out our blood"), considering the religious commitment to be the more fundamental ("we invariably held to the religion of Jesus Christ in whom our confidence rests").[56] Their religion, in fact, inspired their love of country: religion will be national only when it identifies itself, without detriment to its principles, with the institutions of the country it claims as its own, when it sanctifies the love of the laws and authorities who govern.[57]

The problem was not the décadi; the problem was making the décadi into its own kind of Sunday: "We are not ignorant of the fact that the enemies of our holy religion would like to destroy our worship and abolish the celebration of Sunday."[58] But by urging the transferal of devotional feasts to the décadi "while making a show of the preservation of Sunday," the government actually placed the décadi in competition with Sunday: "They induce the Christian people to error by making them believe that the décadi has become a religious festival, whereas it is a civil festival."[59] This is not to say that the feast days—as opposed to Sundays—could not be moved to the décadi for the sake of the people: "Does not everything require . . . transferals that would put the majority of religious feasts on the same course as the *fêtes décadaires*, or at least allow for accommodation so that the festivals do not become too heavy a burden for the faithful attached to their obligations?"[60] Sunday work could be proper and even necessary, according to Grégoire, but "only when a great public need or exercise of acts of humanity require that one work on days consecrated to religious solemnities."[61]

In sum, complementarity is the overworked theme. Even toward the end of the Directory period, *Annales de la religion* happily reported that two government officials in the Var promoted celebrations of the festivals where the differences between religious and civil could be clearly recognized. These officials were cited for their perception and good governance, actively maintaining all of the distinctions desired by the constitutional clergy: "Citizen Cruves, the ex-commissioner, and the people respect the law on freedom of worship; and citizen Raibaud, his son-in-law, the actual commissioner, walks in his footsteps: they know how to harmonize the national festivals with the religious festivals; both are celebrated by the citizens; and the administration is so well coordinated with us that the décadi services do not in any way interrupt our religious services."[62]

And so went constitutional participation in the cultural wars under the Directory—although culture was certainly not separate from politics. The continuing struggle of Jacobins and monarchists left the constitutional clergy with the challenge of finding common cause with an ex-Jacobin middle, an acute problem inasmuch as the politicians were not clear enough about their own church–state goals to make common cause possible. The Directory's foreign policy was, very broadly speaking, the invasion of territories surrounding France, centered on the Italian campaign led by the military rising star Napoleon Bonaparte. The constitutional bishops had outlined in their encyclicals a set of priorities and goals that they hoped to realize in future councils, national and ecumenical. Two episcopal personalities who had little or nothing to do with the production of the encyclicals would come to play key, though disparate, roles—Claude Le Coz and Jean-Baptiste Royer.

Chapter Nine

STABILIZING THE CONSTITUTIONAL CHURCH

Claude Le Coz and the Council of 1797

Claude Le Coz was an imposing intellectual and organizational leader. As an intellectual, he promoted the religious values of a Republic and the republican values of religion; as an organizer, he rebuilt the church, physically and morally in his own diocese, with generous attention to challenges elsewhere in the country. Born in Lower Brittany, he received his early education at Quimper, later becoming head of the college he had attended as a youth. Forty-nine when the Revolution occurred, he welcomed it so enthusiastically that he became an immediate and obvious choice for departmental bishop (Ille-et-Vilaine). When the Legislative Assembly was put together in 1791, he was chosen deputy, a voice for moderation and a walking advertisement for the dedicated constitutional clergyman.[1] He presided at the Constitutional Church's Council of 1797, his strong and dramatic signature first on every act and on the recorded minutes of every session.

Le Coz strongly criticized the refractories as an obstacle to church renewal, but was equally harsh on those of his own camp who married. Those who abdicated or married he considered the signal causes of the damage to his own positive Revolution, a strong stand that may have been one of the reasons why he was thrown in the great prison at Mont-Saint-Michel during the Terror. Naturally critical of the pope's lack of understanding and support for the Constitutional Church, he was even more critical of any irreverence toward the pope's office and person. His pastoral letters and essays, his articles in the *Annales de la religion*, documentation from the Constitutional Church councils of 1797 and 1801, and his voluminous correspondence demonstrate that Claude Le Coz found a unique way to activate the values of the constitutional enterprise into a mission that lived on in the church of the Concordat. In his views of church and state he was an authentic constitutional, and in his pastoral concerns he was a devoted bishop. At the two constitutional councils he formally presided without sacrificing his personal reservations, and between the two of them he forcefully aided the United Bishops with special support (and sometimes criticism) of Henri Grégoire. All of this brought him later to reconciliation with Rome on his own terms as an archbishop in the concordatory church.

The Catholic Church in a Republican State

All across the revolutionary decade, Le Coz demonstrated sensitivity to the church–state possibilities unique to the era. His writings were a moral reflection and a practical application that complemented the theology and canon law of Lamourette and Durand de Maillane. The long "Avertissement pastoral du Cen Le Coz, évêque d'Ille-et-Vilaine, sur l'état actuel de la religion catholique" that appeared at the end of the century was a reprise of his promotion and preaching of a Christian republic; he consoled believers in their trials, but promoted a faith strong enough to overcome anxieties.[2]

In 1795, however, Claude Le Coz had produced a long treatise titled *Accord de la religion catholique avec le gouvernement républicain*. But what should have been an "accord" promoted by his constitutionals, the supposed bridge between church and state, was impeded by papal maximalists and extremist republicans: "Right now, two types of men are harmful to the Catholic faith, believers who are poorly trained and confused republicans. They agree to maintain that our holy religion is incompatible with any form of republican government. One group rejects the Republic, because they believe it to be destructive of Catholicism; the others would destroy Catholicism, because they believe it excludes the Republic."[3] Both sides are unpatriotic and dangerous, the former giving irreligion new excuses for action and the latter willingly blind.[4] Accordingly, he wants his treatise to "dissipate both the understandable anxieties of the Catholic and the dangerous prejudice of the republican!"[5] The thesis is discussed in two complementary halves: "(I) A republican government does not bring any destruction in any way to the Catholic religion, (II) The Catholic religion does not exclude a republican government."

Le Coz has no theological problems with republican governments, first of all. In the time of the apostles were there only Old Regime–style monarchies

Figure 28 Bishop Claude Le Coz was one of the strongest and most influential constitutional clergymen after Henri Grégoire. Le Coz had enjoyed relative success in his diocese of Ille-et-Vilaine in Brittany, headquartered at Rennes; pastorally and intellectually active across the Directory years, he was the foundation of the United Bishops' pastoral program and was the natural choice to preside over the first National Council of the reconstituted Constitutional French Catholic church in 1797.

around? Did not the apostles preach to all without concern for the style of government? "Did they withhold the light of the gospel from republics and popular governments? Such an assumption is outrageous. The apostles would have made themselves guilty of criminal disobedience, they would have spurned the formal commands of their divine master."[6] And second, he made a case for Catholicism, that its virtues are so manifest that fanatical republicans will look foolish when order is restored: "You would have it that the Catholic faith excludes the republican Constitution to which you relate your happiness. Will you, when the days of prejudice are passed, when truth will have reclaimed its empire, not blush to have so calumniated a religion so open to fraternity, equality, and liberty, to have wanted to condemn a religion which does not cease to call men back to a common source, to the descent from the same faith, to the same immortality, to the religion that established among men a joyous union of services and benefits, and which raises their thoughts to greatness?"[7]

Even at the beginning of his episcopal career, two weeks after the 20 June 1791 flight of the king, Le Coz had worked out the church–state balance, clearly and simply.[8] Those who are both Christians and citizens will ask, he says, "What are, in these moments of crisis, the obligations that we must fulfill?"[9] But he was painfully aware that the king's flight lost him all credibility with republicans: "Seduced by traitorous insinuations, led astray by vile courtesans who in their bitterness miss all the abuses with which they used to fatten themselves up . . . Louis XVI has let himself be roped into the project of abandoning his people."[10] He works out a parallel between the law of God and the law of the land. As Moses gathered together the Hebrews to swear allegiance to the covenant, so the French people will be gathered together to swear allegiance to the Republic.

When the king was at last deposed, Le Coz threw his support to the Convention: "A republic is the patrimony of all, without being the property of anyone. This common patrimony: each one can and ought to contribute to its defense and improvement; but no one can, without committing a crime, diminish or alter it."[11] At the same time, he sympathizes with citizens who have suffered across the years, first as "victims of the traitorous and bloody court," and then as soldiers defending the borders of a new France. The leaders of the Convention, unimpressed by his support and mindful of his moderation in the Legislative Assembly, pursued Le Coz for refusal to promulgate the laws he had earlier opposed, ordered his arrest, and sent him to prison for fourteen months.

After the Terror, when discussion of a church council began, Le Coz was not so sure that it would work at all. Then, in 1796, he wrote to the ensemble of the United Bishops saying that they should not expect a national church council to do much more than repeat all that had been said already. The usual violent anti-constitutional forces would remain united against them. Heresies can never be extinguished by decree, but must be fought at every turn and with every force. Only the most dedicated constitutionals would be at the council, the refractories assuming that they would be rejected anyway (as they, to begin with, had rejected the constitutionals in 1790). At this point Le Coz believed that the constitutional bishops needed all of their energies in order to take care of their parishioners at home: "To go off elsewhere, in these moments of violent crisis, would be to cast them into despondency; a thousand calumnies made up on the spot would be spread throughout the already shaky communes, and in place of diminishing the evil, we would increase it and lose perhaps, by an indiscreet step, all the fruits of our zeal and extensive work."[12] Given the pope's age and feebleness, he permits himself to think of a successor who may understand them better. He can only hope that another pope, one day, will appreciate what they are trying to do, who "will not have the same interest in supporting a false and disastrous choice [against the constitutionals]."[13]

Le Coz had also remained apart from the production of the encyclicals. There, too, he could speak to the United Bishops as an ensemble, but much more positively: "I have read with the most lively interest your second encyclical; it bears the imprint of genius and piety." He says that a good measure of their success has been "the ranting of the unbelievers."[14] They should shortly receive other, yet more flattering, comments from the friends of religion and humanity. There follows, then, his suggestions for clarification of issues presented in the text.

Pastoral Concerns: Good Liturgies and Religious Freedom

In between the publication of the two encyclicals in 1795 and the opening of the 1797 National Council, Le Coz presented the full gamut of his goals and concerns in *Annales de la religion*, highlighting a liturgical renewal built on solid support for the Constitutional Church. He was able to convince himself that support for Catholicism in this setting was also support for the Constitutional Church: "Worship continues on there, even under the axes of the proconsul executioners; and the citizens, ready for every sacrifice that a wise and generous patriotism can inspire, ask only one thing, guaranteed by the constitution and the laws, freedom of worship, which is the origin of their wisdom, the nourishment of their virtue, their consolation amid privations, and the real support of their labors."[15] Le Coz's good people are definitely not the Chouans of Brittany, who are as likely to kill constitutionals as to kill Jacobins.

Le Coz reported his well-attended liturgies of some size and splendor to *Annales* publisher Desbois de Rochefort: "Passing by Vannes, I officiated there and administered first communion and confirmation. Although this city, so tried by the shootings that followed the Quiberon affair, is completely distraught, we had great crowds for our services and preaching, and it consoled us to see so many tears shed."[16] In another one of his cities he had the same success. Many confessions first of all: "There we found an immense gathering of people. Having arrived at our appointment at seven o'clock in the morning on the fourteenth, after having journeyed for six leagues, we went into the confessional, which we only left regretfully at 12:30 in order to go to lunch. After a light meal we returned until 8 o'clock."[17] The next day, he celebrated a pontifical Mass: "Around noon I went up to the altar: the large church was completely full, there would not have been room for one more chair. . . . At the post communion, I spoke for about half an hour. Oh, dear colleague, what attention, what sensitivity I saw in my large audience!"[18] And finally, a sure punch line for Desbois: "To give you an idea of our work, and of the good we would do if pseudo-philosophy and *chouannisme* did not oppose us without letup."[19] It would all go so well without the extremes around them, the philosophers (read: anti-Christian Enlightenment) and the Chouans.

At one and the same time, Le Coz was pleased by the accession of the courageous and outspoken episcopal vicar Yves-Marie Audrein to the episcopate, and troubled by the retraction of the theretofore influential constitutional bishop François-Thérèse Panisset. He wrote on 24 August 1797, "You already received from Quimper the details of the consecration of citizen Audrein. This ceremony, as beautiful as it was edifying, has brought joy to the majority of the inhabitants of the Finistère. This department, always the first to render the fatherland its share of contributions and zeal, is also perhaps the one that in all of France has maintained the greatest respect and love for our holy religion."[20] When he responded to the retraction of Bishop Panisset, he complained that too much energy was wasted on defending the Constitutional Church against lies and calumnies.[21] Why, he wonders, under the pretext of defending Christian principles, do you harass those who defend them? "Ah! If the true interests of religion are important to you, leave off the useless and scandalous quarreling, and come unite your efforts to ours, to restore the altars of the Catholic religion."[22]

The bête noire of the period was François-Antoine Boissy d'Anglas, who in his anticlericalism was an obvious target for Le Coz the reforming bishop, as he had been for Yves-Marie Audrein, episcopal vicar during the Convention. Boissy was at the beginning of the collapse of the spirited first Constitutional Church, a man of the kind that "closed the first church, and caused the closing of all the others in the department, by whom were uttered the first blasphemies against our worship and the first curses against the priests who obeyed the laws."[23] In fact, contra Boissy, wherever priests work with the government there can be good results: "In the Finistère, many curés accepted the position of commissaire [*du pouvoir exécutif*]; and in their cantons especially you see the rule of order, respect for laws, and sincere love of the fatherland."[24]

Responding to an attempt by Directory legislator Rallier to limit the role of religion in society, Le Coz says he would not suspect the man of plotting against religion, but wonders why he took on the subject of religion at all, not having the necessary expertise.[25] A simple apologetic for the truth of Christianity would be preferable. In a second letter to Rallier he tries to defuse a challenge to infallibility, saying that there is nothing in church tradition that forbids examining the grounds for such a belief.[26] Saint Peter himself "commends the faithful to be always ready to justify their hope to those who ask."[27] Of course it all had to be done with simplicity and modesty. Christ himself and the Jewish converts urged fidelity to the scriptures, so there would have been no possibility for heterodox teachings (e.g., infallibility) in the early church.

And again in 1796 Le Coz reviewed some of the challenges facing the church in an open letter to the faithful published in *Annales de la religion.*[28] He insists that the Gallican Church did not have to seek confirmation of new bishops by the pope. Why is this way of operating now called schismatic? Le Coz cites legislation as far back as the early 1400s. And a related problem: How is the Civil Constitution of the Clergy a presbyterian document? Traditionally the bishops have always consulted their priests (e.g., the Fourth Council of Carthage). In the presbyterian system, the bishops' authority is rejected: "The *civil constitution,* on the contrary, openly recognizes that the *institution of the episcopal order in the church, and the superiority of bishops over priests, are of divine law.*" Accordingly, Le Coz wonders why the author of a recent brochure on the "constitutional schism" does not see that such a calumniating label "tends to provide new weapons for a sect that is one of the main enemies of the Catholic and Roman church."[29] The physical church building could also be a challenge, a discouragement, for any constitutional: "But what sorrow was ours the first time we entered the church, once so beautiful and today so debased! Picture in your mind dirty and disgusting walls, broken windows, statues and sanctuary marbles broken in pieces, the cobblestones ruined by the carts they have dragged by; the altar missing, and the obnoxious odors of tons of tallow, oil, rum, and eau-de-vie. That is my picture, not exaggerated but true and faithful, of the house of the Lord, when they let us go inside."[30] In this case, the faithful cleaned and put all in order and replaced the altar by the following Sunday. In the end, the only interruption of worship was the six months when the priests were in prison. On the Feast of the Circumcision, the full rededication of the church took place—tears everywhere, including his own. Le

Coz's priests were "penetrated by the sublimity of their holy ministry," and their sobs "penetrated every heart."[31]

At the National Council of 1797: Building on the Encyclicals

Claude Le Coz presided at, and assured a full report on, the accomplishments of the constitutionals' National Council of 1797. According to the minutes, the council opened on 15 August in the Notre-Dame Cathedral with an appropriately sizeable congregation—"an immense throng," they called it—that stayed there six hours, leaving no doubt about "the interest they had in the workings of the august assembly."[32] With the president of the assembly properly in his place, the opening discourse was pronounced in Latin; Mass followed, with some elaboration of standard episcopal ceremonial, and then the council meetings began.

There, in August, the council fathers had reason to be optimistic, given events in the first half of 1797. Clément had been elected and consecrated as bishop of Versailles. And it was clear that a number of the constitutional bishops had taken their responsibilities in hand: Nord, Haut-Rhin, Puy-de-Dôme, Vosges, Haute-Saône, Indre-et-Loire, Ardennes, and Aveyron. Elsewhere presbyteries had successfully regrouped, as in Pyrénées-Orientales, the Gard, and the Doubs. Estimates of the number of parishes in which worship had been reestablished went as high as forty thousand (Grégoire's standard estimate was over thirty-two thousand). In secular politics, the successes of Napoleon could be encouraging, and in religious polity, reports that the pope had issued a brief permitting the refractories to swear allegiance to the Directory government continued to circulate. The Paris presbytery continued to supply a full pastoral ministry to the capital with the support of the nearby bishop of Seine-et-Marne. Canonists, although concerned about the authority of their Paris presbytery, had urged the convocation of the 1797 Council as a solution to the biggest challenges facing the French church.[33]

Revision of the encyclicals came to be a principal preoccupation and the center of some controversy: to wit, the recorded complaint that "the congregation seems to be less concerned with revising the encyclicals than with setting up a new system."[34] And on the most practical level, the Constitutional Church needed financial support, for all its criticism of the opulence of the Old Regime church—so a policy document, based, of course, on church history, was entered into the council minutes. Faith and adoration "requires of the faithful sacrifices necessary for the maintenance of worship. The first Christians provided for this by voluntary donations to take care of the poor and the church communities."[35] And later, St. Augustine saw to it that the clergy should be provided for: "Thus was formed the church treasury to help us to understand that the admonition against concern for the morrow does not relieve people of the obligation to hold money in reserve, lest fear of poverty lead to the neglect of justice." The text here is long, indicating how much the council members were preoccupied by this matter *and* how sheepish they were about it: "The [financial] bases adopted here by the council are certainly inferior to those . . . of the earliest centuries."

The always tricky issue of clergy elections was shored up by firm foundational discourse (written into the council minutes twenty-five pages after the first decree on elections):[36] "The church of God, says St. Paul, is established on the foundation of the apostles and the prophets, and on the cornerstone, which is Jesus Christ (Eph. 2:19–20). The links that continued the chain are election and ordination." They are indifferent to the details of election procedures, but strongly condemn past neglect in this domain because of the "tyrannical influence of kings and the court of Rome, as well as the heedlessness of clergy and people." These were "epochs fatal to religion." But the search was on for official church consensus, providing for appropriate elections while maintaining the roles assigned to bishop and priest in the New Testament and the Christian tradition.[37]

Rather than take the pope severely to task, the council preferred to consider him uninformed: "The profound respect that we have for the head of the church ordains that we regard as apocryphal the briefs dated 1790, 1791, and 1792, that have been circulated under his name, because they are not vested with the character of authenticity."[38] On the one hand, authenticity could have been guaranteed only by consent of the government; on the other hand, the pope could not have understood that these laws take away from the rights of the people and that they go against the teachings of Christ himself. Catholics themselves often believe that they can do nothing without the permission of Rome, but the bishops have every hope that the pope will see that they have his best interest at heart. He must act: "The responsibility with which he has been charged as head of the church does not permit him to remain silent."[39] Given the pope's virtue and his past good deeds, they know that he will come around, "that he will unite his efforts to ours to put an end to the scandal of religious dissension that now troubles our church, unless perverse people again manage to get around his wishes and muffle his voice."[40] Even so, the bishops demand an ecumenical council, the decisions of which they submit themselves to, in advance, "recommending to the faithful confided to our care, to wait in silence, prayer, and confidence in the Lord."[41]

As the council began, La Librairie chrétienne, the constitutional press responsible for the *Annales de la religion*, published a *Journal du Concile national de France*, reporting the attempts to improve on the encyclicals and highlighting eloquence and spirituality. The *Journal* assumes that the majority of the readers are familiar with the organization and discipline provided by the encyclicals—in other words, it counts on an engaged and educated readership (who else would be interested in the important doings of the council?). A reliable estimate of readership would be 300 subscribers for the first issue through 1,500 for the last.[42] The *Journal* calls the encyclicals "the work of six bishops that divine providence seemed to have brought together in Paris, not to protect them from persecution, but to make it possible to conjure away the final storms and to summon their confreres to rally with courage." Nor was this the brainstorm of a few, because the majority of the other bishops and the presbyteries backed the project.[43]

There are several improvements that the council members are intent on making, beginning with that very difficult issue of elections, which was explained and set up long before the encyclicals in the Civil Constitution of the Clergy. Then, the Civil Constitution handed over almost completely to the laity the election of priests and bishops, whereas the clergy themselves had and have valuable contributions to make regarding these choices.[44] Subsequently, the encyclicals failed to resolve the problem, so a council committee now proposes to give the clergy the right to draw up the list of candidates—even though the faithful do not have to restrict themselves to this list.

The *Journal* also played up liturgical highlights, both preaching and ceremonial, reporting, for example, that the congregation listened to the bishop of Toulouse, Hyacinthe Sermet, "with all the interest that his rare talents, great zeal, and rich voice deserve." There were even some refractories there listening respectfully.[45] One of the liturgical ceremonies that received special attention was the Eucharist in a Greek rite preserved at the abbey of St. Denis. This was cited as evidence of special concern for the Orthodox churches, though it was not without the traditionally Western Catholic assumptions about the attempts at unity of the 1400s. The hope then was that emphasis on council authority over papal supremacy would get beyond all other differences, and that the common ceremonies at the Council of Florence "marked the extinction of the schism and the union of the church of the East with that of the West"; knowing that it did not last, the reporter hoped that results would be better this time.[46] On the day itself, Bishop Saurine celebrated the liturgy in Greek.

The decrees of the council dealing with marriage, education, and the liturgy were issued in a special booklet.[47] The decadence of post-Tridentine Catholic liturgies had to be reversed. Priests should not be celebrating their private masses at those extra altars in front or along the sides of the churches while the principal service was being conducted. A fortiori, simultaneous masses should be avoided. The council wanted the congregation to be attentive to, and to be a part of, the central prayer. Prayers of petition before the Offertory should be in the vernacular. And apart from the central formularies, the administrations of the sacraments should be in French.[48]

In the decrees on the reform of morality, the council wants it known "that religion makes it a sacred duty for us to love the fatherland, that it is a crime to refuse to take up arms to defend [the fatherland] when it is required by law, and that it is an enormous crime to take up arms against it"—again, an extremely strong underwriting of the French government.[49] The faith has been communicated to the church to be infallibly interpreted, and so the council proposes and declares a series of basic truths that pastors everywhere must teach: insufficiency of natural law, along with the necessity of divine revelation and grace. And so the council dramatically closed with a series of prayers for the church and all humankind, including such diverse figures as Pope Pius VI, the refractories, the persecutors of religion, the council fathers, the benefactors of the National Council, the church of Paris, the legitimate authorities, the Republic, and all the nations of the earth.[50] It would appear to have been a scene both of joy and uncertainty: "These different acclamations are received with great emotion by the faithful who were forming the same good wishes. But the general emotion was best manifested when all the fathers of the council, ready to separate for a long time and perhaps forever, offered one another the holy kiss of peace as a sign of union and of charity."[51] The document was signed by Le Coz, as metropolitan bishop of Rennes (Ille-et-Vilaine) and as president of the Concile national de l'Église de France, and cosigned by the five secretaries.

Across the council sessions, some constitutional priests who were present responded with silence or antagonism; engaged priests wrote open and

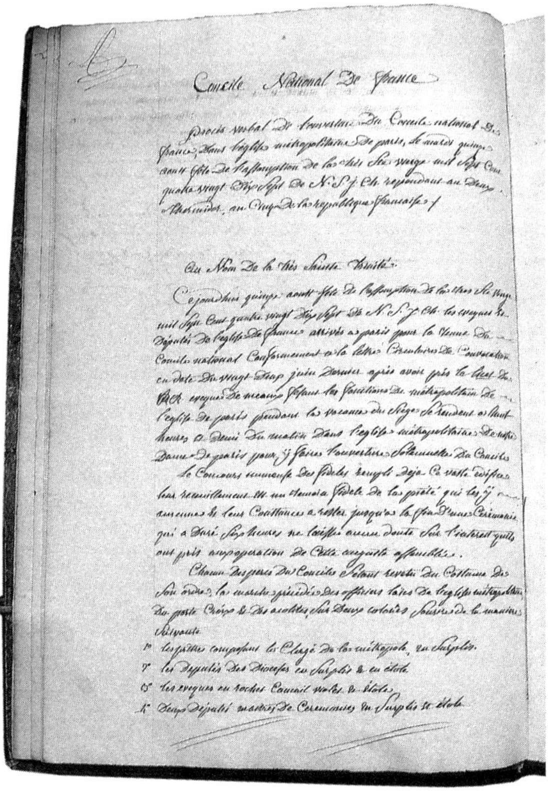
Concile National de France

Au Nom de la très Sainte Trinité

Figure 29 First page of the official minutes of the National Council of 1797, called together by the United Bishops representing the French Catholic Church, formerly set up as the Constitutional Church, in order to revive an authentic Catholicism appropriate for the new political era. The council president was Claude Le Coz.

frank letters. One council priest in particular, the abbé François de Torcy, a delegate of Nicholas Diot, the bishop of Reims, was far and away the most vocal, and epistolary, of the advocates of early church polity and the rights of priests, in the council and in their own dioceses. He believed that the United Bishops, in taking it on themselves to write their encyclicals in 1795, had neglected to include priests in the Constitutional Church reform. The voting in council was not set up such that the majoritarian priests would be heard with the same respect as any random bishop. In the overall group of engaged constitutional priests, none were more central than members of the presbytery of Notre-Dame Cathedral, already distressed that the parishes in Paris were more loyal to Grégoire (of Blois!) than to them.[52]

In the letters and documentation conserved apart from the council minutes, two maverick clergy considered authority and worship from their own novel viewpoints. The Old Regime leftover Bishop La Font de Savine was not attending the council and wrote that he was against attributing to it any legislative authority. He believed that episcopal authority had become confused with civil authority in the first centuries of Christianity. Spiritual authority was extended to the church as a worldly, physical entity, modeled ultimately on the authority of the state: "With more good faith than good sense, they extended a type of sacred privilege to properties, territories, contributions, and other things of an obviously civil and temporal nature; honor, power, authority, and jurisdiction were, accordingly, incorporated into it [the spiritual authority]."[53] Though he knows his ideas will seem a little scandalous, he writes that he "could only see the council as a fraternal gathering of ecclesiastics, called together to discuss the interests of the church, to find means of reconciliation and regeneration." He concludes with an impassioned plea for the rights of refractories. Louis-François Poinsignon, hoping that he and the faithful whom he represents will get a full hearing, writes that his priority is the cessation of violence and the healing of the schism: "But we are deprived of this yearned-for peace, this unity of hearts and minds, so dear to Catholics; to our great misfortune a thousand obstacles oppose it; our evil deeds are the cause . . . ; anxiety mixed with bitterness and derision spread out in our hearts; this affliction of the evil and unfortunate division that reigns in the church gives birth to a number of sects and heresies."[54] Poinsignon was particularly upset by the success of the government-sponsored Deistic cult, Theophilanthropy, which had been trying to get control of the old Royal Chapel at Versailles. There are also pages of details about the Mass and office calendar, and the reverence required for the liturgy. Poinsignon was even willing to adopt and adapt some of the revolutionary festivals in imitation of the early church's transformation of pagan customs. The Fête de la jeunesse could be used to teach scriptural lessons and be placed under the patronage of St. Raphael. In similar fashion the Fête des époux could be used to teach the meaning of the sacrament of marriage; the Fête d'agriculture, the dignity of work. Of course, behind Poinsignon lurked the ever-vigilant constitutional infighter, the bishop of Versailles himself, Auguste Clément. He had already gone through two campaigns, the first to get himself elected to the see of Versailles and the second to safeguard constitutional control of the church of Saint-Louis after a leading refractory had petitioned the Versailles municipal administration for use of the church.

Fortunately for the constitutionals, the radical change at high government levels, the great coup of 18 Fructidor (4 September 1797), ensured a review of the royalism of the Versailles administrators. Reacting to the conservative, in effect monarchist, successes in the legislative elections, members of the old political left on the Directory itself and in the two houses had invalidated the elections and ensured their own stability. Le Coz announced news of the coup and obtained the submission of council members to the new government, but there were problems here. The restructured government demanded an oath of hatred of royalty, a dilemma because the bishops had to justify how "hate could be compatible with Christian teaching." They issued an *Instruction du Concile national sur le serment décrété le 19 fructidor, an V de la République*, suggesting that the oath simply signaled the opposition of the republican regime to any attempt to bring back the monarchy: "There is nothing in this engagement contrary to the law of the gospel and the law of charity; taken in this way, the oath involved is not only legitimate but obligatory."[55] In the months to follow, however, government paranoia led to the imprisonment of government resisters (sixty-five were sent to Guyana) and the renewed suppression of the refractories.

Supporting United Bishops and Grégoire at the Turn of the Century

In a long piece sent to Desbois de Rochefort and Grégoire in 1798 (actually inserted in a letter to Grégoire), Le Coz supported the installation of Jean-Baptiste Royer as bishop of Paris and the reunion of the priests of Notre-Dame and Saint-Gervais, but condemned the antipapal language of a bishop reprinted in *Annales* with "bitter and profound sorrow."[56] Inasmuch as they reprinted the antipapal remarks of the bishop of Tuscany and of citizen "Moyse" (François-Xavier Moïse), they must hear what he has to say. His is, then, a cri de coeur: "O bishops of Jesus Christ, where is then your prudence? You want peace for our church, it seems about to enter, and you stand in the doorway to prevent it from penetrating within. *O Moyse* [Bishop Moïse], what is the meaning of this violent, this indecent diatribe against the first vicar of Jesus Christ?"[57] Le Coz's pro-papalism is hardly celebratory, because the pope is compared to a naked Abraham, mocked by his sons! "You, another Ham, what have you done? Was it your place to draw attention to the pathetic nudity of your father? Should not the curse uttered against your guilty model make you more cautious?"[58] Others, here presumably Grégoire and Desbois de Rochefort, are like Abraham's other sons, who should hasten to cover their father "with the cloak of filial respect."

Le Coz also rejected the easy notion that in the early church priests were married: "Without doubt married men were often raised to sacerdotal functions, but from that moment on, they renounced sexual relations, and their wives also agreed to live in continence."[59] He continues his history of celibacy laws, giving pride of place to Thomassin's paeans of praise for celibacy, a classic reference to the impurities of marriage: "The law of celibacy for ecclesiastics in major orders is as old as the church. The eternal pontiff, who willed to be born of a virgin and who has himself been a virginal host, which he willed to be offered in eternal immolation in his church by those he called to his divine priesthood, willed also that those who offered sacrifice should be imitators of him and offer their bodies with his as a chaste, pure, and innocent victim. According to this plan, he chose apostles, either virgins from the beginning or continent after their call; for this reason the apostles elected as possessors of, and successors to, their royal priesthood only virgins, or, lacking virgins, only persons vowed to permanent celibacy. Finally, for that reason the apostles banished forever from the virginal priesthood those whose continence had been shattered by a second marriage."[60] Clearly Le Coz was sometimes lucky and sometimes unlucky in his historical certainties, not being trained in any methods for separating conjecture from evidence.

The joy Le Coz experienced at the consecration of Audrein had been turned to sorrow by 1800 when the latter was murdered by the Chouans. In a letter addressed to "the author of a historical dictionary," he tries to set the record straight, reporting how years before, the usually timid Audrein braved swords and daggers to place himself between prisoners and their would-be assassins, finally even getting some of them out. It is true that, in a moment of fright, he voted for the death of the king, but placed a restriction on it that virtually annulled the measure. Furthermore, he did his utmost to save other members of the royal family.[61] Audrein was murdered after he had tried, as bishop of the Finistère, to reconcile warring factions, and rebuild and repair the churches. Even when he knew his life was in danger, he could not be restrained from his pastoral visits: "Having done only good in these parts, and having nothing else in view than religion, charity, and concord, he could not believe there would be men awful enough to punish him for it with a dagger."[62] Before reaching his destination, he was pulled from his coach and stabbed to death.

Claude Le Coz never contested the leadership of Henri Grégoire. He tried to both fine-tune Grégoire's leadership and encourage him to further success. He recommends some adjustments to Grégoire's unclear or stern discourse, presuming that his own "candor and zeal" will appeal to a like-minded colleague.[63] And he prepares Grégoire for this criticism by reminding him that the fathers of the church themselves let fall some expressions that were "equivocal or inexact" in matters of history or ethics. Le Coz, a literalist who could not accept the results of some archeological finds, arbitrarily attacks Grégoire's seemingly innocent metaphor in the sentence, "The march of reason, like that of the sea, is only apparent after many centuries," adding that philosophers and unbelievers use the idea that the sea progresses over the face of the earth for their own fell purpose: to deny the flood.[64] But Le Coz's letter to Grégoire at the beginning of the new century was filled with hope for the Constitutional Church, especially in light of Grégoire's election to the Senate of the Consulate: "Dear and venerable colleague, divine providence protects us: your entry into the legislature is a new proof of it. Even the impious notice it [the protection of divine providence], such that they cannot but applaud your nomination. They sense that a man who is the center of the Convention and in the presence of the hounds of atheism, dared to proclaim the divinity of our religion, will not remain silent in face of the aggressive little dogs who have succeeded them [Convention delegates]."[65] And then, praise and a prayer for Napoleon: "May the premier restorer of Catholic worship in France manage to gain for himself the wise freedom that seeks both reason and the national interest!"[66]

Le Coz continues to have at the calendar, praising an author in the *Annales* for his "sortie against the stupid and infernal calendar! He has cited in his fine paper the shameful almanacs where they purport to substitute for the names of saints and for religious feasts the names of the most bizarre and disgusting stuff," which was but one more manifestation of the boundless destruction of the Revolution: "It is time we opened our eyes. More than a hundred thousand French people have been sacrificed to the barbarian fantasy of decatholicizing us; and the blood, which still flows in torrents in those unfortunate regions, is shed, in the last analysis, by the same hands who have devastated our churches and profaned what is most sacred in our religion."[67] All those deaths occurred in the provinces, when the Jacobins who had ruled Paris with a bloody hand sent French soldiers into the countryside to bring populations to order and disperse local militias. The story is going around, too, that Joseph-Marie Lequinio, no more popular with Le Coz than Boissy d'Anglas, "went so far as to feed the hosts to the basest animals. For these horrible scandals and deep wounds, more than palliatives are needed."[68] Le Coz wants help from the consuls against such dechristianizing foolishness.

For all his adroit dedication to the constitutional cause and rejection of exaggerated papal authority, Claude Le Coz always believed a basic reverence for the pope to be theologically correct. He emerged from the constitutional experiment with an important archiepiscopal appointment, unlike Grégoire, who would not compromise with Roman officials (Spina at one time suggested a cardinal's hat), and unlike the constitutional bishop of Paris, whose ministry at the end of the century finally put him at odds with other constitutionals. This latter, Jean-Baptiste Royer, could not find the proper dialogue strategies to preside over his own church of Paris, and his unsuccessful late tenure resulted from his own insufficiencies as an administrator, yes, but also from the fractured existence of the constitutional experiment at the national level.

Chapter Ten

CONSTITUTIONAL IRRESOLUTION IN THE SEE OF PARIS

Jean-Baptiste Royer and the Council of 1801

When Jean-Baptiste Royer accepted the metropolitan see of Paris with its two constitutional power bases, the Paris presbytery and the United Bishops, he faced formidable challenges and in time became the target of sharp criticism. A strong influence during the 1797 Council, the presbytery was officially formed on 26 March 1796 under the leadership of Pierre Brugière, curé of Saint-Paul; Pierre Eugène Clausse, curé of Saint-André-des-Arts; and Jean-Claude Leblanc de Beaulieu, curé of Saint-Séverin. Slowly other curés joined in, some with trepidation. Early on they had to deal with Royer, who, although bishop of Ain at the time, had assumed pastoral responsibilities for the Parisian church of Saint-Médard. He always seemed to be a man of personal flexibility and pastoral dedication.[1]

In fact, Royer was a mild, decent man who took refuge in inaction when confronted by major challenges. Born in 1733 into a medical family, curé of Chavannes-sur-Suran in Franche-Comté, he served as a deputy to the Estates General and member of the Constituent Assembly. He heavily invested his political energies in the Jacobins, even as he militated against insults to and encroachment on church dignity and rights—once having at Jacques-Nicholas Billaud-Varenne on these issues. When on 6 February 1791 he was elected constitutional bishop of the Ain, a region with a heavy concentration of constitutional clergy, he was relatively well received. His own family followed his example in that his priest brothers hastened to take the oath. And when the Revolution turned anti-Christian with its promotion of the Feast of Reason, his niece, Rosalie Royer, was chosen by her municipality to play the role of the goddess Reason. This little adventure was countermanded, whether by Royer or someone in the civil government we do not know; but when Royer passed through the municipality a little later, he appointed another one of his brothers as his vicar general to keep a close eye on such things.[2]

As bishop of Ain, Royer aggressively promoted the Constitutional Church as the legitimate French Catholic church, and as an essential element of the Revolution to bring the "regeneration of this huge empire."[3] The faithful had only to be careful of the troublemaker prelates, who pretend to protect religion but really set brother against sister and virtually revive the wars of religion. Yet he had the greatest reverence for the constitutional monarchy. Condemning the vicious and malicious enemies of the king, he praised Louis because "this magnanimous prince goes freely into the National Assembly, and there declares himself the protector of the revolution and approves in all its parts the Constitution that had been decreed; a solemn day when by a most august oath, we all swore to be faithful to the nation, the law, and the king, and where the dear spouse of Louis the regenerator promised to raise in [faithfulness to] the principles of the Constitution, the presumptive heir to the crown."[4]

On his way to the Convention in September 1792, the month of the Paris massacres of imprisoned aristocrats and priests, Royer wrote to the faithful of his department that he had prayerful high hopes for the government and the role he might play in it: "We will not neglect any of those measures that we believe to be best suited for assuring your peace of mind and obtaining for you the spiritual aid that you have every right to ask for."[5] Yet lawlessness and violence troubled his vision. He did not accuse any political faction directly, but says that "disturbed men . . . seek to aggravate these evils; they try by secret maneuvers and dark plots, to foment a spirit of rebellion among you, and to rob your superiors of the trust that they deserve and have the right to enjoy."[6] As a Convention legislator, Royer voted for the mildest measures against the king: appeal to the people, detention, and banishment. Yet he was a partisan, timid to be sure, of Robespierre, perhaps to serve as a moderating influence. Even as late as August 1793, he was invoking the authority of the apostles and of St. Francis de Sales from the Assembly tribune. After internment and near execution, he helped move the post-Terror Convention to pass measures restoring some religious liberties.

The Paris Ministry

Royer was installed as bishop of Paris on 15 August 1798, but this did not give him or the team of priests, the presbytery of Notre-Dame, total control of the cathedral. The Directory government had conceded use of the front part of the cathedral to the semi-official Deist cult, Theophilanthropy, presided over by Directory chairman La Revellière-Lépeaux, and the municipal décadi celebrations were also held there. Official constitutional Catholic worship was relegated to one of the transepts and had been coordinated around the Theophilanthropy and décadi gatherings. The recalcitrant presbytery, accustomed to its own independence and mistrustful of Grégoire, worked with Bishop Royer because he, too, was an outsider, or at least minor player, among the United Bishops. His election as bishop of Paris had been a challenge from the beginning. Not only were the United Bishops and the presbytery intent on guaranteeing their own rights, but constitutional curés of the other principal Paris churches were themselves dissatisfied with the organization of the presbytery. Several times it looked as if the factions would not be able to come together. In fact, before and during the Council of 1797, the self-assertion of members of the presbytery contributed to a general unpopularity. When calm prevailed, compromises were made, and the only two options were Grégoire and Royer; the more malleable of the two, Royer, was elected.[7]

Royer's acceptance of his election as bishop of Paris was dutifully recorded on 15 June 1798 in the official register of the presbytery, which highlighted the discourse of Pierre Thuin, the long-suffering episcopal substitute in Paris (a sort of suffragan bishop) as bishop of nearby Meaux. First, Royer was presented to all: "Faithful and Christian people, this is he whom you will respect as a kind and attentive father who is sensitive to all your needs; he will ease your bitter sufferings, he will dissipate your sorrows, and he will teach you Christian resignation. He will live among you and his life will edify you. He will work continually to make saints of you."[8] This is about what one would expect in a presentation of a bishop to his flock, whatever Thuin's positive or negative thoughts about Royer. Thuin further wants Royer to assume the most positive attitude, the fullest acceptance from a people who cannot have the slightest idea of what to expect after the confusion and violence of the preceding five years: "And you, honorable pontiff, rejoice in the happiness of seeing the satisfaction and joy depicted in every eye, taste the pure and savory pleasure compared to which all the

Figure 30 Bishop Jean-Baptiste Royer, at first constitutional bishop of the Ain, became the bishop of Paris in 1798, years after the preceding constitutional bishop, Jean-Baptiste Gobel, had resigned. (Bibliothèque nationale de France)

principal titles invented in the past by pride are vain and contemptible and now destroyed by the grand courage of a free nation."[9]

A Reluctant Bishop

Royer's first Paris pastoral, 4 September 1798, was a rather humble letter explaining that the vote went against his wishes when he was elected.[10] He came to recognize it as the will of God, but, still and all, he began the task with "a feeling of terror."[11] When he looks at the talent and dedication of the outstanding Paris priests, he recognizes that he was certainly not the best choice for bishop. But God's ways are not man's ways, and so he bows before the mystery. His contribution will be to get the priests to work together: "Shall I add that God has permitted that I be the only one who, pulling together two-thirds of the votes, brings quickly to an end the difference of opinion that had hitherto divided the clergy?"[12] In fact, he is pleased that the church of Paris has so little to offer by way of worldly rewards: "As in those pristine days of Christianity, it offers only vigils, labors, perhaps even chains to him who has charge of it."[13] Presumably, he can thus be sure that he is working for the right reasons.

The preceding month, a week after his 15 August installation, Royer had addressed himself to an open meeting of the presbytery in these same accents. Evoking the heaviness of the burden, which he believed he shared with all the faithful, he promised the priests to "work in concert" and "rule in common" with them and to take as his model the great bishops such as Cyprian and Augustine: "He declared that he will consider himself to be no more than an executor of the general will, and he congratulated the assembly on the union that reigns among the members and urges it even more to full concord." And he said that if he were an obstacle to peace he would resign. Those present then responded with "a touching silence" and then received the kiss of peace from the bishop.[14]

Attending to the Clergy

Bishop Royer did look after the diocese as such. When the curé of Villetaneuse (Seine-Saint-Denis) wanted to resign, both the bishop and the presbytery went to work to get him to change his mind. Royer "expressed his sorrow about the experiences that brought [the curé] to do it." He displays genuine paternal understanding here, because "he [Royer] sees in the contradictions and suffering that he experienced in the running of the parish a particular mark of the vocation of God, who is calling him to return," and he sees "in the commitment to take care of him a proof that the Holy Spirit has inspired their [the parish members] will in such a way that a priest could hope for a fruitful ministry."[15] The priest had wanted to return to his monastery, and Royer tried to make the point that both the monastic and parish-priest vocations were fundamentally pastoral. He had apparently been imprisoned for a while, and Royer tried to turn this bad experience into a positive motivation to stay the course, "because the grace that God gave him to witness gloriously to his faith and to suffer prison as a confessor of Jesus Christ, would play a great part . . . in gaining him the esteem and veneration of his parishioners."[16] Royer also had standard inter-diocesan problems: some priests asked to come to Paris because they did not like their own bishop. Whatever lay behind this type of case, he was unwilling to get involved, and sent a response in consummate legalese. He was not able to accept their services, and "reminded them of the church discipline to the effect that if they do not get satisfaction from their bishop they should have recourse to a synod and then if necessary to the metropolitan council, and to a national council if one takes place, and that, in any case, they should not leave their dioceses without reference letters."[17]

A vexing problem for Royer in particular was the unauthorized use of French in the pro tem cathedral at Versailles, a fait accompli recently announced to the United Bishops: "We consider this custom to be a dangerous novelty, against which our love for the peace and unity of the church requires us absolutely to object."[18] A priest of Versailles, Louis Poinsignon, the aforementioned episcopal vicar of Bishop Clément, had taken a decree of the 1797 national church council promoting a new edition of the ritual book for the Gallican Church as a mandate or license for a vernacular sacramentary. Therein lay the problem. Had he stayed within his own mandate he would have been worthy of the praise and gratitude of the French clergy and people. Royer is disturbed by the report (he has not seen the whole work) that the baptismal ritual has been tampered with, and he proceeds to tick off a list of scriptural principles on authority and collegiality. Priests work with their bishops; bishops, with their national church; national churches, with the universal church. They also have as their guides the church fathers and the church councils and synods, which occasionally placed serious sanctions on offenders. Royer is indignant: "What! A simple priest, in circumstances as unfortunate as those in which we find ourselves, without observing any of the formalities proscribed by the sacred canons, takes the liberty of introducing in a church where he exercises only a subordinate ministry, an unheard-of innovation that undermines the general and continuing discipline of the Gallican church!"[19] Within the year Royer joined with the bishops of Dax and Amiens in warning that the easy promotion of the vernacular would perpetuate the errors of the Reformation era, and further isolate the Constitutional Church: "The first effect of the use of the vernacular would be to alienate, perhaps forever, the church of Rome and the other churches of the Latin rite, and to perpetuate the schism that is devouring us."[20] Even with these reservations, Royer, it was said, joined in the singing of the Psalms in French with the faithful who had gathered in his private chapel.

Sense of Fulfillment

Despite these internal church failures, Royer could take pride in the successes of the national government.[21] By 1800, he had no qualms about attributing the victories of the French army in Italy to the action of God and God's chief instrument, Napoleon, "the young hero who unites the wisdom and enlightenment of the elders to the value and fearlessness natural to the warriors of France."[22] It is unfortunate that the enemies of France cannot recognize reality here. Appropriately enough, Royer then concludes with words of praise from the Book of Judith, who by the strength of God was able to smite the enemy of Israel.

In 1800 also, he could say in a major pastoral instruction that the Revolution was necessary for the good of France: "If one takes an impartial look at the state to which France was reduced before eighty-nine, one will judge easily that the Revolution was inevitable and in a certain way necessary."[23] The government was incompetent and retrograde; officials were lazy or confused, their efforts only serving to make matters worse. For the church, the problem could be traced back to the sixteenth-century Concordat between the king of France and the pope: "The Concordat, that shameful arrangement [*marche*] concluded between Leo X and Francis I, one of the most catastrophic [*funeste*] sources of all the evils in the church of France, and against which it has perseveringly objected."[24] But now, in place of the old system that so strengthened the power of the high dignitaries of church and state, the French church promotes the potential freedoms of the Republic, and makes it possible to "heal all our church's wounds."[25] At the moment, Royer would have to say that the reform was stalled: "God, whose thoughts are unknowable, has shown us only the possibility of reform, and not permitted the execution of it."[26] He and the constitutional bishops should therefore take on the ministry that others have fled, take the oath, accept their appointments, look to the salvation of the faithful, and safeguard their besieged religion.

Thanksgiving, then, for Napoleon, the brilliant general of the Italian campaign, who, Royer says, has peace as his only goal: "Bonaparte offered peace; they refused it; he has now headed off to win it. No obstacle can stop him. The Alps incline their proud summits before him. Everywhere his invincible army, directed by such a head, sees all his efforts crowned with the most unbelievable successes; and at the center of the brilliant victory that delivered Italy, he demanded peace, the unique object of his desires."[27] God himself has given the victory: "Glory, honor, and thanksgiving to the God of hosts, who alone gives victory, we exclaimed to ourselves in our first transports of joy and gratefulness."[28]

The last part of the instruction is an attack on those who would have him retract his constitutional oath and accept the jurisdiction of de Juigné, the last Old Regime archbishop of Paris. No, says Royer, because he is in the best tradition of the Church of France: "Abjure the Civil Constitution of the Clergy! Far from abjuring its principles, we declare to you that as French bishops and priests, formed in the school of the great Bossuet, glory of our church, we firmly hold to these principles that can only cause the further development of our precious liberties."[29] He needs to hammer away again at that old Francis I/Leo X Concordat, always a harmful and annoying brake on the progress of the Gallican Church, and insist that there are good, practical reasons why he cannot accept the jurisdiction of the refractory archbishop of Paris, Antoine-Éléonore-Léon Leclerc de Juigné. Now in an irregular situation, the former archbishop could not return to the see of Paris. Royer is not even allowed to communicate with him, and so he had no choice: "Now a church cannot last without a bishop, and we must give it one; and he having been recognized canonically must be recognized by all. Such is the spirit and such are the rules of the church."[30] One has only to look back to the difficult times and theological solutions offered by the church fathers for justification of his own reaction to de Juigné: "By virtue of these same principles of the church of Antioch, Gregory was substituted for the Patriarch Anastasius, who was driven out by the Emperor Justin. Gregory exercised this worthy office in peace for twenty-five years until his death. Fleury, who reports this, does not treat Gregory as an *intrus* nor as a false shepherd; he praises him for it and gives him the name of Saint."[31]

Indecision

At the turn of the century, it was above all Royer's irresolute approach to diocesan and national challenges that put him at the center of controversy. "[Opponents] present me to the church as a bishop without zeal or energy, who uses up all his time in activities that are respectable in themselves but of minor importance, while I neglect the absolute essentials," he wrote in a letter to his fellow bishops on 21 April 1801. He had hoped at first that patient endurance would work, but then he saw that he had to protect the dignity of his office: "The honor of the episcopate, insulted in my person, imposes on me the painful obligation of explaining myself on things I would have liked to consign to oblivion."[32] He takes up a series of accusations against him and the difficulties in calling a council. The accusations against him deplored his failure to fill vacant sees (Sens, Orléans, Chartres), to properly inform all the bishops (suffragans) of the upcoming National Council, to set up diocesan and metropolitan synods, and to properly govern his own diocese.

As for the vacant see problem, he assures his colleagues that one of his major concerns was the assignment of bishops to those dioceses that no longer had a bishop, but he was convinced that he could not get correct and canonical elections in the three dioceses (of which he had regional jurisdiction as metropolitan bishop).[33] In fact, when he called together the bishops of his metropole and with them chose three candidates, each priest chosen declined for his own reasons. As for the diocesan synod, he believed it would be superfluous, because he had already arranged regular meetings of his clergy to reflect on the church's needs and to provide solutions. He thought that these meetings were like so many little synods and were well suited to the small size of the territorial jurisdiction. Random bishops, hanging around Paris instead of tending to their own dioceses, had no right to say anything about this. Royer insists that he is in the best position to convoke a synod at the proper time and direct its sessions. As for his negligence in running the diocese: after words to the effect that he is doing his best, he once again invokes the difficulty of the situation. Times are such that he cannot easily correct his misbehaving priests. Amid anarchy, church laws have no force. Bad priests can easily resist persuasiveness, paternal concerns, and even censures.

Finally, as regards the National Council, he obviously wants to avoid the problem of having to do everything over again. When he looks at the topics people want the council to take up, he is aghast: "What! They dare to propose to the fathers who make up the council that they enter into deliberations concerning the Council of Trent, and that they pronounce on all the errors that have come by since that same council."[34] As if the church did not already have enough problems, this would be a crushing burden, igniting all kinds of conflicts and leading to the destruction of the Gallican Church.

The actual criticism in the *Annales*, published toward the end of 1800, had been straightforward, without any particular animosity: "We would like to offer, without reserve, the praise due to the virtues of our bishop; but his humility will allow us without doubt to observe that the established priest has a set of functions different from that of a bishop or metropolitan."[35] In particular, critics were concerned with his penchant for preaching every day, even twice a day, from one end of the year to the other. His health suffers from it, but so does the diocese: "Here it is, the most important diocese in France with the greatest resources, the model for all the others, and it is not even in as good shape as a country parish!" The diocese was not well run, because the priests of the area were not effectively used and the bishop visited neither city nor country parishes: "Why does the bishop, who writes so often and so well, write so seldom and so laconically to his flock?" He provided no Lenten pastoral letter and no diocesan synod, despite all the demands for it. The writer is careful to insist that this criticism in no way contravenes "our respect and our sincere attachment to the bishop of Paris," and that he wants to commend the "virtues of a number of the priests composing the presbytery."[36] The writer has enough compliments to pass them all around: there is a superior group of priests in Paris, and a great number of the simple faithful, who are "as enlightened as they are edifying."

Royer's defensive reactions to the United Bishops stirred up much more severe and formal criticism subsequently. The *Annales* writers feign great surprise, and search to excuse his writing: "One wonders what kind of similarity can be established between a defense and a lampoon. Our first idea was to classify [the letter] in the second way, and to consider it apocryphal, for who is there among us who has not had imputed to him or directed against him some kind of lampoon?"[37] They note that neither the suffragan bishop of Paris nor they themselves received official copies of this letter, as they should have, whereas it was sent to laypeople. Here the United Bishops themselves appear as nothing less than disingenuous, because Royer's text was simply a defense against the accusations they had been making all along.

The bishops of the departments around Paris, who called the necessary council on their own authority, receive signal praise from the United Bishops in 1801, in contrast to Royer, who did not believe a council should be held while the government, that is to say the first consul, was negotiating with Rome: "Precisely because they are negotiating, we have one more reason to hold the council. The Gallican Church should in all things take the dominant stance, and that if any major change in its discipline is proposed it ought to put forward a united front."[38] There is also the problem of rehashing Council of Trent issues. It appears that the council was never accepted in France, and this needs to be examined. Royer had feared that the discussion would get unnecessarily heated, and the United Bishops ask in response, "Is it not to calumniate ahead of time a serious assembly that will be composed of venerable pastors, just like the first council?"[39] These are bishops on the scene who have observed the limited reach of Bishop Royer, for all his supposed contacts with the highest reaches of government. They believe, further, that he has "calumniated the government" and "calumniated the clergy to the government," all of this to take on himself the mantle of a prophet. This particularly harsh attack on Royer was signed by Grégoire, Desbois, Clément, and Wandelaincourt.

The Constitutional Last Stand: The 1801 Council

Bishop Royer could never straightaway accept the initiatives of the United Bishops. When they moved to have a National Council of the French constitutional clergy, he put them off, even though he had previously noted the utility of such an event. To the Paris presbytery he said that "he resolved not to address to the bishops of his region the circular letter of 2 March that four of the United Bishops had addressed to him in order to effect the convocation of a National Council for Ascension Day 1801. He declared that he would in no way recognize the position [*qualité*] of the United Bishops."[40] He fussed about the need for a diocesan synod to prepare a regional synod, which could then help coordinate the convocation of a national synod, but, in fact, he was so slow in organizing it that Clément and Thuin had to do it for him.

In the Shadow of Grégoire and Le Coz

Royer was grousing about the appropriateness of the council just as the Concordat was being worked out, and members of his cathedral administration team were developing their own council procedures. Le Coz and Grégoire, especially concerned to maintain the integrity and authority of the United Bishops, wanted to put their constitutional theory and practice in good form, and so they convoked the council in 1801 with one vital goal: stabilizing the Constitutional Church as the official Catholic church of France. When the council began, Royer officiated at the opening liturgies; his several sermons over the course of the week's liturgies encouraged the colleagues, but did not fully placate Grégoire for his earlier opposition.[41]

In his own opening discourse on 29 June, Grégoire placed their efforts in line with great councils of church history: "One of the most efficacious means to avert and repress the abuses, and to guard the integrity of the faith, morality, and the rights of the hierarchy, is the holding of councils, which are, after holy scripture, the most respected monuments and the purest sources of tradition."[42] He thinks that the lively importance of this council is something he ought to address at the beginning, with special attention to episcopal councils. His conclusion here is that "our principles are those of antiquity, those which in modern times good theologians and canonists have supported: the cardinals Dailly and de Cusa, and above all that Gerson who was the glory of the church of France, the oracle of the council of Constance, and who did not cease to combat false doctrines, to reestablish the ancient form of the Christian republic."[43]

The National Council Grégoire addresses belongs to that great tradition of church councils: "To the Gallican church belongs the glory for having revived the ecclesiastical assemblies. In the last six years it has held around eighty synods, eight metropolitan councils, and the National Council of 1797."[44] Opposing the council are his usual dogs of war: first, the rabid secularists. "There were such obstacles to conquer: because in order to prevent it from taking place, two groups, we noted, made common cause: the destroyers of churches who after having knocked down the crosses erected the scaffolds of the Terror," and then the refractories "who, believing themselves to be the only real Catholics, having both heaven and earth at their beck and call, are abundantly supplied with excommunications."[45]

Citing anonymous attacks in the press, Grégoire vigorously responds: "Against this council they mustered the journalists who know how to substitute bombast for reason; they multiplied the number of anonymous, which is to say, always vile accusations: no one dared admit the authorship of them, and so later they were ready to censure even the title *National Council*."[46] Then he attacks the refractories, noting that they had no problem with Protestant and Jewish councils—strange gripe on his part, given that the contentious French clergy had nothing to do with Protestants and Jews anyway. He insists that the constitutional bishops saved the church in France several times over the last decade: "Without them, religion would have been buried under the remains of its own cradle; but certainly they did not have to complain of an excess of gratitude."[47] Now there is the present council. And some have sacrificed their lives for this cause: "Our eyes will not encounter any of those harvested by a natural death, not those who perished in the horrors of hunger, nor those bishops whom the rage against royalism has massacred. The virtuous Expilly found martyrdom on the revolutionary scaffolds; his successor, on his way to Morlaix to bring the consolations of his ministry to members of his diocese, fell under the assassin's dagger of those men who, at Machecoul, washed themselves in the blood of patriots, on the bodies of whom they dared to celebrate the Holy

Sacrifice."[48] After defending councils in the church, Grégoire broadens out to a defense of religion in the country. He and the constitutional bishops have tried to work for peace and for a balance of church and state.

Resolving the Schism

The council was under the patronage of Royer only in the sense that it was held in his diocese and that he was the primary liturgical celebrant. Grégoire and Le Coz were actually the main personalities, with Le Coz presiding formally, as he had for the Council of 1797. According to the council minutes, concrete organizational problems received first attention. A diocese was for all practical purposes without a bishop because it was technically still the see of the deadbeat bishop François Marbos, who, for all his contempt for the job, would not agree to a replacement; worse, "since that time his negligence has become even more inexcusable, and leaves no doubt that we ought to consider him as definitively deposed and for this reason apply to him all the severity of the church canons."[49] On the problem of the metropolitan sees, the delegate Father François de Torcy said that, although based on civil jurisdictions that existed in the days of the early church, the system still had normative value precisely because it came from the early church. Grégoire, of course, could not let an early church issue go by without a note: "According to the bishop of Blois the metropolitan government is of the earliest antiquity and was highly esteemed by the church." He then brought up the primacy of the see of Lyon, the idea that it might be reestablished, recalling the existence of "the old imperial see of Trier and the measures to take against a metropolitan who would neglect the fulfillment of his duties."[50]

One of the first items on the council agenda was the discussion of the general resignation of all of the French bishops, a key element of the Concordat being worked out by representatives of Napoleon and of the pope (see next chapter). If the Old Regime bishops should prove to be willing to do so, why not the constitutionals? Some of the bishops were positive on resignation, but Grégoire and the United Bishops were not. Too many issues were unresolved for such a move to be safe and effective, but this time around the bishops were able to reiterate their fidelity both to the pope and to the French government. They focused on social questions where a conflict with the government could arise: marriage, divorce, marriage of priests. Then they approved a letter to be sent to the pope asking him to back their

Figure 31 A caricature of the second National Council of the reconstituted Constitutional Church, interpreting the council as a ridiculous, diabolical inversion of the sober, guardedly optimistic gathering that actually took place in Notre-Dame Cathedral. (Bibliothèque nationale de France)

attempts to bring peace to the troubled consciences of the citizens. The church–state relationship was the broad field here, which allowed for a discussion of the celebration of a national festival on 14 July. There were a number of recensions of a letter to Napoleon, with some combination of real and feigned hope in the background: "Your proclamation announces that soon the scandal of religious divisions will cease. This news fills us with joy and we have spread it abroad into our respective dioceses."[51] They are concerned lest there be a reduction of the numbers of bishoprics and lest the parishes be without pastors. They seem only too happy to give the first consul a major role in ecclesiastical decision making, assuming that if they left confirmation of appointments to him they could avoid the illegitimate control that Rome had come to exercise on the French church: "Since that day when the popes had the audacity to appropriate this to themselves, they have held in their hands a major means of subjugating both the church and the state."

A few days later, the medieval hero of the French church, theologian Jean Gerson, was held up for promotion and praise. Desbois de Rochefort petitioned that the council fathers recognize Gerson "as one of the lights of the church, because his memory is still venerated, miracles are worked at the tomb that vandalism has profaned and possibly destroyed." In fact, the speaker expected that one day "this productive and learned doctor" would be canonized.[52] Claude Le Coz joined the praise but did not believe that the council should concern itself with any of this, especially inasmuch as he found Gerson inconsistent on the matter of councils and infallibility.

As August began, a communication on the council deliberations was prepared, along with a brief number of decrees pertaining to the council itself and the invited regional administrations (Belgium and the colonies). One bishop told the assembly that it would be shameful if the Paris constitutionals did not stand up to the overextension of papal authority, when at the same time the churches of Italy were praising the freedoms of the Gallican Church: "The different churches, coming together one day, following the examples of the churches of France and Italy, have hope for an ecumenical council that will effectively reform the universal church."[53]

A table of episcopal reports was put together, a summary of the complaints and hopes of the metropolitan bishops. The see of Lyon laments widow churches in the dioceses of Montblanc, Ain, and several other places, but seems to have it in most for old Bishop Lafont de Savine of Viviers. According to this story, the bishop had not been around for the previous five years, but rather had comfortably retired to Paris. But Paris cannot find priests willing to be consecrated bishops for the region—and this includes Poinsignon of Versailles: "We can only hope that any further holding out on the part of the priests so appointed does not prolong the evils of anarchy in the dioceses."[54] The see of Rennes was still feeling the distress occasioned by the death of Bishop Audrein; Aix, the distress caused by the marriage of Bishop Jean-Baptiste Dumouchel, once bishop of nearby Nîmes in the department of the Gard. In fact, Aix was also sorting out the relative usefulness of bishops situated at Grenoble and Valence. The see of Bourges was finding a way to get ex-Jesuit Michel-Joseph Dufraisse to accept consecration and episcopal duties at Chateauroux. The see of Rouen was haunted by

Figure 32 Jean Gerson statue outside the chapel of the Sorbonne. Gerson was a theologian of the medieval French church and a role model for some of the constitutional clergy. Although a promoter of papal primacy, broadly speaking, he believed in the superiority of an ecumenical council. He clearly articulated the role of French Catholicism within the papal church and, accordingly, has been called the father of Gallicanism. His importance for the Constitutional Church was briefly highlighted at the Council of 1801.

the ghost of Massieu; and the see of Bordeaux, by the notorious abdication of Bishop Gay-Vernon. But Bishop Claude Debertier, compiler of the text, wrote in sum that if it is "in some ways painful, it is also very satisfying in others." And he hopes that at the next great council he will only have consolations to offer.

A final synodal letter was placed in the minutes as a witness to the successful ministry of the Constitutional Church. No doubt they believe that they have accomplished a great revival in the worst of circumstances: "What a wealthy clergy in its prosperous days did not accomplish, was brought about in 1797 by a clergy just out of the prison cells of tyranny and then plunged into the agonies of persecution and extreme poverty."[55] That was when they had their first church council, with its activation of piety and patriotism through reorganization of the church. And they see their accomplishments this time around as direct and ordered: "In the course of the present session, we have several times addressed our words to you in order to outline the principles that united you to Jesus Christ as Christians, to the visible head of the church as Catholics, to the Republic as citizens, to the churches of the countries recently united to France as integral parts of our national church."[56] Caught up in the grandeur of the moment, the council fathers believe they have formally set up the French Catholic church: "We would have presented an outline of errors against faith and morals to those who since the Council of Trent have harmed religion and merited the censures of the church. We would like to reestablish the synodal statutes of all the dioceses in a single code, forcefully reiterate the rules of canonical penance, organize teaching in the seminaries, and achieve a uniformity of the various rites and liturgical books."[57] Ways were thus prepared for an ecumenical council by determining the relationship of dioceses to broad regional authority and of the Gallican Church to "the universal church, the mystical body of Jesus Christ."[58]

Concerned that their resignations would leave the church defenseless against the disorder and divisiveness that the refractories were intent on bringing to the process, council members foregrounded the eternal theme of the liberties of the Gallican Church. A delegation that included Royer was formed to arrange a formal meeting with Napoleon, who with his advisers was just then formulating the Concordat. The concluding discussions in council, no surprise, highlighted modalities of resignation that would preserve those Gallican liberties: each bishop could submit his resignation to his (constitutional) metropolitan, or to Le Coz as president of the council. However, it is clear that Grégoire and a number of others, including Moïse, Clément, and Dufraisse, adhered to the old hard line, protesting that resignation would be in the name of some false charity. Included in the council documentation was a letter written *after* the signing of the Concordat, looking forward to vindication by a future ecumenical council: "Considering the confusion . . . that is placed before us in the supposed *general resignation of the Episcopate of France*, based on the abandonment by several bishops, already accomplished they say, of their sees, we cannot see here anything other than the illegal, the pernicious, and the radically null and void, whatever the pretext—even that of a (false and illusory) peace."[59] It was signed "at Bourges and at Paris with the expectation of the holding of a general council, in the month of November 1801."

Map 3 The revived Constitutional Church—six areas of activity

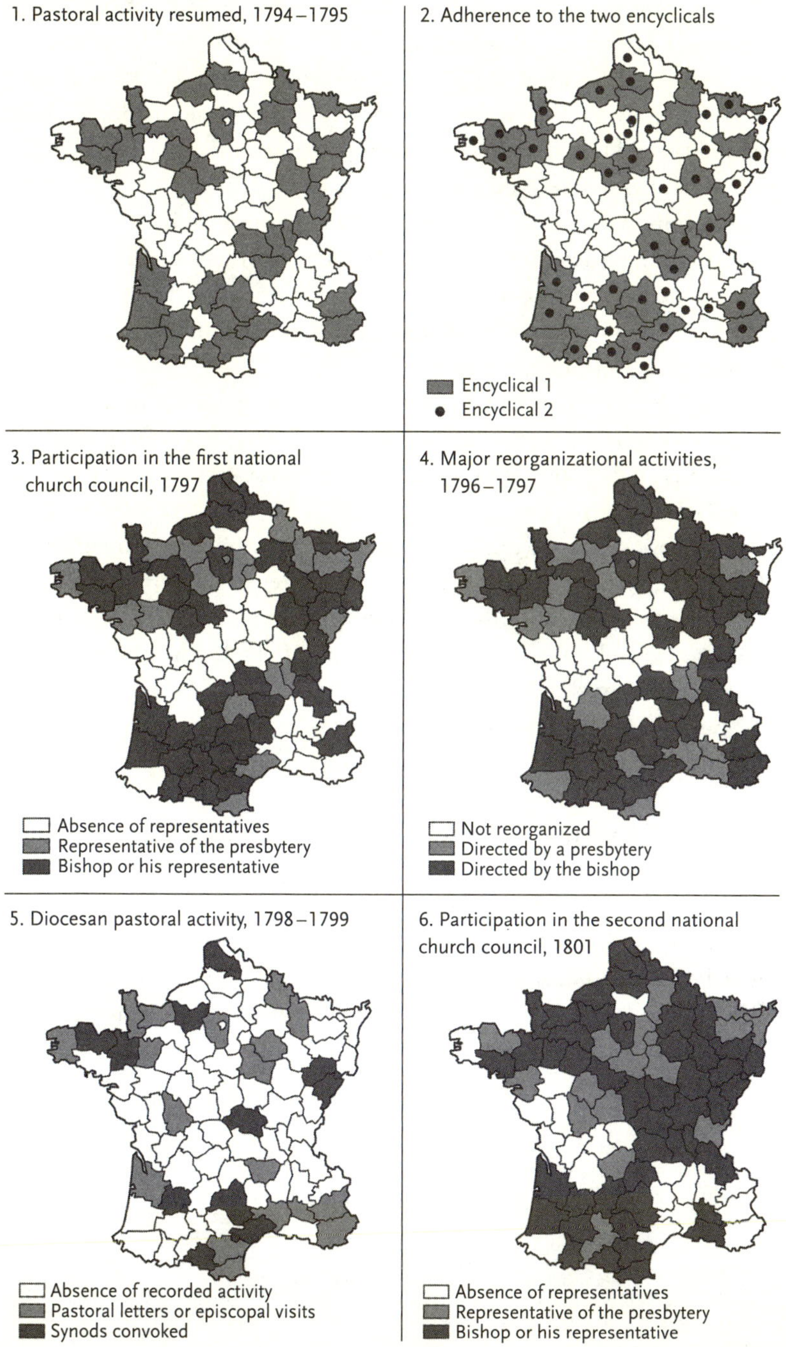

It was clear to the constitutional clergy, as it is clear to historians today, that the second Constitutional Church displayed a genuine vitality, despite its continuing personnel problems and its diminished status. Bernard Plongeron notes that between the Council of 1797 and the Council to 1801, 104 assemblies were held in fifty-five dioceses, and some fifteen to twenty thousand faithful took part in eight metropolitan councils. The council delegates entrusted to the appropriate experts the production of a new ritual text, a new missal, a treaty on marriage. It might be possible to consider the fine and erudite *Traité sur l'uniformité de la liturgie* (1800) to be a crowning achievement. At the Council of 1801 there were more delegates present than in 1797, with better representation from the provinces and delegations from Germany, Spain, and England.[60]

The achievements of the second Constitutional, or Gallican, Church across the years can be graphed for six areas of activity: (1) Resumption of activity in each diocese was signaled by the publication of the local bishop's pastoral letters, and (2) a principal indication of the resumption of activity was the adherence of the local bishop to the two encyclical letters sent out from Paris by the six United Bishops. (3) Representation of individual dioceses was higher still in the first National Council of the constitutional bishops (1797), although twenty-seven out of the eighty-three dioceses were not represented. (4) Reorganization efforts included a majority of dioceses, but in nineteen dioceses neither bishop nor presbytery indicated any resumption of activity; (5) as for major pastoral activities (pastoral letters, episcopal visits, and diocesan synods), only twenty dioceses were represented. (6) However, at the second National Council a larger number of dioceses were represented than at the first National Council (fifty-three out of eighty-three).

Counting on a future general council of the church, the delegates to the Council of 1801 soon saw all their efforts thwarted: Royer's pessimism was not far off the mark, because the Concordat would not be a sure solution for them at all.

Chapter Eleven

CONSTITUTIONAL CLERGY IN THE CHURCH OF NAPOLEON'S CONCORDAT

Pope Pius VII knew that the Catholic Church would be saved from its low estate if Napoleon could reintegrate it into French national life, and accordingly he sent Archbishops Spina and Caselli to Paris from Rome in September 1800. They were given instructions to deal directly with the government, and not with the constitutionals at all. The constitutionals' National Council of 1801, held in the middle of these negotiations, was almost completely ignored. In the series of formal "projects" and responses put together over the following months by the representatives of Paris and Rome, an agreement was slowly fashioned: a combination of written formulations and interpretative maneuvers around the formulations. Representing Napoleon was Bishop Étienne Bernier, politically experienced and astute, who had helped Napoleon end the Vendée crisis.[1] The central documents were labeled the *Projets de convention*, in that they were to represent the "compact" or "convention" of two substantial powers.

Toward the Concordat

With the First Project, bargaining began on the resignation of the episcopacy, with Bishop Bernier recalling the Concordat of Leo X and François I as a model of exchange between the French and papal governments—in total contrast to the oft-expressed viewpoint of the constitutionals. Talleyrand joined Bernier in the negotiations, while in the background preparations were made to send François Cacault, a career diplomat, to Rome to manage Napoleon's interests there. Napoleon, with the help of Joseph

Fouché, surveyed the entire process, reviewing texts and reports on Archbishop Spina's activities. Bernier made it clear to Spina that the pope had to accept the loss of his confiscated territories and the resignation of all loyalist bishops. After twenty-one different drafts and eight months of discussions, the Concordat was signed on 15 July 1801. In response to the First Project, Talleyrand insisted that Catholicism could not be the state religion or the "dominant religion." By the Third Project, Catholicism was called the religion of the majority of French citizens and of the government (but not of the state), and the reconciliation of the constitutionals and married priests was to be left to a delegate. Although this language was acceptable to Spina, Talleyrand insisted that the Third Project was not acceptable either to him or to the first consul, because no formal provisions were made for the constitutional clergy. Napoleon's heightened power and prestige served as the political setting for the successive projects from the victory at Marengo (14 June 1800), five to six months before the development of the First Project in November–December 1800, through the conclusion of the last project, one week before the Treaty of Lunéville.

At this time the constitutional bishops were trying to strengthen their position by the positive reports and arguments in *Annales de la religion.* They were preparing in earnest for their second National Council, and had issued a *Lettre pastorale sur la paix.* A few of them, however, went to see Bernier in hopes of securing an episcopal position for themselves later on, thereby incurring the wrath of Grégoire. In May 1801, Napoleon intensified his demands for the confirmation of the constitutional bishops, acceptance of priests' marriages, silence about the Revolution-era takeover of church properties, and the calling of a National Council of the French church. The Sixth Project, in fact, coincided with the calling of the constitutionals' second National Council. After the touch-ups worked on the Seventh and Eighth Projects, and the interpretations that Cardinal Hercules Consalvi, the papal secretary of state, offered in three counterprojects, the final redaction of the Concordat was completed.

The text was signed on 15 July 1801, ratified in Rome on 15 August and in Paris on 8 September, and then, just as the second National Council was in full swing (it had begun on 29 June and would continue through to the middle of August), the constitutional bishops were shown a draft of the text. Finally, Henri Grégoire and Jean-François Périer were taken to meet Napoleon, who authorized the continuation of the council and attended an official dinner at the Tuileries to mark its closing. After this, Napoleon

Figure 33 The signing of the Concordat between Napoleon's government and the Catholic Church. The figure at the center left is the emperor's brother, Joseph Bonaparte; on the far left is Cardinal Hercules Consalvi, the papal secretary of state. Two figures pictured as priests in this illustration are Étienne Bernier (soon to be bishop of Orléans), who represented Napoleon's interests to the papal delegation in Rome, and Cardinal (by the time the Concordat was signed) Caselli, who was a member of the original delegation. (Bibliothèque nationale de France)

indicated that he did not want demeaning submissions extracted from the constitutionals and that a minimum of twelve constitutional bishops were to be named for the Concordat hierarchy of ten archbishoprics and sixty bishoprics.[2]

The concordatory church as it was finally set up would be governed by bishops chosen by the first consul and invested with authority by the pope. The new layout of dioceses would be the same as the revolutionary division of France into departments. Napoleon expected all the bishops to resign and await the decision of the pope as to their role in the concordatory church. He expected the pope to admit the validity of the ministry of the Constitutional Church and disinherit the Old Regime bishops and other refractories. This, in effect, awarded the pope a tightened rule over French clergy that he never had before, and surrendered the old jealously guarded rights of the Gallican Church to organize ministry and make all hierarchical appointments on its own without interference from Rome.

Between August 1801 and April 1802, rules and procedures for the constitutionals' submission and retraction of errors were at the center of continuing negotiations—and subterfuge. Napoleon knew that many former

Jacobins, and in fact many of his generals, remained quite hostile to the Concordat and to the refractories especially. Cardinal Giovanni Battista Caprara, special legate for reconciling the constitutionals and inactive priests, headed for Paris on 5 September 1801, even as the French bishops, the constitutionals, were deliberating the mode of their resignations and incorporation into the concordatory church. Their reactions to several papal communications and the letters of Archbishop Spina were somewhere between reserved and negative. To elevate the discussions to a higher political register, Napoleon decided to appoint Jean-Étienne-Marie Portalis as the minister of state responsible for church affairs, an office coordinated with the ministry of the interior, headed by Jean-Antoine-Claude Chaptal. This facilitated the agreement on a formula for the resignation of the constitutional bishops, but it did not ensure consistent interpretation and submission on the part of the bishops themselves. Grégoire (along with Moïse, constitutional bishop of the Jura) addressed a letter to Portalis attempting to radically modify the document, and then issued a pastoral letter of his own.[3]

The indefatigable Cardinal Caprara continued to negotiate with the bishops; such are the ways of diplomacy that the constitutionals could say they had been treated as bishops, whereas Caprara wrote in his diary that he did no such thing. From October onward, Portalis was preoccupied with the lists of bishops to be appointed, using the results of a survey begun by Chaptal on 21 July 1801, six days after the signing of the Concordat. Unfortunately the discussion was gerrymandered by Portalis's nephew, the abbé Paul-Thérèse-David d'Astros, who worked out an evaluation of the constitutional bishops that did not correspond to the results obtained by Chaptal from his departmental prefects. Each prefect had established a rostrum, or annotated list (état nominatif), evaluating the personal strengths of the bishops and priests of the department.[4] This was careful and detailed work.

Usable Constitutionals

With periodic insertions of patriotic themes, the prefect from Alpes-Maritimes gives the "reasons why they enjoy public esteem": wisdom and good conduct, civic responsibility, talent, worthiness and selflessness as a curé, good conduct during and loyalty to the Revolution, basic morality, charity, and common sense.[5] Unfortunately, says the prefect in his formal letter, despite a number of good men on the list, it would be hard to find many "men who because of their enlightenment, acceptance by the public, and reputation are capable of leading the ministers of the Catholic religion in the department."[6]

Categories were useful only insofar as they answered the question, "Would this man be an *effective bishop* now?" And the prefect of the Aisne was careful about his subheadings. First, "Priests who by their behavior, their talents, and the esteem they enjoy could well fulfill important functions." There was Father Boussart, once a well-liked professor at the local *collège*, who returned to minister to parishioners in the town of Coucy where his family resided; people can appreciate the wisdom with which he negotiated the revolutionary years. And Father Pennier, the former Norbertine prior, would also be worthwhile: a very moral and well-trained man, a village curé and mayor of Castres. Then, a second subheading: "Priests who have sufficient education and talent to be assigned to the cities," of which a good example would be Father Reiser, with his good morals, good piety, good sense, and wisdom, a constitutional since the beginning. The third subheading: "Priests who are the most noteworthy among those who could be religious leaders in the major villages." Example: Father Matra, a curé before the Revolution, who stayed in his home parish and continued to preside at worship.[7]

Other prefects lined up their choices in similar ways. From the Ardennes, for example, the list of good men begins with the bishops, and continues on in order of dignity and loyalty.[8] Joseph Monin, bishop of the department of the Ardennes (consecrated in 1798),[9] "has talents, good morals, and the esteem of the people, he is attached to the government and has made his submission to it." Joseph Collot, major vicar and curator at the Bibliothèque nationale, is "talented, he enjoys the esteem of his fellow citizens and is attached to the government." In the Gard, the prefect found "distinguished and conciliatory old types." The first name on the list is the Old Regime bishop of Alais, de Bausset, now living in Paris, or so thinks the prefect—he is a "very learned, conciliatory, generally loved and esteemed. I know that the correspondence he engaged in has constantly given proof of his attachment to the government." But Rochemore, an episcopal vicar from the diocese of Nîmes, has broad appeal: "Has made his submission. He is one of the men most respected by all religious groups and people of all viewpoints. He is naturally kind and conciliating. . . . His credit is good with other priests and with every type of citizen."[10]

Superior qualities alone were insufficient for appointment of a constitutional bishop: the local man, often a good person, had been at the center of religious strife, and so would not be an appropriate leader in that area for the future. Bishop François Bécherel (consecrated 1790; later concordatory bishop of Valence), says the prefect of La Manche was a fine man, but it would be better to choose someone else: "A peace-loving spirit, good morals, kindly attitude toward everyone. No one has ever said otherwise."[11] Refractories are, of course, resentful: "Because the non-juring priests have suffered much, some of them have considered [the bishop] an intriguer. In this instance, despite the error of such a viewpoint, should the government want him to exercise an important function, it would be better that he do so in a neighboring department." Likewise, the prefect of the Lot praises the constitutional bishop, but still would not keep him there: "A virtuous and learned man. When, in the trauma of the Terror, the refractory priests were imprisoned, he sold his furniture to feed them. He never stopped trying to lighten their punishment. If all the furniture of the constitutional clergy had been consigned to him there would have been peace in the church long ago."[12] There seemed no way to get rid of the *esprit de parti* in Puy-de-Dôme. Jean-François Périer, the constitutional bishop (consecrated 1791; later concordatory bishop of Avignon), was learned, kindly, prudent, and an able administrator: "If the impressions that help form a partisan attitude were not eradicable, he could be given the responsibilities that he deserves in this department."[13]

Constitutional bishops sometimes impaired their otherwise good reputations by ordaining mediocre priests, even though one could not really blame bad priests on a good bishop. In the Aube, Bishop Louis Belmas (consecrated 1801; later concordatory bishop of Cambrai) "merits esteem and confidence by his talents and the consistency of his conduct; but his clergy being composed of men without morality and resources, it is to be feared that if he were appointed to higher office in the department, partisan spirit would make him chose them [the mediocre priests] for the junior posts."[14] Looking to the future, prefects noted on occasion that there might be a good candidate for bishop but a bad "market": curés are not readily available because they cannot get enough financial support to survive. The prefect of the Charente wrote, "I foresee in this region many obstacles to the roles proposed by the government. Of ten clergy that I have authorized to serve in parishes, six have abandoned their posts for lack of payment on the part of the locals."[15] Or a well-placed constitutional bishop would have to deal with insulting refractories, as in the Gironde: "[Dominique] Lacombe [consecrated 1798; later concordatory bishop of Angoulême] is truly religious, charitable, and full of zeal. . . . He is reproached, nevertheless, for too high a self-esteem and too great an intolerance of the refractory priests, who, in truth, have done all they can to heap insults upon him."[16]

Some prefects find fault with both the refractories and the constitutionals: "Very few of the priests in the department merit complete confidence: those whom we dignify with the name of constitutionals have been forced to deal with, and even to fawn on the most vicious and guilty men. They have always made common cause with those who have undercut and dishonored the Revolution."[17] Not only were they soft on Jacobin extremes, but they were anti-Christian to boot: "They have accepted, and still keep in their ranks those who have renounced any kind of worship." As for the refractories, "I should have dismissed with even greater care those whom incurable pretentiousness made into intolerant enemies of the Revolution and of interior peace." In the Sarthe, the prefect criticized the bishop for playing along with both the revolutionary and religious extremists: "[Jean-Guillaume] Prudhomme [consecrated 1791], the constitutional bishop: ambitious, some reproach him for having taken part in popular movements and subsequently in pious movements. He has been, I believe, a good citizen."[18]

Some prefects clearly developed a *history* of one or another bishop. In the Landes, of course, the prefect had to deal with the high-profile constitutional Jean-Baptiste Saurine (consecrated 1791; later concordatory bishop of Strasbourg). The prefect sent in a long essay titled "Quelques observations sur le culte catholique" with full coverage of the bishop. When Saurine arrived, all was set up in proper fashion, legally and ceremonially. He imported unworthy young men from elsewhere, ordained them, and set them loose: "Citizen Saurine, in a quandary to replenish his clergy, ordained priests from the young men that he brought in from the Pyrénées, who were without education and morality, and were then set up everywhere in response to the citizenry's need for new clergy." All of this made the refractory clergy look good: "The nonconstitutional clergy here were generally very austere in demeanor and very few were known for scandalous conduct. The comparison does not serve to the advantage of the new priests." Worst of all, some citizens were even executed for not supporting the Constitutional Church: "As soon as the persecutions began, [these citizens] were denounced, arrested, and sometimes guillotined for not having assisted at the masses of the constitutional priests." To put it bluntly, nobody likes him, whereas people did appreciate the old bishop, "persecuted" by Saurine. It would not matter that the prefect himself approves of the man: "Not that I do not personally believe him worthy."[19]

And so on: the brief vignettes with simple approval and disapproval. Alexandre-Victor Rouanet (consecrated 1799) of the Hérault is good at the basics: he "enjoys the finest reputation" for his "public spirit" and "morality."[20] Claude Le Coz (consecrated 1791; later concordatory archbishop of Besançon) gets simple praise from the Ille-et-Vilaine prefect: "Called by the people to be bishop of the department of Ille-et-Vilaine, where he has remained. Has many resources, is of irreproachable conduct; esteemed by both sides, he took the first oath."[21] Jean-Joseph Mestadier (consecrated 1790) is criticized in the Deux-Sèvres: "One would put him here only because he once fulfilled important functions. He is worthless and disliked. His ignorance is such that he could not pass the test for primary-grade teacher."[22] Charles-François Dorlodot (consecrated 1799) was an old semi-aristocrat who calmly went through the years as a constitutional curé and then bishop in the Mayenne: "He adopted the principles of the Revolution as a man educated in letters, science, and philosophy. Gentle, tolerant, he united the qualities of heart and mind that make a good ecclesiastic."[23] Jean-Joachim Gausserand (consecrated 1791) of the Tarn was a mediocre preacher: "He has no gift for public speaking."[24] Gabriel-François Moreau, Old Regime bishop of Macon, who had stayed in his diocese all across the decade, and Louis Charrier de la Roche (consecrated 1791), of Seine-Inférieure, both from other regions then, were taken seriously as bishops and (rather solemnly here) as true citizens in Saône-et-Loire: "I surely cannot propose to the government any more complimentary label on their behalf."[25] And the état nominatif says of Charrier de la Roche that "his age encloses in a healthy body a strong spirit, and a head full of good sense and ideas."[26] Jean-Baptiste Flavigny (consecrated 1791) gets high praise in Haute-Saône: "He is endowed with the Christian virtues and has kindly ways about him. His talents and qualities got him named a bishop at the beginning of the Revolution and he has kept the attachment and esteem of everyone."[27] A Jansenist of impeccable credentials, Jean-Claude Leblanc de Beaulieu (consecrated 1800; later concordatory bishop of Soissons), constitutional bishop in Rouen, was the favorite in Seine-Inférieure: "Austere in his behavior, and trained in the principles of Port-Royal, to which he is very much attached.[28] Charles Montault-des-Isles (consecrated 1791; later concordatory bishop of Angers) was written up as gentle-spirit constitutional who seems to have gone into remission. He would go on to become an eminently successful concordatory bishop in a refractory stronghold, Angers: "Constitutional bishop of the department, learned, of gentle comportment, a conciliatory spirit. He has not been active for several years and lives quietly with his family."[29]

Clearly the constitutional bishops favored by the prefects were later given dioceses, however begrudgingly conceded by the pope, in the church of the Concordat. The survey of usable constitutionals was simply the best information available as the details of the 1801 Concordat were being actualized.

The Choice: Reintegration or Retraction?

The constitutionals who were perhaps most ready to work for reintegration into a reunited church wanted to do so on their own terms, and were mightily antagonistic to refractories who would condemn them, and antagonistic also to fellow constitutionals who would retract. *Annales de la religion* records their testimonies.

Reintegration Without Compromise

Constitutionals believed that their refractory antagonists considered "retractions as a type of preliminary step, indispensable in your view for arriving at a final reconciliation," and asked how the refractories could possibly demand this when the oath was a just one to begin with, and had since become a dead letter.[30] The refractories are the ones who have made common cause with émigré campaigns to foment the bloody civil wars that came upon France. They are the ones responsible for "the revival of the most outrageous heresies, the most hateful lies, and the blackest calumnies spread about without restraint."[31] Now the faithful are ready to abandon religion completely, and religion as a whole is about to be proscribed anyway. After another brief list of vile refractory behaviors overlapping with the first list, they, the Paris constitutionals, turn to reconciliation: "O dear and venerable brothers, however hard the truths that we have just recalled, let us nonetheless be always ready for frank and honest reconciliation, as soon as we have the commission to bring it about. . . . Let not our heart ever open up to hate! Let us offer the most humble thanksgiving to providence for the gentle laws that bring them [the refractories] to the bosom of their families and of the fatherland."[32]

The constitutionals were especially frustrated when trouble-making, meddling refractories were called "the good priests," because, far from being "good," they are "unhappy victims of fanaticism and the aristocracy; these latter, who have sworn mortal hate for the Revolution, support them and nourish them [the priests] as long as they have any hope of obtaining their despicable goals."[33] Taking stock of the state of Catholicism in Paris itself, the constitutionals find, in the main, "chaos." Catholicism, the ancient and for centuries the only religion of the Parisians, is lost in a confusion of languages, philosophies, and opinions: "Its voice is constantly muffled by the droning on of so many individuals who can neither hear nor make themselves heard, or who are totally occupied with other goals, or who have conspired to destroy it."[34] On the refractory side, pastoral care "hardly exists anymore; four or five spacious church buildings, rather than full parishes, seem to form the base of this group; the presumed heads have renounced their title of pastor."[35] They have deserted the churches of Paris, thereby forcing people to come all the way to Notre-Dame Cathedral for crowded religious services. But "the pulpits filled by the priests who have made their submission resound with lessons of respect due to law and authority. The constitutional clergy do not have oratories, nor do they try to secure followers."[36] Only the constitutionals have tried to keep the church alive amid the decadent priests who wander the capital: some, married men; some, apostates; some, idlers. Most of all, they have set themselves against those who are, for no good reason, retracting their oaths: "Certain of what should be the case, they [the constitutionals] abandon to remorse of conscience, to public shame, and to whatever dangers the future will bring, the self-interested and unprincipled priest, who after having seen the Revolution from all sides, has the baseness to retract his oath."[37]

Compromise and Retraction

Large numbers of priests who had sworn that oath of loyalty, implying acceptance of the Civil Constitution of the Clergy, retracted it across the years. There were also those who had never taken the oath but who compromised themselves by misbehavior or leaving altogether. They believed they had been seduced by revolutionary ideas and wanted to have a place—not always as members of the clergy—in the papal church. Retractions took various forms: some of them published, some of them making it into government files, some only written down for the papal legation set up in Paris under the headship of Cardinal Caprara upon the demand of Napoleon, whose aides saw in Caprara a conciliatory figure. These retractions run the gamut from extreme guilt to forward-looking proposals for productive secular or religious lives. We preserve intact the names of the retracting priests in the following testimonies: their names and career highlights already figure in a printed repertoire, and so contemporary readers can explore more of the careers and contexts of these men.[38] The following testimonies are striking and representative—for their drama, clarity, or both.

Without denying their guilt, retracting priests would offer some justification of their behavior. Former curés would often say that when they took the oath as constitutionals, they made public or mental reservations—limitations on the fullness of adhesion to the oath.

Michel Gibal began work as a constitutional by hedging his bets: "I took the oath with all the restrictions in favor of the Catholic religion that the circumstances could permit."[39] These restrictions he listed in his sermons and recorded in an official registry of the municipality (which did not protect him from later persecution as a constitutional). His obedience to the new system was at best begrudging; he never paid a formal visit to the constitutional bishop, but rather opposed him in every parish he visited. For three years, though, he did nothing about the ecclesiastical suspension that he had incurred as a constitutional. When after the coup of Fructidor, the church authorities could not come to an agreement, he took the liberty of informing them that, according to the ecclesiastical brief published back in 1791, they had no right to suspend him, for the following reasons: "First, they could not say that I had taken the oath purely and simply; second, I had fulfilled the wish of the legislator and the purpose of the law had been accomplished, and they could not refuse the request for absolution I had made, even if it should be true that I had incurred some censure." But the church authorities insisted that he wait longer. The Gibal petition then shifted into the retracting mode with a bow to papal supremacy. He displayed theological awareness—"I know that it is only on the barque of St. Peter that one can avoid shipwreck"—admitted the validity of canon law, and assumed that he was making up for his faults as much as possible. With the conclusion, "If something is missing, I beseech your eminence to accept new expressions of sorrow," Gibal's self-justification was near total.

It was clear that many of the priests had been dedicated to their parishioners (and at times to their own advancement), with the possibility of

Figure 34 Cardinal Giovanni Battista Caprara and Pope Pius VII in a detail from *The Coronation of Napoleon*, painted by Jacques-Louis David. Cardinal Caprara headed the commission for the reconciliation of the constitutional bishops and priests, and, in fact, for all those French priests who wanted official reintegration into the concordatory church or official dispensation from their clergy obligations—the vow of celibacy in particular.

suffering and imprisonment always in the background. Genuine pastoral concern was their justification, perhaps post-factum sometimes.

Jacques-René Tourteau had taken the oath and thus became eligible for a parish of twelve hundred parishioners in the nearby town of Tuffé (Sarthe), whereas he had previously been administering to a parish of two hundred communicants.[40] It would appear that he wanted to both help people and move up the clerical ladder. He told authorities that he could not submit himself to the new bishops, but they, in their turn, asked him again if he would think about working with the local constitutional bishop. His negative response lost him the pastorate at Tuffé. Then the authorities turned right around and gave him another parish, his reservations about the oath notwithstanding. In the new parish Tourteau took all the new oaths required by the new state of affairs, cavalierly noting that he would have taken whatever oaths were appropriate to a given culture and government: "I took, retook, or renewed [on the given dates] the oaths of loyalty, liberty, equality, and hatred of royalty (as incompatible with a purely democratic state). At Rome, Naples, Madrid, Saint Petersburg, and Constantinople I would have in the same sense sworn hatred of democracy. By that time, if they have asked for a hundred oaths for and against, I would have taken them." He was an utter pragmatist.

Innocence shows through, too: the most natural thing in the world is to continue in the ministry. Honestly looking for help in difficult and confusing times, it seemed right to take the oath, hand over papers, look into marriage, and work productively at some job.

Claude-Nicholas-Joseph Collignon was a Carthusian, who tells a straight story of service to the Constitutional Church as if it were simply in the order of things.[41] "After I lived thirteen years in the Carthusian order, a law forced me to leave that state in life. I took the first oath of fidelity to the laws of the French government, and I exercised the functions of priesthood for the next eight and a half years, until the period when they [the functions] were forbidden." And he would have continued, in all innocence, had he not contracted a fake marriage that was a strategy to save both parties. The young woman had taken refuge in the home of her parents, and on the night before she was to flee the country with her family, she agreed to the formal marriage in order to save him from death. She left as planned, and they never did resume contact. And Guillaume Bruzac took the oath without anxiety, it would appear, but the fear of persecution was more than he could handle.[42] Not knowing what to do, he consulted friends who told him that marriage was the only solution. He "had the weakness" to do this in the presence of a priest and civil official, continuing his pastoral functions for another four or five months. Then came abdication, but, he emphasized, without offense to religion and without handing over the *lettres de prêtrise.* He lists simply and without comment all the actions that he is submitting to reconciliation: the oaths, the acceptance of the constitutional pension, the marriage—from which he has one daughter. All of these actions, however, are presented as the normal state of things. Louis-Alexandre-Pierre Bourdon was not shy about his virtues: "For twenty years . . . his conduct never ceased to merit the esteem of the natives of the canton."[43] Those virtues were at once "the most beautiful adornments of the true pastor" and "the consolation and joy of his flock." He believed it was just natural to go on working where he had exercised his ministry, serving a parish until the height of the Terror, when he went to work at the National Treasury. In fact, he could not really be classified as a constitutional priest at all.

Curés could start as successful and fulfilled constitutional pastors, whether ordained by an Old Regime bishop or a new constitutional bishop. The Constitutional Church was simply *their* church, taken on without soul searching or later agonies, though some do admit to errors or conniving of sorts. Hyacinthe Doux, to begin with, had a vital position in the new

Constitutional Church when he accepted a professorial chair in the constitutional seminary and assisted the bishop at ordinations.[44] He was a constitutional in all innocence, simply continuing his work as if he were still under his Old Regime bishop: "I had not at all left the parish to which I was attached, and having all the faculties needed from the former bishop, I did not demand any from the new one." In this letter of retraction, Doux refers to the Constitutional Church as "us," but looks to full reconciliation: "After the great day of 9 thermidor, 28 July 1794, the mourning of France was ended and the exercise of Catholic worship seemed possible, in order to put an end to the split existing between Rome and us."

Complexity could result from confused involvement in the system or an idiosyncratic religious stance. Pierre Barthélémé Barruel-Labeaume had a very subtle way of reporting his oaths and behavior as a constitutional.[45] He offered an elaborate and sincere justification of his constitutional apostolate. First, the Civil Constitution of the Clergy of 1791 seemed quite correct, respecting religion and the throne. His promotion of the Constitution was intellectual and not heartfelt, and even the intellectual promotion he came to recognize as an error. Seriously ill in 1796, Barruel-Labeaume received viaticum, and of his own will made the following public statement: "I declare before God that all I have said, done, or written about the events of these times, I have done only for the good of religion and peace in the church, but recognizing now my error, I retract sincerely and wholeheartedly all that has been condemned and all that would subsequently be condemned by my judges concerning faith and discipline, protesting that I have submitted in mind and heart to all that is taught by the Catholic, apostolic, and Roman religion—in the bosom of which I wish to live and die—and I ask pardon of God and men for the scandal that could have been given [*des scandales que je puis avoir donnés*]." This, then, was an earlier retraction and one that placed Barruel-Labeaume in the first rank of *retractés*. He did take the later oath of hatred of royalty, in order to continue receiving his pension; but to put everything in order, he formally requests full rehabilitation.

Suffering, however, could be the ultimate justification. And here few constitutionals told as sad and bitter a story as Pierre Vistorte, who suffered at the hands of revolutionaries, just as his wife had suffered at the hands of churchmen. Even so, he begged the Caprara legation that "he not be judged in the greatness of his iniquity"; instead, "he asked for forgiveness and mercy, not to appear innocent, but out of love for the truth," and declared himself ready to accept his punishment.[46] He, too, had hedged his bets on the oath, taking it with restrictions and signing nothing. A reputable clergyman and, for all practical purposes, a refractory, he was "considered a model of religious ministry, as much for his virtues as for his learning," and wanted to ensure that his own behavior did not cause his fellow priests to go astray. He was aware that his public retraction was unclear, but at least he refused to accept the mandate of the new bishop. Then, in the face of persecution, profanation, and deception, he had to take refuge. Parents were no help, "not having offered him a glass of water." A good widow, whose children he had tutored, admitted him to her aristocratic household, where he was not, in fact, safe and sound. When the political clubs set upon them, he remained calm. But for the widow it was different, "fearing for his life, safety, and liberty." Drama then: "She suddenly fainted, and when she came to, she was unwilling to give me up. She did not see any other solution than contracting a marriage with [me]."

Although Vistorte did marry the widow, sinning thereby against church discipline, he continued to defend the true faith. But his conscience tormented him, and he wanted to set things straight. The "good faith" of his wife held him back, however, because she, "was ignorant of the diriment impediment that made his marriage invalid in the eyes of the church," and because he was persuaded "that a church full of tenderness for her children would, in view of the circumstances, extend its mercy to her." Vistorte believed the opportune moment had arrived when the church made peace with the French government, and appeared to be open to the reconciliation of married priests. He revealed his troubled conscience to his wife, who quite willingly agreed to the procedures necessary for reconciliation. At that point, he did not understand that the Caprara legation had full powers of dispensation. So he did not try to have the marriage validated or leave his wife, a missed opportunity all the more unfortunate in view of her final illness: "She [eventually] died as a result of breast cancer, which tormented her, and of moral suffering, which pained her even more." When she knew her illness could not be cured, she begged the curé to offer a Mass for her intentions: the grace to bear her suffering, obtain forgiveness of her sins, and die a happy death. Her request for confession was refused, with Vistorte still trying to make his case: "You who each day pray for pagans and infidels, you refuse to recommend to the prayers of the faithful a dying woman who has great confidence in those prayers." But he finally had to admit that for his wife's well-being, even at the end, they had to part: "[He] went to the sick woman, and with great charity spoke to her thus, 'My dear spouse, you are on the threshold of eternity, the bishop is silent, the priests remain obstinate, so you must not entrust your eternal destiny to chance. . . .' With these words, the hapless couple separated, never to see one another again."

Vistorte ended his petition to the Caprara legation with a simple justification of the life he had lived subsequent to these sad events: a trusted municipal administrator, he was able to insure the safety of his fellow priests. And so he requested the validation of his marriage, the legitimation of his children, and perhaps even, one day, "the joy of saying Mass again before dying."

In sum, a number of the *rétractés* felt pure guilt, with abject contrition, but some offered excuses, too: they took the oath with major reservations, or stayed on as constitutionals because their people needed them, or simply saw nothing wrong in the renewed church (of course, new priests never experienced anything else). It was seldom simple: priests reported complex and confused years when they tried to work it all out. For a few, revolutionary priesthood was nothing but suffering, as much caused by the church as caused by the Revolution. Most of the testimonies we read came after the close of the revolutionary decade itself, but they are expressive of the inner thoughts of the men who failed to bring off an experiment they once considered the best way to meet the era's political, religious, and personal challenges.

The Concordat opened the way to a successful church career for a minority of former constitutional priests and bishops, but in the main it brought no more than closure: a tolerable apostolate for the priests integrated into ministry and dispensation from obligations and censure for those who retracted their mistakes. Hopes died out, mostly in the years following the Concordat.

Chapter Twelve

THE AFTERLIFE OF THE CONSTITUTIONAL CHURCH

Hopes and Reality

French Catholicism was restructured, then, to be acceptable to the Roman (papal) church administration and the French government (the consulate of Napoleon) as the Concordat of 15 July 1801 was implemented. Twelve constitutional bishops were appointed, which represented one-tenth of the 118 bishops who made up this hierarchy over the years. Looked at from another angle, the percentage is one-fifth of the constitutionals, because only sixty of those bishops were alive in 1802.[1] It took a great deal of pushing and pressure to retain so many of the constitutional bishops by the time the final selection was made: François Bécherel, bishop of Valence; Louis Charrier de la Roche, bishop of Versailles; Dominique Lacombe, bishop of Angoulême; Louis Belmas, bishop of Cambrai; Jean-Claude Leblanc de Beaulieu, bishop of Soissons; Claude Le Coz, archbishop of Besançon; Charles Montault-des-Isles, bishop of Poitiers; Jean-François Périer, bishop of Avignon; Claude-François-Marie Primat, bishop of Toulouse; Henri Reymond, bishop of Dijon; Jean-Pierre Saurine, bishop of Strasbourg; and Marc Berdolet, bishop of Aix-la-Chapelle (and so, outside of France).[2] Boudon notes that Napoleon's entourage, with its large representation of old parliamentarians, was favorable to the constitutional clergy who had served the various revolutionary legislatures. Five of the concordatory bishops of France served in the government legislatures: Bécherel, Charrier de la Roche, and Saurine in the Constituent Assembly, Le Coz and Lacombe in the Legislative Assembly; Saurine, of course, was in the Convention, and even continued on in the Directory legislative house, the Five Hundred. These and the others had also faced the Terror bravely; two, Lacombe and Primat, had abdicated, only to reassume their roles quickly afterward.[3]

On paper, the constitutionals appeared to be integral to the concordatory church.

Hopes for the Concordat

A letter of Claude Le Coz to Cardinal Caprara, the pope's delegate to Paris, written five months before the signing of the Concordat, is especially revealing in light of his later position in the concordatory church, where he was the only constitutional bishop to be elevated to archbishop. He gave every evidence of being more pro-papal than other constitutionals, but he still took their part. His profession of loyalty was published in all the faithful constitutional dioceses of France a few years before: "Holy church of Rome, mother of all churches and all the faithful, church chosen by God to unite his children in the same faith and charity, we will secure your unity by a deep faith. If I forget you, church of Rome, may I forget myself! May my tongue dry up and remain immobile in my mouth, if you are not the beginning of all my songs and rejoicing."[4] He makes no bones about his authority in the Constitutional Church. He presided at the two National Councils and is proud of it: "There I have been of some use to the church."[5]

Loyally and with vigor, Le Coz takes up the defense of his constitutional bishops and priests, whose thoughts and goals he knows better than anyone, with this cardinal who was sent from Rome in 1801 to reconcile all French priests with the pope. He assures Caprara, "With heart and mouth they profess all the truths taught by the Catholic church, apostolic and Roman; and all the errors it proscribes they condemn."[6] He fears, however, that Caprara has heard negative reports about the last council and the arguments that took place there. Were the discussions less animated at Trent or the revered earlier councils, he wonders: "Ours [the councils] have displayed a valuable frankness; they reveal the interior of their hearts. And the decrees that have ensured proved clearly that these hearts neither love nor seek anything other than true teachings."[7] There would be many stories to tell, if Caprara would consent to a longer conversation on all this.

Le Coz had to face the complications of taking office in the concordatory church, of course. Right away, on 15 June 1802, he contacted Cardinal Caprara, because it had been reported that the pope gave those bishops in place another six months to leave office, a generosity primarily aimed at the Old Regime bishops. This, Le Coz cries, would cause total confusion, and he is happy to hear that Caprara believes it to have no binding force (*non avenu*).[8] Then, as if there were never any controversy between Rome and the Constitutional Church, Le Coz simply reiterates the constitutional position that the bishops could not have sought institution by the pope because, first of all, they were manacled by the laws of the land: "People dared to say that these bishops were outside the unity of the Catholic Church because they did not have the institution of Pius VI, an institution to which they were not permitted recourse, given the very strict [political] laws."[9] The ultimate excuse, of course, was the chaotic and violent politics of the country. Their "love of peace, as well as their desire and duty to safeguard religion in France kept them, in those days of irreligion and horror, from such recourse."[10] It becomes clear, however, that Le Coz was just being polite. That such papal institution was never the rule had been the constitutional viewpoint since the beginning. With mock horror, Le Coz evokes the condition of the good bishops of history: "Without such institution these bishops were outside of the unity of the church, were they? They were also outside the unity of the church, those numerous archbishops and bishops who for thirteen centuries were the glory of the most illustrious episcopal sees of Christianity? Authorized by the canons of the most respectable councils, they never gave a thought of recourse to [the pope]."[11] No, Caprara should understand that those decade-long attacks, condemnations, and criticisms have been the affliction of all good Catholics, making them look foolish to the rest of the world.

Annales de la religion, the journal of the Constitutional Church, continued to appear after the Concordat, which presumably had dissolved the Constitutional Church into the church of the Concordat. There, a certain abbé Danton (no relation to the great revolutionary, one assumes) wrote optimistically that the faithful will forgive all the turmoil once they realize that zeal for religion and for the faithful themselves impassioned *both* the refractories and the constitutionals: "We have seen zeal operate in diverse ways: it impels some to tear themselves away from their flock, without fearing the fatigue, the journey, and the awkwardness of their departure. Whereas it impels others to unite their fate with that of their flock, without regard for the excesses of every kind that threaten them."[12] To be sure, there followed ten years of mutual accusations, bitterness, and misfortune. Well might the faithful have wondered what would come of religion when the churches were closed and worship was forbidden. It resembled the persecutions of ancient times, and priests were responsible for some of the problems.

But a new era is beginning and the old discord does not have a place in it. The nation itself reaches out to all priests, "to make reparation for so many injustices. In calling you to itself, it wants to console you; it wants to dry your tears. It wants to render to the church its splendor and render to the fatherland its lost children."[13] The suggestion is that after the "shipwreck" of the church, the constitutionals saved the day: "Gathering all the debris, they reconstructed the vessel that they now offer to you, battered but saved from storms even more horrible than the first ones. In peril of their lives a thousand times, they have brought it back to the port where providence now brings you."[14] But both constitutionals and refractories will find one another, because God has guided both groups: "O priests! Learn to appreciate one another's accomplishments; these will gain everyone's admiration. Who would not recognize here the hand of God who brings about good in ways that seem opposed to one another?"[15]

There follows an accounting of all of the accomplishments of the constitutionals: bringing together the Republic and the church, ensuring Catholic sacraments, maintaining a Catholic presence on the great public occasions of war and peace. They influenced both the authorities and public opinion by their church apologetics in general, and in particular by their publication of *Annales*. By the establishment of a periodical consecrated to religion, the authors of *Annales* maintained the spirit and the structures of religion: "by the public sign of the profession of faith by priests and faithful; by that public voice which repeated every time the decrees of the universal church; and by the deposit of the purest gospel morality with which they responded to the writings and discourses of a great number of enemies of all kinds, who continually declared they were against all religion."[16]

In the new era, the value of all of this will be clear, from individual studies to conciliar meetings. National life flows on like a great river that once spilled over its banks, carrying much along with it, but in the end permitting a new order to be put together. The constitutional author, Father Danton, finally promotes the Concordat as a new motivation and not a pacification built out of indifference and isolation: "Woe also to him who, at the wondrous publication of the Concordat, would hold back the organization of the clergy; for the danger has passed."[17] Gone is the general disorder, gone is the general hate. The faith has withstood all, the same way that the great cathedrals withstood all efforts to demolish them, the same way that a great ship finally enters port after a storm. With the Concordat, both clergies are empowered: "O priests, you can all be of service, because you are all equally adopted by the Concordat; from this day onward, further distinctions among you must be condemned."[18]

Post-Concordat Reality

The last volumes of the constitutional journal *Annales de la religion* (1802–4) first highlighted the news that constitutional bishops had been given a place in the concordatory church—witness the remarks of Father Danton—but then recorded a series of disappointments about the suppression of their structures and their style.

There was always strong resistance to any emphasis on, even recognition of, "submission"—in effect, retraction—in the month-to-month efforts to apply the Concordat. The constitutionals still had a strong constitutional identity, and Dominique Lacombe, consecrated bishop only in 1798, was probably the most outspoken among them. So when the heart of Pius VI was buried in the Cathedral at Valence, constitutionals were much tried to say something nice about the prelate who was the cause of all their apostolic frustrations. To read the constitutionals, one would think that papal authority was no more acceptable after the Concordat than it was during the Revolution. The use of the cardinalate by Pius VII to express his controlling authority over the French church brought lively criticism. One curé mounted a formal defense of the whole constitutional operation that functioned during the revolutionary years.

It was clear, then, from the beginning of the Concordat era that the Gallican–ultramontane struggle had abated very little. According to the constitutionals, all *rumors* about submission had to be scotched: "The spirit of discord has not failed to spread it about that the constitutional bishops appointed to the new bishoprics obtained their canonical institution only by retracting the oath they took in 1791."[19] With a twist of the knife, the writer notes that this was an oath to be "faithful to the nation, the law, and the king." How can one say that these priests were guilty of *intrusion*? This was the old stereotype. And if the rumor is that the constitutionals have received absolution for such conduct, one may as well say that they have had to do penance also. Although not speaking officially for the bishops, the author wants readers to know that they accepted neither absolution nor penance. The report that they acquiesced to four or five propositions is completely false; in fact "they have indignantly rejected them." This was not just a matter of polite bickering, because the bishops say that "they would prefer prison time on Guyana," instead of some cowardly denial of what is, in fact, right and just.[20]

Bishop Lacombe, now ensconced in the concordatory church as bishop of Angoulême, was the leading voice opposing any hints of submission and repentance. Writing to a priest about the matter, he highlights his own letter to Cardinal Caprara, now a matter of public record. "*Monsieur le cardinal*, we are French bishops; you do not seem to recognize us," he said. "You propose that we declare to his holiness that we repent of what we did in conformity with the Civil Constitution of the Clergy. Never, no never, will we make this declaration."[21] And so he goes over some of the shenanigans of the last meeting between the cardinal and the constitutional delegation, made up of Bishops Leblanc de Beaulieu, Belmas, and himself. They had been shown a letter of submission, but were not given the time to read it all the way through. The three of them had to reject it, because it was clear to them that this was not what they had originally agreed to. They immediately headed over to the office of Portalis, the minister of worship, who was eventually able to influence Caprara: Portalis told them that he would take care of it, and that "the government did not want a retraction; only pure and simple adherence to the Concordat was required."[22] Portalis asked that all the concordatory constitutionals have a meeting, and then Bernier was called in to mediate. He finally proposed a different letter, and so obtained the agreement of the constitutionals.

Lacombe was, then, a high-profile spokesperson of the now standard constitutional theme that the Civil Constitution was only superseded, not condemned: "Having respected and loved its measures taken, I will always continue to respect and love them; far from blaming myself for having obeyed and remained faithful to them, I regard these accomplishments as the most important of my life."[23] If anyone says that the bishops have retracted, they are lying, and both Bernier and Portalis can bear witness to this. There can be no absolution when its potential recipients neither believe it appropriate nor want it: "You will say with me that Monsieur the [Cardinal] Legate, without giving a thought to the usual rules for administering the sacrament of penance, and without giving a thought to the renowned words of an infinity of popes, *nisi vere contritis et confessis* [unless repented and confessed], has given an absolution that was neither wished nor demanded."[24] When Bishop Bernier brought the decree to the constitutional bishops, they tossed it in the fire in the presence of Portalis, who said he had done the same thing himself. Lacombe authorizes Father Binos, to whom he was addressing this message all along, to say that, although has great reverence for the Holy See, he does not have respect for the political machinations of the church personnel who represent it.

For the solemn occasion, when the heart and organs of the constitutionals' old nemesis, Pope Pius VI, were solemnly transported to Valence, where he had earlier died in exile, constitutionals had to use prudence: "We are still too close to the pontificate of Pius VI to have the right to judge him with assuredness."[25] Some want to make a martyr out of him; others, a political opportunist. The writer does go so far as to say that "if he had possessed the humility, the charity, and the prudence that go with his station, he would have a thousand times subdued the schism within France, and would have contributed triumphantly to the immediate pacification of Europe."[26] True that he showed constancy amid the horrors of the European wars and in the face of much personal abuse, but he, in fact, engaged the papal state in European wars and was, technically, one of the last to lay down arms. Still and all, French Catholics welcomed the passage of the papal relics through their territories. At Valence, they were solemnly received by Bishop Bécherel, the former constitutional, and so, in sum: "It has been a source of consolation for us that the heart [*le coeur et les entrailles*] of Pius VI have been met by Monsieur Bécherel, bishop of Valence, and placed in the church of this worthy prelate. He will bear witness at the foot of the altar and before these precious remains, that the pope never had more submissive children and more faithful friends than the bishops and priests who had the courage to take the oath of 1791."[27] In effect, reverence of the pope today is no different from the reverence expressed in the declarations of the constitutional councils of 1797 and 1801.

Such reverence for Pius VI does not make the constitutionals any more ready to tolerate the repetition of his behavior by the new pope, Pius VII. Constitutionals well remember that an archenemy of the Constitutional Church, the abbé Maury, was made a cardinal in 1794 to win points for the counterrevolutionary movement. The Constitution was opposed to the cardinalate on principle—because the cardinalate does not belong to the original hierarchical structure of the church, it was invariably an expression of opulent worldliness, and it was frequently used by the Holy See to induce exaggerated loyalty. The allocution Pius VII delivered to a closed Roman

Figure 35 Pius VI in a commemorative image lamenting his suffering and celebrating his triumph over the evils of the Enlightenment; the image indicates, too, his death at Valence in 1799. In witness of his death there, his heart was placed in the Cathedral of Valence, then under the jurisdiction of Bishop François Bécherel, the former constitutional who became the concordatory bishop of Valence. Former constitutionals, whatever their private views of the irony of all this, considered the translation of these relics to Valence a consolation. (Bibliothèque nationale de France)

consistory on 17 January 1803 is summarized, to show just how the investiture of cardinals is a controlling mechanism.[28] Responding, *Annales* sees clear evidence here that the Roman court still tries to demonize all those government officials who on their own try to set up diocesan boundaries or any other simple geographical or organizational features of the physical church organization. And they refuse to accept as valid the election of bishops to sees that are, in fact, empty and otherwise impossible to fill.

Although their reverence for the Holy See has had no effect, the constitutionals persist in maintaining the proper balance of respect and independence, both in obedience to Christ and for the sake of Christianity: "Our deep respect for the person of the pope and, even more, our sincere love of peace oblige us to avoid any [further] discussion, and to accept in silence all the accusations that might be made against us."[29] The suffering of churchmen who stayed to serve and console the faithful was undergone in the name of Christ and in order to "contribute to the general peace."[30] It would do more harm than good to make trouble at this point.

Maintaining the Constitutional Vision, 1802–1804

Reading these constitutionals, one would never think that they had anything to do with the split: never wanted it and never agreed to it. They did everything they could to overcome it, they say, even though their open-armed acceptance of their brothers was greeted with silence and disdain. Now the successor of the pope they revered even in the most deadly years of the Revolution is calling for the resignation of everyone. No pope got to do this for the first 1,200 years of Christian history. The notion that he can do so is "a new idea, unheard of across twelve centuries, which teaches that bishops receive their jurisdiction from the pope. . . . It should be banned from Christian teaching. . . . It is an extravagance and an absurdity."[31] Of course, by the time these objections were printed in the *Annales*, it was already too late: the Concordat had been signed and the new roster of bishops had been worked out.

Annales authors had good memories of some of the Old Regime bishops of the Estates General, such as Archbishop Jean-Georges Le Franc de Pompignan of Vienne, who, they thought, prepared the way for the new church. And so *Annales* published a gracious review of his collected works: "We believe that it would render a great service to religion, if the complete works . . . were to be published; this was proposed to the archbishop of Vienne in 1786. He did not reject the idea, but said only to make the edition more interesting by adding several works on which he was just putting the finishing touches."[32] The reviewer admits that Le Franc de Pompignan gave in occasionally to a sort of "bias" (*esprit de parti*). And yes, the archbishop was more submissive to Rome's recent pretensions than he needed to be, given that Rome had tried to overturn the normal just and proper relationships with governments, and governments had most often given in to them. This contributed to a revival of powers that Rome itself had rejected at the better moments of its history.[33]

Promotion of the constitutional vision in the face of its enemies energized two contrasting reviews of the works of Antoine-Hubert Wandelaincourt and Augustin Barruel, the former a constitutional bishop and the latter a troublesome refractory. Reminding readers that Bishop Wandelaincourt had always given education priority of place in his ministry, the reviewer writes that the pastoral letters and education treatises deserve "a distinguished place among the works of this clergyman, who . . . by his learned and useful works, gave us the hope that we might see revived the century of the writers of Port-Royal."[34] Wonderful that a bishop in his seventies, and in ill health, because of an attempt to poison him, keeps himself so busy and can serve as such a good example for the others as he "dedicates the strength that remains . . . to expanding the field of Christian education!"[35] But if Wandelaincourt was on the side of the angels, Barruel, with his book on papal authority, was not. The reviewer says that absolutely nothing comes from the author apart from his "tortured explanations, absurdities, and bad form." Certainly the old *parlements* would not have put up with this kind of talk; nor would contemporary universities. So, what did this old ultramontane write anyway, with his old ideas justly condemnable by both church and state? "In effect . . . you would have to say that the French government for fifteen centuries, and all the administrations from century to century and in these latter times, and our best legal experts were out of their minds; or [admit] that this inert matter [*caput mortuum*] of ultramontanism is sheer lunacy."[36] No criticism is possible of a work so completely flawed: "The basic principles of the Christian and the citizen are all we need to counteract this poison." Given "the flaws the work teems with," the reviewer will not even discuss whether the work ruins the author's reputation.[37] With a final shot at Barruel, the *Annales* author compares his work to the world-religions text by Charles Dupuis (not noting here that Dupuis was an ex-priest) that was a genuine put-down of Christianity: "If we have to compare Dupuis's *Origine des Cultes* and Barruel's *Traité du pape*, we do not know which of these authors would be the most damaging . . . to the interests of the government and the teaching of Jesus Christ."[38]

The "spiritual testament of an eighty-year-old curé" is the witness of a convinced curmudgeon of a constitutional who was facing his last days: for him, the Constitutional Church has gotten its Catholicism right. On the constitutional side "you will find Christian charity and true zeal for the salvation of souls."[39] But now, to add injury to the old insults, when a former constitutional is given a new diocesan assignment, the others "insidiously spread the rumor that he has retracted and secretly submitted to a canonical penance."[40] The old refractories will even hover over an ill and dying constitutional, looking for some kind of capitulation, and, not having obtained it, spread the news that they could not save the poor fellow, who, they say, died in a state of despair. To make sure that this does not happen to him, the old priest sent in a last will and testament to his bishop: "I, François Froment, an oath-taking priest, on the point of taking my leave in order to render account of my conduct to the sovereign judge, implore his mercy, and have every confidence in his justice. Worn down by infirmities for a number of years, I have not been able to fulfill the functions of a pastoral ministry . . . but I have always offered to God the sacrifice of a pure heart, and I hope that his humble servant will find grace in his presence."[41] He is worried, though, that sentiments which are not his at all will be attributed to him. Trying to avoid this, he delivers here a final punch line: "In 1791, I took the oath required by law, because my conscience and my duty commanded me to do so; and the same compelling motives have ever since made me persevere in my original sentiments. I am firmly persuaded that a priest, more than any other citizen, should give the example of submission to established authority."[42] The oath of allegiance to government and acceptance of the Civil Constitution of the Clergy was a matter of conscience in 1791 and is a matter of conscience again now that he is in his last years. This testament of old François Froment moved the *Annales* commentator to his final exhortation. The constitutionals should not let themselves be dragged down by false doctrine, because they can ultimately count on the esteem of the people and the joys of heaven: "When you are asked to compromise your conscience, your honor, and divine law, recall the example of good Monsieur Froment."[43]

The most notable components of the constitutional vision were highlighted in the obituaries of the bishops and priests presented in the last issues of *Annales*, beginning with Bishop Charles Le Masle, a model of pious poverty. From a poor background himself, he always had a special love for the unfortunate and an indifference to his own personal comfort. When he had nothing at all and was making his way to a hospital for the indigent, a parishioner of some means caught up with him, but then had the worst time in the world to get him to accept a room at his house. Later, after the second National Council, when, in accordance with the Concordat, the jurisdiction of the Constitutional Church was at its end, he was ready to live with the sick and poor in the hospital at Nantes, saying, "I give to this institution the few possessions I have, and I will spend my last days with the poor, exercising my ministry among them."[44] Unto the end he maintained his identity as a constitutional, being much troubled by the provisions of the Concordat. When it was promulgated, "[t]he bishop of Vannes [Le Masle] did not fool himself about the damage it did to the real authority of the Gallican church, and to its rights and exemptions. . . . He submitted to it with great complaint, and was one of the first to resign his see to the metropolitan bishop of Rennes."[45] There followed in *Annales* a somewhat ordered necrology, with entries of priests who "have not tarnished by any weakness the holy and truly noble cause that they have defended."[46]

Finale: Vigilance for the Future

Although encouraged by the project of Portalis, the minister of worship, to guarantee the vitality of Gallicanism—"every French ecclesiastic should try to learn the maxims of the Gallican church"[47]—constitutionals were mightily tried by pseudo-conciliatory publications of refractories emoting about the beauties of retraction as a form of reconciliation. Even in the semiofficial *Manuel des prêtres* the author cavalierly sweeps aside a number of things held dear by the constitutionals, somehow assuming that he was being conciliatory: "Gentleness and the spirit of reconciliation seem to direct the pen of the writer; he wants nothing of controversies, disputes, or quarrels."[48] He just supposes that the Revolution was repugnant and that the constitutionals were "intruders, schismatics, excommunicated!"[49] *Annales* responds that, in fact, they were the "priests who remained faithful to the fatherland."

"On the Mind and Viewpoints of the Former Clergy" was a long, groaning set of observations in *Annales* on life since the Concordat. The reunion of hearts and minds is more apparent than real, and the government should know this: that it can only count on the old constitutionals for loyalty. Proof lies in examining how the old refractories have behaved since the Concordat. The author works an elaborate comparison of constitutional behavior to the behavior of the Anglican bishops and priests as they submitted to Henry VIII and then proceeded to restructure Catholicism in England. The Civil Constitution of the Clergy, in contrast to the Anglican program, "did not seem to alarm consciences, because there was no change in the dogma and public worship of the dominant religion; far from giving birth to a schism, it recognized the supremacy of the pope."[50] The *Annales* author delivers an elaborate diatribe against the essential destructiveness of the nonjurors, who did not recognize this catholicity: "Was not the war in the Vendée the result of their fanatical preaching? Were they not seen at the head of a blinded people, impelled by their mad zeal, and did they not excite [the people] to violence at a period before worship was forbidden and churches closed?" He poses, then, a final vexed question: "Was this the example that so many martyrs had given, above all the Christian legion that let itself be disarmed and decimated without posing the least resistance to the orders of the emperors?"[51]

The behavior of the constitutionals was, on the contrary, the essence of charity: "Not only did they help them [the refractories] and succor them in their needs; but in their synodal assemblies they openly declared that they had accepted the positions of the deportees so that the faithful would not lack the consolations of religion, and that they were ready to sacrifice these positions and give them back to those who once held them."[52] People have only to compare the behavior of the two clergies to see which group operated on Christian principles—in other words, that refractory behavior has hurt the people at every turn. For example, children from marriages that were not solemnized by the church because of the small number of active and available priests do not have official civil status. This is the case for at least those children born to parents who knew nothing of the need to legitimize their children by fulfilling certain state requirements, but placed their trust in the refractory clergy, who insisted that the nuptial blessing was all they needed. Or to take a different example, by the time the second oath—hatred of royalty—came along, refractory priests resisted simply because they did not like the government and wanted it to fail (i.e., not for any theological reason). Rather, they rejoiced in the successes of the Russian army invading Switzerland and menacing France. Too bad for them, of course, because "these enemies were driven back from our territories, and the Eighteenth Brumaire, reestablishing order and justice in all areas of government, took away all hope for their movement."[53]

Those Old Regime bishops who were appointed to sees in the concordatory church also took it upon themselves to require of the former constitutionals more than the Concordat allowed: "We cannot ignore the humiliating ways by which the oath-taking priests have been accepted into communion with some of the old bishops."[54] They not only required adherence to the Concordat and loyalty to the bishop, but they got out the bulls of Pius VI and subsequently required former constitutionals to obtain absolution after humiliating penances. They could not go back to their former assignments nor obtain new ones, unless former refractories refused to go to some parishes. In general, former constitutionals were treated as pariahs by the former refractories, who, as before, made their people stay away from sacraments administered by their former enemies: "They forbid those in their charge to hear [a constitutional] mass; they do not care for the sick who have confessed to [constitutionals], unless they repeat their confession: finally, they always try to disparage them in the minds of the people."[55] Nothing has changed, then. These priests even want to destroy the present government of Napoleon, and the nobles are only too happy to make common cause with them.[56] They have been appointed to the largest and best parishes, often in city centers; they have gone after the women and old folks, proselytizing in every direction. There exists a concerted and very determined effort to coordinate the old refractories, "which proves that they have not renounced their schemes, and that they carry on a secret correspondence among themselves and with specially appointed representatives."[57]

A dramatic finale in the *Annales de la religion* showed how papal authority spoiled things at every turn. Rome probably could have hung on to some of the Protestant countries at the time of the Reformation: "Rome has lost through its own fault England, Denmark, and Sweden; and it let other churches perish rather than renounce its own pretensions."[58] After having tried to establish direct power over governments, Roman authorities turned to attempts to indirectly control governments; but it was still power they were looking for. What a goofy principle, that the papacy should be the arbiter of its own power: "We have been appalled in reading [Robert] Bellarmine that the pope in virtue of his own infallibility is the judge of the limits to his own power."[59] Two depressing features of Roman authority come out of all this. First, "Rome does not abjure its errors, the renowned Melchior Cano considered it to be incurable. . . . The aggression of Clement XIII in our own time (1769) against the duke of Parma is a proof of this, the progressive march toward enlightenment seems to stop at the banks of the Tiber." Second, the pope uses the bishops as extensions of himself, and cleverly uses the cardinalate as a means of putting down or controlling the bishops: "The episcopacy, trampled underfoot by the cardinalate, is in his eyes only a [papal] delegation; so he refuses to establish dioceses in mission countries, precisely where they are most necessary."[60] It is clear that the authors are foregrounding the Constitutional Church as the only community *within* the Catholic Church to stand up to papal exaggerations: "France alone has the glory of having held across eight years, twenty-four synods, eight metropolitan councils, and two national councils."[61] Ecumenical councils, such as those of Florence and Bâle, tried to bring balance and order. Theological faculties, such as that of Paris in 1497, after the censure of John XXII, believed that if the pope did not convene a council every ten years, leading prelates should do so for him. And now the punch line: "Rome, then, is in revolt against the church."[62]

If they can finally get to a new ecumenical council, there will be a basic agenda: "Give to the metropolitans the right to set up bishops; reduce the cardinals to the number required and to their appropriate functions as pastors of the city of Rome; suppress the artificial dating of documents [*la daterie*] and the whole apparatus of simony that accompanies it; wipe out the existing inquisition that is a blot on the good name of the church; bring back to the center of unity the societies that indignation over abuses, as much as schism and heresy, holds apart. Such operations without doubt highlight the works of such an assembly."[63] And the final words of this final article of the final volume of *Annales de la religion*: "Let us end this essay with the words of Saint Bernard, 'Who will grant me to see before I die the church of God as it was in the first centuries!'"[64]

The combination of retraction and reconciliation proffered by the constitutional bishops of the concordatory church was haphazard and inconsistent. Claude Le Coz held out until the last, precisely because he was, for all his reverence toward individual popes, most insistent on the traditional roles of bishop and pope, and therefore, the most consistent in his dealings with the papacy.[65] Pius VII had one high card to play, when he insisted that the formalities of retraction and reconciliation should be completed before his arrival in Paris for a grand finale, the coronation of Napoleon Bonaparte as emperor of the French and of the French Republic. Between the date of the pope's departure from Rome, 2 November 1804, and the ceremony at Notre-Dame Cathedral on 2 December, the negotiations continued, complicated by the new archbishop of Bordeaux, Charles-François d'Aviau du Bois-de-Sanzay, who carefully and critically denounced the theology and attitudes of the former constitutionals.[66] Last-minute interventions by Joseph Fouché, former Oratorian and Napoleon's minister of police, helped speed the negotiations. Without full satisfaction, Pius went on with the coronation, but then had to wait almost three weeks, until 22 December 1804, before he got satisfaction from Le Coz.

In the years that followed, doubts lingered as to whether Le Coz—and, for that matter, Saurine, Lacombe, Belmas, Périer, and Reymond—ever really agreed to what Pius thought they agreed to: retraction of their oath and submission to the universal jurisdiction of the pope. The theological and disciplinary goals of Pius VII were not fully realized until many years later, when the first Council of the Vatican met at Rome in 1870. By that time, the Gallican temperament among the French hierarchy had waned considerably. Almost twenty years of persistent efforts by Pius IX and his entourage had prepared the way for a declaration of papal infallibility that attributed to Pius and his successors the charisma and authority that the constitutional clergy, and many others previously and subsequently, considered unhistorical, and so, untrue.

Within the Catholic system, however, this Constitutional Church, in its original form and as reconstituted, was a reform attempt that went beyond any others in early modern and modern Europe. With all their hang-ups and hopes, the revolutionary priests opted for a restructuring of the French church that would coordinate with the new government; they were engaged in the transformation of both church and state. When the transformation was nothing at all like they planned, priests and bishops sought to salvage their political engagement, sometimes surviving as priests, sometimes as revolutionaries, sometimes as both: politically republican and religiously Catholic. With the passing of the radical revolution, those who had survived as both priests and advocates of a republican government attempted to revive the church, searching for a new order that could be built on their old theological and political goals and in effect be the real church. Their work was endangered when the post-republican government of Napoleon elaborated its Concordat with papal Catholicism. Although they hoped for positive incorporation into the concordatory church, they were soon subjected to the maximalist version of papal authority that was the natural outcome of the Concordat. But constitutional ideas on a church loyal to Rome, though not subject to its direct administrative control, never completely died out.[67] Such ideas found further expression in the Gallican Catholicism that survived into the middle of the nineteenth century. And such ideas are today reflected (1) in the decrees of the Second Vatican Council (1962–65) on the traditional role of local episcopates, where loyalty to Rome is combined with regional autonomy, still to be worked out in its details; and (2) in the statements by Orthodox church authorities willing to grant to future bishops of Rome who would not claim universal jurisdiction a distinct primacy of honor.

Appendix

ADMINISTRATION OF THE CONSTITUTIONAL CHURCH AND OATH ADHERENCE BY DEPARTMENT

Each of the following administrative divisions of the Constitutional Church (metropolitan sees subdivided into departmental sees) contains the names of the bishops who were able to take official possession of their dioceses. Often, constitutional priests in these regions had to fend for themselves, sometimes organizing a unified apostolate and sometimes not, when there was no bishop actively administrating. Here readers can find the names of the constitutional bishops highlighted or mentioned in the text, who will be marked here by an asterisk, as well as all the others (the alphabetical index will point readers to only the names with asterisks). At the same time, readers can see the level of constitutional participation of individual departments in the first years of the Revolution (i.e., the percentages of those who took the oath of fidelity to the nation, the law, and the king, implying acceptance of the Civil Constitution of the Clergy). The whole is based on information and tables provided in the two currently standard references: Paul Pisani, *Répertoire biographique de l'épiscopat constitutionnel (1791–1802)* (Paris, 1907); and Timothy Tackett, *Religion, Revolution, and Regional Culture in Eighteenth-Century France: The Ecclesiastical Oath of 1791* (Princeton, 1986). For this list, I have adopted the ordering of Pisani, who followed a certain geographical logic rather than listing dioceses alphabetically; the metropolitan see is always the first diocese listed. As noted in the body of the current text, a new dictionary of the constitutional bishops is in preparation.

Métropole de Paris
- Seine
  - Administration
    - *Gobel, Jean Baptiste. 1791–93. b. 1727; d. 1794
    - *Royer, Jean-Baptiste. 1798–1801. b. 1733; d. 1807
  - Oath Adherence (January–Spring, 1791)
    - Curés—86 (75%)
    - Vicaires—78 (66%)
- Aube
  - Administration
    - Sibille, Augustin. 1791–97. b. 1724; d. 1798
    - Blampoix, Jean-Baptiste. 1799–1801. b. 1740; d. 1820
  - Oath Adherence (January–Spring, 1791)
    - Curés—250 (68%)
    - Vicaires—46 (58%)
- Eure-et-Loir
  - Administration
    - Bonnet, Charles. 1791–93. b. 1721?; d. 1793
  - Oath Adherence (January–Spring, 1791)
    - Curés—403 (84%)
    - Vicaires—160 (88%)
- Loiret
  - Administration
    - *Jarente de Senac d'Orgeval, Louis-François-Alexandre. 1791–93. b. 1746; d. 1810
  - Oath Adherence (January–Spring, 1791)
    - Curés—331 (91%)
    - Vicaires—100 (94%)
- Seine-et-Marne
  - Administration
    - *Thuin, Pierre. 1791–1801. b. 1731; d. 1808
  - Oath Adherence (January–Spring, 1791)
    - Curés—346 (74%)
    - Vicaires—71 (72%)
- Seine-et-Oise
  - Administration
    - Avoine, Jean-Julien. 1791–93. b. 1741; d. 1793
    - *Clément, Augustin-Jean-Charles. 1796–1801. b. 1717; d. 1804

Oath Adherence (January–Spring, 1791)

Curés—552 (83%)

Vicaires—223 (80%)

Yonne

Administration

*Brienne, Étienne-Charles de Loménie de. 1761–93. b. 1727; d. 1794

*Poinsignon, Louis François (elected but not consecrated)

Oath Adherence (January–Spring, 1791)

Curés—370 (89%)

Vicaires—57 (92%)

Métropole du Centre

Cher

Administration

*Torné, Pierre Athanase. 1791–93. b. 1727; d. 1797

*Dufraisse, Michel-Joseph. 1798–1801. b. 1728; d. 1802

Oath Adherence (January–Spring, 1791)

Curés—213 (76%)

Vicaires—41 (82%)

Allier

Administration

Laurent, François-Xavier. 1791–93. b. 1744; d. 1821

Butaud-Dupoux, Antoine. 1798–1802. b. 1730; d. 1802

Oath Adherence (January–Spring, 1791)

Curés—312 (89%)

Vicaires—76 (79%)

Creuse

Administration

*Huguet, Marc Antoine. 1791–93. b. 1757; d. 1802

Oath Adherence (January–Spring, 1791)

Curés—223 (76%)

Vicaires—79 (74%)

Indre

Administration

Héraudin, René. 1791–1800. b. 1722; d. 1800

Oath Adherence (January–Spring, 1791)

Curés—237 (89%)

Vicaires—54 (79%)
Indre-et-Loire
Administration
Suzor, Pierre. 1791–1801. b. 1733; d. 1801
Oath Adherence (January–Spring, 1791)
Curés—176 (54%)
Vicaires—93 (62%)
Loir-et-Cher
Administration
*Grégoire, Henri. 1791–1801(2). b. 1750; d. 1831
Oath Adherence (January–Spring, 1791)
Both clergies—277 (65%)
Nièvre
Administration
Tollet, Guillaume. 1791–1801. b. 1735; d. 1805
Oath Adherence (January–Spring, 1791)
Both clergies—236 (72%)
Vienne
Administration
Lecesve, René. 1791. b. 1733; d. 1791
*Montault-des-Isles, Charles. 1791–95. b. 1755; d. 1839
Oath Adherence (January–Spring, 1791)
Curés—257 (69%)
Vicaires—84 (66%)

Mètropole du Nord-Ouest
Ille-et-Vilaine
Administration
*Le Coz, Claude. 1791–1801. b. 1740; d. 1815
Oath Adherence (January–Spring, 1791)
Curés—65 (18%)
Vicaires—67 (16%)
Côtes-du-Nord
Administration
Jacob, Jean-Marie. 1791–1801. b. 1741; d. 1801
Oath Adherence (January–Spring, 1791)
Curés—84 (27%)
Vicaires—89 (26%)

Finistère

Administration

*Expilly, Louis-Alexandre. 1791–94. b. 1742; d. 1794

*Audrein, Yves-Marie. 1798–1800. b. 1741; d. 1800

Oath Adherence (January–Spring, 1791)

Curés—58 (24%)

Vicaires—64 (19%)

Loire-Inférieure

Administration

Minée, Julien. 1791–93. b. 1738; d. 1808

Oath Adherence (January–Spring, 1791)

Curés—47 (22%)

Vicaires—59 (22%)

Maine-et-Loire

Administration

Pelletier, Hugues. 1791–93. b. 1729; d. 1794

Oath Adherence (January–Spring, 1791)

Curés—189 (47%)

Vicaires—161 (43%)

Mayenne

Administration

*Villar, Noel-Gabriel-Luce de. 1791–98. b. 1748; d. 1826

*Dorlodot, Jean-François. 1799–1801. b. 1756; d. 1816

Oath Adherence (January–Spring, 1791)

Curés—84 (30%)

Vicaires—95 (28%)

Morbihan

Administration

*Le Masle, Charles. 1791–1801. b. 1723; d. 1812

Oath Adherence (January–Spring, 1791)

Curés—26 (13%)

Vicaires—214 (19%)

Métropole des Côtes de la Manche

Seine-Inférieure

Administration

*Charrier de la Roche, Louis. 1791–91. b. 1758; d. 1827

Gratien, Jean-Baptiste Guillaume. 1792–99. b. 1747; d. 1799

*Leblanc de Beaulieu, Jean-Claude. 1800–1801. b. 1753; d. 1825
Oath Adherence (January–Spring, 1791)
Curés—542 (50%)
Vicaires—298 (50%)
Calvados
Administration
*Fauchet, Claude. 1791–93. b. 1744; d. 1793
Duchemin, Julien-Jean-Baptiste. 1799. b. 1742; d. 1799
Bisson, Louis-Charles. 1799–1801. b. 1742; d. 1820
Oath Adherence (January–Spring, 1791)
Curés—402 (41%)
Vicaires—144 (33%)
Eure
Administration
*Lindet, Robert-Thomas. 1791–93. b. 1743; d. 1823
Oath Adherence (January–Spring, 1791)
Curés—573 (63%)
Vicaires—214 (62%)
Manche
Administration
*Bécherel, François. 1791–1801. b. 1732; d. 1816
Oath Adherence (January–Spring, 1791)
Curés—383 (53%)
Vicaires—358 (50%)
Oise
Administration
*Massieu, Jean-Baptiste. 1791–94. b. 1743; d. 1818
Oath Adherence (January–Spring, 1791)
Curés—554 (79%)
Vicaires—141 (79%)
Orne
Administration
*Lefessier, André-Jacques-Simon. 1792–1801. b. 1738; d. 1806
Oath Adherence (January–Spring, 1791)
Curés—302 (46%)
Vicaires—166 (45%)
Pas-de-Calais
Administration

*Porion, Pierre-Joseph. 1791–94? b. 1743; d. 1830
Asselin, Mathieu. 1797–1801. b. 1736; d. 1825
Oath Adherence (January–Spring, 1791)
Curés—142 (17%)
Vicaires—50 (20%)
Somme
Administration
*Desbois de Rochefort, Éléonor-Marie. 1791–1801. b. 1749; d. 1807
Oath Adherence (January–Spring, 1791)
Curés—485 (60%)
Vicaires—114 (60%)

Métropole du Nord-Est
Marne
Administration
*Diot, Nicholas. 1791–1801. b. 1744; d. 1802
Oath Adherence (January–Spring, 1791)
Curés—339 (79%)
Vicaires—52 (71%) (No figures for district around Reims.)
Aisne
Administration
*Marolles, Claude-Eustache-François. 1791–93. b. 1753; d. 1794
Oath Adherence (January–Spring, 1791)
Curés—592 (77%)
Vicaires—(No figures.)
Ardennes
Administration
Philbert, Nicholas. 1791–97. b. 1724; d. 1797
*Monin, Joseph. 1798–1801. b. 1741; d. 1805
Oath Adherence (January–Spring, 1791)
Curés—223 (66%)
Vicaires—57 (66%)
Meurthe
Administration
*Lalande, Luc-François. 1791–92. b. 1732; d. 1805
Nicholas, François. 1800–1801. b. 1741; d. 1807
Oath Adherence (January–Spring, 1791)

Curés—223 (46%)
Vicaires—29 (29%)
Meuse
Administration
Aubry, Jean-Baptiste. 1791–1801. b. 1733; d. 1813
Oath Adherence (January–Spring, 1791)
Curés—273 (83%)
Vicaires—81 (87%)
Moselle
Administration
Francin, Nicholas. 1791–1801. b. 1735; d. 1802
Oath Adherence (January–Spring, 1791)
Curés—172 (39%)
Vicaires—26 (22%)
Nord
Administration
*Primat, Claude-François-Marie. 1791–1801. b. 1747; d. 1816
Schelle, Jacques-Joseph. 1800–1801. b. 1747; d. 1803
Oath Adherence (January–Spring, 1791)
Both clergies—190 (15%)

Métropole de l'Est
Doubs
Administration
*Séguin, Philippe-Charles-François. 1791–96. b. 1741; d. 1812
Oath Adherence (January–Spring, 1791)
Curés—88 (40%)
Vicaires—18 (17%)
Bas-Rhin
Administration
Brendel, François Antoine. 1791–97. b. 1736; d. 1799
Oath Adherence (January–Spring, 1791)
Curés—28 (10%)
Vicaires—5 (5%)
Côte-d'Or
Administration
*Volfius, Jean-Baptiste. 1795–1801. b. 1734; d. 1823
Oath Adherence (January–Spring, 1791)

Curés—311 (63%)
Vicaires—90 (61%)
Haute-Marne
Administration
*Wandelaincourt, Antoine-Hubert. 1791–1801. b. 1731; d. 1819
Oath Adherence (January–Spring, 1791)
Curés—252 (65%)
Vicaires—71 (51%)
Haut-Rhin
Administration
Martin, Arbogast. 1791–94. b. 1731; d. 1794
*Berdolet, Marc-Antoine. 1796–1801. b. 1740; d. 1819
Oath Adherence (January–Spring, 1791)
Curés—119 (39%)
Vicaires—57 (43%)
Haute-Saône
Administration
*Flavigny, Jean-Baptiste. 1791–1801. b. 1732; d. 1813
Oath Adherence (January–Spring, 1791)
Curés—118 (40%)
Vicaires—37 (24%)
Jura
Administration
*Moïse, François-Xavier. 1791–1801. b. 1742; d. 1813
Oath Adherence (January–Spring, 1791)
Curés—101 (45%)
Vicaires—3 (4%)
Vosges
Administration
Maudru, Jean-Antoine. 1791–1801. b. 1748; d. 1820
Oath Adherence (January–Spring, 1791)
Curés—199 (68%)
Vicaires—135 (62%)

Métropole du Sud-Est
Rhône-et-Loire
Administration
*Lamourette, Antoine-Adrien. 1791–94. b. 1742; d. 1794

Oath Adherence (January–Spring, 1791)
Curés—256 (89%)
Vicaires—140 (76%)

Ain

Administration
*Royer, Jean-Baptiste. 1791–98. b. 1733; d. 1807

Oath Adherence (January–Spring, 1791)
Curés—336 (88%)
Vicaires—170 (86%)

Ardeche

Administration
*Savine, Charles de La Font de. 1791–1801. b. 1742; d. 1815

Oath Adherence (January–Spring, 1791)
Curés—160 (58%)
Vicaires—77 (38%)

Cantal

Administration
*Thibault, Anne-Alexandre-Marie. 1791–93. b. 1747; d. 1813
Bertin, Louis. 1800–1801. b. 1751; d. 1822

Oath Adherence (January–Spring, 1791)
Curés—143 (55%)
Vicaires—109 (60%)

Haute-Loire

Administration
Delcher, Étienne. 1791–1801. b. 1732; d. 1806

Oath Adherence (January–Spring, 1791)
Curés—67 (58%)
Vicaires—32 (60%)

Isère

Administration
Pouchot, Joseph. 1791–92. b. 1720; d. 1792
*Reymond, Henri. 1793–1801. b. 1737; d. 1820

Oath Adherence (January–Spring, 1791)
Curés—460 (84%)
Vicaires—122 (84%)

Mont-Blanc

Administration
*Panisset, François-Thérèse. 1793–96. b. 1729; d. 1809

Oath Adherence (January–Spring, 1791)
(No figures available.)
Puy-de-Dôme
Administration
*Périer, Jean-François. 1791–1801. b. 1740; d. 1824
Oath Adherence (January–Spring, 1791)
Curés—218 (48%)
Vicaires—116 (49%)
Saône-et-Loire
Administration
*Talleyrand, Charles-Maurice de
*Gouttes, Jean-Louis. 1791–94. b. 1739; d. 1794
*Poullard, Thomas-Juste. 1801. b. 1754; d. 1833
Oath Adherence (January–Spring, 1791)
Curés—354 (63%)
Vicaires—54 (48%)

Métropole des Côtes de la Méditerranée
Bouches-du-Rhône
Administration
Roux, Charles-Benoît. 1791–94. b. 1738; d. 1794
Aubert, Jean-Baptiste-Siméon. 1798–1801. b. 1731; d. 1816
Oath Adherence (January–Spring, 1791)
Curés—108 (69%)
Vicaires—140 (66%)
Basses-Alpes
Administration
*Villaneuve, Jean-Baptiste-Romé de. 1791–98. b. 1727; d. 1798
Champsaud, André. 1799–1801. b. 1738; d. 1826
Oath Adherence (January–Spring, 1791)
Curés—228 (91%)
Vicaires—108 (89%)
Corse
Administration
Guasco, Ignace-François. 1791–93. b. 1720; d. 1802
Oath Adherence (January–Spring, 1791)
Curés—479 (92%)

Drôme
- Administration
  - *Marbos, François. 1791–1801. b. 1739; d. 1825
- Oath Adherence (January–Spring, 1791)
  - Curés—312 (84%)
  - Vicaires—114 (86%)

Gard
- Administration
  - *Dumouchel, Jean-Baptiste. 1791–93. b. 1748; d. 1820
- Oath Adherence (January–Spring, 1791)
  - Curés—128 (36%)
  - Vicaires—39 (32%)

Hautes-Alpes
- Administration
  - *Cazeneuve, Ignace de. 1791–98. b. 1747; d. 1806
  - *Garnier, André. 1800–1801. b. 1727; d. 1816
- Oath Adherence (January–Spring, 1791)
  - Curés—157 (89%)
  - Vicaires—82 (88%)

Hérault
- Administration
  - Pouderous, Dominique. 1791–99. b. 1721; d. 1799
  - *Rouanet, Alexandre-Victor. 1799–1801. b. 1747; d. 1821
- Oath Adherence (January–Spring, 1791)
  - Curés—182 (46%)
  - Vicaires—49 (37%)

Lozère
- Administration
  - Nogaret, Étienne. 1791–1801. b. 1726; d. 1804
- Oath Adherence (January–Spring, 1791)
  - Curés—31 (17%)
  - Vicaires—16 (14%)

Var
- Administration
  - Rigouard, Jean-Joseph. 1791–1800. b. 1735; d. 1800
- Oath Adherence (January–Spring, 1791)
  - Curés—188 (91%)
  - Vicaires—259 (95%)

Vaucluse
Administration
Rovère, Siméon-Stylite-François-Régis. 1793–1801 (1794). b. 1756; d. 1818
Étienne, François. 1798–1801. b. 1763; d. 1836
Oath Adherence (January–Spring, 1791)
(Figures not available.)

Métropole du Sud
Haute-Garonne
Administration
*Sermet, Antoine-Pascal-Hyacinthe. 1791–1801. b. 1732; d. 1808
Oath Adherence (January–Spring, 1791)
473 (43%) (Figures not available to differentiate functions.)
Ariège
Administration
Font, Bernard. 1791–1800. b. 1723; d. 1800
Lemercier, François-Louis. 1801. b. 1729; d. 1804
Oath Adherence (January–Spring, 1791)
Curés—152 (66%)
Vicaires—86 (64%)
Aude
Administration
Besaucèle, Guillaume. 1791–1800. b. 1712; d. 1801
*Belmas, Louis. 1801. b. 1857; d. 1841
Oath Adherence (January–Spring, 1791)
Curés—318 (71%)
Vicaires—102 (68%)
Aveyron
Administration
*Debertier, Claude. 1791–1801. b. 1750; d. 1831
Oath Adherence (January–Spring, 1791)
Curés—137 (23%)
Vicaires—108 (25%)
Basses-Pyrénées
Administration
Sanadon, Barthélemy-Jean-Baptiste. 1791–96. b. 1729; d. 1796
Oath Adherence (January–Spring, 1791)
Old Regime diocese 1 (Lascar)—157 (63%)

Old Regime diocese 2 (Bayonne)—152 (40%)
(Figures not available to differentiate functions.)

Gers

Administration

Barthe, Paul-Benoît. 1791–1801. b. 1739; d. 1809

Oath Adherence (January–Spring, 1791)

Curés—205 (40%)

Vicaires—78 (28%)

Hautes-Pyrénées

Administration

Molinier, Jean-Guillaume. 1791–1801. b. 1733; d. 1814

Oath Adherence (January–Spring, 1791)

Curés—264 (80%)

Vicaires—129 (72%)

Lot

Administration

Danglars, Jean. 1791–1801. b. 1739; d. 1814

Oath Adherence (January–Spring, 1791)

Curés—191 (40%)

Vicaires—78 (48%)

Pyrénées-Orientales

Administration

Deville, Gabriel. 1791–94. b. 1749; d. 1796

Villa, Dominique-Paul. 1798–1801. b. 1735; d. 1801

Oath Adherence (January–Spring, 1791)

Curés—57 (28%)

Vicaires—26 (32%)

Tarn

Administration

*Gausserand, Jean-Joachim. 1791–1801. b. 1749; d. 1820

Oath Adherence (January–Spring, 1791)

Curés—49 (18%)

Vicaires—27 (13%)

Métropole du Sud-Ouest

Gironde

Administration

Pacareau, Pierre. 1791–97. b. 1711; d. 1797

*Lacombe, Dominique. 1798–1801. b. 1749; d. 1823
Oath Adherence (January–Spring, 1791)
Curés—343 (63%)
Vicaires—62 (44%)
Charente
Administration
Joubert, Pierre-Mathieu. 1791–92. b. 1748; d. 1815
Oath Adherence (January–Spring, 1791)
Curés—354 (78%)
Vicaires—55 (71%)
Charente-Inférieure
Administration
Robinet, Isaac-Étienne. 1791–93. b. 1731; d. 1797
Oath Adherence (January–Spring, 1791)
Curés—322 (65%)
Vicaires—49 (51%)
Corrèze
Administration
Brival, Jean-Jacques. 1791–1801. b. 1727; d. 1802
Oath Adherence (January–Spring, 1791)
Curés—158 (51%)
Vicaires—62 (39%)
Deux-Sèvres
Administration
*Mestadier, Jean-Joseph. 1791–95. b. 1739; d. 1803
Oath Adherence (January–Spring, 1791)
Curés—223 (80%)
Vicaires—13 (50%)
Dordogne
Administration
*Pontard, Pierre. 1791–93. b. 1749; d. 1832
Bouchier, Antoine. 1801. b. 1741; d. 1801
Oath Adherence (January–Spring, 1791)
Curés—88 (40%)
Vicaires—18 (17%)
Haute-Vienne
Administration
*Gay-Vernon, Léonard. 1791–93. b. 1748; d. 1822

Oath Adherence (January–Spring, 1791)
Curés—166 (65%)
Vicaires—91 (65%)
Landes
Administration
*Saurine, Jean-Pierre. 1791–1801. b. 1735; d. 1811
Oath Adherence (January–Spring, 1791)
Curés—114 (36–38%)
Vicaires—18 (26%)
Lot-et-Garonne
Administration
*Constant, André. 1791–1801. b. 1736; d. 1811
Oath Adherence (January–Spring, 1791)
Curés—299 (77%)
Vicaires—88 (65%)
Vendée
Administration
Rodrigue, François-Auguste. 1791–93. b. 1730; d. 1813
Oath Adherence (January–Spring, 1791)
Curés—112 (35%)
Vicaires—45 (30%)

Colonial Dioceses
Cayenne (Guyane)
Jacquemin, Nicholas. 1798–1801. b. 1727; d. 1819
Cayes (Saint-Domingue)
Mauviel, Guillaume. 1800–1801. b. 1757; d. 1814

Notes

PROLOGUE

1. See Claude Langlois and Timothy Tackett, "Ecclesiastical Structures and Clerical Geography on the Eve of the French Revolution," *French Historical Studies* 11 (1980): 352–70. The authors calculated these numbers from the 1817 list of clerical pensioners. Total religious personnel, including nuns, was approximately 170,000, of which "slightly more than one third was directly involved in pastoral care in the parishes (i.e., the *curés* and *vicaires*)" (353). This means that approximately 56,000 priests were obligated to the oath of loyalty to the revolutionary government. I have not dealt in this book with issues that arose when priests were members of religious orders, congregations, or societies (sometimes called "regulars" because they follow a *regula*, or rule), although for comparative purposes I have studied the letters written by Benedictines, Cistercians, Dominicans, and Oratorians to the Comité des assemblées; see AN, DXIX 1, 13–15. See, however, the basic work of Bernard Plongeron, *Les Réguliers de Paris devant le serment constitutionnel* (Paris, 1964); and the recent study of female religious orders, Gwénaël Murphy, *Les Religieuses dans la Révolution française* (Paris, 2005).

2. "More than half" according to the calculations of Langlois and Tackett in "Ecclesiastical Origins and Clerical Geography"; and "as high as 61 percent" according to the calculations communicated to me by Rodney J. Dean. For his major studies of the Constitutional Church, see note 7 below.

3. See the recent dissertation of Gérard Pelletier published as *Rome et la Révolution française: La théologie et la politique du saint siège devant la Révolution française (1789–1799)* (Rome, 2004). On the development of the role of the pope in Catholic history, see Hans Kung, *Infallible? An Unresolved Inquiry* (New York, 1994).

4. See the classic Albert Soboul, "Classes populaires et Rousseauisme sous la Révolution," *Annales historiques de la Révolution française* 34 (1962): 421–38; the appropriate essays in Roger Chartier, *Les Origines culturelles de la Révolution française* (Paris, 1990); and Nigel Aston, *Religion and Revolution in France, 1780–1804* (Washington, D.C., 2000), chap. 4: "The Church and the Enlightenment."

5. John McManners, *The French Revolution and the Church* (London, 1969).

6. To establish a full narrative presentation of the personalities and events I study over the revolutionary years, a systematic review of the three major publications of the revolutionary era would be mandatory: *Le Moniteur Universel* for daily reports of the events considered newsworthy; *Les Archives Parlementaires* (which includes regular selections from the *Moniteur*) for daily discussions of the national assemblies; and the *Annales de la religion* for biweekly news and views of leading Constitutional Church writers. I have done this selectively, relying more on archival inventories and the leads established by some of my predecessors and colleagues. Accordingly, I have highlighted elements

in a number of series in the Archives nationales: the files of the work committees of the National Assembly represent the religious issues that came to the attention of the central government administration; the dossiers of abdicating priests and of retracting priests provide a cross-section view of the experiences of priests, who were formally disengaging or reengaging themselves from/to the church; and, of course, the series F19 (*cultes*) and F7 (*police générale*) contain widely scattered testimony to societal/religious turmoil. Printed primary sources, many of them available only in the original printings (and so, at the Bibliothèque nationale and in the collections of the appropriate departmental archives), included the pastoral letters of the leading constitutional bishops and revolutionary-era publications where religion was a genuine concern (e.g., *La Feuille villageoise*).

7. A colloquium to initiate these projects, *Gouverner une église en révolution: Histoires et mémoires de l'épiscopat constitutionnel français*, was held under the auspices of the Université de Lyon III, 9–10 June 2012; papers are to be published in 2014 in *Chrétiens et sociétés*, a review edited at the university. The executive committee comprised Bernard Plongeron, Jacques-Olivier Boudon, Philippe Bourdin, Paul Chopelin, and myself.

8. See Rodney J. Dean, *L'Église constitutionnelle, Napoléon et le Concordat de 1801* (Paris, 2004), and *L'Abbé Grégoire et l'Église constitutionnelle après la Terreur, 1794–1797* (Paris, 2008); Bernard Plongeron, *Les Réguliers de Paris devant le serment constitutionnel* (Paris, 1964), ed., *Les Défis de la modernité*, volume 10 of *Histoire du Christianisme* (Paris, 1997), esp. 301–453, and *Des Résistances religieuses à Napoléon (1799–1813)* (Paris, 2006); Timothy Tackett, *Religion, Revolution, and Regional Culture in Eighteenth-Century France: The Ecclesiastical Oath of 1791* (Princeton, 1986), as well as Claude Langlois, Timothy Tackett, and Michel Vovelle, eds., *Religion*, vol. 9 of *Atlas de la Révolution française* (Paris, 1996). The earlier references are Augustin Sicard, *Le Clergé de France pendant la Révolution*, 2 vols. (Paris, 1912–27, focusing on work that he had done at the beginning of the century); Dom H. Leclercq, *L'Église constitutionnelle (juillet 1790–avril 1791)* (Paris, 1934); Jean Boussoulade, *L'Église de Paris du 9 thermidor au Concordat* (Paris, 1950); Paul Pisani, *Répertoire biographique de l'épiscopat constitutionnel* (Paris, 1907), and *L'Église de Paris et la Révolution* (Paris, 1908–11). Especially see McManners, *The French Revolution and the Church.* Nigel Aston's volumes are *The End of an Elite: The French Bishops and the Coming of the Revolution, 1786–1790* (Oxford, 1992), and *Religion and Revolution in France*. See also Dale Van Kley in *The Religious Origins of the French Revolution: From Calvin to the Civil Constitution, 1560–1791* (New Haven, 1996), esp. chap. 6; and Suzanne Desan in *Reclaiming the Sacred: Lay Religion and Popular Politics in Revolutionary France* (Ithaca, 1990). Finally, see Paul Chopelin, *Ville patriote et ville martyre: Lyon, l'église et la Révolution, 1788–1805* (Paris: 2010); and Caroline Chopelin-Blanc, *De l'apologétique à l'Église constitutionnelle: Adrien Lamourette (1742–1794)* (Paris, 2009).

9. Twentieth-century study of the phenomenon was given major impetus by the writings of the proto-sociologist Max Weber. Relevant sections of Weber's *Wirtschaft und Gesellschaft* (1922) are translated as *The Sociology of Religion*, trans. Ephraim Fischoff with introd. by Talcott Parsons (Boston, 1963); and the Weberian style can still be seen in Stephen Sharot, *A Comparative Sociology of World Religions: Virtuosos, Priests, and Popular Religion* (New York, 2001). See, then, the summary of intervening interpretations in John Jay Hughes, "Christian Priesthood," in *The Encyclopedia of Religion*, 16 vols., ed. Mircea Eliade (New York, 1987), 11:536–39.

10. See Catherine Vincent, "De la mission à la pastorale" (chap. 1) and "Les temps des prêtres de paroisse (VIIIe–XIIe siècle)" (chap. 2), in *Histoire des curés*, ed. Nicole Lemaitre (Paris, 2002). In particular, see Gabriel Fournier, "La mise en place du cadre paroissial et l'évolution du peuplement," in *Cristianizzazione ed organizzazione ecclesiastica delle campagne nell'alto medioevo: Espansione e resistenze*, vol. 1 (Spoleto, 1982), 495–563.

11. See Catherine Vincent, "La Naissance du curé (fin XIIe–XIIIe siècle)" (chap. 3) and "Limites, concurrences et contestations (XIIIe–XVe siècle)" (chap. 4), in Lemaitre, *Histoire des curés*. On the organization of clerical preaching in particular, see Jean Longère, "La Prédication et l'instruction des fidèles selon les conciles et les statuts synodaux depuis l'Antiquité tardive jusqu'au XIIIe siècle," in *L'Encadrement religieux des fidèles au Moyen Âge et jusqu'au concile de Trente*, vol. 1 (Paris, 1985), 391–418.

12. Quoted in Nicole Lemaitre, "Des curés tridentins militants?" 182–83, in Lemaitre, *Histoire des curés*. All translations from the French, unless otherwise indicated, are mine.

13. The twentieth-century classic on the French school of spirituality beginning with Bérulle is Henri Brémond, *Histoire littéraire du sentiment religieux en France*, 5 vols., ed. François Tremolières, 1st ed., 12 vols., 1916–33 (Grenoble, 2006). Leszek Kolakowski's brilliant *Chrétiens sans églises: La conscience religieuse et le lien confessionnel au XVIIe siècle*, trans. Anna Posner (Paris, 1969) sets Bérulle and others in a dialectic between religious conscience and church allegiance, making Bérulle a master of both.

14. See Catherine Maire, *De la cause de Dieu à la cause de la Nation: Le jansénisme au XVIIIe siècle* (Paris 1998); and Edmond Préclin, *Jansénistes au XVIIIe siècle et la Constitution Civil du clergé: Le développement du Richerisme, sa propagation dans le bas clergé, 1713–1791* (Paris, 1923). For one view of the complex interplay of theology and politics from the Council of Trent through the Revolution, see Van Kley, *The Religious Origins of the French Revolution*. On scholarly exaggeration of the importance of a quasi-consistent Jansenism in histories of the constitutional clergy, see Paul Chopelin and Caroline Chopelin-Blanc, "L'Héritage janséniste dans l'Église constitutionnelle: Débats historiques et perspectives de recherché" (MS, n.d.).

15. Bernard Plongeron, *La Vie quotidienne du clergé français au XVIIIe siècle* (Paris, 1989), 55.

16. Ibid., 54.

17. Ibid., 57.

18. Ibid., 58–59.

19. John McManners, *Church and Society in Eighteenth-Century France*, 2 vols. (Oxford, 1998), 1:359–83.

20. Ibid., 1:381.

21. Ibid., 1:346.

22. Father Dominique Chaix from the diocese of Gap in the Dauphiné is a clear example of a faithful and refined curé in the generation leading up to the Revolution. See the vignette presented by Timothy Tackett in *Priest and Parish in Eighteenth-Century France: A Social and Political Study of the Curés in a Diocese of Dauphiné, 1750–1791* (Princeton, 1977), 86–95. Chaix received better than the usual clerical education, attaining even a university degree. In his small mountain village, he apparently had no difficulty combining the cultivation of his expertise in botany and his dedication to the service of his parishioners. Given that he did not see any conflict between religion and science, he

was in particular angered by the writings of Voltaire and Buffon: "I admire the depth of [the philosophers'] bearing, but I abhor their proud and shameful obsessions" (94–95).

23. McManners, *Church and Society*, 1:214.

24. Ibid., 241.

25. There is no full and sure chronology of religious events across the revolutionary decade. The chronologies established by Alfred Fierro in *Histoire et dictionnaire de la Révolution française, 1789–1799*, with Jean Tulard and Jean-François Fayard (Paris, 1987), 311–410; and Yann Fauchois in *Chronologie politique de la Révolution, 1789–1799* (Paris, 1989) are, however, useful.

CHAPTER 1

1. Jean-Denis Bredin, *Sieyès: La clé de la Révolution française* (Paris, 1988), 75.

2. With the recent Emmanuel de Waresquiel, *Talleyrand: Le prince immobile* (Paris, 2006) as orientation, see the much older, and only, text on Talleyrand as bishop, Bernard Lacombe, *Talleyrand, évêque d'Autun, d'après des documents inédits* (Paris, 1903). For Fouché, see Jean Tulard, *Joseph Fouché* (Paris, 1998). Recent editions of the memoirs of both men are Charles-Maurice de Talleyrand-Périgord, *Mémoires complets et authentiques*, ed. Adolphe Fourier de Bacourt (Paris, 1990); and Joseph Fouché, *Mémoires*, presented by Michel Vovelle (Paris, 1992). If only for the title, note also Henri Noëll, *De la soutane au bonnet phrygien et à l'habit de cours: Sieyès, Fouché, Talleyrand* (Paris, 1947).

3. Alyssa Sepinwall, *The Abbé Grégoire and the French Revolution: The Making of Modern Universalism* (Berkeley, 2005), 52–54. For greater emphasis on the Jansenist leanings of Grégoire, see Jean Dubray, *La Pensée de l'abbé Grégoire: Despotisme et liberté* (Oxford, 2008).

4. See McManners, *Church and Society*, 1:321–83.

5. See Bredin, *Sieyès*, 24–25.

6. See Paul Bastid, *Sieyès et sa pensée* (Paris, 1970), chap. 1; and Christine Fauré, Jacques Guilhaumou, and Jacques Valier, *Des Manuscrits de Sieyès, 1773–1799* (Paris, 1999), 101n56, where this work, *Sur Dieu ultramètre*, is mentioned and other references given. The Archives nationales has a vital, major collection of Sieyès material; see Robert Marquant, ed., *Les Archives Sieyès aux Archives nationales* (Paris, 1970).

7. Sieyès's life and career are outlined in the *Notice sur la vie de Sieyès* (Paris, 1794), reprinted in the modern *Oeuvres de Sieyès* (Paris, 1989), vol. 1. Sieyès corrected and edited this piece himself.

8. C.-A. Sainte-Beuve, *Causéries de lundi*, vol. 5, 3rd ed. (Paris, n.d.), 190.

9. Ibid., 195.

10. Quoted in ibid., 194.

11. Sieyès, *Notice sur la vie de Sieyès*, 9.

12. Bastid, *Sieyès*, 49.

13. Quoted in ibid., 39.

14. Ibid.

15. However, philosophical metaphysics also served as a basis for a quantitative science. Guilhaumou finds that, in Sieyès, a principle of individual immanence ("self-constitution of the ego") interacts with a principle of the *optimum* (i.e., highest level of

attainment possible), and that this interaction is "well suited to account for the infinity of actions and for the best possible actions." See Jacques Guilhaumou, *Sieyès et l'ordre de la langue: L'invention de la politique moderne* (Paris, 2002), 53. More recently, Guilhaumou has further highlighted the relationship of Sieyès's metaphysics of the concrete ego and all his writings on the political order. See "Sieyès et la figure nominaliste du métaphysicien: Du *Grand cahier métaphysique* aux *Vues analytiques*," in *Figures de Sieyès*, ed. Pierre-Yves Quiviger, Vincent Denis, and Jean Salem (Paris, 2008), 241–53.

16. Fauré, Guilhaumou, and Valier, *Manuscrits de Sieyès*, 101n56.

17. Quoted in ibid., 101.

18. Quoted in ibid., 102. One work in particular was probably Sieyès's theology sourcebook: M. de Prémontval, *La Théologie de l'être ou chaîne d'idées de l'être jusqu'à Dieu (choix des mémoires et abrégé de l'histoire de l'Académie de Berlin)*, vol. 3 (Berlin, 1764), which he refers to, along with other works by the same author, under the heading "Sur la philosophie en général et morceaux détachées," in the *Bibliographies* of his *Grand cahier.* See ibid., 102n58; as well as AN, AS 284 AP 1, d. 3, *Projet de bibliothèque ou bibliographie.*

19. Quoted in Fauré, Guilhaumou, and Valier, *Manuscrits de Sieyès*, 102.

20. Jacques Guilhaumou, "Fragments d'un discours sur Dieu: Sieyès et la religion," in *Mélanges Vovelle* (Aix-en-Provence, 1997), 257. Guilhaumou has more recently stated, in a communication to me, that the dating of this document is far from certain. The "fibre" of the title labels a disposition to one or another sensibility or sentiment, a definition that is clarified in the contemporary *Dictionnaire des expressions et locutions*: the metaphor comes from early anatomical terminology, where *fibers* can designate the nerves, the tendons, the ligaments, from which membranes and body parts are made (*entretissues*). At first they spoke of *fibers of being, of the heart*, and so forth, mythical organs of sensibility; then *fiber* in the singular represented more abstractly the aptitude for sensing. See Alain Rey and Sophie Chantreau, eds., *Dictionnaire des expressions et locutions*, 2nd ed. (Paris, 1993), s.v. "fibre."

21. Guilhaumou, "Fragments d'un discours sur Dieu," 258. With some slight changes, I have followed Guilhaumou in this presentation, but I have also worked directly from the complete manuscript, *Sur Dieu ultramètre et sur la fibre religieuse de l'homme* (1780), AN, AS 284 AP 2, d. 3, c. 6, p. 236; I use here the numbering of papers in the archival manuscripts, where each number covers a paper page, both front and back. Jacques Guilhaumou has very generously put at my disposal his own transcription of the entire manuscript, thus enabling me to verify and correct the small, select set of pages that I transcribed myself, and to read a full version of this important text. Publication of this and several other related manuscripts is still several years away.

22. *Sur Dieu ultramètre*, quoted in Fauré, Guilhaumou, and Valier, *Des Manuscrits de Sieyès*, 102n57.

23. *Sur Dieu ultramètre*, AN, AS 284 AP 2, d. 3, c. 6, 236.

24. Guilhaumou, "Fragments d'un discours," 259–60.

25. AN, AS 284 AP 2, d. 3, c. 6, 237–38.

26. Ibid., 238.

27. Guilhaumou, "Fragments d'un discours," 260.

28. AN, AS 284 AP 2, d. 3, c. 6, 243.

29. Ibid., 240.

30. Ibid., 242.

31. Ibid., 250.
32. Ibid., 251.
33. Ibid.
34. Ibid., 252.
35. Guilhaumou, "Fragments d'un discours," 264.
36. Emmanuel-Joseph Sieyès, *Qu'est-ce que c'est le tiers état?* (Paris, 1789).
37. Ibid., 8.
38. Ibid., 2, 3.
39. Ibid., 6.
40. Ibid., 8.
41. Ibid., 18.
42. Ibid., 22.
43. Ibid., 31.
44. Ibid., 43.
45. Ibid., 53.
46. Ibid., 56.
47. Ibid., 98.
48. Ibid., 109.
49. Henri Grégoire, *Mémoires de Grégoire, suivies de la Notice historique sur Grégoire d'Hippolyte Carnot*, 1st ed. 1808 (Paris, 1989), 49–50.
50. Antoine Sutter, *Les Années de jeunesse de l'abbé Grégoire: Son itinéraire jusqu'à la Révolution* (Sarreguemines, 1992), 16, citing a footnote in Louis Maggiolo to this effect.
51. Grégoire, *Mémoires de Grégoire*, 50.
52. Ibid., 51.
53. Ibid., 52.
54. Sutter, *Les Années de jeunesse*, 24.
55. Sepinwall, *Grégoire*, 24.
56. Henri Grégoire, *Éloge de la poésie, discours qui a remporté le prix . . . de la Société royale des Sciences et Belles-lettres de Nancy* (Nancy, 1773), 3. I use a transcription of elements of the text made by Alyssa Goldstein Sepinwall, which she has graciously placed at my disposal. All quotations and pagination are from this transcription of the original text, unless they are cited in Sepinwall's major study, *The Abbé Grégoire and the French Revolution*, in which case I give the page of the original text and as it is cited in the Sepinwall study.
57. Grégoire, *Éloge*, 7.
58. Ibid., 29, quoted in Sepinwall, *Grégoire*, 23.
59. Ibid., 29, quoted in Sepinwall, *Grégoire*, 24.
60. Ibid., 29, quoted in Sepinwall, *Grégoire*, 23–24.
61. Sepinwall, *Grégoire*, 24.
62. Grégoire, *Éloge*, 32.
63. Ibid., 41.
64. Ibid., 56, quoted in Sepinwall, *Grégoire*, 24.
65. Sutter, *Les Années de jeunesse*, 29.
66. Grégoire, *Mémoires de Grégoire*, 118.
67. Henri Grégoire, *Essai sur la régénération physique, morale et politique des juifs*, 1st ed. 1788 (Metz, 1789).

68. Ibid., 15.

69. Ibid., 17.

70. Ibid., 43.

71. Ibid., 70.

72. Ibid., 74.

73. Ibid., 106.

74. Ibid., 141.

75. Ibid., 146.

76. Ibid., 194.

77. "Motion en faveur des juifs," quoted in Frank Paul Bowman, ed., *L'Abbé Grégoire, évêque des Lumières* (Paris, 1988), 26.

78. Sepinwall, *Grégoire*, 91.

CHAPTER 2

1. The labels *bailliage* and *sénéchaussée* have the same meaning; their use depends on the region of France where the electoral district is situated.

2. See Aston, *The End of an Elite*, chap. 7, "Bishops versus Curés: Clerical Elections to the Estates General, Spring 1789."

3. Tackett, *Religion, Revolution, and Regional Culture*, 146–55. Indirectly—and Charles-Louis Chassin emphasized this (see note 8 below)—the *cahiers* of the Third Estate can be used as partial witness to the attitudes of curés: hence, the vital research of John Markoff on the parish *cahiers* (not to be confused with the *cahiers* of the clergy) and the standard *cahiers* of the Third Estate (which contain some evidence of the goals of the lower clergy). See Markoff, *The Abolition of Feudalism: Peasants, Lords, and Legislators in the French Revolution* (University Park, Pa., 1996).

4. See Tackett, *Religion, Revolution and Regional Culture*, 152n87, for a list of grievances and their frequency of appearance in the clerical *cahiers*.

5. Philippe Grateau, *Les Cahiers de doléances: Une relecture culturelle*, cited in Rodney Dean, *La Naissance de l'église constitutionnelle sous l'Assemblée constituante, 1789–1791*, chap. 1. I am grateful to Rodney Dean for sharing the text of his forthcoming book with me. See also Aston, *Religion and Revolution in France*, 117.

6. Tackett, *Religion, Revolution, and Regional Culture*, 154.

7. Ibid., 150.

8. Charles-Louis Chassin, *Les Cahiers des curés, étude historique d'après les brochures, les cahiers imprimés et les procès-verbaux manuscrits* (Paris, 1882). Chassin examined the *cahiers*' content relative to the early history of the Revolution, from the curé "insurrection" in the Dauphiné through the Tennis Court Oath, concluding with a rapid thematizing of events following 1789. He used the *cahiers* published in the *Archives Parlementaires*, supplementing them with documents from series B III in the Archives nationales.

9. Chassin, *Cahiers des curés*, 204.

10. Ibid., 204, 207.

11. Ibid., 210–11.

12. Ibid., 217.

13. Ibid., 221.

14. Ibid., 228, 232.
15. Ibid., 250.
16. Ibid., 254.
17. Ibid., 255.
18. Ibid., 256.
19. Ibid., 260.
20. Ibid., 245.
21. Ibid., 225.
22. Ibid., 270.
23. Ibid., 267.
24. Ibid., 269–70.
25. Ibid., 214.
26. Ibid., 216.
27. Ibid., 265.
28. Ibid., 275.
29. M. G. Hutt, "The Role of the Curés in the Estates General of 1789," *Journal of Ecclesiastical History* 6 (1955): 191. Hutt also lists several memoirs in manuscript that are available in departmental archives. For a survey of events and personalities that builds on Hutt, see Ruth F. Necheles, "The Curés of the Estates General of 1789," *Journal of Modern History* 46 (1974): 425–44.
30. Albert Houtin, ed., *Les Séances des députés du clergé aux États Généraux de 1789: Journaux du Curé Thibault et du Chanoine Coster* (Paris, 1916), xvii; Jacques Rangeard, *Procès-verbal historique des actes du clergé deputé à l'Assemblée des États-Généraux des années 1789 et 1790* (Paris, 1791). See in particular pp. 15–16.
31. Jacques Jallet, *Journal inédit de Jallet, précédé d'une notice historique par J. J. Brethé* (Fontenay-le-Comte, 1871), 55.
32. Ibid., 60–61.
33. Ibid., 68.
34. Ibid., 86.
35. Ibid., 93.
36. Ibid.
37. Ibid.
38. Ibid., 97.
39. Ibid., 98.
40. Ibid., 103.
41. Ibid., 112–13.
42. Ibid., 121, 122, 123.
43. Ibid., 141.
44. Ibid., 143.
45. Ibid., 151. Jallet, having put so much of his personality into these accounts, was elected bishop of the department of the Deux-Sèvres in 1790, but refused the office and died of a stroke in August 1791. See Pisani, *Répertoire biographique de l'épiscopat constitutionnel*, 422.
46. Hutt, "Role of the Curés," 193.
47. Ibid., 202.
48. Ibid., 203.

49. See ibid., 206–8.

50. Ibid., 209.

51. Aston, *The End of an Elite*, 172n95 (citing both Necheles and Doyle); see also pp. 171–72, 180.

52. Jo Ann Seeley, "The Parish Clergy in the French Constituent Assembly, 1789–1791" (Ph.D. diss., Catholic University of America, 1992), 36–38.

53. Ibid., 130–36.

54. Pierre Durand de Maillane, *Histoire apologétique du comité ecclésiastique de l'Assemblée nationale* (Paris, 1791), 130–31. Jérôme Tissot-Dupont, in "Le Comité ecclésiastique de l'Assemblée nationale constituante (1789–1791): De *L'Histoire apologétique* par Durand de Maillane à la recherche moderne," *Revue d'histoire de l'Église de France* 90 (2004): 427–52, highlights the prejudices and omissions in the *Histoire apologétique*: "Instead of an objective narrative, Durand de Maillane offers an example and defense of his Gallicanism, reinforced by the work of the Constituent Assembly. Durand de Maillane hides the internal and administrative organization of the Comité ecclésiastique. . . . He limits himself to a description of the tasks confided to three sections of the Comité ecclésiastique and to the comité des dîmes."

55. Durand de Maillane, *Histoire apologétique*, 321–22.

56. Ibid., 56.

57. Ibid., 195.

58. Ibid., 276, 277.

59. Ibid., 163.

60. Ibid., 302.

61. Ibid., 303.

62. The text that will undoubtedly be the definitive study of the preparation of the Civil Constitution of the Clergy—Dean, *La Naissance de l'église constitutionnelle sous l'Assemblée constituante*—is still in preparation. I do not presume to quote from it here, and I have already noted my gratitude to the author for sharing the manuscript with me.

63. Keith Baker, ed., "Civil Constitution of the Clergy," in *The Old Regime and the French Revolution*, ed. John W. Boyer and Julius Kirshner, University of Chicago Readings in Western Civilization 7 (Chicago, 1987), 240.

64. Ibid., 241.

65. Ibid.

66. Ibid., 242.

67. See Malcolm Crook, "Citizen Bishops: Episcopal Election in the French Revolution," *Historical Journal* 43 (2000): 955–76.

68. Catherine Maire, *De la cause de Dieu à la cause de la Nation: Le jansénisme au XVIIIe siècle* (Paris, 1998), 585. See also Van Kley, *The Religious Origins of the French Revolution*, 354. Speaking of the principles on which the new legislation was based, he writes, "Even if some of these principles were strictly speaking more Gallican than Jansenist, they bear witness to a Gallicanism so radicalized by contact with Jansenism in the course of the eighteenth century's *Unigenitus*-related conflicts that they may be thought of as just as Jansenist as Gallican."

69. See chap. 7, "The Civil Constitution," in Aston, *Religion and Revolution in France*, for details on the bishops' *partis pris*.

70. See Pelletier, *Rome et la Révolution française*, chap. 6.

71. See chap. 12, "The Meaning of the Oath," in Tackett, *Religion, Revolution, and Regional Culture*, for a summary of attitudes and motivations.

72. Ibid., 95.

73. Here Jean Leflon is at pains to correct Paul Pisani, who counted eighty-three elected bishops. Only eighty were required because three Old Regime bishops remained as heads of their dioceses. Pisani had counted eighty-two new heads at another point by listing two of the new bishops twice. See Leflon, *La Crise révolutionnaire, 1789–1846* (Paris, 1951), 74n3.

74. This was, in any case, the effect on the refractory priests of the law proposed by Isaac-René Le Chapelier forbidding citizens of the same profession to form public associations. Le Chapelier was a founder of the Breton Club, an early version of the Jacobins. The classic study of yet earlier local versions of this group is Augustin Cochin, *Les Sociétés de pensée et la Révolution en Bretagne* (Paris, 1925).

75. AN, F19 470, *Mémoire au Conseil général du département de Paris par Monsieur Gobel, Évêque du dit département concernant l'établissement d'un séminaire diocésain dans cette capitale* (n.d.).

CHAPTER 3

1. Gary Kates, *The Cercle Social, the Girondins, and the French Revolution* (Princeton, 1985), 27; Edna Hindie Lemay, ed., *Dictionnaire des legislateurs, 1791–1792*, 2 vols. (Paris, 2007), 2:293.

2. See Tackett, *Religion, Revolution, and Regional Culture*, 354–55.

3. Claude Fauchet, *Discours sur la liberté française*, 5 August 1789, cited in Jules Charrier, *Claude Fauchet, évêque constitutionnel du Calvados, député à l'Assemblée législative et à la Convention (1744–1793)*, 2 vols. (Paris, 1909), 1:83–84.

4. Claude Fauchet, *Discours prononcé aux Quinze-Vingts*, 25 June 1790, cited in ibid., 84.

5. *Journal des Amis* 1 (1793), cited in ibid. The minutes of an assembly of electors in Paris record the event as one continuous movement: "The permanent committee of the Paris militia, believing that there should be no military force at Paris not under the jurisdiction of the city, charged the deputies to address themselves to the Bastille commander and ask if he would be disposed to receive there the troops of the Paris militia, who would guard it in concert with the troops already there." The group presented itself in the Orme courtyard, but their signals were not noticed. When they returned to the foot of the towers on the rue du Faubourg Saint-Antoine side of the Bastille, they saw that some members of the crowd had been injured. Afterward, they made their way back to the Hôtel de Ville. *Procès-verbal des séances et délibérations de l'Assemblée générale des électeurs de Paris, réunis à l'Hôtel de Ville*, 14 July 1789, vol. 1, p. 217, cited in ibid., 84–85n4.

6. Claude Fauchet, *Discourse à l'autel de la Patrie, pendant la cérémonie de la fédération générale du département* (Caen, 1791), 1–2.

7. Ibid., 2.

8. Ibid.

9. Ibid.

10. Charrier, *Claude Fauchet*, 1:3.

11. Ibid., 1:22.

12. Quoted in ibid., 1:43.

13. Ibid., 1:59.

14. Ibid., 1:60.

15. Ibid., vol. 1, chap. 4.

16. Quoted in ibid., 1:65.

17. Quoted in ibid.

18. Quoted in ibid., 1:67.

19. Quoted in ibid., 1:113.

20. Ibid., 1:138.

21. Quoted in ibid., 1:178.

22. For an orientation to the *Bulletin de la Bouche de fer* and the Imprimérie du Cercle social, see Kates, *The Cercle Social*, 82–84.

23. Claude Fauchet, "Premier discours prononcé par M. l'abbé Fauchet, pour l'inauguration de la Confédération universelle des amis de la vérité," in *La Bouche de fer, 1790–1791*, 2 vols. (Paris, 1981), 1:20.

24. Claude Fauchet, "Deuxième discours, prononcé par Claude Fauchet, procureur-général du cercle social, à l'assemblée de la Confédération universelle des amis de la vérité," in *La Bouche de fer*, 1:106–7.

25. Ibid., 1:107.

26. Ibid., 1:110–11.

27. Ibid., 1:111.

28. Claude Fauchet, "Suite du discours du Claude Fauchet, prononcé le 20 octobre, à la deuxieme séance de l'Assemblée fédérative," in *La Bouche de fer*, 1:116.

29. Ibid., 1:116–17.

30. Ibid., 1:117.

31. "Troisième discours, prononcé par Claude Fauchet, procureur-général du Cercle social, à l'assemblée de la Confédération universelle des amis de la vérité," in *La Bouche de fer*, 1:168.

32. Ibid., 1:173.

33. Ibid., 1:174.

34. Ibid., 1:179.

35. "Claude Fauchet à M. Cloots," in *La Bouche de fer*, 1:157.

36. Ibid.

37. Ibid.

38. Ibid.

39. Ibid.

40. Ibid.

41. Ibid., 1:159.

42. Ibid., 1:159; and see 1:260–61 for a second Cloots letter that simply thanks the man for a letter he himself wrote to *La Bouche de fer* praising the journal.

43. Charrier, *Claude Fauchet*, 1:269.

44. Claude Fauchet, *Lettre pastorale et la traduction de sa lettre de communion adressée à NSP le pape* (Bayeux, 1791), 1.

45. Ibid., 10.

46. Ibid.

47. Ibid.
48. Ibid., 11.
49. Ibid.
50. Ibid., 13.
51. Ibid.
52. Ibid., 13–14.
53. Ibid., 15.
54. For a presentation and interpretation of this speech, see Caroline Chopelin-Blanc, "Discours de Fauchet contre les prêtres insermentés (26 octobre 1791)," *Parlement(s)* 6 (2006): 165–73. The Fauchet–de Lessart antagonism is explained in Rita Hermon-Belot, "L'Abbé Fauchet," in *La Gironde et les Girondins*, ed. François Furet and Mona Ozouf (Paris, 1991).
55. Charrier, *Claude Fauchet*, 2:179.
56. Ibid., 2:181.
57. Claude Fauchet, *Lettre pastorale aux pasteurs et aux fidèles du diocèse* (Bayeux, 1792), 1.
58. Ibid., 2.
59. Ibid.
60. Ibid.

CHAPTER 4

1. Chopelin-Blanc, *De l'apologétique à l'Église constitutionnelle*. For the Mirabeau–Lamourette connection, Chopelin-Blanc sends readers to Daniele Menozzi, *Philosophes et Chrétiens éclairés: Politica e religione nella collaborazione G-H Mirabeau e A-A Lamourette* (Brescia, 1976). Also useful is Léon Berthe, "Grégoire, élève de l'abbé Lamourette," *Revue du Nord* 44 (1962): 39–46.
2. See Munro Price, "Mirabeau and the Court: Some New Evidence," *French Historical Studies* 29 (2006): 37–75, for a presentation of Mirabeau's hopes to save the monarchy, even by civil war if necessary, at the same time as he worked to save the Constitution. Price does not cross over a demarcation line marked out by Guy Chaussinand-Nogaret in his classic *Mirabeau* (Paris, 1982): Mirabeau might have countenanced violence and a temporary flight of the king to save the monarchy, "but to set the king against France with the help of the Austrians, there is nothing, neither in his acts nor in his writings, that permits us to impute that to him" (264–65).
3. Abbé Liébault, *Lamourette, prêtre et évêque assermenté, 1742–1794* (Nancy, 1894), 22–23.
4. Ibid., 25.
5. Ibid., 70 (citing *Extrait des observation de M. Camus, sur deux Brefs du Pape, en date du 10 mars et du 13 avril 1791*).
6. On Camus, see David C. Miller, "A.-G. Camus and the Civil Constitution of the Clergy," *Catholic Historical Review* 76 (1990): 481–505. Pierre Préteux, *Armand-Gaston Camus, 1740–1803* (Paris, 1932) is still helpful as well.
7. *Revue du Lyonnais*, cited in Pisani, *Répertoire biographique de l'épiscopat constitutionnel*, 278. The equivocal features of the election of Lamourette receive detailed analysis

in Paul Chopelin, "L'Élection de l'évêque constitutionnel de Rhône-et-Loire (1er mars 1791)," *Revue d'histoire de l'Église de France* 89 (2003): 385–418.

8. Adrien-Antoine Lamourette, *Instruction pastorale de M. l'évêque du département de Rhône et Loire, au clergé et aux Fidèles de son Diocèse* (Lyon, 1791).

9. "Polity" is formally defined as the form of government of a religious organization.

10. Lamourette, *Instruction pastorale,* 19.

11. Ibid., 19–20.

12. Ibid., 21.

13. Ibid., 25.

14. Ibid.

15. Ibid., 26.

16. Ibid., 27.

17. Ibid., 34.

18. Ibid., 39.

19. Ibid., 40.

20. Ibid., 56.

21. Ibid.

22. Ibid., 60.

23. Ibid., 69.

24. Guy Chaussinand-Nogaret, *Mirabeau entre le roi et la Révolution: Notes à la cour suivies de Discours* (Paris, 1986). For an analysis of the Voidel speech, see Rodney J. Dean, "Les Débats à l'Assemblée nationale des 26 et 27 novembre 1790" (MS, n.d.).

25. Chaussinand-Nogaret, *Mirabeau entre le roi et la revolution,* 353–54.

26. Ibid., 356.

27. Ibid., 362.

28. Ibid.

29. Ibid., 366.

30. Camus, *Obervations sur les deux brefs du pape,* cited in Lamourette, *Instruction pastorale,* 84.

31. Ibid., 85.

32. Ibid.

33. Ibid., 85–86.

34. Ibid., 86.

35. Ibid., 89.

36. Ibid., 91.

37. Ibid.

38. Ibid., 53.

39. Adrien-Antoine Lamourette, *Discours pour la fête des canonniers volontaires de l'armée parisienne, prononcé en l'église de Notre-Dame, le dimanche 4 décembre 1791* (Paris, 1791).

40. Ibid., 6.

41. Ibid.

42. Ibid., 9.

43. Ibid., 12.

44. Adrien-Antoine Lamourette, *Projet de réunion entre les membres de l'Assemblée nationale* (Paris, 1792). And see the *Archives Parlementaires, recueil complet des débats législatifs et politiques des Chambres françaises, première série, 1787 à 1799,* ed. Jérôme Mavidal and Émile

Laurent, 82 vols. (Paris, 1867–1913) (hereafter *AP*), Jérôme Mavidal and Émile Laurent, vol. 46: *Du 30 juin au soir au 20 juillet 1792 au soir*, 7 July 1792, 212–13. For an authoritative analysis of this dramatic moment, see Caroline Chopelin-Blanc, "Le 'Baiser Lamourette' (7 juillet 1792)," *Annales historiques de la Révolution française*, January–March 2009, 73–100.

45. Lamourette, *Projet*, 3–4.

46. Ibid., 4.

47. Ibid.

48. Ibid.

49. *AP*, 46:212.

CHAPTER 5

1. The Comité des recherches was set up by the Constituent Assembly to handle some of the police issues, including requests, complaints, and denunciations; consequently, it processed the greatest number of constitutional complaints. The Comité d'instruction publique that was set up by the Legislative Assembly looked to the organization of education, of course, but also fielded concerns about archives, libraries, museums, monuments, and even revolutionary festivals and public worship. The Comité de législation was set up by the Constituent Assembly to handle controversies that would arise out of legislative and judicial action.

2. AN, DXXIX 22, d. 235, lettre d'Expilly, évêque du Finistère, à Lanjuinais, Quimper, 21–22 avril 1791.

3. On Expilly as constitutional bishop, see R. Daniel, "Études sur les difficultés d'un évêque constitutionnel et le recrutement d'un nouveau clergé: Expilly, évêque constitutionnel du Finistère et les 'expilliens,'" *Bulletin de la Société archéologique du Finistère* 94 (1968): 80–134. For more on earlier accomplishments, see Jeanne L'Herron, *Un Morlaisien dans la Révolution: LA Expilly: Recteur de Saint-Martin* (Morlaix, 1989).

4. AN, DXXIX 22, d. 236, lettre de Saurine, évêque du Landes, au Msgr. De La Neufville, évêque du Dax, 20–24 avril 1791.

5. AN, DXXIX 23, d. 246, lettre de Cazeneuve, évêque du département des Hautes-Alpes, et délibérations du même et de son conseil, 12 juin 1791.

6. AN, DXXIX 8, d. 78, Morbihan: lettre de Le Masle, évêque constitutionnel, 26 mai 1791.

7. AN, DXXIX 22, d. 242, lettre, non signée de "plusieurs prêtres nouvellement élus curés" au département du Jura, 3 mai 1791.

8. AN, DXXIX 25, d. 252, lettre du sieur Mortier, ci-devant chanoine du chapitre de Luzarches (Seine-et-Oise), 5 décembre 1790.

9. AN, DXXIX 20, d. 216, lettre de Delaville, curé de Courmenil, évêché de l'Orne, 2 janvier 1791.

10. AN, DXXIX 22, d. 234, lettre, addressée à Voidel et signée "Les fonctionnaires assermentés du district de Brioude," au sujet des prêtres réfractaires, 14 avril 1791.

11. AN, DXXIX 23, d. 245, lettre du sieur Lepage, cure de Gisors, au président du Comité ecclésiastique, 24 mai 1791.

12. See Caroline Chopelin-Blanc, "La prise de parole des évêques-députés à l'Assemblée législative (1791–1792)," *Parlement(s)* 6 (2006): 118–34.

13. See Fauchois, *Chronologie politique de la Révolution.*

14. Pierre Pontard, *Lettre de P. Pontard, évêque du département de Dordogne, en réponse à l'ordonnance de M. Grossoles-Flamarens, évêque, datée de Paris, le 14 avril 1791* (n.p., 1791).

15. Ibid., 1.

16. Ibid., 3.

17. Ibid., 4.

18. Ibid., 5.

19. Ibid., 9.

20. Ibid.

21. Ibid.

22. Ibid., 11.

23. *AP*, 34:334–35.

24. Ibid., 38:565.

25. Pontard was one of the editors/writers for a bulletin that began publication as the Convention began its sessions. The *Poste du matin; ou, L'ami de la patrie, de la liberté, des moeurs et de l'égalité* was called an *Ouvrage périodique, auquel on a réuni le Bulletin de la Convention Nationale, l'extrait des nouvelles de la Guerre, le Journal Prophétique, et celui de la Correspondance civique et morale*, 2 vols. (Paris, 1792). According to the *Prospectus*, the intention was "to get out the journal, composed of eight pages in octavo every morning," but it never came close to a daily appearance and probably lasted less than a year. It offered readers the insights of Pierre Pontard, "bishop and deputy from the first legislature, [who] will be responsible for *prophetic issues* and *basic theology*." But there is apparently only one piece, extended and aggressive, by Pontard in this volume. Sounding like a Franciscan spiritualist, he wants the church, if not the state, to disappear temporally and somehow exist spiritually: "The church in the name of which so much has been said, has been weighed down without ever undergoing change beneath the scaffolding of a so-called representative of God and of a monster body called the *clergy*." He counts on an inner awareness, a gnostic awareness, as he cites his favorite "Illuminés" of the era: "Let us offer as a preamble here what the author of *The Divine Instinct* . . . said in 1727. The predictions of the Misses Labrousse and Brounhe having already been in the main fulfilled, they have acquired thereby a certain right to be believed." See *Poste du matin*, 1:31.

Two biographies of Pontard may be consulted: P. J. Credot, *Pierre Pontard: Évêque constitutionnel de la Dordogne* (Paris, 1893); and Henri Lacape, *Pierre Pontard, évêque constitutionnel de la Dordogne* (Bordeaux, 1952). On Franciscan spiritualism, see David Burr, *Spiritual Franciscans: From Protest to Persecution in the Century after Saint Francis* (University Park, Pa., 2003).

26. Pierre-Anastase Torné, *Discours prononcé à Bourges le 14 juillet 1791, sur l'Autel de la Patrie, par Monsieur Torné, evêque de la métropole du Centre* (Bourges, 1791).

27. Ibid., 3.

28. Ibid., 4.

29. *AP*, 34:445.

30. Ibid., 34:446.

31. Ibid.

32. Ibid., 34:447.

33. Ibid., 34:448.

34. *AP*, 49:679.
35. Ibid., 49:680–81.
36. Ibid., 49:684.
37. Ibid., 49:685.
38. Ibid., 49:686.
39. Ibid., 49:688.
40. Ibid., 49:690.
41. *La Feuille villageoise*, adressé chaque semaine à tous les villages de la France pour les instruire des loix, des evénements, des découvertes qui intéressent tout Citoyen: proposée par souscription aux propriétaires, fermiers, pasteurs, habitans et amis des campagnes (1790–94) (hereafter *LFV*), title page.
42. Melvin Allen Edelstein, *La Feuille villageoise: Communication et modernisation dans les régions rurales pendant la Révolution* (Paris, 1977), esp. 68–69, 72, 74–75. See also the discussion in Serge Bianchi, "Les curés rouges dans la Révolution française," *Annales historiques de la Révolution française* 54 (1982): 364–92.
43. *LFV* 3, no. 2 (6 octobre 1791): 26.
44. *LFV* 3, no. 10 (1 décembre 1791): 223.
45. *LFV* 3, no. 7 (10 novembre 1791): 155–56.
46. *LFV* 3, no. 10 (10 novembre 1791): 157.
47. *LFV* 5, no. 13 (27 décembre 1792): 293–94.
48. *LFV* 6, no. 44 (1 août 1793): 416.
49. Ibid., 417.
50. *LFV* 4, no. 36 (31 mai 1792): 228.
51. *LFV* 4, no. 27 (29 mars 1792): 9.
52. Ibid., 9–10. For the language controversy during the Revolution, see Michel de Certeau, Dominique Julia, and Jacques Revel, *Une politique de la langue: La Révolution française et les patois* (Paris, 1975).
53. *LFV* 4, no. 50 (13 septembre 1792): 558–60.
54. *LFV* 5, no. 16 (17 janvier 1793): 361.
55. *LFV* 6, no. 43 (25 juillet 1793): 377–88.
56. *LFV* 8, no. 27 (Quartidi, 14 Germinal, l'an 2, 3 avril 1794), 12.
57. Ibid.
58. Ibid.
59. Ibid., 12–13.
60. Ibid., 13.
61. Ibid., 35.
62. Ibid., 35–36.

CHAPTER 6

1. Leflon, *La Crise révolutionnaire*, 106.
2. Quoted in ibid., 109.
3. See the complex, at times virtually self-contradictory arguments of Albert Mathiez in his *Études sur Robespierre (1758–1794)* (Paris, 1988), chap. 7.
4. Quoted in Leflon, *La Crise révolutionnaire*, 115.

5. Henri Grégoire, *Mémoires de Grégoire, ancien évêque de Blois, député à l'Assemblée Constituante et à la Convention Nationale, Sénateur, membre de l'Institut,* 1st ed. 1840 (Paris, 1989), 127.

6. The entries in August Kuscinski, *Dictionnaire des conventionnels* (Paris, 1916–18), indicate that the dedication and efficiency of Jacques-Léonard Goyré-Laplanche, episcopal vicar of the constitutional bishop of Nièvre, served him well in the Convention as delegate from Nièvre (305–6). After his election, he paraded his efforts to combat refractory priests back in the Nièvre; he also publicized his fidelity to the government and his resolutions to safeguard liberty. He was indefatigable in the pursuit of unruly functionaries and recalcitrant priests, sending a number of them to their deaths. Jean-Baptiste-Benoît Monestier, episcopal vicar of Puy-de-Dôme, made a special fuss of his renunciation of Catholicism (459). For Monestier even the Civil Constitution of the Clergy should be tossed into the flames, "antirepublican" document that it was. Philibert Simond was the episcopal vicar of the bishop of Bas-Rhin and even helped Grégoire reorganize church efforts in the department of Mont-Blanc (569). He was called "Simond-Limon" (Simond-Slime) after he groused about the Vendéens and *their* revolt, suggesting that they should be added to the slime at the bottom of the Loire; paradoxically, he was executed even so. Of course, there were priests in the Convention who were not episcopal vicars, and one of them, Pierre-Jacques-Michel Châles, stands out for his violence (125). He was against the establishment of the Bureau d'Esprit Public, against the Girondins, and, to be sure, against priesthood: "They reproached me for being a priest; but I congratulate myself for having been a priest, because by living among them, that is, with all that is most corrupt in this world, I learned to despise and combat the scoundrels we call priests" (125). Accused of misdoing in the army and stereotyped by his enemies as an "ex-chanoine," he publicized his service to the fatherland loudly enough to acquire serious backing. See Claude Pichois and Jean Dautry, *Le Conventionnel Chasles et ses idées démocratiques* (Aix-en-Provence, 1958), which deals very little with his priestly career.

7. Ruth Graham, "The Secularization of the Ecclesiastical Deputies to the National Convention, 1792–1794," *Proceedings of the Consortium on Revolutionary Europe, 1750–1850* (1974): 65–79.

8. Quoted in Kuscinski, *Dictionnaire des conventionnels*, 122.

9. "Yves-Marie Audrein," in *Dictionnaire des parlementaires français depuis le 1er Mai 1789 jusqu'au 1er Mai 1889*, ed. Robert Adolphe, Edgar Bourloton, and Gaston Cougny (Paris, 1889–91).

10. Yves-Marie Audrein, *Discours patriotique, à l'occasion du renouvellement du serment civique fait par M. M. les vicaires de M. l'évêque du Morbihan, dans l'église cathédrale & paroissiale de Vannes, le 29 mai 1791* (Vannes, 1791).

11. Ibid., 1.

12. Ibid., 11.

13. Ibid.

14. Ibid.

15. Ibid., 14.

16. Yves-Marie Audrein, *Éloge des armées françaises* (Paris, n.d.).

17. Ibid., 1.

18. Ibid., 4.

19. Ibid., 4–5.

20. Ibid., 5.
21. Ibid.
22. Ibid.
23. *Procès-verbaux du Comité d'Instruction publique de la Convention nationale*, ed. M. J. Guillaume, vol. 2, 15 October 1792–2 July 1793 (Paris, 1891), 152.
24. Yves-Marie Audrein, *Un quatrième mot à ses collègues ou Boissy D'anglas, cité au tribunal* (Paris, n.d.), 1.
25. Ibid., 2.
26. Ibid.
27. Ibid., 3.
28. Ibid.
29. Yves-Marie Audrein, *Dernier mot au Convention nationale sur la liberté des cultes* (Paris, 1794), 1.
30. Ibid., 1–2.
31. Ibid., 3.
32. Ibid.
33. Ibid.
34. Ibid.
35. Ibid., 5–6.
36. Ibid., 6.
37. Ibid., 8.
38. Ibid.
39. Ibid.
40. P. Hémon, *Audrein, Yves-Marie, Député du Morbihan à L'Assemblée législative et à la Convention nationale, évêque constitutionnel de Finistère* (Paris, 1903).
41. Chabot's early years are presented in the Vicomte de Bonald, *François Chabot: Membre de la Convention (1756–1794)*, 2nd ed. (Paris, 1908), chap. 1.
42. Ibid.
43. Quoted in Kuscinski, *Dictionnaire des conventionnels*, 122.
44. Quoted in ibid.
45. For this reason, Albert Mathiez edited the only accessible edition of *François Chabot, représentant du peuple à ses concitoyens qui sont les juges de sa vie politique (plûviose an II)* (Paris, 1914), 1.
46. Norman Hampson, "François Chabot and His Plot," *Transactions of the Royal Historical Society*, 5th ser., 26 (1976): 14.
47. Quoted in Kuscinski, *Dictionnaire des conventionnels*, 123.
48. Mathiez, *François Chabot*, 3–4.
49. Ibid., 9.
50. Ibid., 28.
51. See Jules Guiffrey, *Les Conventionnels, listés par départements et par ordre alphabétique des députés et des suppléants à la Convention nationale* (Paris, 1889); Pisani, *Repertoire biographique de l'épiscopat constitutionnel*; and Kuscinski, *Dictionnaire des conventionnels*.
52. Kuscinski, *Dictionnaire des conventionnels*, 557.
53. See Jean-Pierre Laulom, "Mgr Jean-Pierre Saurine (1733–1813), Evêque constitutionnel des Landes," *Bulletin de la Société Borda* 378 (1980): 239–312; 386 (1982): 187–95.

54. For an example of his minor interventions in the Convention, see *AP*, 65:707.

55. Jean-Pierre Saurine, *Discours prononcé par le C. Jean-Pierre Saurine, évêque du département des Landes, député à la Convention, pendant la messe qu'il célébroit le troisième dimanche du Carême, 18 ventôse (8 mars 1795)* (Paris, 1795), 3–4.

56. Jean-Pierre Saurine, *Lettre pastorale de l'évêque du diocèse de Landes* (Paris, 1796–97), 5–6.

57. Ibid., 6–7.

58. Ibid., 20.

59. Ibid., 23.

60. *AP*, 57:67, 357.

61. Antoine-Hubert Wandelaincourt, *Eléments de morale; ou, Devoirs de l'homme et du citoyen* (Paris, 1793).

62. Ibid., 8.

63. Antoine-Hubert Wandelaincourt, *Plan d'éducation publique* (three pamphlets bound together) (Paris, n.d.). See *AP*, 68:222, 333.

64. Wandelaincourt, *Plan d'éducation publique*, 1–2.

65. Ibid.

66. Ibid., 9.

67. Ibid., 21.

68. Antoine-Hubert Wandelaincourt, *Suite des observations sur le plan de constitution* (Paris, 1793). This text was presented to the Convention on 24 June 1793. See *AP*, 67:415.

69. Wandelaincourt, *Suite des observations*, 1–2.

70. Ibid., 6.

71. Jean-Baptiste Massieu, *Lettre pastorale de Jean-Baptiste Massieu, évêque du département de l'Oise, à l'occasion du décret de l'Assemblée nationale, qui déclare la patrie en danger* (Beauvais, 1792), 3–4. The Legislative Assembly, facing threats from within and without, issued the "Patrie en danger" proclamation on 11 July 1792. Surveillance committees were to be set up in all departments, districts, and communes, and the National Guard was to be placed on alert.

72. Ibid., 4.

73. Ibid.

74. Ibid.

75. Ibid., 5.

76. Ibid.

77. Ibid.

78. *AP*, 54:706; *AP*, 70:505–6.

79. *AP*, 79:2.

80. *AP*, 82:189.

81. Kuscinski, *Dictionnaire des conventionnels*, 440.

82. Léonard Gay-Vernon, *Lettre pastorale aux Citoyens Pasteurs, et aux Citoyens fidèles du même département (8 février 1793)* (Paris, 1793).

83. Ibid., 2.

84. Ibid.

85. Ibid., 3.

86. Ibid.

87. Ibid., 8.

88. Ibid.

89. *AP*, 72:555.

90. *AP*, 78:552.

91. At the end of the revolutionary decade, Gay-Vernon was still a moralist. Examples come from two letters that he wrote as a government official, one preaching unity and another attacking Pius VI. In the first, long after his renunciation of the priesthood, he was still concerned with the value of morality for social good, specifically the return of peace to France and all of Europe. With a reflexive plug for republicanism, he says that royalism keeps the country in a state of dangerous upset. See Philippe Pauchet and René Vaillant, eds., *La Correspondance de Gay-Vernon en 1799* (Amiens, 1988), 6. And in another letter, he declares that the pope, recently deceased, is to be damned for ruining the constitutional experiment, and, later, for leading the forces of reaction: "That wicked man, surrounded by the personification of every vice . . . has covered our fatherland with blood and carnage. He had his emissaries preach everywhere in the name of God, murder and the assassination of free and virtuous men" (26).

92. *Journal des Amis*, 12 January 1793, 79, cited in Charrier, *Claude Fauchet*, 2:196.

93. Quoted without reference in ibid., 212.

94. Quoted in ibid., 213, citing "Opinion de Claude Fauchet, député du Calvados, sur le jugement du ci-devant roi," *AP*, 53:393–405.

95. Quoted in Charrier, *Claude Fauchet*, 2:321, citing the last issue of *Journal des Amis*, 2nd ser., 15 June 1793, 161–74.

96. Ibid., 2:323.

97. Ibid., 2:323–24.

98. Ibid., 2:324.

99. Ibid.

100. Jean-Claude Beugnot, *Mémoires de Comte Beugnot, 1779–1815*, ed. Robert Lacour-Gayer (Paris, 1959), 128–29.

101. Ibid., 129.

102. Ibid.

103. Ibid.

104. Ibid.

105. See chapter 5, note 25, regarding Pontard's millenarianism.

106. Ibid., 149.

107. Ibid.

108. Ibid.

109. Ibid.

110. Ibid., 150. Beugnot was repeating the oversimplified notion that the oath to the nation, the law, and the king, implying acceptance of the Civil Constitution of the Clergy, was actually an oath *to* the Civil Constitution.

111. Ibid., 151.

112. Ibid., 149–50.

113. Adrien-Antoine Lamourette, *Déclaration et rétractation d'Adrien Lamourette, évêque constitutionnel du département de Rhône et Loire*, in *Déclaration et rétractation de François-Thérèse Panisset, extraite des "Annales religieuses" du samedi 4 juin 1796* (Toulouse, n.d.).

114. Ibid., 18.

115. Ibid.
116. Henri Grégoire, *Mémoires de l'abbé Grégoire,* 1st ed. 1801 (Paris, 1989), 76.
117. Henri Grégoire, *Lettre pastorale, 12 mars 1795–22 ventôse an 3* (Paris, 1795), 1.
118. Ibid.
119. Ibid., 14.
120. Ibid., 14–15.
121. See Prologue, "Priesthood: The Catholic and French Heritage."

CHAPTER 7

1. McManners, *The French Revolution and the Church,* 90.

2. Maurice Dommanget, *Enragés et curés rouges en 1793* (Paris, 1993); André Berland, *Un grand révolutionnaire charentais, L'Abbé Jacques Roux: Les débuts en Angoumois et en Saintonge du futur chef des Enragés (1752–1794)* (Paris, 1988). These texts are completed and usefully ordered in Jean-Marc Le Guillou, *Jacques Roux, 1752–1794* (Paris, 2000). On the issue of *curés rouges*, see the preface by Michel Vovelle in Dommanget, *Enragés et curés rouges*, which sums up the issues and the research as they appeared, principally, in *Annales historiques de la Révolution française.* See as a primary example Bianchi, "Les curés rouges dans la Révolution française." At issue was the priest's mission to eliminate elite control of the economy, but as much analytical effort was put into justifying the anachronistic notion of Marxist and *Red* as was put into direct profiles of deeds and words. We leave aside the question of whether Jacques Roux and the other *curés rouges* were proto-Marxist and proto-*Red*, going directly instead to their political and quasi-religious expression.

3. Cited in Berland, *Un grand révolutionnaire,* 49.

4. Ibid., 51–54.

5. Cited in ibid., 15.

6. R. B. Rose, *The Enragés: Socialists of the French Revolution* (Melbourne, 1965), chap. 3; Walter Markov, ed., *Jacques Roux: Scripta et acta* (Berlin, 1969). Markov's edition of the works of Roux can be complemented by his idiosyncratic (East German Marxist) biographical study *Die Freiheiten des Priesters Roux* (Berlin, 1967).

7. Jacques Roux, "Le Triomphe des braves Parisiens sur les ennemis du bien public," in Markov, *Jacques Roux,* 8.

8. Ibid.

9. Ibid., 9–10.

10. Ibid., 13.

11. Ibid., 16.

12. Ibid.

13. Ibid.

14. Ibid., 18.

15. Jacques Roux, "L'Apôtre martyr de la Révolution; ou, Discours d'un curé patriote, qui vient d'être assassiné par dix-huit aristocrates," in Markov, *Jacques Roux,* 20–44.

16. Le Guillou, *Jacques Roux,* 58.

17. Jacques Roux, "L'Apôtre martyr de la Révolution," 23.

18. Ibid., 25.

19. Ibid.

20. Ibid., 31.

21. Ibid., 31–32.

22. Ibid., 32–33.

23. Jacques Roux, "Discours sur les moyens de sauver la France et la Liberté," in Markov, *Jacques Roux*, 49–78.

24. Ibid., 51.

25. Ibid., 52.

26. Ibid., 52–53.

27. Ibid., 53.

28. Jacques Roux, "Discours sur le jugement de Louis-le-dernier, sur la poursuite des agioteurs, des accapareurs et des traîtres," in Markov, *Jacques Roux*, 79–85.

29. Ibid., 82.

30. Ibid., 83.

31. Ibid.

32. Ibid.

33. Jacques Roux, "Exécution de Louis XVI, Rapport de Jacques Roux au Conseil général de la Commune (1793)," in Markov, *Jacques Roux*, 87–88. The last sentence is not found in all printed versions.

34. Jacques Roux, *Manifeste des Enragés*, quoted in Berland, *Un grand révolutionnaire*, 20.

35. Ibid., 22.

36. Ibid., 27.

37. Ibid.

38. There is a presentation, however, of several brief, shining moments of Roux's career in Morris Slavin, "Jacques Roux: A Victim of Vilification," *French Historical Studies* 3 (1964): 527–37.

39. Quoted in McManners, *The French Revolution and the Church*, 60.

40. A.-J. Paris, *Histoire de Joseph Le Bon et des tribunaux révolutionnaires d'Arras et de Cambrai* (Arras, 1879). The most recent book is a popular text built on A. J. Paris: Ivan Gobry, *Joseph Le Bon: La Terreur dans le nord de la France* (Paris, 1991).

41. Paris, *Histoire de Joseph Le Bon*, 7.

42. See ibid., 8.

43. Quoted in ibid., 9–10.

44. Émile Le Bon, *Joseph Le Bon dans sa vie privée et dans sa carrière politique* (Paris, 1861), 181–82. This is taken from a letter to Barthélemy Masson, then a young Oratorian, who remained a teacher across the years and married Le Bon's sister. After the execution of Le Bon and his wife, this man raised their son (Émile Le Bon).

45. Quoted in Paris, *Histoire de Joseph Le Bon*, 19.

46. Ibid., 21.

47. Ibid., 39.

48. Ibid., 42.

49. Ibid., 54.

50. Ibid., 105.

51. Ibid.

52. Ibid., 106–7.

53. Ibid., 107.

54. Quoted in Le Bon, *Joseph Le Bon*, 199.

55. Ibid., 200.

56. McManners, *The French Revolution and the Church*, 91.

57. The foundation studies of the *abdicataires* appeared in 1964, when Marcel Reinhard presented a research methodology for a quantitative and qualitative analysis of the abdications of 1793–94. Bernard Plongeron, Maurice Bordes, Michel Vovelle, Mlle Rebouillat, and M. L. Fracart presented statistics and analysis for the city of Paris, Provence, and the departments of Gers, Allier, and the Deux-Sèvres. All based their work, in part, on the same series in the Archives nationales, F19 872–93, *Lettres de prêtres classes, démissions données devant diverses administrations*, pairing these cartons with appropriate documentation in departmental and private archives, and I follow their lead. By and large, dossiers of individual priests were collected under their own names by the national government offices, and summaries of abdication activity came in from regional headquarters. These outstanding studies were revalorized when Timothy Tackett published *Religion, Revolution, and Regional Culture*. Reinhard, Tackett, and subsequent studies are resumed in Langlois, Tackett, and Vovelle, *Religion*. See Marcel Reinhard, ed., *Actes de quatre-vingt neuvième congrès national des sociétés savantes* (Paris, 1964). For a recent discussion of clerical marriage during the period, see Claire Cage, "'Celibacy Is a Social Crime': The Politics of Clerical Marriage, 1793–1797," *French Historical Studies* 36 (2013): 601–28.

58. Bernard Plongeron, "Les Abdicataires parisiens," in Reinhard, *Actes*, 47.

59. AN, F19 873, Beulazet. The Beulazet dossier is discussed in Bianchi, "Les curés rouges dans la Révolution française."

60. Ibid.

61. AN, F19 876, Courtonne.

62. AN, F19 880, Gillard.

63. AN, F19 891, Saint-Didier.

64. Ibid.

65. AN, F19 889, Paintandre.

66. AN, F19 876, Courbec.

67. AN, F19 889, Paintandre.

68. AN, F19 872, Abadie.

69. AN, F19 884 Lacombe.

70. AN, F19 883, Julien. Here with an asterisk he footnoted his text, "I sent a small work to the printer in 1790, which was entitled *Le mariage des prêtres; ou, Le célibat détruit*, in which I had to rebuke the foolish and exalt the wise."

71. Ibid.

72. Ibid.

73. AN, F19 877, Destremour.

74. AN, F19 878, Dyvincourt.

75. AN, F19 891, Sousciat.

76. AN, F 19 891, Surdraud.

77. AN, F19 878, Douchin.

78. Ibid.

79. AN, F19 873, Baudin.

80. AN, F19 879, Le Forestier.

81. AN, F19 884, Lacouture.

82. AN, F19 880, Géruzez.

83. AN, F19 872 , Allaire.
84. AN, F19 880, Genet.
85. AN, F19 889, Pasquer.
86. Ibid.
87. Ibid.

CHAPTER 8

1. Charles Saillant, a medical doctor ordained a priest in 1796, reported this in his *Mémoire secret sur la Vie de M. Clément, évêque de Versailles* (Paris, 1812), cited in Dean, *L'Abbé Grégoire et l'Église constitutionnelle*, 4. On pp. 8–11 Dean places in full relief the initiatives of both Clément and Saillant. See also Boussoulade, *L'Église de Paris du 9 thermidor au Concordat*, 30.

2. On the constitutional hierarchy, see Pisani, *Répertoire biographique de l'épiscopat constitutionel.* For a brief summary of the ecclesiastical and political policies of the Constitutional Church under the United Bishops, see Ruth F. Necheles, "The Constitutional Church, 1794–1802: An Essay in Voluntarism," in *The Consortium on Revolutionary Europe, 1750–1850: Proceedings, 1794* (Gainesville, Fla., 1978), 80–90.

3. See Dean, *L'Abbé Grégoire et l'Église constitutionnelle*, 57–58.

4. Quoted in Pisani, *L'Église de Paris et la Révolution*, 2:185.

5. Évêques réunis, *Lettre encyclique de plusieurs évêques de France*, 4th ed. (Paris, 1795). A variety of position papers, written by Clément, Saillant, and others, are preserved in the Bibliothèque de l'Arsenal. Essential for understanding the genesis of the first encyclical, they are presented in Dean, *L'Abbé Grégoire et l'Église constitutionnelle*, 26–34.

6. Évêques réunis, *Lettre encyclique*, 3.

7. Ibid.

8. Ibid., 4.

9. Ibid.

10. Ibid., 5.

11. Ibid.

12. Ibid., 6.

13. On False Decretals and other documents that have misrepresented, even misconstrued, the prerogatives of Rome, see the essays of Stephan Kuttner, *Medieval Councils, Decretals, and Collections of Canon Law* (Brookfield, Vt., 1992).

14. Évêques réunis, *Lettre encyclique*, 6.

15. Ibid., 7.

16. Ibid., 8.

17. I summarize their presentation without reference to numbering.

18. Ibid.

19. *Concile de Nicée*, par. 5, canon 4, quoted in ibid., 9–10.

20. *Concile de Nicée*, par. 23, canons 6 and 7, quoted in ibid., 10.

21. Ibid.

22. See ibid., 13–14.

23. Ibid., 16.

24. Ibid., 21–22.

25. Ibid., 23–24.

26. Ibid., 25–26.

27. Évêques réunis, *Seconde lettre encyclique de plusieurs évêques de France, réunis à Paris, à leurs confrères les autres évêques, et aux églises veuves: Contenant un règlement pour servir au rétablissement de la discipline de l'Église gallicane* (Paris, 1795).

28. Ibid., 4.

29. Ibid., 9.

30. Ibid., 70. For mention of Clement XIV relative to Anglican orders, see Montague R. Butler, *Rome's Tribute to Anglican Orders: A Defense of the Episcopal Succession and Priesthood of the Church of England, Founded on the Testimony of the Best Roman Catholic Authorities* (London, 1894), 17.

31. Ibid., 73.

32. Ibid., 89.

33. Ibid., 90.

34. Ibid.

35. Ibid., 104.

36. Ibid.

37. Ibid., 115.

38. Ibid., 189.

39. Ibid., 211.

40. Ibid., 213–14.

41. I have explored the calendar preoccupations of the constitutional clergy before in "Three Ways of Imagining Sacrality: Promoting, Regulating, and Rejecting the French Revolutionary Festivals," in *Studia Anselmiana: Imaginer l'Église catholique* (Festschrift in honor of Dom Ghislain Lafont, OSB) (Rome, 2000), 189–200. The issue has been dealt with subsequently in Noah Shusterman, *Religion and the Politics of Time: Holidays in France from Louis XIV through Napoleon* (Washington, D.C., 2010); and Matthew Shaw, *Time and the French Revolution: The Republican Calendar* (Rochester, N.Y., 2011).

42. *Annales de la religion* (hereafter *AR*) 5: 127–28. And see, of course, Albert Mathiez, *La Théophilanthopie et le culte décadaire* (Paris, 1903).

43. *AR* 7: 124 (1). Vol. 7 is divided into two parts, each having its own pagination.

44. Ibid.

45. Ibid.

46. *AR* 7: 158 (1).

47. *AR* 8: 181 (3). Vol. 8 is divided into five parts, each having its own pagination.

48. *AR* 8: 181–82 (3).

49. *AR* 7: 396 (2).

50. *AR* 7: 397 (2).

51. *AR* 8: 12 (3).

52. *AR* 8: 64 (3).

53. *AR* 8: 65 (3).

54. *AR* 6: 102.

55. *AR* 7: 75 (1).

56. Ibid.

57. *AR* 7: 104 (1).

58. *AR* 8: 26 (5).

59. Ibid.

60. *AR* 8: 112 (3).

61. *AR* 6: 200.

62. *AR* 9: 375. Apart from actually moving Sundays to the décadi, an arrangement could be worked out: "In the one, you gather together without distinction all the citizens to hear the laws of government that they should know about, in the other you gather Christians together to meditate on the noble truths of the gospel." See *AR* 8: 154 (3).

CHAPTER 9

1. The old biography of Le Coz by Alfred Roussel is fundamental and I have used it to complement and support my work with the *Annales de la religion* and Roussel's own edition of the letters of Le Coz. See Alfred Roussel, *Un évêque assermenté (1790–1802): Le Coz, évêque d'Ille-et-Vilaine, métropolitain du nord-ouest* (Paris, 1898).

2. Claude Le Coz, "Avertissement pastoral du Cen Le Coz, évêque d'Ille-et-Vilaine, sur l'état actuel de la religion catholique," *AR* 11: 3.

3. Claude Le Coz, *Accord de la religion catholique avec le gouvernement républicain* (Rennes, n.d.), 1–2. No date, yes, but there was a review of the text in *AR* 1: 386, and so 1795. The *Accord* was an erudite presentation of the history and theology of the Constitutional Church, parallel to the texts of Lamourette and Grégoire, with opening sections on the oath and on the laws of the church, and reflections on elections, the Western church, and the Gallican Church's mission and jurisdiction. In the *Dictionnaire de biographie* entry for "Le Coz," the text, apparently signed in 1791 by eighteen constitutional bishops, is attributed to a former Theatine priest named Lebreton.

4. Le Coz, *Accord de la religion catholique*, 2.

5. Ibid.

6. Ibid., 6.

7. Ibid., 48.

8. Claude Le Coz, *Lettre de l'évêque métropolitain du nord-est, 5 juillet 1791* (Rennes, 1791).

9. Ibid., 1.

10. Ibid., 23.

11. Claude Le Coz, *Lettre pastorale du citoyen évêque métropolitain du nord-est, 13 octobre 1792* (Rennes, 1792), 1–2.

12. A. Roussel, ed., *Correspondance de Le Coz, évêque constitutionnel d'Ille-et-Vilaine*, 2 vols. (Paris, 1900–1903), 1:162, lettre 79: aux Évêques réunis, 10 février 1796.

13. Ibid.

14. Ibid., 1:167, lettre 82: aux Évêques réunis, 1796.

15. Ibid., 1:283, lettre 131: à Desbois de Rochefort, 24 août 1797. After three thousand insurgents debarked by the British at Quiberon in the Morbihan attempted an invasion, they were captured by the government forces under General Hoche, and 748 of them were executed.

16. Ibid., 1:285.

17. Ibid.

18. Ibid.

19. Ibid., 1:286.

20. Ibid., 1:283.

21. "Avis au Schismatisans; ou, Réponse du citoyen Le Coz, évêque d'Ille-et-Vilaine, à un écrit intitulé, réponse au citoyen Le Coz, sur la rétraction de son confrère Panisset; par un auteur célèbre," *AR* 4: 337.

22. Ibid., 338.

23. Roussel, *Correspondance*, 1:284, lettre 131: au Desbois de Rochefort, 24 août 1797.

24. Ibid., 1:283. For a description of Le Coz's consecration of Audrein, see Roussel, *Un évêque assermenté*, chap. 9.

25. "Réflexions sur les Lettres du citoyen Rallier; member du conseil des anciens, au citoyen Crégoire, membre du conseil des cinq-cents," *AR* 3: 169.

26. "Au Cit. Rallier, membre du conseil des anciens," *AR* 3: 433.

27. Ibid., 434.

28. "Suite de la Lettre du citoyen Le Coz, évêque d'Ille-et-Vilaine, à tous les catholiques, etc.," *AR* 3: 369.

29. Ibid., 370.

30. "Réinstallation édifiante du culte à Port-Liberté, au rédacteur des *Annales de la religion*, 18 janvier, 1797, an V," *AR* 4: 359.

31. Ibid.

32. Bibliothèque de Port-Royal (hereafter BPR), Régistre du Concile de 1797, séance du 15 août.

33. See Dean, *L'Abbé Grégoire et l'Église constitutionnelle*, 245–60.

34. BPR, Régistre du Concile de 1797, séance du 20 septembre.

35. Ibid., séance du 31 octobre.

36. Ibid., 106.

37. For a presentation of some of the highlights of elections and episcopal decision making in specific dioceses across the decade, see Bernard Plongeron, "Théologie et applications de la collégialité dans l'Église constitutionnelle de France (1790–1801)," *Annales historiques de la Révolution française* 45 (1973): 71–84.

38. Concile national de France, *Quatrième lettre synodique du Concile national de France aux pasteurs et aux fidèles, pour leur annoncer la fin de la session* (Paris, 1797), 6.

39. Ibid., 7.

40. Ibid.

41. Ibid., 8.

42. On the establishment and diffusion of the *Journal du Concile national de France*, see Bernard Plongeron, "L'Église constitutionnelle [gallicane] à l'épreuve du Directoire: Réorganisation, liberté des cultes et Concile national de 1797," in *Du Directoire au Consulat*, 2 vols., ed. Hervé Leuwers (Lille, 2000), 1:149–64. The *Journal* appeared every four days in eight-page brochures from 18 August 1797 to 15 November 1797 (twenty-two issues). In fact, with the simultaneous publishing of the *Journal* and the *Annales de la religion*, some divisions within the constitutional leadership came to light—such as between the printer Rebour and the United Bishops. Plongeron writes (159) that the main tension was produced by the Directory, where legislators took the constitutionals to be poor republicans, indeed, for not integrating married priests into the church apostolate. Somewhat vengefully they published a *Précis historique et politique sur le Concile national de Paris* (27 September 1797), which, in fact, pleased the refractory clergy.

43. *Journal du Concile national de France* (Paris, 1797), 89.

44. Ibid., 90.

45. Ibid., 107.

46. Ibid., 108. I deal with views and relationships of the constitutional bishops and clergy with the Protestant and Orthodox churches in "Les Évêques constitutionnels face à l'orthodoxie et au protestantisme," *Chrétiens et Sociétés* (2014).

47. Concile national de France, *Décrets du Concile national de France: Proclamés dans la cinquième (et la sixième) session solemnelle du Concile, dans l'Église métropolitaine de Notre-Dame de Paris, le 5 novembre, l'an de Jésus-Christ 1797 (5 brumaire, l'an VI de la République française, une et indivisible)* (Paris, 1797).

48. Ibid., 10–13.

49. Ibid., 15.

50. Ibid., 19, 20, 21.

51. Ibid., 21–22.

52. Boussoulade, *L'Église de Paris du 9 thermidor au Concordat*, 106–7, 111–15.

53. BPR, Concile de 1797, carton 1.

54. Ibid., d. "minutes de procès-verbaux."

55. *Instruction du Concile national sur le serment décrété le 19 fructidor, an V de la République*, cited in Plongeron, "L'Église constitutionnelle [gallicane] à l'épreuve du Directoire," 163.

56. Roussel, *Correspondance*, 1:301, to citizens Grégoire and Desbois, bishops; inserted in lettre 134: à Grégoire, 28 septembre 1798.

57. Ibid., 302.

58. Ibid., 302–3.

59. Ibid., 306.

60. Ibid.

61. Ibid., 374–75, lettre 157, à l'auteur d'un dictionnaire historique (n.d.)

62. Ibid., 376.

63. "Lettre du Citoyen Lecoz, évêque de Rennes, au Citoyen Grégoire, évêque de Blois," *AR* 7: 117 (2).

64. Ibid., 118.

65. Roussel, *Correspondance*, 1:352, lettre 148: à Grégoire, 4 février 1800.

66. Ibid.

67. Ibid., 352.

68. Ibid., 353.

CHAPTER 10

1. See Dean, *L'Abbé Grégoire et l'Église constitutionnelle*, 99–114.

2. The story is told in Pisani, *Répertoire biographique de l'épiscopat constitutionnel*, 61; and in comte Marc de Seyssel, *Jean-Baptiste Royer, évêque constitutionnel de l'Ain, puis métropolitain de Paris, 1732–1807* (Belley, 1911), 22.

3. Jean-Baptiste Royer, *Lettre pastorale de M. l'évêque du département de l'Ain, 7 avril 1791* (Paris, 1791), 1–2.

4. Ibid., 7.

5. Jean-Baptiste Royer, *Lettre pastorale de M. l'évêque du département de l'Ain, 11 septembre 1792* (Belley, 1792), 2.

6. Ibid., 2–3.

7. See Pisani, *L'Église de Paris et la Révolution,* 1:225–58. The definitive study of Royer's election, including the controversies and charged negotiations leading to it, is Rodney Dean's as yet unpublished "L'élection de Jean-Baptiste Royer comme évêque constitutionnel et métropolitain de Paris en 1798" (MS). I am grateful to the author for permission to use the manuscript as a complement and correction to the Pisani text.

8. BPR, Régistre du presbytère de Paris, 1795–1801, séance du 15 juin 1798, 189.

9. Ibid.

10. Jean-Baptiste Royer, *Lettre pastorale de l'évêque de l'église métropolitaine de Paris, 4 septembre 1798* (Paris, 1798).

11. Ibid., 3.

12. Ibid., 20.

13. Ibid.

14. BPR, Régistre du presbytère de Paris, 1795–1801, séance du 22 août 1798.

15. Ibid., séance du 11 février 1800.

16. Ibid.

17. Ibid., séance du 6 mai 1800.

18. "Jean-Baptiste Royer, évêque de l'église métropolitaine de Paris, et les pasteurs formant son presbytère, au rédacteur des *Annales de la religion,*" *AR* 9: 461–62.

19. Ibid., 465.

20. "Adhésion des évêques de Paris et d'Amiens," *AR* 10: 96.

21. "Mandement de l'évêque de Paris," *AR* 11: 168.

22. Ibid., 169.

23. Jean-Baptiste Royer, *Instruction pastorale du révérendissime évêque métropolitain de Paris sur la paix civile et religieuse* (Paris, 1800), 5.

24. Ibid., 9.

25. Ibid., 10.

26. Ibid.

27. Ibid., 20.

28. Ibid.

29. Ibid., 45.

30. Ibid., 49.

31. Ibid., 49–50.

32. Jean-Baptiste Royer, *Lettre circulaire du R.R. évêque métropolitain de Paris aux R.R. évêques de l'Église gallicane, en réponse à plusieurs évêques qui lui ont écrit sur les inculpations dirigées contre lui dans les Annales et sur la tenue projetée d'un Concile national, 21 avril 1801* (Paris, 1801), 2.

33. Vacant sees, dioceses that still had no constitutional bishop, were a problem elsewhere in France, because priests competent enough and willing to be consecrated had to be sought out; Royer, however, was responsible for filling the very visible vacant sees for which he was metropolitan (i.e., a bishop with regional jurisdiction).

34. Royer, *Lettre circulaire,* 12.

35. *AR* 12: 578.

36. Ibid., 579.

37. *AR* 13: 41.
38. Ibid., 45.
39. Ibid., 46.
40. BPR, Régistre du presbytère de Paris, séance du 6 mai 1800, 287.
41. See Dean, *L'Église constitutionnelle, Napoléon et le Concordat de 1801*, 223.
42. Henri Grégoire, *Discours pour l'Ouverture du Concile national de France, prononcé le 29 juin 1801 (10 Messidor an 9) en l'Église métropolitaine de Paris* (Paris, 1801), 3.
43. Ibid., 21.
44. Ibid., 26.
45. Ibid., 26–27.
46. Ibid., 27.
47. Ibid., 28.
48. Ibid., 29. For a full study of the extended drama at Machecoul, see Edward J. Woell, *Small-Town Martyrs and Murderers: Religious Revolution and Counterrevolution in Western France, 1774–1914* (Milwaukee, 2006).
49. BPR, Actes du Concile de 1801, séance du 15 juillet.
50. Ibid., séance du 23 juillet.
51. BPR, Concile of 1801, carton 1, GR 2405.
52. BPR, Actes du Concile de 1801, séance du 29 juillet.
53. Ibid., séance du 11 août.
54. BPR, Concile de 1801, carton 1, GR 2334, Rapport du bn. promoteur sur l'état des diverses métropoles de l'église de France.
55. BPR, Actes du Concile de 1801, séance du 16 août.
56. Ibid.
57. Ibid.
58. Ibid., 149.
59. BPR, Concile de 1801, carton 1, GR 2317.
60. See Bernard Plongeron, "L'Église constitutionnelle [gallicane] à l'épreuve du Directoire," 1:164.

CHAPTER 11

1. See Jean Leflon, *Étienne-Alexandre Bernier, évêque d'Orléans (1762–1806)* (Paris, 1938).
2. Dean, *L'Église constitutionnelle, Napoléon et le Concordat de 1801*, chaps. 4 and 5.
3. Ibid., chap. 8.
4. AN, F19 865–66, *Renseignements sur les ecclésiastiques qui méritent la confiance du gouvernement (an IX–an X)*. I have researched these dossiers and organized my presentation here separately from Dean, *L'Église constitutionnelle, Napoléon et le Concordat de 1801*, 355–67, but I have benefited from his work and my discussions with him.
5. AN, F19 865, Alpes-Maritimes, état nominatif.
6. AN, F19 865, Le préfet du département des Alpes-maritimes au ministre de l'Intérieur, 15 vendémiaire l'an 10.
7. AN, F19 865, Aisnes, état nominatif.
8. AN, F19 865, Ardennes, état nominatif.

9. Dates of consecration in parentheses are not included in the original document but are inserted here from Pisani, *Répertoire biographique de l'épiscopat constitutionnel.* As noted above, the definitive study of Royer's election, is Dean's manuscript "L'Élection de Jean-Baptiste Royer comme évêque constitutionnel et métropolitain de Paris en 1798." I am grateful to the author for permission to use the manuscript as a complement and corrective to the writings of Jean Boussolade.

10. AN, F19 865, Gard, état nominatif.

11. AN, F19 866, La Manche, état nominatif.

12. AN, F19 866, Lot, état nominatif.

13. AN, F19 866, Puy-de-Dôme, état nominatif.

14. AN, F19 865, Aube, état nominatif.

15. AN, F19 865, Le préfet du département de la Charente au ministre de l'Intérieur, 16 thermidor an 9.

16. AN, F19 865, Gironde, état nominatif, Prêtres de Bordeaux jouissants de l'estime publique (here the états are listed by arrondissement).

17. AN, F19 866, Le préfet du département du Haute-Marne au ministre de l'Intérieur, 7 thermidor an 9.

18. AN, F19 866, Sarthe, état nominatif.

19. AN, F19 865. Le préfet du Landes, "Quelques observations sur le culte catholique."

20. AN, F19 865, Hérault, état nominatif.

21. AN, F19 865, Ille-et-Vilaine, état nominatif.

22. AN, F19 866, Deux-Sèvres, état nominatif.

23. AN, F19 866, Mayenne, état nominatif.

24. AN, F19 866, Seine-et-Oise, état nominatif (reporting on the constitutional bishop of the Tarn).

25. AN, F19 866. Saône-et-Loire, Le préfet du département de Saône et Loire au ministre de l'Intérieur, 21 brumaire an 10.

26. AN, F19 866, Saône-et-Loire, état nominatif.

27. AN, F19 866, Haute-Saône, état nominatif.

28. AN, F19 866, Seine-Inférieure, état nominatif.

29. AN, F19 866, Vienne, état nominatif.

30. *AR* 10: 256.

31. Ibid.

32. *AR* 10: 297.

33. *AR* 12: 50.

34. *AR* 12: 569.

35. *AR* 12: 570.

36. *AR* 12: 577.

37. Ibid.

38. Sources used for this study include selected cartons from the Archives nationales, series F19, AN microfilms of the *dossiers Caprara* (AF IV 1897, 1898), and the two Jeannine Charon-Bordas volumes on the Caprara legation published by the Archives nationales: *Inventaire des archives de la Légation en France du cardinal Caprara (1801–1808)* (Paris, 1975); and *La Légation en France du cardinal Caprara (1801–1808): Répertoire de demandes de réconciliation avec l'Église* (Paris, 1979). About every tenth petition was in Latin. I have not

included any Latin petitions because the formality of writing in Latin seemed to preclude the possibility of subtle self-expression.

39. AN, AF IV 1897, d. 1, *Absolutiones et rehabilitationes juratis, intrusis, ordinatis a constitutionalibus aliisque, a die prima augusti 1802 ad totum decembrem 1802*, piéce 41, Michel Gibal.

40. AN, AF IV 1897, d. 5, *Absolutiones et rehabilitationes ecclesiasticorum secundi ordinis traditorum litterarum ordinationis et civiliter conjugatorum, a die prima januarii 1802 usque ad diem 30 julii ejusdem anni*, pièces 62–63, Jacques René Tourteau.

41. AN, AF IV 1897, d. 3, *Pétitions émanant de prêtres séculiers et réguliers demandant l'absolution des censures encourues (serment d'adhésion à la constitution civile du clergé, de haine à la royauté, etc., mariage) et la réintégration dans leurs fonctions ecclésiastiques*, pièce 74, Claude-Nicholas-Joseph Collignon.

42. AN, AF IV 1897, d. 3, pièce 27, Guillaume Bruzac.

43. AN, AF IV 1897, d. 4, *Demandes d'absolution formulées par des prêtres séculiers et réguliers, des religieux et des religieuses: Adhésion à la Constitution civile du clergé, ordres sacrés conférés par des évêques constitutionnels, service aux armées, désobéissance au voeu de pauvreté*, pièces 114–15, Louis-Alexandre-Pierre Bourdon.

44. AN, AF IV 1897, d. 1, pièce 36, Hyacinthe Doux.

45. AN, AF IV 1897, d. 3, pièce 53, Pierre Barthélémé Barruel-Labeaume.

46. AN, AF IV 1898, d. 2, *Absolutiones ecclesiasticorum qui matrimonium attentaverunt vel ecclesiasticam professionem ejuraverunt, a die prima januarii ad totum aprilem 1803*, pièces 81–82, Pierre Vistorte.

CHAPTER 12

1. Jacques-Olivier Boudon, *L'Épiscopat français à l'époque concordataire: Origines, formation, nomination* (Paris, 1996), 298.

2. For summaries of their episcopates under the First Empire, see Jacques-Olivier Boudon, *Les Élites religieuses à l'époque de Napoléon: Dictionnaire des évêques et vicaires généraux du Premier Empire* (Paris, 2002).

3. Boudon, *L'Épiscopat français*, 299; but the calculations, Boudon makes clear, come from Pisani, *Répertoire biographique de l'épiscopat constitutionnel.*

4. Roussel, *Correspondance de Le Coz*, 1:402, lettre 168: à Cardinal Caprara, 14 février 1801.

5. Ibid.

6. Ibid.

7. Ibid., 1:403.

8. Ibid., 2:11, lettre 4: à Cardinal Caprara, 15 juin 1802.

9. Ibid., 2:12.

10. Ibid.

11. Ibid.

12. *AR* 15: 435.

13. *AR* 15: 442.

14. *AR* 15: 442–43.

15. *AR* 15: 444.

16. Ibid.
17. *AR* 15: 451.
18. *AR* 15: 461.
19. *AR* 15: 91.
20. *AR* 15: 92.
21. *AR* 15: 135.
22. *AR* 15: 136.
23. *AR* 15: 137.
24. *AR* 15: 139.
25. *AR* 16: 554.
26. *AR* 16: 555.
27. *AR* 16: 558.
28. *AR* 16: 565.
29. Ibid.
30. *AR* 16: 566.
31. *AR* 17: 31–32.
32. *AR* 17: 558.
33. Ibid.
34. *AR* 17: 559.
35. *AR* 17: 560.
36. *AR* 17: 561.
37. *AR* 17: 562.
38. *AR* 17: 565.
39. *AR* 18: 18.
40. *AR* 18: 20.
41. *AR* 18: 20.
42. *AR* 18: 21.
43. *AR* 18: 22.
44. *AR* 18: 213.
45. *AR* 18: 215.
46. *AR* 18: 219.
47. *AR* 18: 474.
48. *AR* 18: 448.
49. *AR* 18: 449.
50. *AR* 18: 499.
51. *AR* 18: 510.
52. *AR* 18: 512.
53. *AR* 18: 519.
54. *AR* 18: 521.
55. *AR* 18: 522.
56. *AR* 18: 525.
57. *AR* 18: 529.
58. *AR* 18: 552.
59. Ibid.
60. Ibid.
61. *AR* 18: 553.

62. *AR* 18: 561.

63. *AR* 18: 563.

64. *AR* 18: 570.

65. For the terms and calendar of these reconciliations, see Dean, *L'Église constitutionnelle, Napoléon et le Concordat de 1801*, chaps. 13–15, who cites, among others, the important Simon Delacroix, *Les Nominations d'évêques et la liquidation du passé*, vol. 1 of *La Réorganisation de l'Église de France après la Révolution (1801–1809)* (Paris, 1962), 336–59.

66. This drama has only recently been brought to light by Dean, *L'Église constitutionnelle, Napoléon et le Concordat de 1801*, 659–62.

67. Certainly, former constitutionals suffered prejudice for decades after the Revolution, with the situation of some of them being notably difficult under the Restoration. Grégoire himself was prevented from taking his place in the Restoration parliament as a delegate from the Isère. Constitutional bishops who were integrated into the concordatory church managed to carry on for years, Bishop Belmas surviving as bishop of Cambrai until 1841. One notable participant in a later, minor and idiosyncratic, Gallican movement was Thomas-Juste Poullard, the last consecrated of the constitutional bishops, who ordained priests for the so-called Église française of the abbé Chatel in 1830 and 1831.

Bibliography

MANUSCRIPT SOURCES

Archives nationales

AF IV 1897, dossier 1. *Absolutiones et rehabilitationes juratis, intrusis, ordinatis a constitutionalibus aliisque, a die prima augusti 1802 ad totum decembrem 1802.*

AF IV 1897, dossier 3. *Pétitions émanant de prêtres séculiers et réguliers demandant l'absolution des censures encourues (serment d'adhésion à la constitution civile du clergé, de haine à la royauté, etc., mariage) et la réintégration dans leurs fonctions ecclésiastiques.*

AF IV 1897, dossier 4. *Demandes d'absolution formulées par des prêtres séculiers et réguliers, des religieux et des religieuses: Adhésion à la Constitution civile du clergé, ordres sacrés conférés par des évêques constitutionnels, service aux armées, désobéissance au voeu de pauvreté.*

AF IV 1897, dossier 5. *Absolutiones et rehabilitationes ecclesiasticorum secundi ordinis traditorum litterarum ordinationis et civiliter conjugatorum, a die prima januarii 1802 usque ad diem 30 julii ejusdem anni.*

AF IV 1898, dossier 2. *Absolutiones ecclesiasticorum qui matrimonium attentaverunt vel ecclesiasticam professionem ejuraverunt, a die prima januarii ad totum aprilem 1803.*

DIII 361–66. *Mémoires, projets, et pétitions sur des questions de droit et d'administration, 1789–an IV.*

DXIX 1, 13–16. *Lettres, adresses et représentations de religieux, de communautés, corporations et particuliers sur les décrets qui concernent la suppression des ordres religieux.*

DXIX 23–26. *Lettres et adresses de municipalités et d'ecclésiastiques sur la nouvelle organisation du clergé (1789–1790); mémoires et adresses relatives à la circonscription des paroisses et à l'établisement ou la conservation d'évêchés (notamment l'évêché de Comminges).*

DXXIX 1–23. *Lettres et mémoires, dénonciations diverses, dont certaines émanant de municipalités, menées séditieuses et complots contre l'ordre public, troubles dans les départements, en particulier à cause des subsistances (ordre chronologique), juillet 1789–juin 1791.*

DXXXVIII 1–2. *Bureaux et correspondance de la commission, analyses d'arrêtés des comités de Salut public et de Législation, 1792–an VII.*

F19 398–481. *Affaires des cultes dans les départements, en particulier pour la période révolutionnaire (classement départemental), 1788–1838.*

F19 862–71. *Personnel ecclésiastique: Annuaire du clergé (1821–1837); états des religieux et religieuses des couvents de Paris en 1790; renseignements sur les ecclésiastiques qui méritent la confiance du gouvernement (an IX–an X); curés et pasteurs dans les départements étrangers (Premier Empire).*

F19 872–93. *Lettres de prêtres classés, démissions données devant diverses administrations.*

Archives Sieyès

AS 284 AP 1, dossier 3. Emmanuel-Joseph Sieyès, *Projet de bibliothèque ou bibliographie.*

AS 284 AP 2, dossier 3, cahier 6. Emmanuel-Joseph Sieyès, *Sur Dieu ultramètre et sur la fibre religieuse de l'homme* (1780).

Bibliothèque de Port-Royal

Actes du Concile de 1801.

Concile de 1797, carton 1.

Concile de 1801, carton 1.

Concile de 1801, carton 2.

Régistre du Concile de 1797.

Régistre du presbytère de Paris, 1795–1801.

PRINTED SOURCES

Annales de la religion 1–18 (1795–1804).

Archives Parlementaires, recueil complet des débats législatifs et politiques des Chambres françaises, première série, 1787–1799. Edited by Jérôme Mavidal and Émile Laurent. 82 vols. Paris, 1867–1913.

Audrein, Yves-Marie. *Dernier mot au Convention nationale sur la liberté des cultes.* Paris, 1794.

———. *Discours patriotique, à l'occasion du renouvellement du serment civique fait par M. M. les vicaires de M. l'évêque du Morbihan, dans l'église cathédrale & paroissiale de Vannes, le 29 mai 1791.* Vannes, 1791.

———. *Discours prononcé au tribunal de police correctionnelle de Quimper, pour la défense de cinq prêtres patriotes prévenus d'avoir enfreint la loi sur la police extérieure des cultes.* Quimper, n.d.

———. *Éloge des armées françaises.* Paris, n.d.

———. *Protestation du représentant du peuple, Audrein, contre une prétendue réunion, entre les prêtres dits assermentés et les prêtres insermentés.* Paris, n.d.

———. *Un quatrième mot à ses collègues ou Boissy D'anglas, cité au tribunal.* Paris, n.d.

Baker, Keith, ed. "Civil Constitution of the Clergy." In *The Old Regime and the French Revolution*, edited by John W. Boyer and Julius Kirshner, 239–42. University of Chicago Readings in Western Civilization 7. Chicago, 1987.

Beugnot, Jacques-Claude. *Mémoires du Comte Beugnot, 1779–1815.* Edited by Robert Lacour-Gayet. Paris, 1959.

Bulletin de la Bouche de fer, 1–3 (1790). Reprint, Paris, 1981.

[Chabot, François]. *François Chabot, représentant du peuple à ses concitoyens qui sont les juges de sa vie politique (plûviose an II).* Edited by Albert Mathiez. Paris, 1914.

Concile national de France. *Décrets du Concile national de France: Proclamés dans la cinquième (et la sixième) session solemnelle du Concile, dans l'Église métropolitaine de Notre-Dame de Paris, le 5 novembre, l'an de Jésus-Christ 1797 (5 brumaire, l'an VI de la République française, une et indivisible).* Paris, 1797.

———. *Quatrième lettre synodique du Concile national de France aux pasteurs et aux fidèles, pour leur annoncer la fin de sa session.* Paris, 1797.

Durand de Maillane, Pierre. *Histoire apologétique du comité ecclésiastique de l'Assemblée nationale.* Paris, 1791.

Évêques réunis. *Lettre encyclique de plusieurs évêques de France.* 4th ed. Paris, 1795.

———. *Seconde lettre encyclique de plusieurs évêques de France, réunis à Paris, à leurs confrères les autres évêques, et aux églises veuves: Contenant un règlement pour servir au rétablissement de la discipline de l'Église gallicane.* Paris, 1795.

Fauchet, Claude. *De la religion nationale.* Paris, 1789.

———. *Discours à l'autel de la Patrie pendant la cérémonie de la fédération générale du département.* Caen, 1791.

———. *Lettre pastorale aux pasteurs et aux fidèles du diocèse.* Bayeux, 1792.

———. *Lettre pastorale et la traduction de sa lettre de communion adressée à NSP le pape.* Bayeux, 1791.

La Feuille villageoise, adressé chaque semaine à tous les villages de la France pour les instruire des loix, des evénements des découvertes qui intéressent tout Citoyen: proposée par souscription aux propriétaires, fermiers, pasteurs, habitans et amis des campagnes (1790–94).

Fouché, Joseph. *Mémoires.* Presented by Michel Vovelle. Paris, 1992.

Gay-Vernon, Léonard. *Lettre pastorale aux Citoyens Pasteurs, et aux Citoyens fidèles du même département (8 février 1793).* Paris, 1793.

———. *Lettre pastorale de M. l'évêque du département de la Haute-Vienne.* Rennes, 1792.

Grégoire, Henri. *Discours pour l'Ouverture du Concile national de France, prononcé le 29 juin 1801 (10 Messidor an 9) en l'Église métropolitaine de Paris.* Paris, 1801.

———. *Éloge de la poésie, discours qui a remporté le prix . . . de la Société royale des Sciences et Belles-lettres de Nancy.* Nancy, 1773.

———. *Essai sur la régénération physique, morale et politique des juifs.* 1st ed. 1788. Metz, 1789.

———. *Lettre pastorale, 12 mars 1795–22 ventôse an 3.* Paris, 1795.

———. *Lettre pastorale aux pasteurs et aux fidèles de son diocèse sur le payement des contributions publiques.* Blois, 1792.

———. *Lettre pastorale de M. l'évêque du département de Loir-et-Cher, 24 mars 1791.* Paris, 1791.

———. *Mémoires de Grégoire, ancien évêque de Blois, député à l'Assemblée Constituante et à la Convention Nationale, Sénateur, membre de l'Institut.* 1st ed. 1840. Paris, 1989.

———. *Mémoires de Grégoire, suivies de la Notice historique sur Grégoire d'Hippolyte Carnot.* 1st ed. 1808. Paris, 1989.

———. *Mémoires de l'abbé Grégoire.* 1st ed. 1801. Paris, 1989.

Grégoire, Henri (attrib.). *Accéssoire au Parnasse ou Nouvelle méthode pour former l'esprit et le goût.* Paris, 1769.

Houtin, Albert, ed. *Les Séances des députés du clergé aux États Généraux de 1789: Journaux du Curé Thibault et du Chanoine Coster.* Paris, 1916.

Jallet, Jacques. *Journal inédit de Jallet, précédé d'une notice historique par J. J. Brethé.* Fontenay-le-Comte, 1871.

Journal du Concile national de France. Paris, 1797.

Lamourette, Adrien-Antoine. *Déclaration et rétractation d'Adrien Lamourette, évêque constitutionnel du département de Rhône et Loire.* In *Déclaration et rétractation de François-Thérèse Panisset, extraite des "Annales religieuses" du samedi 4 juin 1796.* Toulouse, n.d.

———. *Discours pour la fête des canonniers volontaires de l'armée parisienne, prononcé en l'église de Notre-Dame, le dimanche 4 décembre 1791.* Paris, 1791.

———. *Instruction pastorale de M. l'évêque du département de Rhône et Loire, au clergé et aux Fidèles de son Diocèse.* Lyon, 1791.

———. *Projet de réunion entre les membres de l'Assemblée nationale.* Paris, 1792.

Le Bon, Émile. *Joseph Le Bon dans sa vie privée et dans sa carrière politique.* Paris, 1861.

Le Coz, Claude. *Accord de la religion catholique avec le gouvernement républicain.* Rennes, n.d.

———. *Lettre de l'évêque métropolitain du nord-est, 5 juillet 1791.* Rennes, 1791.

———. *Lettre pastorale du citoyen évêque métropolitain du nord-est, 13 octobre 1792.* Rennes, 1792.

Markov, Walter, ed. *Jacques Roux: Scripta et acta.* Berlin, 1967.

Massieu, Jean-Baptiste. *Lettre pastorale, 24 mars 1791.* Paris, 1791.

———. *Lettre pastorale de Jean-Baptiste Massieu, évêque du département de l'Oise, à l'occasion du décret de l'Assemblée nationale, qui déclare la patrie en danger.* Beauvais, 1792.

Mathiez, Albert, ed. *François Chabot, représentant du peuple à ses concitoyens qui sont les juges de sa vie politique (plûviose an II).* Paris, 1914.

Le Moniteur Universel (24 November 1789–1800).

Pauchet, Philippe, and René Vaillant, eds. *La Correspondance de Gay-Vernon en 1799.* Amiens, 1988.

Pontard, Pierre. *Adresse aux religieuses du département de la Dordogne.* N.p., 1791.

———. *Lettre de P. Pontard, évêque du département de la Dordogne, en réponse à l'ordonnance de M. Grossoles-Flamarens, évêque de Paris, le 14 avril 1791.* N.p., 1791.

———. *Poste du matin; ou, L'ami de la patrie, de la liberté des moeurs et de l'égalité: Ouvrage périodique, auquel on a réuni le Bulletin de la Convention nationale, l'extrait des nouvelles de la Guerre, le Journal Prophétique, et celui de la Correspondance civique et morale.* 2 vols. Paris, 1792.

Procès-verbaux du Comité d'Instruction publique de la Convention nationale. Edited by M. J. Guillaume. Vol. 2, 15 October 1792–2 July 1793. Paris, 1891.

Rangeard, Jacques. *Procès-verbal historique des actes du clergé deputé à l'Assemblée des États-Généraux des années 1789 et 1790.* Paris, 1791.

Royer, Jean-Baptiste. *Discours sur les biens du clergé.* Paris, 1790.

———. *Instruction pastorale du révérendissime évêque métropolitain de Paris sur la paix civile et religieuse.* Paris, 1800.

———. *Lettre circulaire du R.R. évêque métropolitain de Paris aux R.R. évêques de l'Église gallicane, en réponse à plusieurs évêques qui lui ont écrit sur les inculpations dirigées contre lui dans les Annales et sur la tenue projetée d'un Concile national, 21 avril 1801.* Paris, 1801.

———. *Lettre pastorale de l'évêque de l'église métropolitaine de Paris, 4 septembre 1798.* Paris, 1798.

———. *Lettre pastorale de M. l'évêque du département de l'Ain, 7 avril 1791.* Paris, 1791.

———. *Lettre pastorale de M. l'évêque du département de l'Ain, 11 septembre 1792.* Belley, 1792.

Saurine, Jean-Pierre. *Discours prononcé par le C. Jean-Pierre Saurine, évêque du département des Landes, député à la Convention, pendant la messe qu'il célébroit le troisième dimanche du Carême, 18 ventôse (8 mars 1795).* Paris, 1795.

———. *Lettre à un curé réfractaire.* Bordeaux, n.d.

———. *Lettre pastorale de l'évêque du diocèse de Landes.* Paris, 1796–97.

———. *Lettre pastorale de M. l'évêque du département des Landes, 26 mars 1791.* Paris, 1791.

Sieyès, Emmanuel-Joseph. *Qu'est-ce que c'est le tiers état?* Paris, 1789.

Sieyès, Emmanuel-Joseph (attrib.). *Notice sur la vie de Sieyès.* Paris, 1794. Reprinted in the modern *Oeuvres de Sieyès*, vol. 1. Paris, 1989.

Talleyrand-Périgord, Charles-Maurice de. *Mémoires complets et authentiques.* Edited by Adolphe Fourier de Bacourt. Paris, 1990.

Torné, Pierre-Anastase. *Discours prononcé à Bourges le 14 juillet 1791, sur l'Autel de la Patrie, par Monsieur Torné, évêque de la métropole du Centre.* Bourges, 1791.

Wandelaincourt, Antoine-Hubert. *Éléments de morale; ou, Devoirs de l'homme et du citoyen.* Paris, 1793.

———. *Instruction pastorale.* Chaumont, 1792.

———. *Plan d'éducation publique* [three pamphlets bound together]. Paris, n.d.

———. *Suite des observations sur le plan de constitution.* Paris, 1793.

STUDIES

Aston, Nigel. *The End of an Elite: The French Bishops and the Coming of the Revolution, 1786–1790.* Oxford, 1992.

———. *Religion and Revolution in France, 1780–1804.* Washington, D.C., 2000.

Bastid, Paul. *Sieyès et sa pensée.* Paris, 1970.

Berland, André. *Un grand révolutionnaire charentais, L'Abbé Jacques Roux: Les débuts en Angoumois et en Saintonge du future chef des Enragés (1752–1794).* Paris, 2000.

Berthe, Léon. "Grégoire, élève de l'abbé Lamourette." *Revue du Nord* 44 (1962): 39–46.

Bianchi, Serge. "Les curés rouges dans la Révolution française." *Annales historiques de la Révolution française* 54 (1982): 365–92.

Boudon, Jacques-Olivier. *Les Élites religieuses à l'époque de Napoléon: Dictionnaire des évêques et vicaires généraux du Premier Empire.* Paris, 2002.

———. *L'Épiscopat français à l'époque concordataire: Origines, formation, nomination.* Paris, 1996.

Boussoulade, Jean, *L'Église de Paris du 9 thermidor au Concordat.* Paris, 1950.

Bowman, Frank Paul, ed. *L'Abbé Grégoire, évêque des lumières.* Paris, 1988.

Bredin, Jean-Denis. *Sieyès: La clé de la Révolution française.* Paris, 1988.

Brémond, Henri. *Histoire littéraire du sentiment religieux en France.* 5 vols. Edited by François Tremolières. 1st ed., 12 vols., 1916–33. Grenoble, 2006.

Brown, Raymond. *Priest and Bishop: Biblical Reflections.* New York, 1970.

Burr, David. *Spiritual Franciscans: From Protest to Persecution in the Century after Saint Francis*. University Park, Pa., 2003.

Byrnes, Joseph F. *Catholic and French Forever: Religious and National Identity in Modern France*. University Park, Pa., 2005.

———. "Three Ways of Imagining Sacrality: Promoting, Regulating, and Rejecting the French Revolutionary Festivals." In *Studia Anselmiana: Imaginer l'Église catholique* (Festschrift in honor of Dom Ghislain Lafont, OSB), 189–200. Rome, 2000.

Cage, Claire. "'Celibacy Is a Social Crime': The Politics of Clerical Marriage, 1793–1797." *French Historical Studies* 36 (2013): 601–28.

Charon-Bordas, Jeannine. *Inventaire des archives de la Légation en France du cardinal Caprara (1801–1808)*. Paris, 1975.

———. *La Légation en France du Cardinal Caprara, 1801–1808: Répertoire des demandes de réconciliation avec l'Église*. Paris, 1979.

Charrier, Jules. *Claude Fauchet, évêque constitutionnel du Calvados, député à l'Assemblée législative et à la Convention (1744–1793)*. 2 vols. Paris, 1909.

Chartier, Roger. *Les Origines culturelles de la Révolution française*. Paris, 1990.

Chassin, Charles-Louis. *Les Cahiers des curés, étude historique d'après les brochures, les cahiers imprimés et les procès-verbaux manuscrits*. Paris, 1882.

Chaussinand-Nogaret, Guy. *Mirabeau*. Paris, 1982.

———. *Mirabeau entre le roi et la Révolution: Notes à la cour suivies de Discours*. Paris, 1986.

Chopelin, Paul. "L'Élection de l'évêque constitutionnel de Rhône-et-Loire (1er mars 1791." *Revue d'histoire de l'Église de France* 89 (2003): 385–418.

———. *Ville patriote et ville martyre: Lyon, l'église et la Révolution, 1788–1805*. Paris, 2010.

Chopelin, Paul, and Caroline Chopelin-Blanc. "L'Héritage janséniste dans l'église constitutionnelle: Débats historiographiques et perspectives de recherches." Manuscript, n.d.

———. *L'Obscurantisme et les Lumières: Itinéraire de l'abbé Grégoire, évêque révolutionnaire*. Paris, 2013.

Chopelin-Blanc, Caroline. *De l'apologétique à l'Église constitutionnelle: Adrien Lamourette (1742–1794)*. Paris, 2009.

———. "Discours de Fauchet contre les prêtres insermentés (26 octobre 1791)." *Parlement(s)* 6 (2006): 165–73.

———. "Le 'Baiser Lamourette' (7 juillet 1792)." *Annales historiques de la Révolution française*, January–March 2009, 73–100.

———. "La prise de parole des évêques-députés à l'Assemblée législative (1791–1792)." *Parlement(s)* 6 (2006): 118–34.

Christophe, Paul. *1789: Les Prêtres dans la Révolution*. Paris, 1986.

Cochin, Augustin. *Les Sociétés de pensée et la Révolution en Bretagne*. Paris, 1925.

Credot, P. J. *Pierre Pontard: Évêque constitutionnel de la Dordogne*. Paris, 1893.

Crook, Malcolm. "Citizen Bishops: Episcopal Election in the French Revolution." *Historical Journal* 43 (2000): 955–76.

Daniel, R. "Études sur les difficultés d'un évêque constitutionnel et le recrutement d'un nouveau clergé: Expilly, évêque constitutionnel du Finistère et les 'expilliens.'" *Bulletin de la Société archéologique du Finistère* 94 (1968): 80–134.

Dean, Rodney J. *L'Abbé Grégoire et l'Église constitutionnelle après la Terreur, 1794–1797*. Preface by Jean Dubray. Paris, 2008.
———. "Les débats à l'Assemblée nationale des 26 et 27 novembre 1790." Manuscript, n.d.
———. *L'Église constitutionnelle, Napoléon et le Concordat de 1801*. Paris, 2004.
———. "L'Élection de Jean-Baptiste Royer comme évêque constitutionnel et métropolitain de Paris en 1798." Manuscript, n.d.
———. *Histoire de l'Église constitutionnelle dans la métropole de Paris depuis la fin de la Terreur en juillet 1794, jusqu'à la clôture du premier Concile national en novembre 1797*. Lille, 1988.
De Bonald, Vicomte. *François Chabot: Membre de la Convention (1756–1794)*. 2nd ed. Paris, 1908.
De Certeau, Michel, Dominique Julia, and Jacques Revel. *Une politique de la langue: La Révolution française et les patois*. Paris, 1975.
Delacroix, Simon. *Les Nominations d'évêques et la liquidation du passé*. Vol. 1 of *La Réorganisation de l'Église de France après la Révolution (1801–1809)*. Paris, 1962.
Deprun, Jean. "À la fête de l'Être suprême, les 'Noms divins' dans deux discours de Robespierre." *Annales historiques de la Révolution française* 44 (1972): 161–80.
Desan, Suzanne. *Reclaiming the Sacred: Lay Religion and Popular Politics in Revolutionary France*. Ithaca, 1990.
Dommanget, Maurice. *Enragés et curés rouges en 1793*. Paris, 1993.
Dubray, Jean. *La Pensée de l'abbé Grégoire: Despotisme et liberté*. Oxford, 2008.
Edelstein, Melvin Allen. *La Feuille villageoise: Communication et modernisation dans les régions rurales pendant la Révolution*. Paris, 1977.
Fauchois, Yann. *Chronologie politique de la Révolution, 1789–1799*. Paris, 1989.
Fauré, Christine, Jacques Guilhaumou, and Jacques Valier. *Des Manuscrits de Sieyès, 1773–1799*. Paris, 1999.
Fenster, Kenneth R. "The Abdicating Clergy in the Gironde." *Catholic Historical Review* 85 (1999): 541–65.
Fierro, Alfred, with Jean Tulard and Jean-François Fayard. *Histoire et dictionnaire de la Révolution française, 1789–1799*. Paris, 1987.
Fournier, Gabriel. "La mise en place du cadre paroissial et l'évolution du peuplement." In *Cristianizzazione ed organizzazione ecclesiastica delle campagne nell'alto medioevo: Espansione e resistenze*, vol. 1, 496–563. Spoleto, 1982.
Frijhoff, Willem, and Dominique Julia. "Les Oratoriens de France sous l'ancien régime: Premiers résultats d'une enquête." *Revue d'histoire de l'Église de France* 45 (1979): 225–65.
Gobry, Ivan. *Joseph Le Bon: La Terreur dans le nord de la France*. Paris, 1991.
Graham, Ruth. "The Secularization of the Ecclesiastical Deputies to the National Convention, 1792–1794." *Proceedings of the Consortium on Revolutionary Europe, 1750–1850* (1974): 65–79.
Guiffrey, Jules. *Les Conventionnels, listés par départements et par ordre alphabétique des députés et des suppléants à la Convention nationale*. Paris, 1889.
Guilhaumou, Jacques. "Fragments d'un discours sur Dieu: Sieyès et la religion." In *Mélanges Vovelle*, 257–65. Aix-en-Provence, 1997.

———. "Sieyès et la figure nominaliste du metaphysician: Du *Grand cahier métaphysique* aux *Vues analytiques*." In *Figures de Sieyès*, edited by Pierre-Yves Quiviger, Vincent Denis, and Jean Salem, 241–53. Paris, 2008.

———. *Sieyès et l'ordre de la langue: L'invention de la politique moderne*. Paris, 2002.

Hampson, Norman. "François Chabot and His Plot." *Transactions of the Royal Historical Society*, 5th ser., 26 (1976): 1–14.

Hanson, R. P. C. *The Search for the Christian Doctrine of God: The Arian Controversy, 318–381*. Edinburgh, 1988.

Hémon, P. *Audrein, Yves-Marie, Député du Morbihan à l'Assemblée législative et à la Convention nationale, évêque constitutionnel du Finistère*. Paris, 1903.

Hermon-Belot, Rita. "L'Abbé Fauchet." In *La Gironde et les Girondins*, edited by François Furet and Mona Ozouf. Paris, 1991.

———. *L'Abbé Grégoire: La politique et la vérité*. Paris, 2000.

Hughes, John Jay. "Christian Priesthood." In *The Encyclopedia of Religion*, 16 vols., edited by Mircea Eliade, 11:536–39. New York, 1987.

Hutt, M. G. "The Role of the Curés in the Estates General of 1789." *Journal of Ecclesiastical History* 6 (1955): 190–220.

Kates, Gary. *The Cercle Social, the Girondins, and the French Revolution*. Princeton, 1985.

Kolakowski, Leszek. *Chrétiens sans églises: La conscience religieuse et le lien confessionnel au XVIIe siècle*. Translated by Anna Posner. Paris, 1969.

Kung, Hans. *Infallible? An Unresolved Inquiry*. New York, 1994.

Kuscinski, Auguste. *Dictionnaire des conventionnels*. Paris, 1916–19.

Kuttner, Stephan. *Medieval Councils, Decretals, and Collections of Canon Law*. Brookfield, Vt., 1992.

Lacape, Henri. *Pierre Pontard, évêque constitutionnel de la Dordogne*. Bordeaux, 1952.

Lacombe, Bernard. *Talleyrand, évêque d'Autun, d'après des documents inédits*. Paris, 1903.

Langlois, Claude, and Timothy Tackett. "Ecclesiastical Structures and Clerical Geography on the Eve of the French Revolution." *French Historical Studies* 11 (1980): 352–70.

Langlois, Claude, Timothy Tackett, and Michel Vovelle, eds. *Religion*. Vol. 9 of *Atlas de la Révolution française*. Paris, 1996.

Laulom, Jean-Pierre. "Mgr Jean-Pierre Saurine (1733–1813), Évêque constitutionnel des Landes." *Bulletin de la Société Borda* 378 (1980): 239–312; 386 (1982): 187–95.

Leclercq, Dom H. *L'Église constitutionnelle (juillet 1790–avril 1791)*. Paris, 1934.

Leflon, Jean. *La Crise révolutionnaire, 1789–1846*. Paris, 1951.

———. *Étienne-Alexandre Bernier, évêque d'Orléans (1762–1806)*. Paris, 1938.

———. *Monsieur Émery: L'église de l'ancien régime et la Révolution*. Paris, 1944.

Le Guillou, Jean-Marc. *Jacques Roux, 1752–1794*. Paris, 2000.

Lemaitre, Nicole, ed. *Histoire des curés*. Paris, 2002.

Lemay, Edna Hindie, ed. *Dictionnaire des Constituants, 1789–1791*. Preface by François Furet. 2 vols. Paris, 1991.

———. *Dictionnaire des Législateurs, 1791–1792*. Preface by Mona Ozouf. 2 vols. Paris, 2007.

L'Herron, Jeanne. *Un Morlaisien dans la Révolution: LA Expilly: Recteur de Saint-Martin*. Morlaix, 1989.

Liébault, Abbé. *Lamourette, Prêtre et évêque assermenté, 1742–1794*. Nancy, 1894.
Longère, Jean. "La Prédication et l'instruction des fidèles selon les conciles et les statuts synodaux depuis l'Antiquité tardive jusqu'au XIIIe siècle." In *L'Encadrement religieux des fidèles au Moyen Âge et jusqu'au concile de Trente*, vol. 1, 391–418. Paris, 1985.
Maire, Catherine. *De la cause de Dieu à la cause de la Nation: Le jansénisme au XVIIe siècle*. Paris, 1998.
Markoff, John. *The Abolition of Feudalism: Peasants, Lords, and Legislators in the French Revolution*. University Park, Pa., 1996.
Markov, Walter. *Die Freiheiten des Priesters Roux*. Berlin, 1967.
Marquant, Robert, ed. *Les Archives Sieyès aux Archives nationales*. Paris, 1970.
Mathiez, Albert. *Études sur Robespierre (1758–1794)*. Paris, 1988.
———. *La Théophilanthropie et le culte décadaire*. Paris, 1903.
McGinn, Bernard. *Calabrian Abbot: Joachim of Fiore in the History of Western Thought*. New York, 1985.
McManners, John. *Church and Society in Eighteenth-Century France*. 2 vols. Oxford, 1998.
———. *The French Revolution and the Church*. London, 1969.
Menozzi, Daniele. *Philosophes et Chrétiens éclairés: Politica e religione nella collaborazione G-H Mirabeau e A-A Lamourette*. Brescia, 1976.
Miller, David C. "A.-G. Camus and the Civil Constitution of the Clergy." *Catholic Historical Review* 76 (1990): 481–505.
Murphy, Gwénaël. *Les Religieuses dans la Révolution française*. Paris, 2005.
Necheles, Ruth F. *The Abbé Grégoire, 1787–1831: The Odyssey of an Egalitarian*. Westport, Conn., 1971.
———. "The Constitutional Church, 1794–1802: An Essay in Voluntarism." In *The Consortium on Revolutionary Europe, 1750–1850: Proceedings, 1794*, 80–90. Gainesville, Fla., 1974.
———. "The Curés of the Estates General of 1789." *Journal of Modern History* 46 (1974): 425–44.
Noëll, Henri. *De la soutane au bonnet phrygien et à l'habit de cour: Sieyès, Fouché, Talleyrand*. Paris, 1947.
Paris, A.-J. *Histoire de Joseph Le Bon et des tribunaux révolutionnaires d'Arras et de Cambrai*. Arras, 1879.
Pauchet, Philippe, and René Vaillant, eds. *La Correspondance de Gay-Vernon en 1799*. Amiens, 1988.
Pelletier, Gérard. *Rome et la Révolution française: La théologie et la politique du saint siège devant la Révolution française (1789–1799)*. Rome, 2004.
Picard, Augustin. *Le Clergé de France pendant la Révolution*. 2 vols. Paris, 1912–27.
Pichois, Claude, and Jean Dautry. *Le Conventionnel Chasles et ses idées démocratiques*. Aix-en-Provence, 1958.
Pisani, Paul. *L'Église de Paris et la Révolution française*. 4 vols. Paris, 1908–11.
———. *Répertoire biographique de l'épiscopat constitutionnel (1791–1802)*. Paris, 1907.
Plongeron, Bernard. *Des Résistances religieuses à Napoléon (1799–1813)*. Paris, 2006.
———. "Face au Concordat (1801): Résistances des évêques anciens constitutionnels." *Annales historiques de la Révolution française* 76 (2004): 85–115.

———, ed. *Les Défis de la modernité.* Vol. 10 of *Histoire de Christianisme.* Edited by Bernard Plongeron. Paris, 1997.
———. "L'Église constitutionnelle [gallicane] à l'épreuve du Directoire: Réorganisation, liberté des cultes et Concile national de 1797." In *Du Directoire au Consulat,* 2 vols., edited by Hervé Leuwers, 1:149–64. Lille, 2000.
———. "La première séparation de l'Église et de l'État sous la Révolution, a-t-elle eu lieu?" *Revue d'histoire de l'Église de France* 91 (2005): 231–63.
———. *Les Réguliers de Paris devant le serment constitutionnel.* Paris, 1964.
———. "Théologie et applications de la collégialité dans l'Église constitutionnelle de France (1790–1801)." *Annales historiques de la Révolution française* 45 (1973): 71–84.
———. *La Vie quotidienne du clergé français au XVIIIe siècle.* Paris, 1989.
Préclin, Edmond. *Jansénistes au XVIIe siècle et la Constitution civile du clergé: Le développement du Richerisme, sa propagation dans le bas clergé, 1713–1791.* Paris, 1923.
Préteux, Pierre. *Armand-Gaston Camus, 1740–1803.* Paris, 1932.
Price, Munro. "Mirabeau and the Court: Some New Evidence." *French Historical Studies* 29 (2006): 37–75.
Reinhard, Marcel, ed. *Actes de quatre-vingt neuvième congrès national des sociétés savantes.* Paris, 1964.
Rey, Alain, and Sophie Chantreau, eds. *Dictionnaire des expressions et locutions.* 2nd ed. Paris, 1993.
Robert, Adolphe, Edgar Bourloton, and Gaston Cougny, eds. *Dictionnaire des parlementaires français depuis le 1er Mai 1789 jusqu'au 1er Mai 1889.* Paris, 1889–91.
Rose, R. B. *The Enragés: Socialists of the French Revolution.* Melbourne, 1965.
Roussel, Alfred, ed. *Correspondance de Le Coz, évêque constitutionnel d'Ille-et-Vilaine.* 2 vols. Paris, 1900–1903.
———. *Un évêque assermenté (1790–1802): Le Coz, évêque d'Ille-et-Vilaine, métropolitain du nord-ouest.* Paris, 1898.
Sainte-Beuve, C.-A. *Causéries de lundi.* Vol. 5. 3rd ed. Paris, n.d.
Seeley, Jo Ann. "The Parish Clergy in the French Constituent Assembly, 1789–1791." Ph.D. diss., Catholic University of America, 1992.
Sepinwall, Alyssa Goldstein. *The Abbé Grégoire and the French Revolution: The Making of Modern Universalism.* Berkeley, 2005.
Seyssel, comte Marc de. *Jean-Baptiste Royer, évêque constitutionnel de l'Ain, puis métropolitain de Paris, 1732–1807.* Belley, 1911.
Sharot, Stephen. *A Comparative Sociology of World Religions: Virtuosos, Priests, and Popular Religion.* New York, 2001.
Shaw, Matthew. *Time and the French Revolution: The Republican Calendar.* Rochester, N.Y., 2011.
Shusterman, Noah. *Religion and the Politics of Time: Holidays in France from Louis XIV through Napoleon.* Washington, D.C., 2010.
Sicard, Augustin. *Le Clergé de France pendant la Révolution.* 2 vols. Paris, 1912–27.
Slavin, Morris. "Jacques Roux: A Victim of Vilification." *French Historical Studies* 3 (1964): 527–37.
Soboul, Albert. "Classes populaires et Rousseauisme sous la Révolution." *Annales historiques de la Révolution française* 34 (1962): 421–38.

Sutter, Antoine, *Les Années de jeunesse de l'abbé Grégoire: Son itinéraire jusqu'à la Révolution*. Sarreguemines, 1992.

Tackett, Timothy. *Becoming a Revolutionary: The Deputies of the French National Assembly and the Emergence of a Revolutionary Culture (1789–1790)*. Princeton, 1996.

———. *Priest and Parish in Eighteenth-Century France: A Social and Political Study of the Curés in a Diocese of Dauphiné, 1750–1791*. Princeton, 1977.

———. *Religion, Revolution, and Regional Culture in Eighteenth-Century France: The Ecclesiastical Oath of 1791*. Princeton, 1986.

Tissot-Dupont, Jérôme. "Le Comité ecclésiastique de l'Assemblée nationale constituante (1789–1791): De *L'Histoire apologétique* par Durand de Maillane à la recherche moderne." *Revue d'histoire de l'Église de France* 90 (2004): 427–52.

Tulard, Jean. *Joseph Fouché*. Paris, 1998.

Van Kley, Dale K. *The Religious Origins of the French Revolution: From Calvin to the Civil Constitution, 1560–1791*. New Haven, 1996.

Von Campenhausen, Hans. *Ecclesiastical Authority and Spiritual Power in the Church of the First Three Centuries*. Translated by J. A. Baker. 1st German ed. 1953. Stanford, CA., 1969.

Vovelle, Michel. *La Révolution contre l'église: De la Raison à l'Être suprême*. Paris, 1988.

Waresquiel, Emmanuel de. *Talleyrand: Le prince immobile*. Paris, 2006.

Weber, Max. *The Sociology of Religion*. Translated by Ephraim Fischoff, introduction by Talcott Parsons. Boston, 1963.

Williams, Rowan. *Arius: Heresy and Tradition*. London, 1987.

Woell, Edward J. *Small-Town Martyrs and Murderers: Religious Revolution and Counterrevolution in Western France, 1774–1914*. Milwaukee, 2006.

Index

Page numbers in *italics* indicate figures.

abdicataires of 1793–1794, 142–49, *143, 146*
Annales de la religion (journal)
after Concordat, 229–34
on Catholic ceremonies, 170
constitutional vision in, 235–38
cover of, *160*
criticisms of Royer in, 200–202
Desbois de Rochefort and, 158–60
on festivals, 172
Le Coz writing in, 179–82
obituaries in, 237–38
"On the Mind and Viewpoints of the Former Clergy," 238–40
as source, 259 n. 6
testimonies recorded in, 219–26
United Bishops and, 158
Asseline, Jean-René, xxv
Aston, Nigel, xix, 29, 36
Astros, Paul-Thérèse-David d', 214
atheism, Sieyès on, 14, 15–16
Audrein, Yves-Marie
death of, 206
diocese of, 247
in Jacobin procession, *105*
Le Coz on, 180
murder of, 189
opinions of, 103–8
Aviau du Bois-de-Sanzay, Charles-François d', 241

Barruel, Augustin, 235, 236
Barruel-Labeaume, Pierre Barthélémé, 224
Bastid, Paul, 11–12
Bastille, Fauchet at, 47–48, *49*
Bécherel, François, 216, 227, 233, 248
Bellarmine, Robert, 240
Belmas, Louis
as constitutional bishop, 232, 241, 292 n. 67
diocese of, 255
prefect on, 216
retention of, 227
Berdolet, Marc-Antoine, 227, 251
Bernier, Étienne, 211, 212, *213*, 232–33
Bérulle, Pierre de, xxii
Beugnot, Jean-Claude, 122–24
Beulazet, François, 142–44
Billaud-Varenne, Jacques-Nicholas, 192
Binos, Father, 233
bishops
appendix of, xvii–xviii
Bernier and, 212
Civil Constitution of the Clergy and, 41–42
of concordatory church, 213
Convention and, 76, 102, 111–20
dictionary of, xvii
election of, 52, 165, 167–69, 183
Legislative Assembly and, 87–94
Mirabeau on, 66–68
oath and, 42
opposition to, 30
Pontard on, 88–90
refractory, 82–84, 86
resignations of, 204, 208, 213, 235
selection and consecration of, 44
in 1789, xxv–xxvi
See also constitutional bishops; United Bishops; *specific bishops*
Boisgelin, Raymond de, 2, 36, 41, 63
Boissy D'Anglas, François-Antoine, 106–7, 180
Bonaparte, Joseph, *213*
Bonaparte, Napoleon
coronation of, 241
depiction of, *213*
Italian campaign of, 174
Le Coz on, 190

Bonaparte, Napoleon (*continued*)
negotiations with pope of, 211–14
Royer and, 197–98, 208
successes of, 152, 182, 212
Boudon, Jacques-Olivier, 227
Bourdon, Louis-Alexandre-Pierre, 223
Boussart, Father, 215
Boussoulade, Jean, xix
Bredin, Jean-Denis, 7
Breton Club, 268 n. 74
Brézé, marquis de, 34
de Brienne, Étienne-Charles de Loménie, 42, 245
Brissotins, 144. *See also* Girondins
Brugière, Pierre, 192
Bruzac, Guillaume, 223
Bulletin de la Bouche de fer (journal), 52–56, *55*

Cacault, François, 211
cahiers de doléances, 1, 28–31, 47
Camus, Armand-Gaston, 40, 60, 61, 68–71, *70*
Caprara, Giovanni Battista, 214, 221, *222,* 228, 232
Castera de Larrière, Noël, 158
Catholicism
church-state relationship, 176–79, 204–6
Old Regime, xiv
political crises and, xix–xx
reform of, 2
See also Council of Trent; papacy/pope
Cazeneuve, Ignace de, 84, 112, 254
celibacy
Fauchet and, 52
Le Coz on, 189
priests' opinions on, 96
United Bishops on, 164
See also marriage
Chabot, François, 103, 108–11, *110,* 120
Chaix, Dominique, 261–62 n. 22
Chaptal, Jean-Antoine-Claude, 214
Charrier, Jules, 49, 56, 57
Charrier de la Roche, Louis, 44–45, 218, 227, 247
Chassin, Charles, 29, 30
Chopelin, Paul, xix
Chopelin-Blanc, Caroline, xix, 60, 88
chronology
engagement, 4–6
revival, 155–57
survival, 79–81
church-state relationship, 176–79, 204–6
Civil Constitution of the Clergy
approval of, 2
Le Bon and, 138
Le Coz on, 181
overview of, xiv, 40–46
retractions and, 220–26
swearing of oath and, *xv*
civil religion, xiv, 101, 169–74
Clausse, Pierre Eugène, 192
Clément, Augustin-Jean-Charles
as bishop, 182
as constitutional in-fighter, 187
diocese of, 244–45
leadership of, 158
resignations and, 208
Royer and, 202
Clement XIII, 240
Cloots, Anacharsis, Fauchet on, 55–56
Collignon, Claude-Nicholas-Joseph, 223
Collot, Joseph, 215
Comité de recherches, 86
Comité ecclésiastique, 37–40, 116
Concordat of 1516, xxi, 52, 198
Concordat of 1801
constitutionals and, 214–19
hopes for, 228–31
implementation of, 227–28
Le Coz and, 228–29
negotiations toward, 211–14
reality after, 231–34
signing of, *213*
Consalvi, Hercules, 212, *213*
Constant, André, 258
Constituent Assembly
committees of, 272 n. 1
Estates General and, 36–37
formation of, 26–27
Grégoire before, *26*
illustration of, *89*
See also Civil Constitution of the Clergy
constitutional bishops
in concordatory church, 214–19, 227, 228–29
opinions of prefects regarding, 214–19

retraction and reconciliation offered by, 241
retractions of, 220–26
vigilance for future of, 238–42
See also specific bishops
Constitutional Church
achievements of, *209,* 210
administrative divisions of, 243
Audrein on, 104
high and low moments of, 111–12
Lamourette on, 61–65
Mirabeau and, 65–68
National Council of 1797, 182–88
National Council of 1801, 202–8, *209,* 210
overview of, xiii–xiv
pope and, 70
as reform attempt, 242
constitutional vision, maintenance of, 235–38
Convention
Audrein and, 106, 107
bishops of, 76, 102, 111–20
dechristianization measures and, 100–101
Gay-Vernon and, 120
Le Coz and, 178
outcomes of, 126
role of, 100
Royer and, 193
Convention, post-Thermidorian, 151
Coster, Sigisbert-Etienne, 31
Couet, curé, 97
Council of Trent, xxi–xxii, 7, 58, 163, 201
coup of 18 Fructidor, 187–88
Courtonne, Louis, 144
Cousin, Father, 29
curés. *See* priests

Danton, abbé, 229–31
David, Jacques-Louis, *8,* 9
Dean, Rodney J., xviii
Debertier, Claude, 207, 255
décadi, 169, *171,* 173–74
dechristianization measures, 100–101, 102, 172, 190–91
Declaration of the Rights of Man and of the Citizen, 1, 37
deistic religion/deism, xiv, 76. *See also* Theophilanthropy
De la religion nationale (Fauchet), 50–52, *51*
Desan, Suzanne, xix
Desbois de Rochefort, Éléonor-Marie
décadi and, 173
diocese of, 249
on Gerson, 206
Legislative Assembly and, 88
Royer and, 202
United Bishops and, 158, 159
Desmoulins, Camille, 103, 111
dictionary of bishops, xvii
Diot, Nicholas, 186, 249
Directory government
foreign policy of, 174
Notre-Dame Cathedral and, 194
overview of, 151–52
refractories and, 182
revolutionary calendar and, 169–70
divorce, laws on, 100, 164
Dommanget, Maurice, 131
Dorlodot, Jean-François, 218, 247
Doux, Hyacinthe, 223–24
Doyle, William, 36
Dubourg-Miroudot, Jean-Baptiste, 42, 44
Dufraisse, Michel-Joseph, 206, 208, 245
Dumouchel, Jean-Baptiste, 206, 254
Dupont, Jacob, 106
Dupuis, Charles, 236
Dupuis, curé, 95, 96, 97, 98–99
Durand de Maillane, Pierre, 37, *38,* 38–40

ecclesiastical committee of National Assembly, 37–40
ecumenical councils, 167, 241
Edelstein, Melvin, 94
Edict of Nantes, xxi
education
for priesthood, xxiii–xxiv, 7
Wandelaincourt on, 115
election
of bishops, 52, 165, 167–69, 183
of priests, 168, 183
Émery, Father, 124
engagement
chronology of, 4–6
overview of, 1–4

Estates General
clergy journals during, 31–37
Grégoire and, 27
as official legislature, xiv
opening of, 1, 28
Expilly, Louis-Alexandre
as bishop, *83*
consecration of, 44
diocese of, 247
ecclesiastical committee and, 37
as martyr, 203
on refractories, 82–83

Fauchet, Claude
Bastille and, 47–48, *49*
Beugnot on, 123
Bulletin de la Bouche de fer, 52–56
Camus and, 40
career of, 47, 49–56
as constitutional bishop, 56–59
Convention and, 76, 112
in Convention era, 120–23
De la religion nationale, 50–52, *51*
diocese of, 248
Lamourette and, 59, 60
Legislative Assembly and, 88
pastoral letters of, 57–58, 59
on politics, 52–54
Fauchois, Yann, 88
festivals, 170, 172–74, 194
Feuillants, 37
First Estate, xiv, 1
Flavigny, Jean-Baptiste, 218, 251
Fouché, Joseph, 7–8, 102, 211–12, 241
Francis I, xxi, 52, 198
Franklin, Benjamin, *66*
Freemasons, Fauchet on, 53
Froment, François, 236–37

Gallican Church
Durand de Maillane on, 39
overview of, xvi
survival of, 242
See also Constitutional Church
Gallicanism
Civil Constitution of the Clergy and, 41
ecclesiastical committee and, 38
fundamentals of, 163–64
Gerson and, 207
influence of, xxiii
overview of, xxii
Garnier, André, 254
Gausserand, Jean-Joachim, 218, 256
Gautier, canon, 21
Gay-Vernon, Léonard, 88, 112, 118–20, 207, 257–58
Gerle, Christophe, *8,* 9
Gerson, Jean, 164, 203, 206, *207*
Géruzez, Jean-Baptiste, 147
Gibal, Michel, 221
Gillard, Claude-Damas, 144
Girondins, 76, 100, 109
Gobel, Jean-Baptiste
abdication of, 102
as bishop, 44–46
Cazeneuve and, 84
consecration of bishops by, 44
diocese of, 244
Lamourette and, 61
oath and, 42
resignation of, 195
Saurine and, 83
Gouttes, Jean-Louis, 35, 253
Goyré-Laplanche, Jacques, 103
Graham, Ruth, 103
Grateau, Philippe, 29
Grégoire, Henri
Camus and, 40
Chabot and, 103, 109
before Constituent Assembly, *26*
Constitutional Church and, 111
Convention and, 112
décadi and, 173–74
diocese of, 246
discrimination against, 292 n. 67
educational and spiritual formation of, 7, 20
election to Convention, 76
election to Estates General, 27
Éloge de la poésie, 21–22
father of, 36
on first oath, xvi
from humanist to pastor, 21–23
Lamourette and, 60
leadership of, 158
Le Coz and, 189–90
Napoleon and, 212
National Assembly and, 34

National Council of 1801 and, 202–4
oath and, 42
pastoral letter of, 125–26
Portalis and, 214
on reforms, 32
on regenerated political society, 23–25
on religious freedom, 102
resignations and, 208
Royer and, 202
Sieyès compared to, 9
Tennis Court Oath and, *8*
writings of, 8–9
Grignion de Montfort, Louis, xxii
Grossoles-Flamarens, bishop, 88
Guiffrey, Jules, 112
Guilhaumou, Jacques, 13, 263 n. 20, 263 n. 21
Guilleminet, Father, 30

Hampson, Norman, 109
Hébert, Jacques-René, 101
Hémon, P., 108
Huguet, Marc Antoine, 88, 112, 245
Hutt, Maurice, 36

iereus, xx

Jacobin Club, 37
Jacobins
Fauchet and, 57, 59
Massieu and, 116
Royer and, 192
self-labeling as, 144
Jallet, Jacques, 31–35, *33,* 36
Jansenism, xxii–xxiii, 20
Jarent de Senac d'Orgeval, Louis-François-Alexandre, 42, 244
Jews, Grégoire on, 23–25
Journal des Amis (review), 121–22
Journal du Concile national de France, 184

Kiss of Lamourette, 71–73, *72,* 82
Kuscinski, August, 112

Lacombe, Dominique
as constitutional bishop, 231, 232–33, 241
diocese of, 257
Legislative Assembly and, 88
prefect on, 216–17
retention of, 227
La Font de Savine, Charles de, 42, 186–87, 206, 252
La Feuille villageoise (journal), 94–99, *95,* 147
Lalande, Luc-François, 112, 249
Lamourette, Antoine-Adrien
Beugnot and, 123–24
as bishop, *62*
Camus and, 40
career of, 60
diocese of, 251–52
Fauchet and, 59, 60
Grégoire and, 21
Legislative Assembly and, 76, 88
as legislator and bishop, 71–73
Mirabeau and, 60–61
pastoral instruction of, 62–65
retraction of, 124–25
theology of church of, 61–65
Langlois, Claude, xviii
language for worship, 96–97, 184–85, 197
Lanjuinais, Jean-Denis, 37, 82
La Revellière-Lépeaux, Louis-Marie de, 170, 194
La Rochefoucauld, cardinal de, 34, 36
Launay, marquis de, 47
Laurent, curé, 36
Leblanc de Beaulieu, Jean-Claude, 192, 218, 227, 232, 248
Le Bon, Joseph
Chabot and, 109
death of, 142
as executioner, *141*
as mayor, 140–41
oath and, xvi
as priest, 137–39
as promoter of violence, 127–28, 137
wife of, 141–42
Le Chapelier, Isaac-René, 268 n. 74
Le Chapelier Law, 4, 268 n. 74
Leclerc de Juigné, Antoine-Éléonore-Léon, 199
Leclerq, Henri, xviii
Le Coz, Claude
Accord de la religion catholique avec le gouvernement républicain, 176–77
on church-state balance, 176–79

Le Coz, Claude (*continued*)
  Condordat and, 228–29
  depiction of, *177*
  diocese of, 246
  on first oath, xvi
  Gerson and, 206
  Grégoire and, 189–90
  leadership of, 175–76
  Legislative Assembly and, 88
  National Council of 1797 and, 185
  National Council of 1801 and, 202
  papacy and, 241
  prefect of Ille-et-Vilaine on, 218
  retention of, 227
  United Bishops and, 158, 159, 178–79, 188–91
  writings of in *Annales de la religion,* 179–82
Lefessier, André-Jacques-Simon, 88, 248
Leflon, Jean, 100
Le Franc de Pompignan, Jean-Georges, 235
Legislative Assembly
  bishops and, 87–94
  Chabot and, 109
  competition with king, 75
  Kiss of Lamourette in, 71–73, *72,* 82
  Le Coz and, 175
  Pontard and, 90–91
  role of, 100
Le Masle, Charles, 84–85, 237, 247
Leo X, xxi, 52, 198
Lequinio, Joseph-Marie, 190–91
Lessart, Jean-Marie de, 58
Librairie chrétienne, 184
Ligurian Republic of North Italy, 172
Lindet, Robert-Thomas, 112, 248
Louis XIII, xxii
Louis XV, xxiii
Louis XVI
  attempted escape of, 75
  Audrein and, 108
  depiction of farewell of, *135*
  Estates General and, 1, 34
  Fauchet on, 121
  Gay-Vernon and, 119, 120
  Jallet on, 35
  Lamourette and, 71
  Le Coz and, 178
  Massieu and, 118
  Mirabeau and, 60
  Roux and, 130, 133–34, 134–35, *135*
  Royer on, 193
  Saurine and, 113–14
  Torné on, 92–94
Lubersac, Jean-Baptiste de, 11, 12, 32

Maire, Catherine, 41
Marat, Jean-Paul, 101–2, 118
Marbos, François, 112, 204, 254
Marie Antoinette, xxv, 76, 118
Markov, Walter, 129
Marolles, Claude-Eustache-François, 44, 249
marriage
  divorce, laws on, 100, 164
  of former priests, 109–10, 142, 146–47
  Gay-Vernon on, 119–20
  Le Coz on, 189
  National Council of 1797 on, 185
  refractory priests and, 239
  United Bishops on, 164
  See also celibacy
Martial de Loménie, Pierre-François, 42
Massieu, Jean-Baptiste
  Convention and, 112
  diocese of, 248
  ecclesiastical committee and, 37
  as promoter of revolution, 116–18
  sketch of, *117*
  see of Rouen and, 206–7
Mathiez, Albert, 101, 109, 131, 135
Matra, Father, 215
Maury, abbé, 32, 33, 50, 233
McManners, John, xvii, xix, xxiv, xxv, 127, 137, 142
Mestadier, Jean-Joseph, 218, 257
metropolitans, 165
Mirabeau, Honoré-Gabriel Riquetti, comte de
  Camus and, 40
  Lamourette and, 60–61
  mythic representation of, *66*
  National Assembly and, 34
  Sur la Constitution civile du clergé, 65–68
  Third Estate and, 20

Moïse, François-Xavier, 188, 208, 214, 251
monarchy
  Fauchet on, 121
  Legislative Assembly and, 100
  Roux on, 132
  Royer on, 193
  Torné on, 92–94
  See also specific monarchs
Monestier, Jean-Baptiste, 103
Monin, Joseph, 215, 249
Montault-des-Isles, Charles, 218–19, 227, 246
Montesquieu, 115
Moreau, Gabriel-François, 218

Narbonne, Louis-Marie de, 120
National Constituent Assembly
  ecclesiastical committee of, 37–40
  Fauchet on, 58
  secretaries for, 34
  Third Estate and, 20
National Council of 1797, 182–88, *186*
National Council of 1801
  depiction of, *205*
  Grégoire and, 202–4
  Napoleon and, 212–13
  pope and, 211
  Royer and, 200, 201, 204
  schism and, 204–8, *209,* 210
Necheles, Ruth, 36
Necker, Jacques, 28, 30
Newton, Isaac, 170
Notre-Dame Cathedral, 151, 182, 194

oath of hatred of royalty, 188, 239
oath of loyalty to nation
  resistance to, *87*
  retractions of, 220–26
  taking of, 42–44, *43, 45*
  See also refractory priests
Oberlin, Jean-Frédéric, 22
obituaries, 237–38
Old Regime Catholicism and pope, xiv
Olier, Jean-Jacques, xxii, 10
"On the Mind and Viewpoints of the Former Clergy," 238–40
ordination papers, *146*
Orléans, Philippe d', 50

Paintandre, Alexandre, 144, 145
Panisset, François-Thèrése, 180, 252–53
papacy/pope
  Annales authors on, 240–41
  Audrein on, 104
  Camus on, 68–70
  Lamourette on, 63–65
  Le Coz on, 188, 191
  Mirabeau on, 68
  National Council of 1797 and, 183–84
  National Council of 1801 and, 211
  refractory priests and, 182
  reverence and respect for, 233–34
  See also specific popes
Parent, curé, 96, 98
Paris presbytery, 192
Pasquer, Father, 148–49
Pennier, Father, 215
Père Duchesne (periodical), 101
Périer, Jean-François, 212, 216, 227, 241, 253
Philippe Egalité, 50
Pisani, Paul, xviii–xix, 112, 243
Pitt, William, 104
Pius VI, 229, 231, 233, *234*
Pius VII, 211, *222,* 231, 233–34, 241
Pius IX, 242
Plongeron, Bernard, xviii, 142, 210
Ponsignon, Louis-François, 186–87, 197, 206, 245
Pontard, Pierre, 88–90, 90–91, 257
pope. *See* papacy/pope
Porion, Pierre-Joseph, 249
Portalis, Jean-Étienne-Marie, 214, 232, 233, 238
Poullard, Thomas-Juste, 253, 292 n. 67
presbyteros, xx
presbytery, 165
priests
  abdicataires, 142–49, *143, 146*
  acceptance or rejection of by people, 44
  commitment and behavior of, xvi–xvii
  concerns of, 84–87
  of Convention, 103–11
  election of, 168, 183
  Le Coz defense of, 228
  oath and, 42–44, *43*
  ordination papers of, *146*

priests (*continued*)
origins of, 36–37
Roux on, 132–33, 136
Royer and, 196–97
in 1789, xxiii–xxvi
as terrorists, 127–28
tradition of, xix–xxiii
United Bishops and, 158
See also refractory priests; *specific priests*
Primat, Claude-François-Marie, 227, 250
projets de convention, 211–14
Prudhomme, Jean-Guillaume, 217

Rabaut Saint-Etienne, Jean-Paul, *8*
Rangeard, Jacques, 31
reason, former priests' praise of, 147–48
reforms
of Catholicism, 2
Constitutional Church as attempt at, 242
Grégoire on, 32
priests' opinions on, 96–97
refractory priests
Annales authors on, 238–40
concerns about, 85–87
constitutional priests' opinions of, 219–20
definition of, xvii
Directory government and, 182
Expilly on, 82–83
Fauchet and, 58
suppression of, 188
Torné on, 91–92
Reiser, Father, 215
religion
Audrein on, 103–8
civil, xiv, 101, 169–74
deistic/deism, xiv, 76
Fauchet on, 50–52
former priests' attacks on, 145–47, 148–49
republican civil, 169–74
Sieyès on, 13–18
See also Catholicism; Theophilanthropy
Republic, defense of by priests, 97–99
republican Christianity, United Bishops on, 166–69
republican civil religion, 169–74
Restif de la Bretonne, Edmé-Nicholas, xxiv
retractions, 220–26
revival
chronology of, 155–57
overview of, 151–54
revolutionary calendar, 125, 169–70, *171,* 190
revolutionary priesthood, polarities of, 25–27
Reymond, Henri, 227, 241, 252
Richelieu, cardinal, xxii
Richer, Edmond, xxiii
Richerism, xxiii, 21, 50
Robespierre, Maximilien
Audrein and, 103
Chabot and, 109
civil religion and, xiv
Fauchet on, 120–21
Gay-Vernon and, 120
Le Bon and, 140
Roux and, 127
Royer and, 193
on support for church, 100–101
Terror and, 76–77
Rohan, Louis de, xxv
Romme, Gilbert, 125
Rose, R. B., 129
Rouanet, Alexandre-Victor, 218, 254
Rousseau, Jean-Jacques, xiv, 54, 97, 101
Roux, Jacques
Affaire Mioulle and, 128–29
"Discours sur le jugement de Louis-le-dernier," 133–34
"Discours sur les moyens de sauver la France et la Liberté," 132–33
"L'Apôtre martyr da la Révolution," 131–32
Louis XVI and, 134–35, *135*
Manifeste des Enragés, 135–36
oath and, xvi
as promoter of violence, 127
on revolution and regicide, 133–36
sermons of, 129–33
suicide of, 136
as teacher, 128–29
Roux, Louis-Félix, 118
Royer, Jean-Baptiste
as bishop of Paris, 194–99
career of, 192–93, 199–202
Convention and, 112
depiction of, *195*

diocese of, 244, 252
Le Coz and, 188–89
Napoleon and, 208
National Council of 1801 and, 200, 201, 204
United Bishops and, 158, 159
Royer, Rosalie, 192

Sainte-Beuve, Charles-Augustin, 11
Saint-Sulpice seminary, xxiv, 10
Sanadon, Barthélemy-Jean-Baptiste, 112, 255
sans-culottes
after 1795, 151
Roux and, 129, 134
self-labeling as, 144
Saurine, Jean-Pierre
as accommodator, 112–14
Concordat and, 241
Convention and, 112
depiction of, *113*
diocese of, 258
Greek liturgy of, 185
prefect of Landes on, 217
on refractory bishops, 83–84
retention of, 227
United Bishops and, 158
Second Constitutional Church, xvi. *See also* Gallican Church
Second Estate, 1
Second Vatican Council, 242
Séguin, Philippe-Charles-François, 112, 250
seminary education, xxiii–xxiv, 7
Sepinwall, Alyssa, 21–22, 25
Sermet, Antoine-Pascal-Hyacinthe, 184, 255
sex, Chabot on, 110–11. *See also* celibacy
Sicard, Augustin, xviii
Sieyès, Emmanuel-Joseph
clerical life of, 10–13
educational and spiritual formations of, 7, 9–10
Grand cahier métaphysique, 13–14
Grégoire compared to, 9
image of, *12*
oath and, xvi
political commitment of, 18–20
Qu'est-ce que c'est le tiers état?, 18–20, 26
as secretary for National Assembly, 34–35
Sur Dieu ultramètre et sur la fibre religieuse de l'homme, 14–18, 25–26
Tennis Court Oath and, *8*
votes for, 45
writings of, 8–9, 13–18
Sieyès, Honoré, 10
Simond, Philibert, 103
Solignac, Pierre-Joseph de, 21
Spina, Archbishop, 211, 212, 214
Stanislas, King, 22
submission of bishops, rejection of, 231–34
Sur la Constitution civile du clergé (Mirabeau), 65–68
survival
chronology, 79–81
overview of, 75–78
Sutter, Antoine, 21

Tackett, Timothy, xviii, 28–29, 42, 43–44, 243
Talleyrand-Périgord, Charles-Maurice de
as alternative to Sieyès, 7–8
consecration of bishops by, 2, 44
diocese of, 253
Le Bon and, 138
negotiations with pope of, 211, 212
oath and, 42
as scoundrel, xxv
Tennis Court Oath, *8,* 9, 27, 125
terminology, xvi–xvii
Theophilanthropy, 152, 186–87, 194
Thibault, Anne-Alexandre-Marie, 31, 36, 37, 112, 252
Third Estate, xiv, 1, 18–20, 26
Thomassin (theologian), 162, 189
Thuin, Pierre, 194–95, 244
Torcy, François de, 186, 204
Torné, Pierre Athanase, 88, 91–94, 112, 245
Tourteau, Jacques-René, 222
Traité sur l'uniformité de la liturgie, 210
Treilhard, Jean-Baptiste, 37, 40

union of orders, 34, 35–37
United Bishops
décadi and, 173–74
first encyclical letter of, 160–66
on fundamentals of Gallicanism, 163–64
Le Coz and, 178–79, 188–91
overview of, 158–60

United Bishops (*continued*)
post-persecution policies of, 164–65
reorganization of dioceses by, 165–66
on restoration of discipline, 161–63
Royer and, 201, 202
second encyclical letter of, 166–69

Valmy, victory at, 76
Van Kley, Dale, xix
vernacular, worship in, 96–97
vicars, episcopal, 103
Villaneuve, Jean-Baptiste Romé de, 253
Villar, Noel-Gabriel-Luce de, 112, 247
Vistorte, Pierre, 224–26
Volfius, Jean-Baptiste, 138, 250
Voltaire, 54, 56, 170
Vovelle, Michel, xviii

Wandelaincourt, Antoine-Hubert
as accommodator, 112, 114–16
constitutional vision of, 235–36
Convention and, 112
diocese of, 251
Royer and, 202